HAWAII

T R A V **B U G S**
TRAVEL GUIDES

Project Editors:	Bina Maniar
Editors:	Mary Lee
	Aileen Lau
	Emma Tan
DTP Design & Production:	Sares Kanapathy
DTP Assistant:	Janet Moraes
Illustrations:	Eric Yeo
Cover Artwork:	Susan Harmer
Maps:	Rebecca Fong

The publishers gratefully acknowledge the kind assistance of the Hawaii State Archives, Douglas Peebles and Bennett Hymer in the production of this book.

Co-Published by MPH Publishing (S) Pte Ltd and Sun Tree Publishing Ltd

Titles 1993/1994
Alaska – America SW – Australia – Bali – California – Canada – Caribbean – England – Florida – France – Germany – Greece – Hawaii – Italy – India – Indonesia – Ireland – Japan – Kenya – Malaysia – Mexico – Nepal – New England – New York – Pacific Northwest USA – Singapore – Spain – Thailand – Turkey – Vietnam

Marketing & Sales
International Sales & Foreign Rights:
Sun Tree Publishing
Block 6, Level 3, 152 Tagore Lane
off Upper Thomson Road
Singapore 2678
Tel: (65) 452 2677
Fax: (65) 455 3758

Singapore & Malaysia Sales
MPH Distributors (S) Pte Ltd
MPH House
12 Tagore Drive
Singapore 2678
Tel: (65) 453 8200
Fax: (65) 457 0314

ISBN: 981 00 3096 7
Printed in Singapore

HAWAII

Text by Arnold Schuchter

Project Editors
Aileen Lau
Mary Lee
Bina Maniar
Emma Tan

MPH Publishing (S) Pte Ltd

Sun Tree Publishing Ltd

C O N T E N T S

C O N T E N T S

C O N T E N T S

C O N T E N T S

Gentle ways, lovely leis, heavenly breezes, sweet leilanis, enchanting

smiles, ... Hawaiians have warm and generous ways to welcome any visitor.

Hawaii's generous climate and rich volcanic soil hosts myriad varieties of flowers

greenery, birds and animals – the islands are filled with flora and fauna of volcanic tropics.

Catch it or watch it, surfing and sailing above

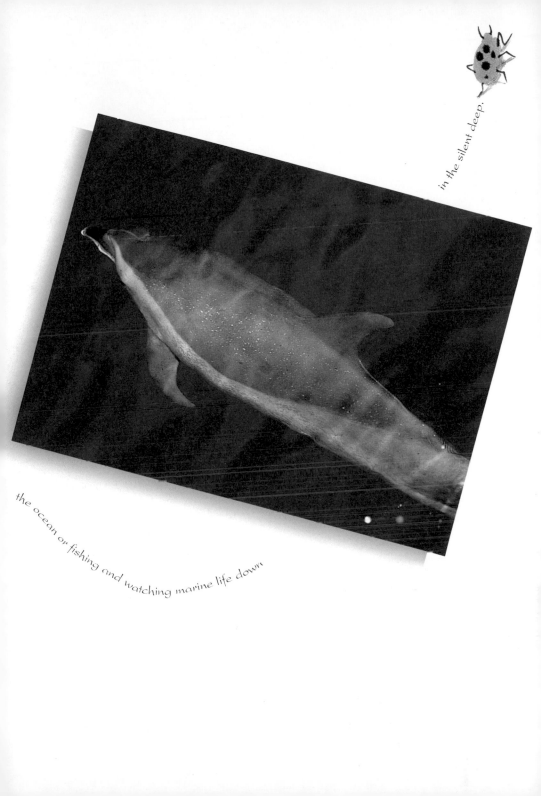

in the silent deep.

the ocean or fishing and watching marine life down

Capture the aloha spirit in those breezy, lingering and

romantic Hawaiian sunsets through swaying palms.

Was it pure accident that Polynesian voyagers who first discovered Hawaii landed on little Kauai at the northwest end of the curving archipelago? Kauai is the closest reminder of the remote Marquesas Islands, northeast of Tahiti, where Polynesian migrations across the Pacific began. The forces of nature and the human spirit have combined across Hawaiian history to embody the *aloha* spirit in many ways – charming, gentle, yet strong and powerful.

Centuries later, Tahitian explorers and their pantheon of gods arrived in double-hulled canoes at the southern tip of a mid-ocean volcano–the fire goddess *Pele's* home – the Big Island. Was this landing, on the only island volcanically erupting at the time, an accidental

Ukelele, grass skirts, leis and a warm Hawaiian welcome.

1

"Aloha" in coral laid out on lava.

event, too? The Big Island's volcanic activity embodies *mana* (spiritual power) central to Hawaiian and Polynesian culture. This *mana* filters into the *aloha* spirit in indefinable ways.

In The Beginning...

From the beginning, the islands that were to become the last frontier in the United States embodied spiritual harmony with nature. No two islands in Hawaii are alike, even in part. Mountains and vistas do not resemble one another from island to island, and they rarely look the same even at the same time of day. Dozens of picturesque and secluded beaches – white, black, salt-and-pepper, red and even green – many of them truly beautiful and untrammeled, all quite unique in shape. Surrounding landscape and foliage, action of the sea against rocks, headlands, cliffs and sand, in many instances have been changed very little by development.

Beauty & Grandeur

Flora and *aloha* are very closely interwoven in Hawaiian culture. Floral garlands placed around the neck of a friend or loved one truly express the *aloha* spirit. The *lei* is the arms of a child around the mother's neck. When you arrive in Hawaii and someone local

serene beauty of *aloha* in waterfalls streaming into verdant jungles and the blue expanse of the Pacific Ocean, in the splendor of sunsets painted with a palette of a thousand colors, and especially in the spirit of the local people. Lindbergh chose to live in his beloved and remote Kipahulu and Kipahulu Valley is one of the truly precious *aloha* places left in Hawaii, preserved today largely as a result of his passionate initiative.

Ann Morrow, Lindbergh's wife and a famous author in her own right, summed up the *aloha* spirit she and Charles Lindbergh found in Kipahulu in her book **Gift from the Sea**: "Simplicity of living, as much as possible, to retain a true awareness of life...life of the spirit, creative life and the life of human relationships." Awareness of human relationships is at the heart of the *aloha* spirit. Visitors to Hawaii may not be aware of it at first, but their hosts are exercising Hawaiian values in ways intended to *soften* newcomers. This *softening* is what Lindbergh learned from "talking story" with field hands and house workers – plain folk living in Kipahulu, so wild and lush, truly heaven on earth.

places a *lei* around your neck, this greeting means much more than a routine gesture. It is an invitation to discover and cherish *aloha* in Hawaii. Open yourself to intimate contact with the beauty and grandeur of Hawaii: waterfalls cascading into pools of chilled water; surf clashing with volcanic stone; waves washing gently on white beaches; protea petals catching the morning slant of light; cloud layers resting on verdant cliffs; golden *koi* gliding through intricate lagoons; lush foliage blanketing jungle forests and gorgeous man-made gardens; the experience of seeing and tasting distinctive Hawaiian cuisine's abundance of fresh local fruits, vegetables and grains and so much more.

The legendary pilot, Charles Lindbergh, was one of those who, in "heavenly Hana" on Maui, found the

Multicultural Mix

A remarkable multicultural mix, Hawaii exhibits inevitable rough edges after the intrusion for over 200 years of some of the less pleasant aspects of

Hawaiian beauties.

western civilization. But stories about these problems as they affect tourists tend to be exaggerated. Considering the number of hyper-stressed tourists descending daily into this multiethnic maze, the quality of the prevailing *aloha* certainly defies the odds.

The *Aloha* Spirit

The *aloha* spirit transplanted by ancient Polynesian settlers, the spirit of friendliness and generosity nourished by bountiful Hawaii, has miraculously survived abuse and exploitation by foreigners. Immeasurably enriched by elements of its imported ethnic and cultural diversity, a Hawaiian cultural renaissance is reaching back before Captain Cook to link pre-contact heritage with contemporary Hawaiian identity.

What does modernization mean for sightseeing pleasures in Hawaii? Only one area of Hawaii thus far is literally damaged by overdevelopment – Waikiki – but even Waikiki is a shopper's paradise with some of the best, most accessible swimming beaches in Hawaii. For every complaint about Waikiki's disfigurement, there are several raves about its vacation values, especially for budget-minded travelers. And several of the best kept scenic secrets in Hawaii are found elsewhere, within a few hour's drive from Waikiki, on much-maligned Oahu. Less crowded Neighbor Islands are only slowly being discovered as tourism numbers inch upward. Subsidized inter-island flights make the Outer Islands' diverse attractions accessible and affordable. Hawaii Volcanoes National Park on the Big Island, Haleakala National Park on Maui and the Na Pali coast on Kauai attract the most tourists. None of them are yet overrun by hoards of tourists. Crowds of people – more than a million visitors annually, make Oahu their vacation destination because it offers so much. Well-heeled tourists no longer arrive with their steamer trunks and servants for month-long getaways. Sidewalks of Waikiki choked with pedestrians and bumper-to-bumper traffic have replaced them. But Oahu still is beautiful along its more than 50 miles of shoreline and parallel Koolau and Waianae Mountains. Ringed by more than 100 beaches and a third of the state's surfing spots, Hawaii's 3rd largest island abounds in natural attractions laced with colorful history.

Metropolitan Meandering

Honolulu, the nation's 11th largest metropolitan area, would be worth visiting even if Waikiki did not exist. Restored old buildings fit more or less harmoniously with the new. When shoreline playgrounds grow a bit tiresome, Hawaii's early royalty can be glimpsed at Iolani Palace, the nation's only palace, a few minutes drive from old-world Chinatown and a moving remembrance of the bombing of Pearl Harbor that triggered US entry into World War II.

Outside of Honolulu and Waikiki, the five parts of Oahu might as well be on another island: Diamond Head to Hanauma Bay and Makapuu Beach Park, serene panoramas and great snorkelling and surfing just southeast of Waikiki; the Windward or east coast between the Koolaus and the Pacific, beautiful flora and beaches ending at the Polynesian Cultural Center in Laia; the North Shore famous for giant waves out to rocky Kaena Point, the turning point to the Waianae Coast, the most native part of Oahu and Hawaii; and the central area between Koolau and Waianae Mountains – pineapple country and Schofield Barracks, setting for the movie *From Here to Eternity*.

Unspoilt Beauty & More...

There much to see and do; the best known attractions, resorts and hotels are easy to find and this book hopes to provide you with an insight into the Hawaiian ways, and what to expect from a vacation in any of the different islands and their individual cultures. In particularly we give our recommendations to discovering the less-trodden paths and savouring the glorious unspoilt beauty of the islands.

Try completely new activities, to get in closer touch with Hawaii's incredible environs, under and above the water.

Above all make an effort to experience the serenity that is so much a part of Hawaii's paradise lifestyle – *Aloha*.

In the cool Hawaiian Tropical Botanical Garden.

Each of the island's *pali* (mountains) and volcanoes that you gaze at, climb or drive up are emerged in splendid isolation from the "hot-spots" on the ocean floor and are over 2,000 miles from any continent or landfall. For millions of years, no plants grew on these volcanic islands, no birds sang, the land was utterly inhospitable with raw and barren rock.

An aged statue near Sunset beach in Oahu.

Over eons they rose from the sea floor as bloating domes before erupting explosively on combustible contact with surface oxygen. Subsiding gradually, while at the same time feeding their height and girth to enormous dense weight, they sealed their spewing volcanic mouths, forcing fiery fluids to find new seams of escape. Choked with basalt, their long deep throats collapsed and finally volcanoes sank into caldera. Thus, huge mounds of raw lava were ready to be sculpted by wind and water into steep crevices, transforming rotund masses into sharp mountain forms, ridges, valleys and cliffs. Still more molten lava poured down steep slopes, black silicon fingers reaching for white skeletal polyps at the steaming edge of the sea.

Ropy or rough and spiny, the lava was porous, preventing lakes from forming at the surface but trapping precious water in dense lower layers ready to gush and ooze forth in countless fresh-water springs that would feed thousands of as yet undisturbed endemic plants found nowhere else on earth. (See *Flora and Fauna*, p 63)

The Discovery

The Hawaiian Archipelago was first found by the world's finest sailors – Polynesians. Two waves of these people arrived in Hawaii about 600 years apart, each perhaps pushing toward the furthest limits of a dimly remembered legend. The first Polynesian natives came as early as 500 AD and the second wave around 1100 AD.

Legend credits a great Polynesian chief named *Hawaii Loa* for this astonishing discovery of the volcanic pinpoints in the Pacific Ocean. A minute error and the seafarers would have been hopelessly lost. Guiding them to the legendary "heavenly homeland of the north" were stars and prevailing wind patterns, the shape and movement of cloud formations, certain kinds of birds or whales and most important, the navigators' own instinct and the faith that it

would work because it had worked for their Polynesian ancestors for over 5,000 years.

From Southeast Asia, through Indonesia, eastward to Micronesia and southwest to Fiji, the Polynesians had moved on to Samoa, Tonga, Tahiti and the far reaches of the "Polynesian Triangle", from New Zealand's Maoris in the south to Easter Island in the east.

Ancient seafarers in the first and later expeditions probably came from the Marquesas Islands and the Society Islands (Tahiti, Raiatea and Bora Bora). The remains of fish ponds, walls and irrigation canals on Kauai are thought to be the work of an incredibly industrious group of elf-like people, *Menehunes*, who preceded latter Polynesian settlers.

All we know for sure is that, long before Columbus, without compass or sextant, Polynesians in 60 to 80-foot double-hulled canoes transported to Hawaii household goods, food, animals and plants, a culture, religious beliefs and deities and a powerful caste system. The lives of Hawaiians were ruled by *kapus* (religious taboos), which included a strict division of labor between the sexes. Men handled *taro*, traditionally held sacred among Polynesians, pounded *poi* and served it; and built houses and canoes, wall and

An early 19th century heiau and tomb.

ditches. Women could not enter the man's house or eat with men. Breaking a *kapu* meant death.

Polynesians also brought with them a unique creative art, songs and *hula* dancing; and a primary god, *Kane*, whose invoked aid probably made the long journey possible. Countless accompanying spirits imbued everything animate and inanimate in the new land.

Further from any landmass than almost any place in the world, how did the Polynesians get to Hawaii? Why? History, archeology and anthropology cannot as yet supply complete answers to these questions "How shall we account for this (Polynesian) nation," Cook wrote in his journal, "having spread itself to so many detached islands so widely disjoined from each other in every quarter of the Pacific Ocean?...by far the most extensive nation on earth."

Captain James Cook

In January 1778, Captain James Cook sighted Oahu and then sailed into Kauai's Waimea Bay in two white-winged "floating islands", HMS *Resolution* and HMS *Discovery*. Hawaii was one of the last places on earth to be discovered by the west, strategically located between east and west. On his 3rd Pacific voyage, Cook had been searching for a Northwest Passage to link the Pacific and the Atlantic. He named the place he accidently found the *Sandwich*

An offering before Captain Cook and his party on Sandwich Islands.

– Islands, in honour of his voyage's patron.

There is the distinct possibility that Spanish explorers discovered Hawaii long before Captain Cook, but the timing of Captain Cook's arrival on the *Sandwich Islands* was, to say the least, uncanny. The discovery of Hawaii and the culmination of Cook's life exploring the vast Polynesian Pacific, would contribute significantly to Kamehameha's prophesied unification of the archipelago.

According to legend,*Lono*, the god of *Makahiki* (the Harvest Festival) had left the island of Hawaii after mistakenly killing his wife for infidelity, promising to return on a "floating island". During the annual celebration of Makahiki, Captain Cook fatefully sailed into a sacred bay called *Kealakekua*, the pathway of the god, on what *kahuna* (priests) proclaimed as "floating islands." The ship's masts with their sails furled looked remarkably like Lono's idol, a tall crosspole draped with white *tapa* cloth banners. Cook became "Lono returned," worshipped as a god until circumstances stripped him of his godliness and caused his death.

Kamehameha's Dynasty and Unification

Several great chiefs in the islands constantly warred among themselves. No one monarch had ever controlled all

Queen Kaahumanu

Kaahumanu's rebellious spirit came from a fiery lineage. Her mother Namahana, wife of Kamehameha Nui, the King of Maui, rejected custom and, after the king died, refused to become the consort of the King's brother. Instead, she married Keeaumoku who had rebelled against his Big Island king and had to flee to Maui as a result. Kaahumanu was born in a hidden cave near Hana where her mother and father had fled to avoid pursuit. Returning to the Big Island, her father took his family to live in the Kau district where Kaahumanu grew up.

As a young visitor to Kau, Kamehameha fell in love with Kaahumanu and married her when she was 17 years old, about 10 years after he first saw her.

Athletic, hot-blooded, tempestuous, Kaahumanu vied successfully for the role of "favorite wife". Keopuolani, "Sacred Wife", had a higher royal lineage and became the mother of Kamehameha's successors, Kamehameha II and III. Kaahumanu remained childless and formed a very close friendship with Keopuolani, Kamehameha's favorite Queen and a bold, brilliant politician who named herself Hawaii's first regent when Kamehameha died. It was Kaahumanu who emerged from Kamehameha's tent to announce his death and that his successor would be his son, Liholiho. Kaahumanu ruled on equal terms with Kamehameha II. He was only too glad to have her run the kngdom.

Loved and respected by the people, Kaahumanu had even dared to wear the king's cloak. She knew that the old ways were *pau* (finished). While Kamehameha was alive, she had infuriated him by eating forbidden foods, sleeping with other chiefs, drinking, running away and otherwise proving independent and uncontrollable.

Kapus – which restricted women's rights – deeply offended her. She persuaded the new young king to eat with her and Queen Keopuolani at a public feast, thus breaking a very important *kapu* which prevented men and women from eating together. In a few days, *kapus* were no longer enforced and *heiaus* (temples) and religious images were destroyed by royal decree. Hawaiian's religious systems and laws were gone.

One of Kaahumanu's triumphs was the abduction of handsome Kaumualii, Kauai's King, whom Kamehameha had never conquered. With Liholiho performing the trickery that brought Kaumualii to her royal tent in Honolulu, Kaahumanu married the Kauaian chieftain and thereby finally succeeded in bringing Kauai into the kingdom, (a feat which even Kamehameha had not been able to do). She even married Kaumualii's 21 year old son, in order to avert any revolutionary activities on Kauai!

the islands. When Cook made his first landfall in 1778, the prevailing goal of Kamehameha's warring royal relatives on various islands was a multi-island Hawaiian kingdom. A massive, six feet six inch, "savage looking" Kamehameha, in his mid-20's, was one of the *ali'i* (royalty) who boarded Cook's ship for an overnight visit with "Lono returned." The ship's weaponry, cannons and muskets, captured Kamehameha's attention. Later on, the cannons that fired on Kamehameha and supposedly injured him and other Hawaiians after Cook's death at Kealakekua Bay in 1779, spoke an unforgettable message of power.

Kamehameha was born at the tip of North Kohala, only a quarter of a mile from a great temple, *Mookini Heiau*, dedicated to the war god, *Ku*. The gods seemed to be on Kamehameha's side from the day of his birth rites. Empowered by his uncle, King Kalaniopuu, as

Kamehameha I

keeper of the family war god, *Ku*, Kamehameha knew that with these weapons he could conquer Hawaii and be king. Within 10 years after Cook's death, assisted by two captured Americans, Isaac Davis and John Young, Kamehameha had double-hulled canoes rigged with sails and cannons on the foredeck.

Kamehameha cannonaded Maui and subdued Kahekili, ruler of Maui, Molokai. Lanai and Oahu, who also controlled Kauai through his half-brother, Kaeo.

Were the gods on Kamehameha's side? Just look at the strange fate of Keoua, Kamehameha's Big Island rival. Routed by Kamehameha's weaponry near Honokaa, on the lush east coast,

Keoua and his warriors were crossing the barren Kau desert in their home district on the southern slopes of Kilauea when a huge cloud of fire, steam, poison gas and mud-ash spewed on them, killing a large contingent of Keoua's warriors and their families.

A demoralized Keoua understandably took this horrendous event as an ultimate sign of rejection by the gods. About a year later, in 1792, he accepted Kamehameha's invitation to talk peace at Puukohola Heiau. On the advice of his *kahuna* (priest and prophet), Kamehameha had built this temple, dedicated to his war god and a unified kingdom. Kamehameha ordered Keoua to be killed before his boat even landed. Keoua's death initiated this huge sacrificial *heiau* (temple), which you will see on Big Island (see Big Island, p 199).

By 1795, Kamehameha's artillery and superior numbers secured control over all the islands except Kauai, which took another 15 years, several abortive invasion attempts, and finally peaceful negotiations, to incorporate in his island kingdom. Kamehameha the Great restored the kingdom to peace and established trade with the United States and Europe before he died in 1819.

Western practices clearly were taking hold in Hawaii. Fortunes were being made in stripping Hawaii's forests of sandalwood for China-bound merchants. The arrival of foreigners and their blatant violation of *kapus* helped to bring on the downfall of Hawaii's system of religion.

Kamehameha II

Among Hawaiians, the greatest exposure to *haoles* (Caucasians) and their life without any *kapus* was experienced by women. It should not be a surprise, therefore, that women eventually led the overthrow of Hawaiian *kapus* (see box on Queen Kaahumanu, p 23). Among Kamehameha's 21 wives, Queen Keopuolani of Maui actually outranked him in royal lineage and

gave him two sons, Liholiho and Kauikeaouli, who succeeded him to the throne. Liholiho later became Kamehameha II.

The first whalers arrived in Hawaiian waters in the same year that Kamehameha died, one year before the missionaries. Hawaii became the mid-Pacific station for refitting whaleships heading for or returning from sperm whale fishing grounds off Japan. Honolulu and then Lahaina became favored places for whalers to drink and raise hell.

Missionaries landed in Kailua on the Big Island in 1820, fast spreading out to Honolulu and Lahaina. They built missions, schools and churches, developed the Hawaiian alphabet, created a written language, translated the Bible into Hawaiian and converted the natives. In long-sleeved woollens and ankle-length dresses in the tropics, they self-righteously rejected island food, fruit and lifestyles. Conscientiously, indeed fanatically, the missionaries devoted themselves to fundamentally changing

A 19th century missionary preaching to the natives at Kailua.

Hawaiian history.

Kaahumanu, the powerful queen regent, and other Hawaiian leaders soon converted to Christianity. Missionaries became government advisers and otherwise involved themselves in Hawaiian politics until they were pushed aside by American and British merchants and fortune-hunters.

However, in the 1870s, second-generation missionaries would gain the ascendancy once more after Hawaii adopted a Western system of private property and they could control the agricultural land essential to huge sugar plantations.

Kanoe, one of the queens of Sandwich Island.

Kamehameha III

Five years after Kamehameha the Great died, Liholiho and his wife, Kamamalu, died in London of measles. Liholiho's 10-year-old brother, Kauikeaouli, (Kamehameha's sole surviving son), became Kamehameha III and reigned from 1824 to 1854.

In the early 1820s, Chieftess Kapiolani's denunciation of fire goddess *Pele* on the very rim of Halemaumau in Kilauea's caldera was symptomatic of the times. Calvanist missionaries saw to it that females were draped in Mother Hubbard dresses and even managed to have the ancient *hula* banned as "lewd". Missionaries and merchants were able to control the regime of Kamehameha III, under Kaahumanu's influence until she died in 1832, and then briefly under

his half-sister, another high chief, Kinau, who lived until 1839. Young Kauikeaouli's life reflected Hawaii's cultural disarray. Like several Kamehamehas and other Hawaiian rulers after him, his life was complicated by alcoholism. His strong feelings toward his younger sister, Princess Nahienaena, could not result in the expected marriage and a child of the highest rank, as it would have in the old days. His attempted suicide, Nahienaena's marriage and the death of her child a few hours after birth, her illness and death at the age of 20 a few months later, all make a tragic tale.

Within four years, Kamehameha's governance had produced Hawaii's first Constitution which created upper and

The Merrie Monarch

Kalakaua travelled around the world to meet other monarchs throughout Asia, the Middle East and Europe, returning home to a grand coronation ceremony and celebration. This intelligent and charming king, scholar, poet and musician became the first reigning monarch to visit the US. In 1875, Kalakaua succeeded where Kamehameha IV and V as well as Lunalilo had failed in negotiating a Reciprocity Treaty giving Hawaii "favored nation" duty concessions and eliminating a tariff on sugar. Ironically, however, he strengthened the economic and political position of the very sugar planters who were calling for the United States to annex Hawaii.

"Kalakua Rex" (as he called himself) entertained lavishly at home, rebuilt the royal residence into the splendid Iolani Palace, and presented gala balls and *hula* events. *Hula* spectacles, previously banned for about 50 years, were celebrations of Kalakaua's pride in being Hawaiian and part of his efforts to restore suppressed and nearly extinct Hawaiian cultural traditions.

In addition to being a patron of the arts and reviving the *hula*, King Kalakaua wrote the words to "*Hawaii Pono*" that became the national anthem of Hawaii and later the state anthem. He had the *Kumulipo* — the Hawaiian creation chant — transcribed, salvaged hundreds of other chants that otherwise would have been lost forever, wrote many new chants himself, and created a classic book of Hawaiian legends and myths.

Having become too beholden to his leading political adviser, Walter Murray Gibson, and wealthy California "sugar king" Claus Spreckels, a politically weakened Kalakaua was subjected to a bloodless coup, including the signing of a new Constitution, the Bayonet Constitution, that curtailed his power, made him a mere figurehead, established discriminatory voting requirements based on property ownership, and shifted power to a few *haole* landowners.

The new cabinet renegotiated the Reciprocity Treaty to grant the US exclusive use of Pearl Harbor. Kalakaua was forced to sign the concession. The last king to reign in Hawaii, the ailing King Kalakaua died in San Francisco in January 1891 while on a convalescent visit.

lower houses of representatives, the latter to be elected by common people. In 1843, after an ill-fated attempt to seize Honolulu by an overzealous British frigate commander, the United States, France and England officially recognized Hawaii as a sovereign nation. A year later, Kamehameha III moved the nation's capital from Lahaina, the tawdry whaling capital of the Pacific, to Honolulu.

The king initiated a land reform plan, the *Great Mahele*, that would change Hawaii forever. Whereas all of Hawaii's land was owned by the kings and administered by their chiefs, under the *Mahele* only one-third goes to the king and his heirs (crown lands), with the rest divided between the government (public lands) and the common people. Two years later foreigners were given the privilege of buying and owning property.

Native Hawaiians, inexperienced in property management, lost their land by neglecting to register title or pay taxes, or they sold their holdings for a case of whiskey or a little cash. The entire island of Niihau, for example, still owned by the Robinson family, was sold for $10,000. Commoners' land and cheap government lands sold subsequently went mainly to *haoles* (caucasians), including many second-generation missionary families.

What started out as beneficent land reform turned into large landholdings that became sugar plantations as the California Gold Rush of 1849 and its aftermath created a growing market. In 1850, the Masters and Servants Act was passed, establishing an immigration board to import cheap plantation labor. Hawaii as a meeting place of east and west was launched.

Kamehameha's Dynasty Ends

When the handsome and elegant Alexander Liholiho, nephew of Kamehameha III became Kamehameha IV, the Hawaiian economy was in its 3rd decade of economic dependence on

Captain Cook.

whaling. However, by the mid-1850s, cheaper petroleum and coal for heating and lighting and the onslaught of the Civil War in 1861 sunk the industry. But the Civil War created a demand for Hawaiian sugar to replace the Confederate sugar supply. However, after the Civil War, the price of sugar fell and Hawaii's sugar needed to enter US ports without paying duty. In turn, Hawaii would offer the same privilege to certain American goods. Reciprocity legislation passed by the US Congress in 1876 was a boon to Hawaii's sugar industry.

A sugar plantation economy created a huge demand for foreign labor to do back-breaking work for low wages. Chinese, Japanese, Portuguese, Filipino and other contract workers poured into

Chinese workers hauling sugar cane.

Hawaii over the next quarter of a century, as the native population decreased by over 60 per cent! When the contracts of plantation workers were over, most of them stayed in Hawaii, some acquired land, others started businesses, many eventually intermarried with Hawaiians, as the native Hawaiian population continued to decrease.

In addition to rampant venereal disease, cholera, smallpox and leprosy (the latest imported scourge which decimated the population), Kamehameha IV's reign was marked by several personal catastrophic events. In a drunken and jealous rage, he shot his secretary and close friend, Henry Neilson, who died slowly over a two-year period; and two years later, his four-year-old son,

Prince Albert, died of an undiagnosed fever only days after his father treated him in an unkindly way. After the king's untimely death the following year at the age of 29, his elder brother, Lot, took over as Kamehameha V.

A stronger nativist than his younger brother, Kamehameha V proceeded to abolish the old Constitution to strengthen the monarchy, and revive dormant native traditions such as the previously banned *hula*. His British-influenced Constitution enacted in 1864 lasted 23 years. His forceful nine-year reign was to be the end of the Kamehameha Dynasty when he died a bachelor on his 42nd birthday at the close of 1872 without naming a successor.

A general plebiscite in 1873 selected

Prince Lunalilo, "Prince Bill", over Prince Kalakaua. Lunalilo's year-long reign was uneventful, but the United States clearly was eyeing the kingdom of Hawaii which possessed the largest natural harbor in the North Pacific, Pearl Harbor. Like his predecessor, Kamehameha V, Lunalilo died a bachelor, leaving it to the legislative assembly to select a successor.

In February 1874, high chief David Kalakaua was elected King of Hawaii, beating Queen Emma, widow of Kamehameha IV, by a wide margin. Irate supporters of Queen Emma rioted, but Kalakaua overcame that shaky start to his kingship in a grand courtly tradition that earned him the nickname of Hawaii's "Merrie Monarch" (see box story, p 27). Unfortunately, by the end of his

Liliuokalani, sister of King Kalakaua.

reign, King Kalakaua had to witness the loss of native rights and powers that he had worked so hard to restore.

King Kalakaua's strong-willed sister, heir-apparent Princess Lydia Liliuokalani (regent during his absence in San Francisco), became Hawaii's first reigning Queen, and last reigning monarch. Even more adamant than her brother about restoring native Hawaiian rights, she opposed the Bayonet Constitution and the puppet cabinet. She intended to overturn the constitution and allow only Hawaiians to vote. She is mostly remembered today as the musically talented queen who added many songs to Hawaii's musical repertoire, including the famous "Aloha-Oe".

The Republic of Hawaii

In 1883, the US government negated the Reciprocity Treaty with the award of a bounty on sugar production to domestic producers. This step significantly increased the pressure for annexation in Hawaii among Americans.

With the help of the US Minister in Hawaii, John Stevens, and a contingent of US Marines, the so-called Annexation Club, consisting of about 30 American businessmen, overthrew the Hawaiian monarchy and established a provisional government on 17 January 1893. Queen Liliuokalani stepped down to avoid bloodshed and to await reinstatement by the US Government. President Grover Cleveland's investigator reported that a "great wrong had been done to Hawaiians". President Cleveland's message to Congress said: "It appears that Hawaii was taken possession of by the United States forces without the consent or wish of the Government of the Islands."

The President's request to the US Senate to adopt measures to reverse this annexation was ignored. On 4 July 1894, the "Provisional Government" declared itself to be the Republic of Hawaii, appointed Sanford Dole as its first President and adopted a Constitution. The Republic of Hawaii was little more than name. An armed opposition attempt supported by the Queen failed, she was convicted of treason and placed under house arrest. Freed two years later, in 1896, Liliuokalani made a trip to Washington for an appeal to the US Government which was interested in Hawaii as a base of Pacific operations as the US was getting ready to implement its "Manifest Destiny" policies in the Philippines and the Spanish American War in Cuba. Admiral Dewey's victory in the Philippines dramatized the importance of a Pacific territory to the United States.

President William McKinley signed a Resolution of Annexation on 7 July 1898, and about a month later the United States received a "transfer of sovereignty" from President Sanford Dole on behalf of the Republic. A few days later, American troops arrived at a site next to Waikiki Beach, which was named Camp McKinley. Two years later, in 1900, with the signing of the Organic Act, Hawaii

Jonah Kuhio Kalanianaole,
Congress delegate, 1902-1922.

became a US territory, placing administrative and legislative control of Hawaii in Washington rather than locally

Sanford Dole became the first governor. The leader of two abortive revolts, Robert Wilcox was elected the first delegate to Congress, followed by Prince Jonah Kuhio Kalanianaole, who was elected 10 times. Prince Kuhio introduced the first statehood bill in 1919, which took 40 years for passage. The Territory of Hawaii had no vote in Congress but Prince Jonah Kuhio Kalanianaole, the territorial delegate to Congress, sponsored a Hawaiian Homes Commission Act in 1920 that set aside 200,000 acres of land for lease to needy Hawaii people with half or more native blood. When Prince Kuhio died in 1922, he took with him the last vestige of political power in the royal Hawaiian family. In recognition of his devotion to the cause of native Hawaiian rights, Prince Kuhio's birthday, 26 March, is a state holiday.

Sugar and pineapple production were Hawaii's great income earners, and economic and political power were increasingly concentrated in Hawaii's Big Five sugar companies (Alexander & Baldwin, Castle & Cooke, C Brewer and Co, Theo H Davies and Co, and American Factors) along with the Dillingham Corporation. This cartel owned the docks, shipping companies, stores, housing, police and Hawaii's Republican Party which was in power.

Atrocious working conditions in plantations boiled over in 1909 with a strike by Japanese workers. For 20 years the Japanese had worked long hours for low pay and degrading treatment. In 1910, after the strike, sugar and pineapple planters turned to the Philippines for a labor force that would accept abominable working conditions controlled by the Big Five. The Territory's colonial heritage safeguarded by a small elite even survived the Depression when sugar, pineapple and tourism collapsed.

World War II

Before World War II, the islands were becoming more multiethnic and racial. Japanese constituted over 40 per cent of the population by the time that Congress passed a law (1924) to stop the flow of Japanese workers and their families. About 100,000 Filipinos had arrived in the 40 years before World War II. Hawaii had the distinction of possessing the largest military bases in the United States: Pearl Harbor for the Navy, Hickam Field for the Air Force and Schofield Barracks for the Army. During World War Ii, the islands became the supply and training headquarters for the entire Pacific war effort and the

Crater of Kilauea.

military population jumped to over 400,000.

The disastrous surprise Japanese attack on Pearl Harbor on 7 December 1941 precipitated America's entry into World War II. The threat of the Japanese invasion led to an immediate declaration of martial law which remained in effect until 24 October 1944. For almost three years nearly all constitutional rights were suspended and the US Army took control of all public functions of the territorial and county governments, (right down to garbage collection)!

During the war, Daniel Inouye, a member of the most highly decorated combat unit in the US armed forces – the all Japanese-American 442nd Regimental Combat Team, lost his arm fighting in Italy. Inouye would go on to be elected to the territorial legislature, then become the state's first Congressman after ratification of statehood and eventually Senator. The lifting of martial law and Japan's unconditional surrender on 14 August 1945, opened a new era of change and internal tensions for Hawaii.

Unrest among plantation workers and militant unionism led by the International Longshoremen's and Warehousemen's Union (ILWU) led to a major strike against the sugar industry in 1946. Two years after this 79-day strike, a 178-day strike of the ILWU crippled the island's economy. During this period, allegations of communist infiltration and control of the ILWU slowed the progress of statehood.

Democratic Party strength grew enough for a sweep of the territorial legislature in 1954. Japanese Americans in the vanguard of the Democratic Party won half of the legislature's seats.

Aloha Statehood

Alaskan statehood in January 1959 finally put to rest questions about Hawaii's qualifications for statehood. Within six months, Hawaii's citizens endorsed Congress' bill, and the territorial legislature ratified Congress' approval unanimously except for the Island of Niihau. On 21 August 1959, President Dwight D Eisenhower proclaimed Hawaii the 50th state. In this year, regular jet services began between Los Angeles and Honolulu.

Statehood brought an economic boom, especially in tourism. Mainland *haoles* become the largest minority in Hawaii with over 30 per cent of the population, followed by Japanese Americans with about 25 per cent. Only 30 per cent of Hawaii's 1.3 million population have Hawaiian blood.

In 1976, sugar and US defense spending were dethroned by tourism. Receipts from sugar, pineapple and other agricultural production amounted to about half a billion in 1976. In 1976, the large double-hulled sailing canoe *Hokule'a*, a recreation of the canoe used by the first Polynesian settlers in the islands, sailed from Hawaii to Tahiti.

Government

"The Sandwich Islands" began to take shape as an idea in the 1850s. The overthrow of the monarchy in the 1890s triggered statehood as a serious proposal for the next 50 years. Congressional and especially southern, opposition only crumbled after 132,900 people in Hawaii voted in favor of statehood (with only 7,800 opposed). President Eisenhower signed the Hawaii State Bill on August 21, 1959, to make Hawaii the 50th state.

Like other states, Hawaii elects a governor and a lieutenant governor to head the Executive Branch. Based on population, 25 members are elected to the State Senate and 51 members to the House of Representatives. Inevitably, Oahu, with the largest number of vot-

State of Hawaii seal.

ers, dominates the House and Senate. Meeting during a once-yearly legislative session that begins in January, the legislative branch completes its work in about 90 days. Otherwise, however, Hawaii is different than any other state in its governmental structure. There are only two levels of state government – state and county and not city or town governments. For administrative purposes, the state is divided into four counties: Kauai covering Kauai and Niihau; the City and County of Honolulu, including Oahu and the Northwestern Islands; the County of Hawaii, just the Big Island; and the County of Maui, which includes Molokai and Lanai in addition to Maui. Perhaps the most significant event in Hawaii's recent political history was the creation in 1979 of the Office of Hawaii Affairs (OHA). The OHA gives some voice to native Hawaiian political activism. OHA members are elected by the people and not appointed by the Governor. After the monarchy was overthrown, 1.8 million acres of crown lands passed on to the Republic, then to the Protectorate, and finally to the state in 1959. Although the US government denies any involvement in the overthrow of the monarchy and any responsibility for reparations to Hawaiian people for land taken, under the state constitution Hawaiians are eligible to receive money for "ceded lands." The restitution process has been slow, impeded by the question of "what is a native Hawaiian?"

As a collection of islands and the only such state, Hawaii is an unusual economy, quite unlike any other state in the United States.

Its largest company, in terms of revenue ($3.9 billion in 1990), is a foreign company: Pacific Resource, owned by Australian-based BHP Petroleum. When oil prices rise, as they did in connection with the Gulf War, revenues jumped by 70 per cent.

The next largest company (previously holding the title of largest), was Castle and Cook, the state's largest land holder with more than four times the revenue of the second largest landholder, Alexander & Baldwin. C&C recently divested itself of the Dole Food Company and became much smaller

Kona coffee beans.

Times of Change

Another unique and governing aspect of the Hawaiian economy is that a handful of landowners own most of Hawaiian land, originally purchased at low prices.

Today, these companies are not under great pressure to de-

Koloa sugar mill in Kauai.

velop these lands for housing or other purposes.

Green & Rural

The sign at the Lanai Airport – Lanai the

Pineapple Island, The World's Largest Pineapple Plantation, may still be there but Castle and Cook has two hotels on Lanai and diversified agriculture as pineapple fields are phased out. Life has changed dramatically for pineapple workers, especially those employed by the hotels. About 5,000 acres are currently devoted to farming and ranching. One benefit is that Lanai will stay green and rural and Lanai City is likely to remain a quiet plantation town for the foreseeable future. Lanai is a microcosm of Hawaii where growth and progress are moving forward in a more cautious and planned way than ever before.

Another economic powerhouse and a major landowner (fated to be scaled down in the future), is the military. The military will continue to be a major source of revenue for the local economy. Nearly 125,000 military personnel, about half in the US Navy, and their dependents spend almost 2 billion dollars annually. On Oahu, more than 25 per cent of the island's land is controlled by the military. The Pearl Harbor Naval Shipyard, next door to the Pearl Harbor Naval Base, has the largest civilian payroll in the state and is the state's biggest industrial operation. Like the overall military and related civilian defense establishment in the United States, cutbacks are inevitable but probably less drastic in Hawaii. Construction is also nearly a $2 billion industry. Since the early 1960s, construction grew phenomenally, only slowing down at the end of 1990, as it did everywhere in the US. In the 1990s, the construction industry and the political system have to face issues of preserving the natural environment on each island.

Environmental protection and development of the *aloha* states' economy are intertwined issues focused on tourism as it rapidly replaces agriculture as the state's primary moneyearner.

Agriculture and Real Estate Development

At the start of the 1990s, there were more than a dozen sugar companies and hundreds of independent growers on 185,000 acres of cane fields. But, both sugar and pineapple are steadily being cutback. Sugar plantations on the Big Island's Hamakua coast have been drastically shrinking and phasing down. It takes a ton of water to produce one pound of raw sugar. Consequently, water shortages threaten Hawaiian sugar, too.

The crowded international sugar market, with more than a 100 nations producing sugarcane, sugar beets, and other sugar products and substitutes has created a glut of sugar and lower prices. From 40 sugar plantations 25 years ago, only 12 plantation operate today, thanks to price supports. Sugar price supports are up for renewal in the mid-1990s. Only a handful of plantations are expected to survive, with or without price supports. Pineapple growers have reduced their acreage by 12,000 acres over the 1980s and pineapple grown for canning is being phased out on Oahu and Lanai, the state's main source of pineapple production.

Today, the situation of sugar on Oahu exemplifies the industry's dilemma. There are 12,000 acres of sugarcane fields on the Ewa plain outside Honolulu. Historically these are some of the most productive cane fields in the world—in fact, 1985 broke the world record for sugar production per acre (21.62 tons versus 11.4 tons). However these fields lie in the way of Honolulu's expansion. Some 5,500 acres of cane fields are scheduled to be used for Kapolei, Oahu's "second city". The pace of development has been slowed only by the recent recession. There are 4.1 million acres of land in the Hawaiian Islands of which only 8 per cent is flat enough to raise crops. These same lands are the cheapest and the most accessible for residential, commercial and industrial development. About 4 per cent of the land in the state is zoned for urban development. That means that urban or large-scale construction is banned on about half of the land most suitable for development.

Only six large land owners own nearly 40 per cent of the land in Hawaii. Without strict land use laws preserving agriculture, much of the open space on Oahu and Neighbor Islands might rapidly disappear. Since the 1960s, about 90,000 acres of agricultural land has been taken out of cultivation.

However, only about 10% has gone into housing, 33,000 into diversified agriculture, including 22,000 acres in macadamia nuts and a successful flower and nursery business (and not including marijuana, an illegal billion dollar export crop) and the rest lies fallow or is used for grazing purposes.

On Oahu, where about 75 per cent of the state's population lives, 8 per cent of the land is zoned for housing. This is a sore spot for developers, a relief for people that want to limit or slow the rate of growth, and a gloomy prospect for people hoping for affordable housing. Developers and others argue that only 15,000 people or less are employed in agriculture (often neglecting to mention that about seven jobs are created for every job on the plantation). Since the shortage of land for building raises the price of land and everyone's mortgage and rent payments, questions are raised about the reservation of so much land for agriculture in the future. The issue became even more sharply focused when Castle and Cook announced termination of their Dole Pineapple operation on Lanai in September 1990. A senior official of the company stated at the time, "Plantation agriculture in Hawaii is a thing of the past." An even more controversial statement was made that diversified agriculture in the state only has a "limited future." He cautioned against the state being "geared for an industry that no longer exists".

Ironically, in 1989, agriculture in Hawaii enjoyed its 2nd best year. Sugar and pineapple generated more than $835 million, the largest revenues for the state after tourism and federal spending. Of the $577 million of unprocessed farm products, nearly 50 per cent was from "diversified agricultural products"– coffee, macadamia nuts, flowers, fruit and other crops. Lanai itself had

Pineapple plantation.

Aloha week parade, a treat for tourists.

launched diversified agriculture.

However, the prospects for these crops are still uncertain. For example macadamia nuts have been hit hard by Australian and other imports that make it difficult for growers to earn a profit. Kona Coffee exports suffer from time-consuming growing, roasting and processing that makes the nearly pure Kona coffee an expensive luxury item for consumers everywhere.

Nevertheless, 20 years ago no one would have predicted that Kona coffee would become so popular in blends. With better blends and marketing, Kona coffee may even make more money for growers and processors. Where Kona coffee is grown on the heights over Kailua-Kona at least it is not threatened by golf courses. However, mountainside coffee farm real estate is some of the most attractive and lucrative on the Big Island.

Even Castle and Cooke's critics, have had to sell off lands to developers in order to survive, some of whom have been strong advocates of developing new products from sugar to cattle feed, pharmaceuticals and other industrial and manufactured products.

Loaded under more than $100 million in debt, nearly 4,000 acres of Hamakua Sugar's most scenic acreage, around beautiful and sacred Waipio Canyon, has been rezoned for resort and golf course development, in order to raise enough money to keep the other half of the plantation in operation.

Tourism

With the dramatic decline of agricultural production, state and local governments are increasingly dependent on tourism for revenue. Today, more than 4 million Americans and 2 million foreigners (including 1.7 million Japanese) visit Hawaii annually, spending over $10 billion. That's almost 3 million more visitors than 15 years ago, a 50 per cent increase in this period.

With only one-eighth of the population of Oahu, Maui attracted 2.5 million tourists in 1990, only 800,000 fewer than Honolulu. Maui's visitors spent more money per capita than on Oahu. Until recently, Maui's goal has been eight million tourists by the year 2002. Maui is happy about this situation but Mauians are not completely positive.

The constant crowd are the high price that Hawaii pays to enjoy increased tourism. Construction of a $170 million international airport at Kahalui, double of the size of Wailea and thousands of other new hotel rooms, 10,000 more housing units, the proliferation of golf courses and the construction of new road and infrastructure projects constitutes a second great wave of construction after the 1960-75 building boom.

Tourism from the US mainland and other places in the world of course is directly related to their nation's business cycle and the level of consumer confidence, as the 1990-92 recession has demonstrated once again. With the

January 16, 1991 airstrike in Kuwait, reduced tourism, sluggish sales and revenues declines were even more adversely affected. However, the overall impact on Hawaii was less than it was on the mainland in 1991, until 1992.

In 1990, the top 250 companies in Hawaii, as reported by *Hawaii Business* magazine, showed $19.4 billion revenues, up 11.2 per cent over 1989. However, many companies in Hawaii that had posted continuous growth figures since the 1950s had flat or declining revenues in 1991. In some sectors, like construction, air and ground traffic related to tourism and the hotel business, business was off as much as 20 per cent. Hotel occupancy levels were dragging below 60 per cent. According to Hawaii's Department of Business, Economic Development and Tourism, expectations for 1991-92 were only 2.2 per cent whereas in 1990 the state's inflation-adjusted gain in gross state product was 4.8 per cent.

The Future

Hawaii faces several strategic economic dilemmas. Real estate values are rising so rapidly that affordable housing is becoming an increasing problem, a more extreme version of a major problem which Southern California is also experiencing but with the advantage of more usable land resources.

Another problem is that manufacturing and construction jobs are being replaced by lower paid service and retailing jobs. In part this results from the growth of a resort economy. Consequently, unemployment has been quite low in Hawaii although total wages have not risen in recent years.

Preservation & Protection

Another concern is the preservation and protection of the precious environment that attracts visitors and sustains the well-being of residents. Kauai is a prototype of the issues involved.

When Alexander and Baldwin announced its massive Kukuiula Project on the southside of Kauai, adding 3,500 units and 10,000 new people (more than doubling the population of rural Koloa), some affordable housing had to be included. However, more local residents were concerned that the southside, adjoining the growing Poipu Beach area, would never be the same again. Another case in point was the $200 million, 605-room Hyatt Regency Kauai, adjoining Poipu Beach, opened in 1991. The Mahaulepu area, previously owned by Grove Farm, was used by locals as an escape for decades. Some of Hawaii's best "hidden" beaches started at Mahaulepu. Residents fought the hotel's golf course all the way to the state's Supreme Court and lost. Southside shoreline is rich in archaeological features, artifacts and burial sites.

Native Hawaiians protested and, like the Ritz Carlton site on the Kapalua

Resort on Maui, a compromise was reached to fund the maintenance of historic sites and the relocation of burial sites. The adjacent 220-unit condominium development, Keoneoloa Bay Villas, also had to be redesigned to preserve numerous ancient burial sites. A Kauai County Burial Society was formed to create a preservation area and deal with other similar problems elsewhere.

Like the Mauna Kea and Mauna Lani resorts on the Big Island, archaeological features have become a part of the tourist environment. The key features of the resolution of these problems hold promise for the future – communication and the spirit of mutual accommodation. These qualities have become trademarks of Hawaiian life and the greatest hope for the future evolution of a satisfying Hawaiian lifestyle.

Hawaii is in the process of confronting the issues of growth management – pacing and guiding the level and type of economic growth toward a future where the quality of life is high and diversified. Today, a center of Asian and Pacific studies, Hawaii can become a center for bringing this knowledge together and using it for international betterment – an East-West meeting place.

Crossroads of the Pacific

Since the 19th Century, Hawaii has envisioned itself as "the crossroads of the Pacific" and the transshipment point for the Pacific. However, ships and planes

The military is a substantial contributor to Hawaii's economy.

no longer need to stop off in Hawaii on their way to Tokyo, Hong Kong, Singapore, and the rest of Asia and the Pacific. Hawaii's role has to be different. That role is more of a Pacific-Asian communication center.

Hawaii is part of the Pacific Region as well as part of the US and has the opportunity to play a unique and leading international role as the US increasingly turns its economic future towards Asia and the Pacific area and Asia seeks to bridge the Pacific to North America. The mix of eastern and western cultures in Hawaii is a great asset, especially since multi-cultural Hawaiians have learned so many valuable lessons over the past two centuries.

A 5¹/₂ hour flight westward from the West Coast of the United States is the shortest trip by jet to the eight islands of Hawaii: Kauai, Niihau, Oahu, Molokai, Maui, Lanai, Kahoolawe, and Hawaii (the Big Island). Stretching across reefs and atolls for 1,600 miles, Hawaii's nearest neighbor is the Christmas Island chain, a few rocks protruding from the sea 2,000 miles to the south. No surprise, therefore, that this remoteness and isolation remained undisturbed until the 6th century.

Lava faucets spill its molten load into the ocean.

Hawaii's islands are the youngest in a chain of 132 volcanic mountains that have been pushed up from the ocean floor over the past 25 to 40 million years as one of the earth's tectonic plates (the Pacific Plate), shifted minutely to the northwest.

The oldest volcanic remains are an eroded reef near Kure Atoll far north of the Big Island's Kilauea,

Geography & Climate

37

Black is beautiful at Kaimu.

the newest volcano, 200 miles southeast of Honolulu. The newest emerging volcanic island lies 30 miles south of Kilauea, 16,000 feet high but still 3,000 feet below the ocean's surface.

One theory suggests that hot magma from multiple stationary vents pushed through fissures in shifting plates in a manner that new volcanoes are created just south of the preceding ones. Another theory asserts that only one "hot spot" did all the work. However for Hawaiians, the explanation is that *Pele*, the fire goddess, after creating volcanoes on Kauai, Oahu, Maui and Hawaii, is still searching for the perfect home to live in harmony with her lover, high chief *Lohiau*.

Big Island

The Big Island, as the island of Hawaii is usually referred to, spreads over 4,038 square miles and is more than twice the size of all the other islands combined, but is home to only 125,000 people! About three-quarters of them live in the city of Hilo and the small towns of Kailua-Kona and Kamuela. For close touch with the awesome power of volcanoes and the creation and spirit of Hawaiiana, the Big Island is unsurpassed.

The road that loops 300 miles around the geologically youngest Hawaiian island embraces five volcanoes (Mauna Loa, Mauna Kea, Hualalai, Kohala and Kilauea), four of them lie

Hamakua waterfall on Hawaii Island cools and moistens the air.

dormant. Twin volcanic peaks, Mauna Kea and Mauna Loa, surpass in size any mountains or island in the world. The mountains are divided by a lava wasteland except for the heavily wooded eastern section. From the Saddle Road passing between the mountains, roads branch towards both peaks.

Snowcapped in the winter, the 13,796-foot dormant volcano Mauna Kea on the northeast side of the island has sugarcane fields on its lower eastern slopes all year-round. Between Mauna Kea and the Kohala Mountain ridge

Tsunamis

On 1 April 1946, the northern and eastern shores of the Hawaiian Islands were violently struck by the largest *tsunami* (tidal wave) in local history.

Generated by an earthquake off the northern Aleutian Islands, the massive wall of water killed more than 170 people as it smashed ashore at Hilo on the Big Island. Hilo had been struck by a similar wave on 2 April 1868, 78 years and 1 day earlier and was struck again in 1960, killing another 75 people, despite the fact that people along the shore were warned two hours previously.

Tsunami is a Japanese word for "long wave in a harbor". Earthquakes themselves do not cause *tsunamis*. Movement of the earth's crust sometimes causes a seismic wave of energy in the sea.

In the open sea, the distance between crests can be 50-60 miles apart and hardly noticeable as they travel over 400 miles per hour. In shallow water, however, speeds slows down and height builds up, especially around large island landmasses.

The 1946 wave only took 4 $^1/_2$ hours to reach Hawaii from Alaska. Originally over 120 feet high in Alaska, the wave was 35-feet high when it hit Hilo with the speed and force of a freight train. Water washing back into the sea sucks everything with it.

The second wave often is larger than the first with a stronger washback and the waves can continue for several more cycles.

After the 1946 disaster, the State of Hawaii installed an advanced warning system based on monitoring systems around the Pacific Basin.

However, some undersea fault movements can go undetected and *tsunamis* that originate locally occur too fast for an early warning system to benefit. If a severe earthquake occurs, people in low-lying area need to reach higher ground.

running to the northern tip of the island is the huge 250,000-acre Parker Ranch in Waimea, the largest ranch in the US. Ranch land runs down old lava fields to famous sun-drenched Kona Coast resorts, public beaches and other developments.

Further south, past the beauty of deep tropical gulches in the Hamakua Coast, over 22,000 varieties of orchid thrive in nurseries on the edge of Mauna Loa near the rain-drenched city of Hilo. This lush tropical town normally absorbs about 140 inches of rain a year. In 1990, (the wettest year ever recorded in Hilo), the figure exceeded 210 inches!

Mauna Loa is the world's largest active volcano. Mauna Loa's visible 13,680 feet actually is 32,000 feet from the ocean floor (that makes it higher than Mount Everest). Kilauea, rising from one side of Mauna Loa in Hawaii Volcanoes National Park, is intensely active, covering more and more of the south coast with fiery lava, both consuming and creating black sand beaches in the Puna district. Puna also contains Hawaii's last remaining lowland rainforests.

West of the Puna district, the desert-like Kau district covering the southwestern tip of the island exhibits yet another climate and terrain, drier near the shoreline but still lush along the lower reaches of Mauna Loa.

The dry west side of the island, the Kona and Kohala coasts, are dominated by the town of Kailua-Kona below the dormant Hualalai volcano. Above and south of Kailua-Kona, large numbers of small coffee groves and macadamia nut farms thrive on the climate and soil.

Kahoolawe

A hot and humid, barren, windswept island seven miles off the coast of East Maui, Kahoolawe is inhabited by wild goats who manage to survive on sparse vegetation and minimal water between winter rains. For over 40 years the scrubby landscape of this bleak and totally unappealing island (smallest of the eight major islands) has been used for US naval target practice.

Since the mid-1970s, naval bombardment has aroused protests by native Hawaiians. Named after *Kanaloa*, one of four major Hawaiian gods, Kahoolawe is sacred to Hawaiians. Many Hawaiian chants and legends mention the island which contains many ancient temples and fishing shrines, mostly preserved in excellent condition.

Kauai

Kauai is the oldest and most northwesterly of these islands. Seventy miles northwest of Oahu across a storm-wracked channel, Kauai's varied landscapes across its 33 miles form the garden spot of the Hawaiian chain.

On the eastern, southern and southwest rim of the Garden Isle, sugarcane fields and rich tropical life merge with many of Hawaii's most beautiful, un-

populated and also deceptively treacherous beaches. The Garden Isle's perimeter of beaches is unsurpassed in the South Pacific: from Kee Beach on the north past Hanalei Town to Poipu in the south and Polihale State Park beach in the west.

Sitting in the center of this roughly circular island is the wettest spot on earth – Mt. Waialeale (5,148 ft) – which annually distributes about 500 inches of rain to Kauai's multitude of rivers, streams and waterfalls, including the Wailua River, Hawaii's only navigable river. Wind-and-rain-sculpted valleys running from craggy peaks and towering cliffs 2,700 ft to the boiling surf below, form the unforgettable beauty of Kauai's Na Pali Coast. Just to the west of of the razor-sharp green spires and flower-choked gorges of the Na Pali Coast, the barren landscapes of 3,600-ft deep Waimea Canyon, the Grand Canyon of the Pacific, fall steeply to the coastline. It was here, in 1778 that Captain James Cook became the first westerner to set foot in Hawaii.

Kauai is full of marvelous contrasts and surprises like, intensely green Mt. Waialeale which adjoins a spectacular desert canyon. Many beaches of the Garden Isle are hidden gems that have to be ferreted out of deeply indented shorelines at the end of nameless dirt roads. Still a collection of small towns strung in a narrow band along three coastlines and the lush backdrop of stunning mountains is never far from view.

Discovered only recently as argu-

Dramatic Kauai landscape.

Hiking Safety and Precautions

Hawaii's wet mountainous areas on all the islands are mostly covered by thick vegetation and are either impenetrable, very rough going, or hide dangerous drop-offs. In addition to heavy vegetation, crossing terrain on doubtful trails can lead to even more risky cliffs with soft rock and useless, crumbly hand-holds. Never try to climb a *pali*.

Know where you came from at all times so that you can retrace your steps if you have strayed off the correct trail. When trails peter out, do not try to force your way through the rainforest or follow what *seems to be* a trail. Always stay on trails and don't be ashamed to turn around and go back to a recognizable starting or intermediate point.

If you're lost, look for ridges, rather than gulches, for easier movement and better visibility – of the terrain and yourself.

Wandering off trails in gulches or anywhere is not wise because hunters may mistake you for game. Unless the plan is to camp out and you are prepared for it, head back to your starting point with ample time before nightfall. Stay put if you get lost at night, light a controlled fire, and stay dry.

When streams are running strong, torrential rain upstream may produce dangerous flows or flash floods downstream. Settling your campsite and tent next to a pretty stream can be very dangerous. Certainly, never camp in a dry creek bed. Bathing or relaxing directly under waterfalls can be dangerous due to falling rocks. Assume that flowing water is contaminated by animals or human beings and don't drink from it.

Hikers along seacoasts tend to be lulled into thinking that all waves are the same size. Occasionally much larger waves hit shore with enough power to pull unwary hikers into the sea and snare them in treacherous currents.

Below 2,800 feet, Hawaii has its nuisance mosquitoes. Black widows, poisonous centipedes, and scorpions abound in low areas but at least you won't have to worry about dangerous land snakes. Wild pigs may attack but usually run off.

Carry water everywhere or be prepared to purify it. Drink enough water to avoid dehydration. (Much more water is needed to restore body water than to maintain it). Carry your own food. Do not even think about "living off the land." Do not eat any fruits or plants than you do not know. Even then, think twice about it.

Carry a stove if you intend to cook since firewood is scarce. **Be very careful with camp fires**. Peat soils in rainforests make fires very difficult to control. Gear should include a tent with rain-fly, broken-in boots, long pants, sunscreen as needed, rain gear, plastic ground cover, a first-aid kit, compass, plenty of insect repellent for frequent applications, an accurate map, a flashlight and extra batteries.

Carry your trash out and leave the forest or other terrain as you found it. Perhaps more of a problem than animals are humans.

Do not leave valuables in locked cars (or unlocked ones) at trailheads. If you come across what looks like marijuana patches while hiking, stay clear of them (another good reason for staying on known trails). Do not hike or camp alone. Do not leave your valuables in a tent. Always leave word with a ranger or official about your hiking plans (itinerary and expected route).

Otherwise, enjoy yourself!

ably the most beautiful Hawaiian island, Kauai offers only a few comparatively small concentrations of resort developments. Furthermore, these resorts are not very visible unless you look for them.

The Westin Kauai, an enormous and grandiose fantasy resort, is hidden from view in an unlikely location on Nawiliwili Bay behind Lihue, the budget accommodation and restaurant haven of Hawaii. A new Hyatt fantasy resort was built near the once remote Shipwreck Beach adjoining Poipu which still sits unperturbed in a sunny enclave under clear skies. Poipu's usual serenity was broken only momentarily by 1982's hurricane *Iwa* and an accompanying tidal wave.

Lanai

Only eight miles from Maui and lying dry in its wind-shadow, the pear-shaped island of Lanai in the heart of the archipelago is still the least known of the major Hawaiian islands. The curved ridge of mountains that rises sharply in the south has deep wet gulches on the east and, about 13 miles away, spectacularly steep cliffs rising up to 2,000 feet on the west.

Except for the uninhabitable east side, Hawaii's smallest and driest island was devoid of vegetation until Jim Dole bought the island in 1922 and piped and pumped precious water into Palawai Basin, creating the world's largest pineapple plantation (15,000 acres or about one-sixth of the island). The plantation town of Lanai City, built by Dole for pineapple workers, lies in the center of the island's tablelands.

In the highlands of the Pineapple Island, a zealous naturalist from New Zealand, George Munro, planted vast areas with Norfolk pines. A rough seven-mile jeep trail named after Munro climbs to 3370-foot Lanaihale, the highest point on Lanai. This road reaches through Norfolk pines and eucalyptus, traversing razorback cliffs and deep gulches, to

expose breathtaking views of neighboring Molokai, Maui and on exquisitely rare days, all the islands.

Pineapple farming was recently discontinued by Castle & Cooke, the new owners and two luxury resorts are transforming a small fraction of the 140-square-mile "hump" (*Lanai* in English) into a tourist destination. Hulopoe Beach, Lanai's finest beach near Manele Bay and its new hotel, are among the best in Hawaii. Isolated beaches on the northern and eastern shores are also among the state's secluded gems.

Maui

Maui has two distinct sides: the west side, focused on the touristy seaport of Lahaina and two major resorts, Kaanapali and Kapalua, beneath the western mountains; and the east side, dominated by the world's largest dormant volcano, Haleakala, surrounded by Haleakala National Park and an upcountry belt of private homes, protea and other farms, and picturesque towns and villages.

Created by two volcanoes whose lava flows came together in a plain between them, West Maui's mountains and valleys are inaccessible and East Maui is dominated by 10,025-ft Haleakala. At the foot of these mountains, along the entire southwest coast, a series of wonderful, sandy beaches stretch from Makena and Wailea on the east to even more secluded Windmill

Beach (Pohakupule Beach) on the west.

It is possible to drive (on sometimes bad roads) around the West Maui mountains, from Napili to Wailuku and around Haleakala, from Paia though Hana to Ulupalakua. These drives, frowned on by rental car companies, open up the geography of Maui off-the-beaten-track.

Beneath West Maui's mountains are two of the island's major coastal resorts, Kaanapali and Kapalua.

The gateway to these resorts is the colorful historic harbor town of Lahaina, retaining some of its old charm while bursting with shopping centers and retail stores.

The third major coastal resort, Wailea, at the southern end of the east coast, is the rapidly expanding gateway to the secluded beaches and roads of Makena and La Perouse Bay.

Above sunny Kihei and Wailea coastal beaches is Maui's upcountry. This covers the central plain with the commercial and port city of Kahului and Wailuku, Maui's charming capital, and the lush northern coast which includes the town of Paia. This verdant belt encircles the middle slopes around about half of Haleakala and includes a winery, ranches, protea farms, several delightful towns centered on Makawao, and the road up to Haleakala Crater. The awesome crater in Haleakala National Park is seven miles long, two miles wide, and 22 miles around.

From Paia to "heavenly" Hana along the northeast coast, the most sce-

nic drive in Hawaii twists and winds 51 miles through more than 600 curves. This road continues to Oh'eo Gulch and around to Uhupalakua Ranch.

Maui is said to be getting too crowded and overbuilt. Actually, only a few small parts of the island geared to tourists are experiencing major new hotel and tourist-oriented development: on the west coast, the semi-restored whaling town of Lahaina and Kapalua;

Not many rivers in Hawaii, but where you find them they can be most pleasant.

and especially the Wailea Resort on the southern coast of the east side of the island.

With about 90,000 residents, Maui houses about twice Kauai's relatively small population and is about 50 percent larger than the Garden Isle. Maui is 123 square miles larger than Oahu and supports about 810,000 fewer residents.

Molokai

Lying 25 miles southeast of Oahu, Molokai shares with Lanai the distinction of occupying the geographic center of the Hawaiian chain. Serenely embedded between Oahu and Maui, in spirit and pace Molokai is the opposite of these more developed islands.

Molokai acquired its infamous image from Kalaupapa, the living hell of exiled lepers that formed Father Damien's leper colony. Fear, however, is the most unlikely emotion that visitors today experience on The Friendly Isle. With the largest proportion of Hawaiians of all the islands, the legacy of old Hawaii, the spirit of *aloha*, is most alive on Molokai.

Only 38 miles long and 10 miles wide, about the size of Manhattan, Molokai was created by three volcanoes which still define the island's geography. Narrow Molokai has three totally contrasting kinds of scenery and climates:

• Deep gorges, rainforests and spectacular cliffs rise along the verdant northeast coast to culminate at the 4970-foot Mount Kamakou before falling more than 2000 feet to the island's western shoreline below;

• Arid Mauna Loa tableland rises to 1381 feet, scrubby cattle grazing lands and pineapple fields on the island's West End, edged on north and south shores by some of Hawaii's most scenic, remote beaches;

• Flat, rain-and-wind-plagued, lava-encrusted Makanalua Peninsula on the north coast, inaccessible except for a tortuous trail down to this broad lava plain jutting into the Pacific.

Molokai hides its treasures from view and the quest to see them on the island's 261 sq miles (less than half the size of Kauai) will not be easily forgotten. Unlike Kauai's magnificent *pali*, Molokai's comparable *pali* lacks a trail along the face of the cliffs to make them accessible. Lookouts and especially helicopter excursions compensate in their spectacular ways.

Ironically, formerly the most hidden and inaccessible place of all on Molokai, the Kalaupapa Leper Colony on Makanalua Peninsula beneath 2,000-foot cliffs, is more accessible today (by foot, mule or airplane) than the rest of the north coast.

On the east end of the island, Halawa Valley and its beautiful waterfalls require a hike of several hours from the end of the island's access road. In the center of the island, scrub and tough *kiawe* (like mesquite plants) along a four-wheel-drive upland road conceal lush areas at higher elevations in the Molokai Forest Reserve full of ferns, *ohia*, rare birds and plants, and waterfalls.

Relatively few tourists visit the contrasting dry western plateau and mountainous western landscapes of Molokai. Usually missed on this end of the island are several beautiful, remote beaches without many footprints.

Niihau

The most separated from the other Hawaiian Islands, Niihau's plateau of gently rolling grasslands, scrub grass and shallow lakes is only 17 miles to the southwest of Kauai. Hawaii's 72-square-mile "mystery" island is as arid as its neighbor is lush.

Recently opened to heli-tours by its owners, the Robinson family, Niihau supports about 300 Hawaiian plantation workers and their families on its very private 73-square-miles. An enigma that invites curiosity, a brief visit to a limited part of this island mainly opens up contact with a few locals to buy Niihau shell *leis* and "talk-story".

Oahu

Oahu means "gathering place" in Hawaiian. Not much larger than Kauai, Oahu contains more than 900,000 people compared to Kauai's 50,000 population. Three-quarters of Hawaii's population has gathered on the Capital Island and mainly in Honolulu.

Waikiki, the former swamp adjoining Honolulu, has become the tourist center of the Pacific, thanks to its justly famous two-mile stretch of beach. As the political, commercial and cultural center of Hawaii, the rest of the islands are defined as "Outer" or "Neighbor" Islands.

Two parallel mountain ranges, the Koolau and the Waianae, cross Oahu holding the fertile Leilehua Plateau between them. On the plateau are several large military bases and vast pineapple and sugar fields. Honolulu and Waikiki to Diamond Head and Koko Head fill the south coast, reaching up Koolau valleys toward passes to the windward side. Steep vertical valleys in windward

mountain flanks resemble the heart-stopping *pali* of Kauai.

Across the jagged Koolaus from Honolulu is the windward shore and the bedroom communities of Kailua and Kaneohe. Commuting workers from Kailua and Kaneohe see the steep and narrow green folds of these awesomely beautiful mountains every morning from traffic-filled roadways en route over one of two mountain passes and through tunnels to Honolulu.

However, with just a few minutes of patient driving northwest along the Windward Coast, familiar suburban sprawl soon becomes exquisite rural and rustic shorelines, dotted with beautiful white sand beaches and parks, some exposed and others hidden, before reaching the famed North Shore surfing beaches: Waimea Bay, Sunset, and Banzai Pipeline.

Residents of the Neighbor Islands view Oahu and Waikiki as metaphors for all that has gone wrong in paradise in terms of overdevelopment, commercialization, military control and influence and population growth. Many former residents of Oahu, including many artists who previously fled the Mainland, now populate the less crowded Neighbor Islands.

However, the realities of Oahu's landscape run counter to these prevailing notions which equate Honolulu and Waikiki with Oahu. Most of Oahu is not asphalt but a variety of mountainous regions and pastoral countrysides. A visit to Oahu's many beautiful beaches

Koko Crater on Oahu.

demolishes unfounded myths about the superior coastal beauty of the Neighbor Islands. A drive to Tantalus Lookout or the less remote lookout at Punchbowl offers dramatic day and night views of cityscapes found on no other island or any other metropolis in America.

Weather and Climate

Hawaii has two seasons, winter and summer. The main differences are the amount of rain and much less so the temperatures, especially from place to

three degrees for every 1,000 ft of elevation. But it also rains more in the mountains, especially on the windward side.

The weather in the off-season travel period (April through December 15, and especially April to mid-July and September to Christmas) may actually be better than the weather during high-season. However, it can rain hard and long in winter. Even on the dry Kohala coast on the Big Island, it can rain on and off for weeks in January. In the Hilo area, over 210 inches of rain fell in 1990, where it can deluge an inch an hour. Usually it's possible to find at least partly clear skies somewhere on an island even when it's raining somewhere else. Frequently you'll see rainbows along with rain or mist. Starting with summer, from May through mid-October, daytime temperatures are in the 80s and nighttimes from the low 70s to the low 80s. Consistent trade winds keep summer temperatures tolerable. Konas can blow in from the south or west and bring humid, sticky, or sweltering weather and thunderstorms. Showers are short. Days are longer.

Winter runs from mid-October through April. During this period, rains are more frequent, longer and more intense, even on leeward coasts. Daytime temperatures at sea level are in the mid-70s to low 80s. Nighttime temperatures run from the low 60s to the low 70s. Trade winds that usually blow in from the northeast are somewhat erratic and in February, may actually cease for a few weeks.

place. The average temperature year-round is 75°F. Between the warmest weather in August and the coldest weather in January, the daytime temperature may vary 5-7°F. February is the most unpredictable month.

Temperatures depend on elevation. In summer, go over 2,000-ft and it's definitely cooler; temperature drops

One of the most isolated places on earth, Hawaii is thousands of miles from the nearest land in North America and another thousand more miles from Asia. Eons ago, Australia was connected to the Asian continent by a land bridge. Not so Hawaii, born entirely of volcanic material oozing layer upon layer over millions of years from a "hot spot" deep in the ocean floor.

Hawaii's famed Bird of Paradise.

The birthing of Hawaii from Mother Earth continues every day. Rivers of fire from deep regions beneath the Earth's surface pour out from a seam torn in Kilauea's side on the Big Island. Kilauea's lava flows in a sense are reclaiming volcanic land it originally created, thereby adding new and larger surfaces for plants and animal life. At all altitudes, invisible to the naked eye, this ostensibly barren volcanic material is actually very much alive with new species creating complex new living

Flora and Fauna

53

communities or ecosystems.

Long before man arrived, life from older islands gradually colonized newer islands rising from the ocean in the Hawaiian Archipelago. Prehistoric colonization of Hawaii by plant and animal life was slow indeed: one plant or animal successfully colonized Hawaii once every tens of thousands of years. Over vast amounts of time, however, ocean-borne, bird-borne or wind-borne plants, insects, snails and birds did island-hop down the archipelago, changing with each new environment they occupied.

Herbs with small seeds had an easier time making it over the ocean to Hawaii than trees with large ones, taking hold more successfully and evolving into a large variety of shrubs and trees. Cooled *pahoehoe* (ropy) lava and its crevices providing shade and water became special-ized niches for pioneering herbs and ferns to gain a foothold on the islands.

Without a land bridge to traverse, animals had to drift or fly thousands of miles to the Hawaiian islands. Those that made it flourished: 15 bird species evolved into over 70. The wild goose, a former water bird, became a land bird, the *Nene*, today living only on volcanic slopes on Maui and the Big Island. It's easy to recognize: a goose with claws (much more useful on lava flows) in-

stead of webs. From a single finch or *tanager*, dozens of species of Hawaii's honeycreepers developed.

Mountains & Winds

Hawaii's mountains attract moist trade winds that cling to their windward slopes forming rain clouds. The leeward sides stay relatively dry. Certain mountains, like Waialeale on Kauai and Puu Kukui on West Maui act like giant rain magnets. Thus, perfect growing conditions await the arrival of a very select assortment of plants, insects and birds. Each windward or leeward fold, twist, turn and cut of the landform at different altitudes would create a unique habitat for flora and creatures that could miraculously survive immense ocean journeys.

New Species

Perhaps only a few hundred select seeds, light, small enough to be moved by wind, wing or water, and self-fertilizing ("bisexual"), like lobeliods and silversword plants, managed to bridge the

Fern forest in Volcano National Park.

mighty Pacific, germinate quickly and weed-like, set down roots in these different habitats. These botanical colonists found an utterly foreign, potentially hostile and highly differentiated ecosystems, requiring incredibly swift and specific adaptation in order to survive. Sometimes new species were strikingly different from kindred species in another niche on the same island.

Seed-bearing plants numbering only 275 spawned the over 2,000 species that the islands boast of today. This vegetation has found suitable niches somewhere, from desert to jungle, from sea-level to over 13,000 ft, without the normal burdens of ecological controls and of endemic dangers back on their ancestral homeground.

No big vertebrates and few small ones arrived (that is, until man came about 1,400 years ago). Some invertebrates (insects, spiders and snails) multiplied amazingly well: 25 land snails became over a thousand; and 300 original insect species produced the more than 7,000 kinds we know of. Hawaii has more than 100 described breeds of unique spiders and numerous undescribed ones. For example, amazing "happy face" spiders have evolved in Hawaii's rainforests. An astonishing assortment of masques cover their translucent bodies, only $1/4$ of an inch long.

When new plant species arrived ever so slowly and selectively from various continents, perhaps clinging to the feathers of migratory and marine birds, they

Lush Rainbow Falls, Hilo, Hawaii Island.

found no furry land animals to eat them. Hooks, thorns, poisons and sticky or protective structures proved to have no value. With no protective purpose, Nature disposed of these needless defenses.

Consequently, nettles growing in the Wao Kele O Puna rainforest be-

neath Kilauea on the Big island are not nettlesome; mints that elsewhere in the world have a pungent taste to ward off deer and rabbits are mintless in this rainforest.

Hawaii's native plant and animal world today is full of surprises. Some

flies, contrasted with more than 1,000 species of native moths: the brilliant Kamehameha butterfly, first discovered in the early 19th century and the Blackburn's butterfly, its beautiful light green underwings speckled with black.

Another surprise for visitors to the "Orchid Island" is that only two species of orchids are native to the Big Island. The hundreds of others growing and displayed for sale around Hilo and Puna districts are "foreigners".

Virgin, rich valley niches, criss-crossed by intersecting differences of precipitation and altitude, yielded micro-climates with fantastic opportunities for rapid evolution without biological competition. For example, among Hawaiian flowering plants, the original colonists' small, easily-dispersed seeds were transformed into large fruit and seeds without any of nature's ingenious features that would make them easily dispersible. The floral rule of Hawaiian habitat became "stay put" and formed a hybrid.

Almost the same natural pattern of habitat-bound selectivity and evolutionary inbreeding occurred for insects and birds. Perhaps no more than 150 original insect castaways on the archipelago evolved into more than 10,000 species, many biologically tied to one island habitat and/or plant and most found nowhere else on the planet.

So isolated were these islands that thousands of fragile plants grew, bloomed, twisted and crawled through their evolutionary cycles in this sub-

adaptations were awesome and astonishing. For example, a group of plant-eating caterpillars became viscious meat-eating ones, tiny green hunters with powerful talons perched on leaves or twigs ready to devour flies, spiders and even wasps.

There are other kinds of surprises as well. Only two native species of butter-

Koa trees.

limely perfect climate and nowhere else, along with over 60 endemic birds. The ancient *o'o a'a* bird still exists but you'll be lucky to see one without traveling to upper rainforests. The Hawaiian stilt can be seen on ponds on Kauai and with even more difficulty, on the Big Island. At a bird sanctuary like Kilauea Lighthouse on Kauai, white and red-tailed tropic birds, Laysan gooney birds and frigate birds are easy to spot, but scarce elsewhere.

Vanishing Species

Homo sapiens, of course, were the big, unanticipated surprise in this supremely isolated and pristine setting. In retro-

spect, the loss of Hawaii's isolation was inevitable. Starting over a thousand years ago, the ocean screen was breached by Polynesian explorers, opening the way for a deluge of plants and animals to reach Hawaii.

Native ecosystems were shaken by the impact of man and the swarm of alien organisms that he brought with him. Dry lowland areas were the first and most affected followed by the wet uplands.

The Marquesan seafarers who arrived in their double-hulled canoes more than 600 years before Captain Cook had a profound effect on the insular native flora and fauna. Before Polynesians arrived, there were no pineapples, coconuts, bananas, taro and

sizes and shapes in almost any conditions, from wetland miniatures to giants on high slopes; and Koa, a form of acacia that is less abundant and grows best in deep forests. Its straight, thick hardwood trunk was favored for dugout canoes.

Koa became a valuable commodity after foreign settlers arrived and it was cleared for farms and buildings. In the process, the balance of nature was upset, leaving *koa* and other trees exposed to new insects and other predators. Cattle and pigs grazed and foraged *koa* seedlings out of large tracts. *Koa* trees mostly retreated from lower to higher mountain elevations, as high as 7000 feet. Extinct plants in the Hawaiian islands generally caused extinct insects. And extinct plants and insects in turn have made birds extinct. Fifteen species of birds evolved into 70 native species before the Polynesians arrived, living in small areas, eating only certain plants and insects. Farming and burning of large areas by Polynesians and, later, commercial agriculture and land developers, has done much more damage to birds since the arrival of Capt Cook than the Hawaiian tradition of using bird feathers as featherwork ornaments for royalty. The cumulative impact is that one-third of Hawaii's native bird species are extinct and dozens more are endangered.

Introduced, alien or exotic (terms used interchangeably) plant species, including weeds, have flourished in Hawaii. While foreign weeds choked out

sugarcane and also no mosquitos, flies, fleas, gnats and reptiles. They brought dogs, pigs and uninvited rats that ate away at what was left of flora and birds after forests on the dry leeward slopes were burned and replaced by *pili* grass, valued for house thatching.

When Captain Cook's *Resolution* arrived at Kauai and then Hawaii, there were more than 300,000 Hawaiians, and still more than (or only) 1,200-1,300 species of flowering plants, most found nowhere else in the world. Today about 10 percent of these are extinct. The rest of the native species miraculously survived, but about 30 percent are endangered species, about half of those in the United States.

Among the most visible and prolific survivors are *ohia* trees that grow in all

A feathered friend in technicolour coat.

the 4,000-7,000-ft level of windward Haleakala on Maui, together with the Maui Parrotbill and the Pueo or Hawaiian owl.

Animals

Only two mammals are native to Hawaii: the Hawaiian monk seal (which can be seen at the Waikiki Acquarium) and the Hawaiian bat.

You're more likely to see dolphins and whales on boat cruises or at Sea Life Park on Oahu.

Other mammals mostly are wild game that hunters may shoot during special seasons, including: wild pigs, goats, cattle, sheep, axis deer and pronghorn (mainly on Lanai). The mongoose, brought to Hawaii in the 1880s to control the rat population, roams during the day and sleeps at night, when rats

native plant species, roof rats from whaling ships did in honeycreepers and foreign mosquitos spread bird malaria and pox. The mongoose and rat played a big part in decimating ground-nesting birds.

Alien flora, now numbering some 4,000 species, crowded out native plant species. Native plants below the 1,500-ft level have had the highest rate of extinction and there are few native Hawaiian birds below the 3,000-ft level. Over 40 incredibly varied Hawaiian Honeycreepers, as different as parrots and thrushes, evolved from one species and today the survivors have retreated to

Wildlife observation at Molokai Island Preserve.

are running around. Consequently the mongoose itself became an environmental problem by killing large numbers of ground-nesting birds.

Flowers and Plants

More than a thousand different kinds of flowers thrive in Hawaii between the alpine tundra on the summits of Mauna Loa and Mauna Kea and the lush lowland rainforests along the oceans and in deep valleys where **ohia lehua** loves to grow to majestic proportions, frequently surrounded by huge **hapuu tree** ferns. Sometimes in pink, yellow or cream garb, tufts of red **lehua** stamens dangle delightfully at the end of tight knots of greenish-grey leaves. Down below, tall **oleander** shrubs with clusters of disarmingly similar colors conceal the fact that its single or double flowers clutch the tip of a poisonous plant.

Protea, a hardy plant.

Nowhere is the riches of Hawaii's native and introduced species of flowers and plants shown more brilliantly than at **Foster Botanic Garden**, on N. Vineyard Blvd. adjacent to Honolulu's apartment and office towers. Several thousand plant species cover about 20 acres, including 24 of Hawaii's protected trees.

Bird of paradise, heliconias, yellow and white gingers, huge collections of bromelaids and orchids adjoin nearly 600 species of palm.

The orange and blue sharp petals of the colorful **Bird of Paradise** from South Africa bloom in six stages—a new one emerging on 2-5 ft. stalks every few days. A member of the same family as the Bird of Paradise, the **Lobster Claw Heliconia** has leaves the color and shape of cooked lobster claws. Small green flowers grow within its leaves.

After visiting Foster Botanic Garden, literally complete your botanical education at the 400-acre **Hoomaluhia Park** and **Lyon Arboretum** on Oahu. This botanic park and nature preserve on Windward Oahu (at the end of Luluku Rd. off Likelike Hwy.) is planted into native communities of rare and endangered plant species divided by geographic regions of the tropics. The 124-acre Lyon Arboretum in upper Manoa Valley, a botanical and horticultural research arm of the University of Hawaii, contains over 400 species and cultivars of gingers, taros, palms, figs, orchids, ti and others.

Reason enough to visit Waimea Falls Park, adjacent to Waimea Bay on the North Shore of Oahu, one of the state's primary tourist attractions, is its

Waimea Arboretum, one of the finest in the state and the U.S. About 3000 species of threatened plants native to the U.S. and Hawaii (one-fourth) and displayed in 36 major plant collections are arranged by genus, family and geographical area.

Kalopa State Recreation Area on the rugged north end of the Hamakua Coast, 5 miles south of Honokaa, has a 4-acre arboretum and a guided nature trail through 100-acres of native rain forest. Here you can see ohia, kopiko, kolea, hapuu and other native rainforest species.

Edible Fish

ahi	yellowfin tuna
moi	threadfin
aholehole	mountain bass
'o'io	bonefish
aku	skipjack tuna
ono	wahoo
akule	bigeye scad
opapapaka	pink snapper
'ama'ama	mullet
'opelu	mackerel scad
a'u	marlin, swordfish
'ula'ula	red snapper
awa	milkfish
ulua	jack creval
mahimahi	dolphin fish
weke	goat fish

Bromeliads

The pineapple is the best-known of more than 2,000 bromeliad species. Francisco De Paula Marin, a Spanish interpreter and physician for Kamehameha I, brought the first pineapple to Hawaii from South America. This remarkably varied plant group is at home mostly in subtropical and tropical parts of North and South America from the swamps of Louisiana to the tip of South America. Visible and microscopic scales on their leaves absorb water and minerals from the air and provide protection from heat and wind. Some bromeliads, like Spanish Moss, anchor to trees and others root in the ground or on rocks. It usually takes a year for bromelaids to flower, only once and then the mother plant dies within a year or two. New buds that appear on the base of the mother plant live on.

As colorful as orchids, the hardiness of bromelaids have made them a favorite for house plants. Starting in the 1950s, island growers brought these prolific plants back from Florida, Brazil, Costa Rica and wherever they could find appealing and new varieties. Foster Gardens and the Lyon Arboretum on Oahu, Kiahuna Plantation on Kauai, and other public gardens around the islands display hundreds of species and hybrids of these fascinating plants that are so addictive for growers.

Along the coast, the shrubby beach naupaka and trailing vines grow around many rare native Hawaiian coastal plants. Native trees such as the lama and the naio grow on old lava flows along the coast. Further up the slopes, koa intermingles with fragrant maile that is prized for leis. More well known as a lei flower, the plumeria or

Plumeria is used for in leis and floral decorations.

frangipani graces the end of stubby tree branches with white, yellow, pink or red blooms.

In wet mountain areas fanned by moist winds, a variety of epiphytes cover tree and shrub trunks and limbs. **Bromeliads** and **orchids** are the most familiar kinds. In these same moist regimes, in any season heavily scented **ginger** always display two or three shapes of red, yellow or white. On Maui, the Kula side of Haleakala nourishes several farms that grow mainly the bulbous and incredible shapes of red, yellow, orange and multicolored **protea** from Africa and Australia, but you'll see many bromeliads and ginger, too.

Dry volcanic earth at 6,000-12,000 foot levels on Maui's Haleakala and on the Big Island' Mauna Kea spawns the remarkable six-foot high stalks with silver spike leaves known as the **silversword**. Once in its life, in August, a lovely flower tuft blooms dramatically on this silver sunflower—and then it dies. Another intriguing plant, **Naupaka kuahiwi**, blooms in Kauai's Kokee forest with only half a flower. According to legend this mountain flower is betrothed to a coastal flower,

Precious Opihi

Only a few hardy souls still risk their lives to snatch lowly *opihi*, a small conical-shaped shellfish, from surf-pounded rocks. Called "the fish of death" because so many people have lost their lives while prying *opihi* off rocks, this delicacy cherished by Polynesians is a species of limpet native to Hawaii.

Shorelines that are easier to reach have been scrapped clean of *opihi*. Nowadays *opihi* hunters must scramble onto precarious perches to remove limpets clamping onto their rocky homes with a suction of up to 70 pounds per square inch!

Served raw and sometimes still alive, locals eat them straight from shells — salty, yellow-and-gray morsels, slightly crunchy, rubbery and wiggling all the way down the hatch. Even *Pele* reputedly munched this protein-packed appetizer, when they were far more plentiful. Today, at luau's or other special occasions, scarce *opihi* are rationed, especially at $200 a gallon shucked.

Naupaka kahakai, also with only half a flower.

Definitely drive up Kimo Drive off of Highway 377 on Maui to see the variety of protea at **Upcountry Protea Farm**. Nearby **Kula Botanical Gardens** (near the junction of Kekaulike Rd. and

Silversword plant, a crater inhabitant.

Hibiscus, the yellow variety being
the state flower.

delightful stream pool.

While on Kauai, be sure to see and take a tour of the National Tropical Botanical Garden in Lawai off Highway 50. On Maui, a satellite of the National Tropical Botanical Garden, **Kahuna Gardens**, at Kalahu Point off Hana Highway, offers really worthwhile tours of Hawaii's edible and medicinal plants.

On the way to Hana, you'll be pleasantly surprised at the remarkable variety of white ginger, philodendron, white impatients, elephant-ear taro and other ornamentals that fill the **Keanae Arboretum** in this shaded valley. In Hana itself, **Helani Gardens** has one of the islands' most interesting and eclectic blends of native and foreign species of plants.

The hibiscus indeed has good reason to be concerned about its status. Over 700 varieties of orchid grow commercially and wild on the islands, preferred for *leis* and less fragile than hibiscus.

On the Big Island, you'll see more orchids than anywhere else on earth and also more **anthuriums**. These unforgettable heart-shaped, waxy red creations will surprise you with orange, pink and even white-green varieties that remain shiny and fresh as cut flowers for as long as three weeks.

At **Akatsuta Orchid Gardens** (on Highway 11, 3 miles east of Volcano Village) you can see over 1600 species of plants. Along the 4-mile Scenic Route off Highway. 19, another amazing collection of plants grows in a lush valley

Kula Highway) shows off almost 30 years of growing native and Pacific region flower and plant species.

The **hibiscus** may be the official state flower of Hawaii, but it is taking no chances about being supplanted. Over 5,000 hybrid varieties of familiar red, yellow, pink, white, orange and more bloom 12 hours a day through the islands tempting you to pick them—only to collapse. The poor *Koki'o* is too easily damaged to be used in *lei* making. You can see plenty of yellow-flowered hibiscus in the unusual setting of the **Keahua Forestry Arboretum** adjacent to the Wailaleale Forest Reserve beyond the end of Highway 580 near Wailua on Kauai. The scenic 2-mile Kuilau Trail runs through the arboretum, passing a

Palms and kukui trees.

on the other (North) side of Hilo, **Hawaii Tropical Botanical Garden**.

Some people pass up the **Panaewa Zoo** south of Hilo, located in the Panaewa Forest Reserve, without knowing that it is one of the better places to see native and other plant species. At **Nani Mau Gardens**, 3 miles south of Hilo, and **Rainbow Tropicals** near the Zoo, both off Highway 11, you can see most of the native and imported that you're looking for in Hawaii. Look for the *pikake* (peacock), a fragrant white jasmine that was the favorite flower of Princess Kaiulani, known as the Princess of the Peacocks.

Foreign plants like Brazil's bell-shaped lavender **jacaranda** are happy enough in Hawaii to flower almost any time of year but mostly in spring. Other seasonal plants abound, often showing brilliant red leaves like the **poinsettia** during November and December and the **royal poinciana** on umbrella-like trees in June and July.

The bright gold and yellow flowers of the **gold tree** usually bloom only in spring but sometimes make a special effort to share magnificent blooms even in midwinter.

Seasonal plants are not really strange, even in Hawaii. The nocturnal **night-blooming cereus**, however, does qualify as both strange and seasonal—opening its huge white buds into yellow blossoms between about 8 p.m. and sunrise for about two weeks of blooming between June and October. Like the cereus, which originates on Mexican cacti, most of Hawaii's plants and flowers were brought to the islands and have flourished in over 200 different natural habitats and many of the loveliest and most fascinating gardens in the world.

Fruits and Vegetables

James Dole deserves the credit for importing a fruit native to Latin America, the pineapple, planting it on Oahu at the turn of the 20th century and subsequently making a hybrid variety one of the most popular fruits in the United States.

Production is more profitable elsewhere in Asia, however, the Hawaiian pineapple industry is rapidly shutting down. Purchased in Hawaii, Pineapples often cost more than in some cities on the mainland.

Sugar marketed as the "C&H" (California and Hawaii) brand is the product of cooperative refining by the local sugar companies. This industry made up the heart of Hawaii's 19th and 20th century agricultural economy before tourism. Sugar growing, which takes two years for growing, milling and refining, is being phased out of Hawaii on the Big Island after producing more sugar per acre than than anywhere else in the world.

Papayas benefit from rich volcanic soil, sunshine and water. These delicious fruits grow on unbranched trees and can be picked as soon as they turn

yellow. Summer is the peak harvesting time. Papaya trees grow quickly, have a shorter growing cycles for fruit, and the fruit needs no processing. Production of this fruit loaded with beneficial vitamins and enzymes is rapidly expanding on the Big Island but the fruit is still expensive in Hawaii because much of it is exported. Papaya is a low calorie fruit

Sugar cane fields.

(60 in half a papaya) that is good with any meal.

For those not counting calories, **avocadoes** (over 200 calories in a quarter of one) are plentiful year-round in two varieties: Guatemalan in winter-spring and West Indian in summer-fall.

Some **coconuts** are available in markets but most coconuts are cut down while green to prevent injury and damage when they fall.

Fresh coconut meat is delicious and the meat is very tasty. However, weight-watchers know that one cup of grated coconut amounts to more than 300 calories. Every part of the towering coconut palm is used by Pacific islanders and banana trees are just as useful for making clothing, medicines, roofing, dyes and even alcoholic beverages. Hawaii's delicious tree-ripened **bananas** can barely keep up with demand in local markets, especially the delectable apple bananas.

Mangoes grow on tall shade trees. The fruit ripens in spring and summer. Known as the king of fruits, mangoes in paradise are rare except in people's yards and the stands of street fruit vendors. (Importing mangoes is forbidden because of a weevil in the seed so don't pack any in your luggage.) Make sure that the mango is ripe; only then does it taste sweeter and juicer than peaches. Peel the skin off first.

Guava is grown commercially on Kauai and otherwise grows all year in lots of backyards and in the wild. Its roundish yellow fruits grow on a small shrub or tree and ripen between June and October. It looks like guava but it's really **passion fruit** (*lilikoi*), seedy and tart, but makes the best butter product you've ever tasted (*lilikoi* butter).

Poha, better known on the mainland as the Cape Gooseberry, is a small yellow-green or orange fruit enclosed in a thin, cream-colored, paper-like husk. Its fruit resembles a cherry in size and shape, and the juicy pulp has many small seeds.

A native Brazilian fruit related to the ground cherry and tomatoes, *poha* has grown wild on the Big Island since the mid-19th Century. From seeds, the plants bear fruit in three to four months and peak in six to eight. Plants grow upright for a few feet and then spread out for as much as 10 feet.

No pesticides or other non-organic chemicals are used to grow poha on the Big Island. After harvesting, thousands of poha berries have to be removed from their papery husks, chilled, washed, graded, pureed, pressure-cooked and made into preserves.

Ohelo berries are harvested high up on the Saddle Road and in the Volcano area on the Big Island. *Ohelo* is one of the few native fruits, found only on the Big Island and East Maui, thriving on lava beds in both places. It only grows wild and especially well near Kilauea. Legend says *ohelo* is sacred to *Pele* and that some *ohelo* should be offered to *Pele* before eating any of the fruit.

Macademia nuts are mainly grown in big orchards on all coasts of the Big Island. The largest processing plants are in Honokaa on the Hamakula Coast and Keaau south of Hilo. Production of the nuts and prices have dropped in response to foreign competition. The nuts are sold shelled and salted or unsalted. Either way, their calorie count (25 per kernel) is high.

Maui Onions, grown in Kula in Maui's Upcountry or on Molokai, are big, sweet, and delicious. **Maui russet potatoes** also have become famous in potato chips.

The Himatione Banguinea.

Birding

There are two kinds of islands: Continental and oceanic islands. Continental ones have at some stage been a part of one of the major landmasses - before the tectonic plates of the earth shifted or sealevels rose to cut them off. Oceanic ones have always been islands, most are created from underwater volcanic eruptions. Of all the oceanic islands in the huge Pacific Ocean that cover more area than all the dry land on the earth combined the Hawaiian Islands are the most isolated ones. The nearest continent of North America is 4,200 km away, and not a single rock sticks out of this stretch of open water. To the west and

south of Hawaii there are plenty of other oceanic islands but they are even further from continental land.

A Variety of Endemics

This concept is important when you go birdwatching on Hawaii. Of all the vertebrate land animals only birds have managed to reach and colonize this distant chain of islands. There are no indigenous reptiles and amphibians on Hawaii and only one mammal, the Hoary Bat. The original stock of today's Hawaiian birds flew in from North America several million years ago, some probably also from Asia and Australasia. Isolated on Hawaii they developed into a fascinating variety of endemic species found nowhere else on earth. While there are fewer indigenous bird species on Hawaii than in continental tropical regions the place is regarded as maybe the most fascinating in the world for studying species evolution and diversity.

The large Hawaiian family of honeycreepers is a case in point. Out of the 44 endemic birds on Hawaii 28 belong to this family, Drepanididae. It is thought that they all derived from the same ancestor, a finch. Today they display a startling diversity in colour, size and especially bill-shape - each species having adapted to a seperate biological space. This way they are similar to the famous Darwin's Finches on the Galapagos Islands which Darwin used

Vestiaria Coccinea.

for his studies on how species evolve. In fact Darwin expressed a great interest in the avifauna on Hawaii but never managed to visit the islands himself.

Extinctions

While oceanic islands are often a treasure house for biological research they very easily turn into the conservationist's nightmare! The birdlife that the first Polynesian settlers found on Hawaii when they landed about 1,400 years ago must have been truly amazing. Seven species of geese, two ibises, seven rails, many of these flightless since oceanic island birds often lose their ability to fly. Also three owls, a sea-eagle, 15 additional species of honeycreeper, probably tame birds easy to observe as island birds with no traditional enemies are often completely fearless of man. They are all gone now, known only from fossil remains dug out recently from the kitchen middens of these first humans on Hawaii! At least 39 bird species got exterminated this way before the Europeans arrived, they in turn took out 14 species more. Twenty-four other species, more than half of those endemics that have survived until today, are now so rare that they are regarded as threatened with extinction by the International Council for Bird Preservation.

Not all the birds ended up in the Polynesians' kitchen fires. Most disappeared because their habitats got de-

The unmistakable Hawaiian Nene goose.

stroyed or because they had no resistance to introduced pests. The Polynesians cleared most of the native forests around the coasts of Hawaii shortly after settling. They introduced mammals like pigs, dogs and rats against whom many of the birds had no defenses. After the Europeans arrived practically all the original lowland vegetation cover gave way to pastures for goats, cattle and deer, and later, to tourist development. More alien mammals like rabbits and mongooses caused havoc to the birds and/or their habitat. A further threat was introduced late in the 19th century in the form of a strain of mosquitoes carrying a disease fatal to native birds. Being tropical the mosquitoes thrive in the hot lowlands below 600

meter's elevation where a combination of factors today has done away with practically all endemic Hawaiian birds.

Explore the Highlands

You have to travel up-country to find and see some of the peculiar species of birds found only on Hawaii. The Hawaii National Park gazetted in 1916 is one of the best destinations, it is today subdivided into Haleakala National Park and Hawaii Volcanoes National Park and is an important location for native birds.

A system of State Parks has also been established more recently, the Kokee State park on Hawaii and Waimea Canyon State Park on Kauai are good birding locations. National Wildlife Refuges have been gazetted to protect wetland birds, e.g. the important Alakai Swamp on Kauai. Private landowners and Non-governmental conservation societies like the Audubon Society and the Nature Conservancy have also set aside land as forest bird preserves on all the main islands.

The habitat on the volcanic mountains where the native birds are found today is characterised by what is called ohia forest, a unique type of montane rainforest. The most fertile elevation is between 800 and 2,000 metres a.s.l. Traveling on these steep slopes is tough, the vegetation is dense and it rains a lot; with an annual rainfall of up to 12,000 mm the mountains of the Alakai Plateau on Kauai, the eastern part of Maui and the Hawaii Volcanoes National Park are among the wettest areas in the world. On some of the coastal areas just nearby annual precipitation may be only 300 mm! In dryer elevated areas koa forest is widespread or a combination of ohia and koa, this terrain is home to the remaining true Hawaiian birds.

Some Native Birds

Most of the Hawaiian endemics are passerines, i.e. they belong to the most advanced taxonomic order of perching birds. But there are a few exceptions like the Hawaiian Hawk that is still thinly but widely distributed. Also the Hawaiian Goose or Nene that came so close to

following its relatives into extinction that the population dropped to 30 birds in 1952. A captive breeding and reintroduction program brought the population back up to appox. 2,500 individuals today.

Among the passerines there is still the Hawaiian Crow, the Hawaiian Thrush, the Nihoa Millerbird (a warbler), the Elepaio (a flycatcher), and a few members of the honeyeater family originating from the Australasian region to look out for. And then of course the honeycreepers. Many members of this family are very rare and confined to only certain areas on just one of the Hawaiian islands. Some populations are less than 500 birds, others are so rarely seen they might in fact already be extinct. Vice versa an entirely new species, the Poo Uli, was discovered as recently as in 1973 in a remote part of Maui! Some species have a similar greenish plumage and are difficult to view well when they move about in the top of the ohia forest canopy. The most spectacular ones with huge, down-curved bills are already extinct, it seems that the most specialised birds are always the first to disappear. But some nice species like the Apapane and the Iiwi are still relatively widespread and numerous.

Introduced Aliens

So if they are not Hawaiian birds what are all those birds we see all around town, you might ask? And around the

Fregata Minor.

coast? Well, just like the human settlers brought in their mammals with them when they came to Hawaii so they introduced all their favorite birds, some on purpose others by accident. Aliens, the ornithologists call them, escapees, exotics. They were often deliberately introduced to brighten up the landscape but are today mostly regarded as a biological pollutant creating a uniform and impoverished environment. Introduced birds totally dominate all developed lowland country on Hawaii. One hundred and seventy different species have been recorded at the last count, they by far outnumber the original bird species left! They include many so-called game birds (mostly pheasants), often released for hunting, as well as adaptable species in the starling, pigeon, white-eye, bulbul, finch etc families that have established themselves all over the Pacific region.

A Wealth of Sea Birds

The last category of Hawaiian birds is maybe also the most impresive in a way, by their sheer numbers the sea birds provide some of the most stunning avian spectacles in the world. These birds are not endemic to Hawaii, in fact they can be found all over the Pacific region, but they are indigenous residents or naturally occuring migrants.

It is a geological paradox that the largest, tallest and most mature appearing of the Hawaiian islands are in fact the youngest. The island of Hawaii is the newest and is still volcanically active while Kauai to the west is 10 million years old, heavily eroded and surrounded by coral reefs and Laysan further north-west is ancient at an age of 20 million years, it has no volcanic soil left, only low limestone formations and sand dunes. Oceanic birds don't usually nest on inhabited islands. Some are nesting on isolated cliffs 1-3 km from the main Hawaiian islands. But otherwise sea birds prefer the remote low islands to the west, places like Laysan and all the other shoals and atolls which

form the Northwestern Hawaiian Islands, most of which are included in the Hawaiian Islands National Wildlife Refuge established in 1906 to protect the breeding sea birds from hunters. Twenty-two indigenous oceanic birds breed in Hawaii, including several members of the tropical bird, booby, storm petrel and shearwater families. On Laysan alone there are estimated no less than 3 millions sea birds; there are huge colonies of Laysan Albatross, Great Frigatebird and most numerous of all,

The delicately beautiful Phalaenopsis orchid, one among the numerous orchids which thrive in Hawaii.

Sooty Tern. 2 million Sooty Terns nest on Laysan Island each year, about half the Hawaiian population, making this species the most numerous bird in the state.

Further Information

"Birds of Hawaii" is a classical book by G. C. Munro, now available in a revised edition, Tokyo 1960. Otherwise Hawaiian birdlife is covered in great detail in ... "Hawaiian Birdlife" by Andrew J. Berger, Honolulu 1981. A handy identification guide is available in "A Field Guide to the Birds of Hawaii and the Tropical Pacific", by H. D. Pratt et all, Princeton 1987. More information can be obtained from the Hawaii Audubon Society, P.O. Box 22832, Honolulu, Hawaii 96822.

The Hawaiians

The second of two waves of Polynesians that sailed to Hawaii brought with them a culture, religious beliefs and deities, a powerful caste system, unique creative art, songs and *hula* dancing and a central god-figure, *Ku*, that periodically fueled merciless warfare.

Poetic *mele* (oral traditions) carried all they knew of their history. Countless accompanying spirits imbued everything animate and inanimate on *Hawai'ia* ("Burning Hawaii", the name first given to the Big Island and later adopted by all of the islands) with meaning and measure, generating the stories and legends that nourished a culture without written language but with an endless source of visual and spiritual inspiration. This culture has thrived on the natural beauty of Hawaii. The quintessential Hawaiian culture speaks of reverence for life: *alo* (to face); *ha* (the meaning of life); and *mana* (the spiritual power within life).

Commemorating past Hawaiian royalty in parades.

Offering to the gods an old Hawaiian tradition.

Hawaiian Deities

Ku, who represented the male side of the universe, had many manifestations: bringing prosperity and procreation but also strife, conflict and war and inspiring human sacrifices at special war temples (*hieau*). *Hima*, his wife, was the expression of female fertility and reproduction. Together, they were the parents of all mankind. *Ku's* help usually was sought to make crops grow, fish successfully, and generally to produce prosperity. *Hieaus* were built in honor of *Ku* and the war gods (*Kukailmoku* and *Kuwahailo*). Fierce-looking effigies were carried into battle to win their support for victory. Some examples of these *Ku*, made of mother-of-pearl eyes set in red *i'iwi* feathers with fiercesome mouths of jagged dogs' teeth, can be seen at the Bishop Museum.

Kane, god of life, created earth and heaven, stars, moon and sun, procreator of all life and ancestor of all chiefs and commoners, is central to a legend amazingly similar to Genesis.

Kanaloa, lord of the ocean and its creatures is also ruler of the dead and revered patron god of healing. Kanaloa is frequently coupled with Kane whom, in certain legends, he is said to have rebelled against and in others, travels with about the land to benefit mankind.

Lono, god of fertility, planted flowers, trees and grasses and was also god of thunder, winds, and agriculture. Lono was central to games and celebrations,

Besides seeds and roots of plants for cultivation and their domestic animals strapped to double-hulled canoes, Polynesians also brought with them a belief that any object could possess a spirit or be a god; a patron god and ritual for every activity and every facet of life; a complex collection of myths, laws and taboos (*kapu*) governing daily life and the behavior of the sexes; countless superstitions and the presence of ghosts as well as human spirits moving about separated from their bodies; and a pantheon of hundreds of Tahitian deities.

Polynesians landing on the Hawaiian Islands worshiped gods in the form of idols made from wood, stone or feathers.

Old woodcarvings and heiau tell alot about beliefs and superstitions.

and making Earth beautiful. The fall *makahiki* harvest festival was dedicated to Lono.

Pele, most revered among the gods today in Hawaii, was the volcano goddess who arrived on the islands as a powerful sorceress. After she was killed by an outpouring of lava, she returned to the islands as the lava spirit and eventually found a home in Kilauea Crater on the Big Island after searching all the major islands.

The best known and most popular of the gods, **Maui**, "the trickster", is celebrated among Hawaiians, Tahitians, Samoans and the Maoris of New Zealand. *Maui's* exploits included "lifting the sky," fishing up the Polynesian islands and bringing fire to mankind. In one legend *Maui* lassoed the sun by its rays over Haleakala to make it promise to slow down so that his mother's *tapa* cloth could dry.

Ancient Temples

Hawaiian deities have been worshiped at home and at outdoor temples varying in dimensions from football field-size to smaller stone platforms, terraces and lava stone walls. The original perishable wooden and thatched *heiaus* are gone. Some held the bones and *mana* (power) of dead *ali'i* (chiefs), others were god houses or oracle towers where *kahuna* (priests) prayed on behalf of *ali'i*, conducted ceremonies or made prophecies. Some of these *heiau's*, like Puukohala Heiau on the hillside above Kawaihae Harbor on the Kohala Coast of the Big Island, were built for sacrifices to the war god, *Ku*.

Heiau or temples, the domain of *alii* (chiefs) and *kahunas*, their gods and goddesses and the sanctuaries for violators of *kapus*, were central to ancient Hawaiian life. The ruins of large open temples (*heiau*) can be seen on each of the islands. Huge lava rock platforms, some larger ones 125 by 250 ft, with 13-ft walls rising 30 ft, are usually all that remain. Structures of lashed wood and thatched-grass huts on the upper level served as prayer houses and storage locations for ceremonial materials. Some *heiau* date back to AD 600 and most were abandoned and wrecked when the

Hawaiian Folk Mass, Waikiki.

Park, near Ka-waihae. On Oahu, Puu O Mahuka Hieau stands above Waimea Falls Park and Kaneaki Heiau in Makaha Valley has been thoroughly restored by the Bishop Museum. On Molokai's southeast coast is a large concentration of *heiau* and Iliiliopae near Pukoo is the best preserved.

kapu system was overturned after Kamehameha's death.

Several of the major *heiau* are located on the Big Island: Puuhonua O Honaunau National Historical Park, south of Kailua, a place of refuge sitting on the edge of Honaunau Bay; Mookini Luakini Hieau, a site at the northern tip of Hawaii near an ancient fishing village (Lapakahi Historical State Park) and the birthplace of Kamehameha; and Puukohala and Mailekini Heiaus, next to Spencer Beach

Hawaiian Renaissance

The society that Cook and later *haoles*

Dressing up at festivals.

found in Hawaii was feudal but not primitive or Stone Age. The kings on each major island and their *alii* (chiefs) and advisors (*kahunas*) presided over a complex division of labor, specialization in skills from island to island, great diversity and ingenuity in agriculture and its irrigation systems, ponds for raising fish, medicinal use of herbs,

Festivals are always a great social time.

astronomy and other sciences. For about 30 years, starting with the chronicles of Captain James Cook in 1778, Hawaiians were praised for their strength, intelligence and cleanliess. By the 1820s, after 40 years of contact with westerners, commentators complained about their apathy and laziness. Demoralization and destruction of the culture had begun.

Out of a long history of tribal wars, Kamehameha of the Big Island of Hawaii emerged as overall chief of six of the eight Hawaiian Islands (1795), sixteen years after the arrival of Captain James Cook at Kealakekua Bay (January 17, 1779) on the same Big Island. Disease introduced to Hawaii by westerners in the late 18th and 19th century shrank the Hawaiian population estimated at 300,000 at

Celebrations at University of Hawaii.

the time of Cook's first visit to less than 40,000 about 100 years later. Disease undermined weakened pride

With a high birthrate, Hawaiians are gradually recovering from this decimation. Still, Hawaiians or persons with Hawaiian blood number about 180,000, only 18 percent of Hawaii's population. These *keiki aina,* children of the soil, are vigorously participating in many local efforts to salvage neglected and suppressed Hawaiian traditions, including revival of traditional Hawaiian crafts and the *hula.* Restored *heiau* are often used as settings for cultural awareness. festivities aimed at reviving interest in the islands' heritage of arts, crafts, music, language, and sports.

Hawaiian craftsmen produced the world's finest featherwork and some of its most beautiful wood carving. These craftspeople often receive public recognition, honors and media attention, some of it is only public relations aimed at tourists but most of it is genuine. The most inspiring fact about contemporary Hawaiians may be their claim to have lived in a delicate balance and harmony with nature for a thousand years before western civilization discovered the islands.

A Land Of Minorities

The history of relationships between Hawaiians and *haoles* and Hawaiians and Orientals is characterised by a great deal of distrust and bitterness. But there

Festivals & Special Events

Oahu

The Hula Bowl at Aloha Stadium, usually on the second Saturday in January, brings all-star football players from the mainland to wrap-up the football season on Hawaii.

From Mid-January to late February, the Chinese New Year celebration and the Narcissus Festival, with a queen pageant, traditional lion dances, drums and other festivities can be seen in Chinatown and Honolulu along with the Japanese Cherry Blossom Festival (in late February and early March), including Kabuki Theater, Tea Ceremony and other events.

Easter Sunday's sunrise service at the National Memorial Cemetery of the Pacific, Punchbowl Crater, is a moving and memorable ceremony. Another quite different sunrise ceremony on Buddha Day, April 8, is held in Kapiolani Park with flowers, dancing and pageants. Lively and fun, the Annual Hawaiian Festival of Music covers all types of Hawaiian music at the Waikiki Shell in April, repeated again in June.

The Pacific Handicrafter Guild Fair in Ala Moana Park in May is a "must" for samples of the best crafts in Hawaii from all the islands. The Guild's Christmas Fair in Thomas Square is another major crafts event that is your best place for Christmas shopping. The Festival of the Pacific, a week long celebration of the songs, dances, arts and crafts of 40 Pacific Rim countries happens in early June.

The most spectacular parade in the island, on June 11, Kamehameha the Great Day, passes the king's statue in front of the Judiciary Building hung with 40-foot leis. As part of these celebrations, the Mission Houses Museum Fancy Fair provides another opportunity to see some of the best craft arts in the islands.

The Prince Lot Hula Festival, the Annual Ukulele Festival in Kapiolani Park, and another Pacific Handicrafters Fair, this time in Thomas Square, provides plenty of opportunities at the end of July to see dance, music and visual art from all over Hawaii.

The flower parade from downtown to Waikiki during Aloha Week in the third week of October is the last big parade on Oahu before the end of the year. The Artists of Hawaii annual exhibition in late November offers an opportunity to see the work of a cross-section of some of Hawaii's best artists at the Honolulu Academy of Arts.

Maui

The old-fashioned Makawao Statewide Rodeo at the Oskie Rice Arena over July 4 brings the island together for a rip-roaring good time.

Big Island

The Merry Monarch Festival, in Hilo, in April, is the state's premier ancient and modern hula competition that runs for a week and brings Big Islanders together with visitors from other islands, an otherwise rare occurrence. On June 11, Kamehameha Day, a princess wearing a traditional pau (full skirt) on horseback from each island is represented in the grand parade down Alii Drive in Kailua-Kona.

The Parker Ranch Rodeo and Horse Races on July 4, in Paniolo Park, Waimea, with Hawaii's top cowboys for a Wild West Hawaii day.

The Ironman World Triathalon Championship dominates Kailua-Kona and the Kona-Kohala coast at the end of October.

Four days in early November are set aside for the Annual Kona Coffee Festival in Kailua-Kona which takes you through every phase of coffee growing, processing, and taste-testing, crowning of a Kona Coffee Queen and other special events.

Kauai

Prince Kuhio Festival at the **end of March**

Noise and colour in Chinatown.

...Festivals & Special Events

honors native son Prince Jonah Kuhio Kalanianaole accompanied by Hawaiian pageantry, canoe races and a royal ball.

Buddha Day on Kauai in **April** enjoys extra special festivities, including pageants, flower festivals and dance, because Japanese-Americans constitute the largest segment of the island's population.

Lei Day on **May 1** brings everyone out with leis and inspires fierce lei-making competitions usually held at the Kauai Museum.

Japanese O-Bon Festival from **mid-June through August** consists of a series of weekend ceremonies and dances dedicated to sending ancestors' souls back to Buddha. With *cho-chin* (Japanese paper lanterns) hanging over head to light the path of deceased souls, persons of all races dressed in Kimonos and happi coats dance inside a roped-off circle to the beat of O-Bon drums and taped background music. Food flows from concession stands and games are played until the O-Bon dance ends at midnight. The next day (Sunday) at sunset, boats stocked with food provisions and rafts carrying *cho-chin* are launched into Kukuiula Small Boat Harbor to send ancestors' souls back to Buddha symbolically.

Leeward Oahu, is one of Hawaii's notable exceptions. You can participate in a *hukilau* (net fishing), or play *ulu maika*, a Hawaiian bowling game, Tongan shuffleboard or other games. Demonstrations by the ocean of fiber and coconut weaving (and coconut tree climbing) and other crafts adds special interest. Dancers on three stages perform Tahitian, ancient and modern hula, with the audience having a chance to wiggle their hips, too. The cuisine is only adequate but it doesn't seem to matter.

The Beachside luau at the **Outrigger Hotel** is another luau that stands out for authentic performances and *aloha*.

At the **Old Lahaina Luau** in Maui's Lahaina, the food is catered by a local Hawaiian family, with *kalua* pig, *poi*, *lomi-lomi* salmon, and other Hawaiian delicacies. As the sun sets over Molokai and Lanai, the entertainment begins with Tahitian dances, ancient and modern hula. Best of all, the hula is danced by some of Maui's best Hawaiian dancers. Genuine *aloha* spirit and hospitality prevail.

The only other luau in Hawaii that comes close for excellent and authentic cuisine, atmosphere and entertainment is at **Kona Village** on the Big Island's Kona Coast. More Polynesian than Hawaiian, the Tahitian and other food is magnificent. Dining in an open-air thatched pavilion, with hula dancers on stages across the lagoon, perhaps a moon shining down on the luau, is an unsurpassed experience.

was also considerable intermarriage. Hawaiians have no historic belief in racial superiority. Chinese, Filipinos and Japanese who came to Hawaii without women or were looking for mates found Hawaiian mates and were welcomed into Hawaiian families.

Hawaiian Heritage

Between 1910 and 1930, part-Hawaiians grew to out-number full-blooded Hawaiians. The pattern in the 20 years before World War II became an equal number of inter-marriages and marriages inside the Hawaiian group. Before 1940, most Asian-Hawaiians were part Chinese, producing successful business people and politicians, combining business acumen and a special human touch. Most important, through the intermarriage of Hawaiians and part-Hawaiians, the Hawaiian heritage and the tradition of *aloha* spread further through the population.

Part-Hawaiians have included some of the most prominent members of Hawaiian society: US Congressman Daniel Akaka, Parker Ranch owner Richard Smart, President of the First Hawaiian Bank, John Bellinger and others. The future looks promising based on the ability of Hawaiians to assimilate and be assimilated

Father and daughter of Hawaii.

into many cultures migrating to Hawaii's shores combined with the resurgence of pride in Hawaiian heritage.

Every racial group in Hawaii is a minority, a condition that exists nowhere else in the world. Most of these minorities originated in Asia and Polynesia. Hawaii has done a remarkable job of assimilating these many foreign cultures in a very small physical space.

But Hawaii is not quite the "melting pot" yet in the sense attributed historically to the United States. Minority communities in Hawaii visibly coexist, sharing the same space and mostly the same economy. Increasingly, however, individuals are engaging in interracial marriage. People familiar with Hawaii are amazed at the high marriage rate. It seems as though unmarried Hawaiians are a minority within minorities and at least half of these marriages are interracial. Racial diversity has resulted in a

minimum of overt racial friction. In schools, however, where Caucasian children are in the minority, they sometimes are victims of racial tensions.

Caucasians and Japanese have practically equal proportions of the population (about 30 per cent each); Hawaiians and part Hawaiians are far behind in numbers (18 per cent); Filipinos are less than half of that (10 per cent); and Chinese, 5 per cent; Koreans, Samoans and Blacks are about equal (each about 1 per cent); and 4 per cent who are just "mixed". Hawaii is the only state in the United States in which minorities outnumber whites.

Haole usually denotes Caucasians from outside of Hawaii or even old-time residents (*kamaaina*). Sometimes locals use the term haole to mean Caucasians who do not understand, appreciate or relate to Hawaiian lifestyle. More often *haole* is a casual way locals, usually a

A Filipino is just as much
Hawaiian.

racial and ethnic mixture themselves, refer to whites, both resident and visiting. *Haoles* even refer to themselves as *haoles*, so the term doesn't possess much negative emotional meaning.

The Japanese

The first Japanese arrived in *Tenjiku, "the heavenly place "* (as Hawaii was called in Japan), as contract laborers in 1868. Their numbers did not start to rise rapidly until after 1884, during the reign of King Kalakaua. Three years earlier, Kalakaua visited Japan during a round-the-world tour and initiated treaty discussions focused on the immigration issue.

Kalakaua even boldly suggested to Emperor Matsuhito that one of the Emperor's princes marry his niece and heir to the throne, Princess Kaiulani. The proposal was not accepted but over 7,500 Japanese arrived in Hawaii over the next five years. Within 15 years (by 1900), the Japanese population had passed 60,000, twice the number of Hawaiians or Caucasians. Planters were relying heavily on Japanese labor to get the field work done on plantations that white workers would not do. Up until World War II, Japanese were the lowest paid workers in all occupations.

During World War II, following the Japanese attack on Pearl Harbor, over 1,400 local Japanese were shipped over to the mainland to join thousands of Japanese-Americans placed in concentration camps, interned as potential security threats. As fighting men during the war and in political warfare back home in Hawaii, Japanese-Americans in Hawaii more than made up for the humiliations and deprivation heaped on them during World War II.

By 1975, Hawaii could boast of a Congressman of Japanese descent, a Japanese-American Governor and a President of the University of Hawaii, a local Japanese-language radio station and a television station, several Japanese-language newspapers and other evidence of Japanese presence and influence in Hawaii.

Based on their numbers, positions in the economic and political power centers of the state and economic con-

Chinese ladies chat in Chinatown.

nections to Japanese business and financial sources, Japanese-Americans in Hawaii have become the pivotal racial group in the state at the close of the 20th century.

The Chinese

Like their Japanese counterparts, Chinese contract laborers patiently endured overwork under awful plantation conditions, discrimination and intimidation to become politically, financially, socially and artistically successful in Hawaii. The first Chinese-American in the United States to occupy a seat in the United States Senate was Hawaii's Hiram Fong.

The heavenly place of the Chinese was *Tan Heung Shan—Country of the Fragrant Tree* — for the Chinese because of the big sandalwood trade. Chinese indentured laborers arrived in the "Sandalwood Islands" in 1852, 16 years ahead of the Japanese. Unlike the Japanese, many Chinese endured their five-year contracts and then went off to make money in business, frequently marrying Hawaiian women. A Chinese milled the first sugar in Hawaii, on Lanai, 18 years before missionaries arrived at Kailua. When bubonic plague was rampant in the Chinese community in 1900, the territorial government made the tragic mistake of trying to burn down rat-infested homes to contain the pestilence and instead, most of Chinatown's businesses and homes burned to the ground.

Chinese people still live in Chinatown and run herb shops, acupuncture clinics, noodle factories, and other such businesses. Most Chinese, however, are living in Honolulu's suburban outskirts, such as Makiki Heights, where they moved following WW II.

The Koreans

Despite their small numbers (less than 15,000), Koreans have had a disproportionate impact on business life in Hawaii. Koreans have their own clubs and associations, but they have proven even more mobile and adaptable than other Asian immigrant groups. These ambi-

Young Hawaiians.

tious, perserving and independent people have married out of their ethnic group at a rate second only to Hawaiians, which has increased the spread of Korean culture and influence throughout the islands.

Koreans worked actively for the freedom of their homeland after Japanese occupation. When South Korea gained its independence after World War II, one of the Korean community's residents, Dr Syngman Rhee, became the first president. From the time in 1903 that about 100 Korean men and their families recruited as laborers for the plantations arrived in Honolulu, they have emerged with the highest educational and income level per capita of any ethnic group in Hawaii.

In recent years, with increased Korean immigration to the United States, the number of native-born Korean residents is second only to Los Angeles.

The Filipinos

When Japan voluntarily restricted emigration to Hawaii under the Gentlemen's Agreement of 1907 with the United States and Japanese laborers staged a strike on Oahu in 1909, plantation owners looked to the Philippines for a solution to their labor problems.

In the 20 years between 1910 and 1930, over 100,000 Filipinos were brought to the sugar cane and pineapple fields of Hawaii. Mostly illiterate male workers arrived who left families behind and intended to return home as quickly as possible with money. Less than half eventually did.

A combination of hard work, low pay, poor working and living conditions, frustration, lack of women, failure to establish community life and other negatives plagued Filipinos in Hawaii before WW II. Some of this frustration was channeled into labor organizations like the Filipino Federation of Labor that fought for workers' rights in the 1920s. In the past decades, Filipinos who intermarried over the years have been prominent names in all professions and in state politics, such as Cayetano, De La Cruz and Malapit.

The Portuguese

By the early 1900s, the Portuguese were settled into Hawaii. Perhaps because of their swarthy skin or peasant backgrounds, Portuguese from the Madeiras and Azores were never categorized as *haoles* by anybody in Hawaii but were regarded as European whites.

Next to last on the plantation pay scale, in front of the Japanese, Portuguese could be counted on to work hard as plantation laborers or in any other job, work cheap and accept authority and the prevailing order of things. They were Christian (devout Catholics), came with their families, were content with manual labor (and not determined to get educated like the Chinese), but interested in other occupations besides plantation work. As Europeans, they assimi-

lated more easily than Asians, with much less discrimination.

The Samoans

Samoans have been exercising their Constitutional right to immigrate to the United States since acquiring it in 1951. The Territory of American Samoa consists of six islands 2,600 miles from Honolulu that has been under US jurisdiction since1899. The lifestyle of Hawaii was much faster than back home and language was a barrier.

Otherwise, the Samoans' Hawaiian-like personalities made it easy for them to be accepted and fit in to local ways while maintaining their own customs. One of the main cultural differences was the Samoan view of all property as communal property – share and share alike. Newly-arrived Samoans have had to get used to the idea of private property and people in Hawaii guarding their fruit, food and other belongings, rather than sharing.

Samoan festivities are well known for the colorful *lava-lava* sarongs and *puletasi* dresses, bold tapa cloths and lauhala mats that decorate dance areas and the bowls of kava drunk night and day at these affairs. Samonans party and play hard and their athletes are sought after by high school, college and professional football teams. Other Samoans form a large minority among the Mormon-Samoans living and working in Oahu's Laie area.

Hula music, Hawaii's folk music, is provided by repetitive chants (*mele*) combined with musical instruments (which are not necessary) such as the *ipu* thumped on a mat or hit with a hand, a steady rhythm from a large base drum (*pahu*) made from a hollowed coconut or a breadfruit log covered with a sharkskin membrane, coconut gourds filled with shells (*uli uli*), various other small drums, pebble castanets, rattles, and a nose flute that provided some melody.

Rhythm of the Pacific.

Storytime

The stories told in the monotonous chants were the important aspect of *hula*, not the melody or swaying hips.

Hawaiians didn't sing until the missionaries came along and taught them hymns. Missionaries, who rarely get credit for any positive influences in Hawaii, taught Hawaiians who knew nothing about melody and the

Hula

An all ladies band entertain.

The *hula* is a ritualistic Hawaiian folk dance. In ancient times, entering a *hula* school was akin to entering a convent to learn a way of establishing communication between man and God. The *hula* is a performing art which has fostered the development of crafts and art used in the dance. Without a written language, ancient Hawaiians passed their history, beliefs and culture from generation to generation through chant and the *hula*.

In ancient Hawaii it began as a form of worship during religious ceremonies. Originally performed only by men, women were allowed to learn the *hula*. The *hula heiau* at Haena Point on Kauai's Na Pali Coast became the sacred place for the most graceful and beautiful girls to learn the *hula*. Pupils in this *hula halau* (school) were taught by *kumu* (teachers) to control every part of their bodies and facial expressions as part of the story telling, and to chant (*mele*) correctly stories accompa-

nied by a wide variety of musical instruments.

Traditionally, dances mimed wished-for events, like a successful hunt or fertility. Long chants were recited or sung with or without the accompaniment of drums made from coconut trees, bamboo rattles and pipes, nose flutes, sticks and pebble castanets, calabash gourds, and other *hula* implements made from plant material. When *hula* spread throughout Hawaiian society as a teaching tool and performing art, women shared in the performances. In the early 1800s, missionaries labeled the *hula* obscene and banned them completely. By the 1850s the *hula* had virtually vanished. When King Kalakaua saved the *hula* 40 years later, much had been lost forever. Only in the 1970s did young Hawaiians begin to dance the *hula* again in ancient style.

Today, the *hula* is being revived thanks to fiercely competitive *hula halau* active on each island. Every April these *halau* come together

A great place to be treated to music and dance – Polynesian Cultural Centre.

for a *hula* competition at the Merrie Monarch Festival in Hilo, an event not to be missed. At the end of June, the King Kamehameha Hula and Chant Competition is held at the Neal Blaisdell Center Arena; and in mid-July, the Prince Lot Hula Festival at Moanalua Gardens in Honolulu.

Musical instruments of wood and gourds.

musical scale. When Spanish *vaqueros* came to the islands from California, they taught the Hawaiian cowboys to play guitars (which originally came over earlier with whalers) and ballads too. Later, the Portuguese brought a small 4-string instrument called a *braquino* or *cavaquinho* which became the Hawaiian ukelele ("jumping flea"). The invention of the steel guitar in Hawaii has more stories and arguments connected with it than the guitar has strings. Then Hawaiians took this distinctively Hawaiian instrument and further modified it by a form of tuning called "slack

key" – the strings are tuned to the key that best suits the singer's voice.

Hula Revival

The Merry Monarch King Kalakaua and gifted Queen Liliuokalani revived the hula and brought new heights to Hawaiian music with the song and ballads they composed, such as Kalakaua's "Hawaii Pono," which became the national anthem, and the Queen's beautiful "Aloha Oe." The King's most important contribution to Hawaii's music prob-

Gentle gestures "talk" their stories.

ably was bringing Prussian bandmaster Heinrich Berger from Germany in 1868 to direct the Royal Hawaii Band for almost 45 years. During this time, "the Father of Hawaiian Music" collaborated with Hawaiian musicians to arrange more than 1,000 Hawaiian songs and composed more than 75 songs himself.

Tiny Bubbles et al

Hawaiian music was an international craze before the radio program "Hawaii Calls" broadcast from the Court of the Moana Hotel to over 700 radio stations around the world from 1935 until 1975. Millions of records with *Sweet Leilani*, *Blue Hawaii* (two Bing Crosby hits), *Hawaiian Wedding Song*, and other hits were the rage from the late 1930s to the 1950s, with hundreds of artists recording versions until the Beattles revolutionized music around the world in the 1960s. Don Ho, the lone Hawaiian singing star to keep Hawaiian music alive through the 1960s and 1970s, still can be heard on Waikiki today.

In the meantime, Al Harrington, "the South Pacific Man," Danny Kaleikini's Polynesian revues, the Brothers Cazimera, Henry Kopono, the Peter Moon Band, the Beamer Brothers, and others sing their own distinctive amalgam of "traditional" Hawaiian and contemporary music in Waikiki's hotels.

Inevitably the natural beauty of the Hawaiian islands — delicate and raw, tranquil and volcanically violent — has drawn artists to them. The visual impact of Hawaii's mountains and *pali*, rain forests and very different leeward and windward coastlines evokes and reinforces the islands' spiritual qualities. Beauty is also everywhere in the faces of children that reflect a marvelous mix of racial and ethnic backgrounds.

Arts & Crafts

97

A quilter in Lahaina, Maui.

Artistic Influences

Many contemporary Hawaiian artists are strongly influenced by the values of pre-modern Hawaii, even though consciously they may not pay much attention to these values. In Hawaiian culture, nature had a power that evoked an aesthetic response. The response to a particular rock or piece of wood was a

An artefact of the past in Bishop Museum.

sculpture. This connection in Hawaiian culture between nature and art, wherein nature speaks to the artists, is a very prevalent belief among non-Hawaiian craft and fine artists.

Visibly the "old ways" in Hawaii for the most part disappeared more than a century ago with the "civilizing" of native Hawaiians, but traditions live on quietly, almost secretly, among many Hawaiians, and more openly in the re-

surgence of old Hawaiian dance, art and crafts. Suppressed and banned for a century, ancient Hawaiian traditions today are still emerging from hiding as an underground phenomenon.

Hawaiian stories, chants and vocabulary show they were close observers of nature and expert users of their natural environment. Canoe makers, the most respected artisans, using adzs and pump drills, built canoes from *koa* logs

quality.

Another important influence among contemporary artists is the ancient Hawaiian concept and spirit of *ohana*. *Ohana* is a word derived from *pule ohana*, which in Hawaiian means "gathering for family prayers". In Hawaii's past, the land, rivers and sea – *aina* – provided all the necessities of life, including art and craft materials. The basis of life was family sharing – *ohana* – sharing their livelihoods, material things, the richness and beauty of nature and their deep knowledge of the spiritual and material world.

Kahunas (Hawaiian teachers of ancient knowledge), lore and the healing arts and culture, carry on the heritage of *ohana*. Many contemporary artists in Hawaii revere and draw on the wisdom of these living *kahunas*.

Photographic Art

Photographer Frank Salmoraghi's famous close-up photograph entitled *Wai'pi'o*, which captures droplets of water inside a taro leaf, touches on two elements of *ohana* – taro is a gift from the gods and water is sacred because it has touched the ground. Often Salmoraghi is quoted as saying that one of his aims is to capture the spiritual power of the Hawaiian landscape.

Coming to the islands in 1968 to teach photography at the University of Hawaii, it was not until he moved to the Big Island that he underwent "a series of

that could hold hundreds of people, and double-hulled canoes for trans-Pacific migrations using amazing native navigational techniques. The best canoe makers in Polynesia, Hawaiians also were the best basket makers, using *lauhala*. The highly refined Polynesian art of feather work reached a peak in Hawaii's helmets and capes. Religious beliefs among Polynesians in Hawaii about man's relationship to birds and the universe were translated into new forms of featherwork of an unrivalled

sensitizing experiences that helped me respond to the specialness of the Hawaiian landscape. When I went to the island of Kahoolawe with the *Ohana* in 1976, I saw the kind of reverence that ancient Hawaiians had given to every path, every stone on the island. That kind of feeling inspired me to explore the theme of their relationship with the land."

Traditional Arts & Crafts

Hawaiians were gifted craftspeople in wood, bone, shell, stone and fiber. The standards of excellence in each of these media was extremely high: Hawaiians soared beyond their Polynesian predecessors in fiber art, feather work and basketry. Polynesian culture did not restrict styles or aesthetic values. Thus Hawaii's sculpture, for example, evolved as remarkably bold and vigorous. Indeed, the inventiveness achieved in *kapa* (bark cloth)-making two centuries ago can only be approximated by today's fiber artists.

Hawaii's *kupuna* carry these endangered traditions in the modern world. Typically their craft work is immensely time-consuming and the environment must supply all natural materials. Time is running out for many of these dedicated craftspeople and so are the materials of their crafts. Most of them go unrecognized except by Hawaiians and others who respect the ways of old traditions, such as their devoted students.

The names of these craftspeople are like a legendary roll call, uttered only with utmost respect, almost reverence: feather work – Aunty Mary Louise Kekuewa, Chosaburo Terui, Frank Medeiros and Tsugi Kaima; hula implements – Herman and Freda Gomez; lauhala weaving: Gladys Grace, Andrew Okada, Marcia Omura, Esther Makua'ole and Sophia Kaiawe; *tapa* (*kapa*) making – Moana Eisele; drum maker Kana'e Keawe; and so forth.

Fiber, basketry, and woodcraft made in traditional ways are important parts of all museums in Hawaii, in permanent and special juried exhibits. Outside of the Bishop, Kauai and a few other museums, however, it's rare that you'll find exhibits of traditional Hawaiian crafts of basketry, featherwork, hula implements and *lauhala* weaving.

Hula Implements

Handcrafted *hula* implements are valued for their usefulness and rare representations of traditional Hawaiian art forms. The *ipu* (Hawaiian gourd drum) is the primary *hula* instrument. Made of two carefully dried gourds fastened together, these drumlike instruments come in various styles and sizes. The pear-shaped *ipu* is the most common. Pierced by a nose hole at the stalk end, two or three finger holes are along the side. Holding the whistle in his left hand, the musician brings the stem up to his right nostril, blows airs through the nose hole

Leis of feather make interesting and colourful designs.

and changes the sound with his fingers.

A cord attached to the neck of the *ipu* allows the performer to hold the instrument in one hand while striking it with the other. The manner of striking the *ipu* varies with the sentiment or feeling of the *mele* (chant). The *ipu* is important in the *hula* performance for expressing happiness, anger, grief, passion and other feelings.

The *ului'uli* is a gourd or coconut filled with shells, seeds or pebbles and used like maracas in modern *hula* (Hula Awana) or traditional *hula* (Hula Kahika). The handle is usually decorated with beautiful feathers and sometimes *tapa* cloth. The dancer holds the *ului'uli* in his right hand and shakes and strikes it against his left hand or another part of his body.

Nose flutes (*'ohe hano ihu*) were made from one to two-ft length of bamboo with a natural node on one end, a nose hole near the node, two finger holes further down and an opening on the other end. The musician would blow into the *'ohe* with his right nostril while closing his left nostril with a finger of his left hand. Bamboo pipes called *'ohe ka'eke* of different lengths from one to four-ft would be raised and dropped to the earth to make different sounds.

The hula also uses: percussion instruments, like castanets, called *'ili'ili*; snare drums, the *puniu*, a half-coconut shell covered with sharkskin; dogs teeth tied to a fiber mesh and attached to the dancers leg produced a rythmic sound; triple rattlers of calabash gourds and other instruments from plant materials such as bamboo, coconut, *kamani* seeds and pods. The gourd *mahiole* (Hawaiian gourd mask), one of the many types of helmets used by Hawaiians and still used in some *hula* and these other instruments also are available in miniature.

Making these *hula* instruments is almost a lost art. Many *hula* implements used by *hula halau* are made by **Cioci and Aloha Dalire** (46-024 Kam Highway, Room 208, Kaneohe, HI 96744, 808-247-6188); **Calvin Hoe** (48-140 Kam Highway, Kaneohe, HI 96744, 808-237-8235); and **Herman and Freda Gomes** (84-239 Ikuone Place, Waianae, HI 96792, 808-695-9192) and their students. Freda teaches these skills at the

Bishop Museum. The materials to make *hula* implements, such as coconut, bamboo and seeds and pods of various kinds, have to be gathered in Oahu's forests and fields or grown at home where possible. These miniature or full-sized *hula* implements as gifts or souvenirs can be found in shops like the **Hula Supply Center** (2346 South King Street, Honolulu, HI 96826, 808-941-5379) in Moiliili on Oahu and **Alapaki's** on the Big Island.

Leis

Many of the most valuable aspects of the Hawaiian culture may be lost forever, but the giving and wearing of *leis* lives on and remains at the heart of the Hawaiian experience. The *lei* is a token of love, a very special way to say hello or goodbye, to give thanks, to pray and to mark special achievements. Like the Hawaiian word *aloha*, it means many things.

The ancient and modern Hawaiian tradition of bestowing a *lei* on visitors, accompanied by *aloha* , with or without a kiss, is supposed to help to dispel immediately *malihini* (newcomer or outsider) feelings. *Leis* of sweet-scented *maile* leaves picked in the mountains are the traditional offering to *Laka,* goddess of dance, venerated by *hula* dancers through the ages.

Today many guests in Hawaii are greeted with the *kui lei* of fragrant plumeria, orchids and other lovely blos-

Lei-makers strive for Lei-day celebrations.

soms, or the *haku lei* made of braided leaves, vines, flowers and other colorful plant materials (like red *liko lehua*, shiny leaves of the *ohia* tree), sometimes wound into a base with thread or fiber, known as the *wili lei*.

Marie Leilehus Adams McDonald and her sister Irmalee Pomroy make custom *leis* in their Kapaa shop on Kauai, Irmalee Pomroy Flowers, which set the highest standards for elegance and beauty. McDonald is the author of *Ka Lei, the Leis of Hawaii*, the definitive work on the styles and techniques of *lei*-making.

Leis come in all colors, textures, designs and materials: flower blossoms, parts of flowers, dried protea, *milo* seeds, eucalyptus leaves; some are custom-made individually by master *lei*-makers in their homes, such as Ray Wong on Oahu.

Some are made by anonymous *lei*-makers and sold in supermarkets such as Ooka's (1870 Main Street) in Wailuku on Maui.

Leis are sold from stands and stores throughout the islands. After several days, you'll begin to tell the differences in styles and materials and recognize the artistic qualities of different *lei*-makers.

There are temporary flower *leis*, woven with six different methods (knotting; braiding or plaiting; *haku*, which is another braid method adding greenery to flowers; winding or *wili*; and sewing on a foundation).

Permanent *leis* are made of seeds, feathers, shells, ivory, animal teeth and human hair.

Each island has its own favorite *lei*. The Big Island has the leathery-looking leaves from the *ohia* tree that also produces the fluffy red pompons that make unusual feathery *leis*.

Across the Kaulakahi Channel off Kauai's west coast lies the dry, barren island of Niihau, populated exclusively by a few hundred Hawaiians.

In addition to running a cattle and sheep ranch for descendants of the original owners of the island, the Robinson family, locals gather tiny shells from the beaches, clean and grade, drill holes, and string into exquisite shell *leis* of different colors. (See box: on *Niihau — Forbidden Island*, page **313**.)

Feather *Leis*

Ancient Hawaiians delighted in the brilliant colored feathers of native honeycreeper birds and used them for *leis*, capes, *kahili* and helmets. Feather capes and cloaks were a mark of social status in Hawaiian culture. Only high ranking chief (*ali'i*) or the most outstanding warriors could wear them. Because of their scarcity, yellow bird feathers were the most prized. Countless feathers were used to make these creations — as many as 500,000 feathers from 80,000 Momo birds were used for Kamehameha the Great's magnificent cape.

Today, Hawaiian feather *leis*, hatbands and ornaments are a unique craft. Feathers are not glued to the foundation but secured by individual stitches or a traditional Hawaiian wrapping and knotting process. A green peacock *lei* from Waimea's master *lei* maker *Tsugi Kaiama* can run about $200; a black and white francolin *lei* $175; the prized dark blue feather *lei* costs over $1,000 – a bargain when you consider the skill and work involved.

Feather *lei* hatbands in all shapes, widths, textures and colors are created by varying the feathers used, the part of the feather used and the way they're attached to the foundation. As many as 30 feathers — each perfectly matched to the next — make a single row of stitching. You can see Mary Louise Kekuewa, one of Hawaii's foremost feather workers and teachers, at the Bishop Museum

Basketry of interesting shapes, sizes and weave.

women wove mats baskets, sandals, bed coverings, fans and other things from the materials around them. Aerial rootlets of the 'ie'ie vine were turned into sturdy baskets and helmets and sedge from swampy areas became valued mats. Leaves of *hala* (pandanus) trees, however, were most often used for weaving coarse and fine mats, baskets, bedding, and many other items. It wasn't until the 19th century that Hawaiian women learned to plait European-style hats from coconut leaves and leaves of the pandanus tree.

The colors and textures of hala leaves depended on the tree it came from. Naturally dried ones are picked, rather than green ones

Hala leaves are more pliable and durable than coconut palm leaves. Hawaiians were the only people who wove *lauhala* mats and baskets without a frame or loom.

The key to weaving is the technique for making the leaves soft and pliable. Preparing the leaves for weaving, softening and stripping them, is arduous and time-consuming and requires bleaching done in sun and shade following traditional methods, rather than by chemical bleaching.

The best places to purchase *lauhala* products are: the Honolulu Hat Company, on Oahu and Kimura Lau Hala Shop in Holualoa on the Big Island, the gift shops of Bishop Museum, Mission Houses Museum and the Polynesian Cultural Center and at Pacific Handcrafters Guild fairs.

every Thursday from 9 a.m.-3 p.m. She uses the feathers of pheasants, Canada geese, peacocks and other birds to make feather *leis*, hatbands and other ornaments. You can see and buy these *leis*, including feather *lei* hatbands in all colors, widths, shapes and textures, by special order from Kekuewa, at the Little Hawaiian Craft Shop, in Honolulu, or at Alapaki's on the Big Island. Some of the most beautiful modern feather work designs in Hawaii, made as necklaces, earrings and other ornaments, are by Beth McCormick on the Big Island.

Lauhala

Without loom or frame, Hawaiian

Basketry

Hawaiian culture developed largely in isolation from other Polynesian cultures and their artistic styles and techniques developed without outside influences. The last contact with Polynesia before Captain Cook arrived in 1778 was about 500 years earlier. In the interval, Hawaiians were making fish traps, containers and storage baskets in all sizes and shapes that were some of the most beautifully crafted and decorated baskets in the Pacific.

It is heartening to see people on all of the islands relearning traditional methods of basket-making. The *kahuna* (teacher of craft) tradition broke down years ago, so self-teaching and experimentation flourishes and is spreading. Kaneohe's Pat Horimoto is one craftsworker in Hawaii reviving this art, using traditional forms and weaving patterns. Self-taught by studying baskets at the Bishop Museum, his own work has been displayed at the museum. Pat's one-of-a-kind baskets and other weaving (fish traps, vessels, religious images) are appropriately expensive considering the amount of time required to prepare the material and make the items.

Expert basket makers like Gladys Kukana Grace and Esther Makuaole, traditional master weavers and Mika McCann and Theo Morrison, working in innovative weaving forms and nontraditional materials, are creating aesthetic links to the past and weaving old Hawaii's past into their works.

Quilting

The brig *Thaddeus*, transporting missionaries from Boston April 4, 1820, anchored off Kawaihae on the Big Island. A scouting party returned to the boat with news that King Kamehameha the Great was dead. His eldest son, Prince Liholiho, soon would be crowned Kamehameha II. So on the eve of 2 April 1820, the Captain invited Kalanomoku, the King's Prime Minister, the dowager Queen Kalakua, Liholiho's mother, her sister Queen Namahana, another widow of Kamehameha and two wives of Kalanomoku to come aboard.

The next morning, missionary wives Bingham, Thurstan, Holman, Whitney, Loomis, Ruggles and Chamberlain formed a sewing circle on the deck of the *Thaddeus* with the four Hawaiian ladies. Patchwork quilting in Hawaii was born. Hawaiian quilting as we know it today was yet to come, however, almost 40 years later.

Quilting in Hawaii is linked to the Polynesian heritage of *tapa* (fine bark cloth made from the tender inner bark of the *wauke* plant, a variety of mulberry, and then sewn with *olana* fiber) and mats. In Polynesian culture, the finest *tapa* and mats were a form and measure of wealth, stored or given away to express deepest respect or love. Made by groups of women, *tapa* was an essen-

There are no short cuts to a hand-made quilt.

tial ingredient in many ceremonies commemorating the milestones of life — birth, marriage, coronation and death.

Tapa was pounded and felted into lengths required for the wrap-around (*kikepa*) or skirt (*pa-u*) for women and loin cloth (*malo*) for men. There was no need to cut or sew a garment. Color fast dyes were extracted from sea urchins, seeds, roots, leaves and other natural materials.

Depending on the type of bark used, *tapa* colors ranged from dark brown to brilliant white. Leaves, ferns and flowers were saturated with dyes and impressed on the borders of tapa. In this manner, patterns were built up bit by bit with these "stencils". A stamped *tapa* sheet was used as the top sheet over four white *tapa* bed sheets.

Quality craftsmanship was highly respected in Polynesian society. The finest *tapa* was made by the royal wives of high chiefs. The only problem with *tapa* was that it was not washable; repeated exposure to water caused it to disintegrate.

The original techniques of cutting "snowflake" designs, appliquéing and quilting – the basis of the traditional Hawaiian quilt – were brought to the islands by the first New England missionaries. Missionaries first taught geometric quilting techniques and then echo or contour-style quilting – quilting that radiates out from a core design in rows no less than 1/2-inch apart. Hawaiians were taught these techniques in mission

Sculpture & Woodcraft

Before the arrival of Polynesians and Caucasians, there were approximately 250 species of trees. The tallest, oldest, most beautiful and valuable is the *koa*. (How its heavy seeds originally crossed the Pacific Ocean from Australia or the Indian and Pacific Oceans from Mauritius remains a mystery.) Once abundant, tall, old *koa* trees today are scarce except on the Big Island. Polynesians who arrived in Hawaii around AD 450 were expert woodcrafters. They developed a full appreciation for the forests of Hawaii and the beauty of its wood. So beautiful was *koa* wood that, unlike elsewhere in Polynesia, Hawaiian bowls were not ornamented. Shape, grain, coloration (from pale blond to deep brown), and finish were more important, all of which was achieved with a stone adz (*koi pohaku*). Sixty- or seventy-ft voyaging canoes and huge surfboards were also made from *koa*. In addition to *koa*, *kou* was a favorite wood for making calabashes, dishes and cups. Probably brought to Hawaii by early Polynesians, the soft yet lasting *kou* wood has beautiful grains of wavy dark and light lines.

Hawaiian wood sculpture was the ancient society's most important art form. (Metal working and ceramics were absent.) Wood carving was entirely connected with religion and religious rituals. The sculptor was transmitting sacred knowledge in ways that still are not well understood. Most of the limited number of known Hawaiian sculpture (about 150) are currently in museums or private collections.

The Hawaiian sculptural tradition is carried on by a few contemporary sculptors such as Henry Hopfe and Rocky Jensen. Henry Kila Hopfe, with an ancestral line maternally descended from Kamehameha IV, is deeply rooted in Hawaiian culture. A mainstream advocate for Hawaiian creative expression, Henry exhibits wood, stone and bronze sculptures. Sculptor Rocky Kai'iouliokahihikolo'Ehu Jensen is founder and director of the *Hale Naua III* Society of Hawaiian Arts. King Kalakaua resurrected a *Hale Naua* Society (that originally began in the 13th Century) in order to restore traditional Hawaiian arts and sciences. Rocky has had to fight his own battles as a native Hawaiian artist whose work can best be classified as contemporary with traditional themes.

schools starting in 1820.

Within ten years, starting in the 1830s, Hawaiian designs already had begun to change from small-scale patchwork to large connected patterns produced by folding and cutting fabric in the snowflake-style. Hawaiians adapted imported techniques and geometric designs to familiar *lauhala* weaving patterns, *tapa* designs and contour quilting. *Wawae moa* stitch (chicken foot) was and is popular. Also, the catch stitch, the blind stitch and the overcast stitch.

Shortages of fabrics and batting led to using fabrics and materials of all kinds, adding to the legacy of innovative Hawaiian quilters. The designers of quilt patterns are the true craft artists and innovators. Many Hawaiian quilters borrow patterns designed by other quilters with the understanding that the name of the quilt will not be the same. Quilting clubs, like the one in Wuimea on the Big Island, own hundreds of quilt patterns contributed by members that everyone in the club shares, as long as the resulting quilts have different names.

Although a traditional Hawaiian quilt is thought to have two contrasting colors, there are many examples of quilts with up to six different colors. These colors are bold and striking, for example, brilliant reds, greens and orange on stark white.

Hawaiian quilts are decorative, an art form, and not designed merely for keeping warm. More than simply art, however, the quilts are believed to contain *mana*, the spirit or power of a person. Thus, when a quilter dies, his or her quilts might be destroyed at the quilter's request to avoid damage to their spirit or perpetual spiritual restlessness. Traditionally other *kapus* (taboos) were also imposed, like destroying patterns or designs (*lau*) when the quilt was finished.

Contemporary Hawaiian Art

Hawaii's art and fine craft galleries differ as much as the islands' microclimates, within each island and from island to island. Like hotels, resorts and other tourism-oriented businesses, they usually cluster on sunnier, drier, or leeward sides of the islands, but that's where the similarities end.

Newer galleries, sometimes with headquarters on the mainland, in and near newer resort developments share the territory with older generations of galleries which, for a decade or more, have nurtured and catered to local artists — Village Galleries on Maui, Stone's and Kahana Ki'i Gallery of Koloa on Kauai and The Volcano Art Center on the Big Island.

The Big Island's galleries selling local art in Hilo, Volcano, Kailua-Kona, and Kamuela, don't resemble each other or the galleries in Lihue, Koloa and Hanalei on Kauai. Even resort-based galleries are mostly different in their mixes of local and international art such as those in the Kaanapali and Wailea resorts on Maui; the Mauna Lani, Mauna Kea and Waikoloa on the Big Island; and the Kauai Westin or Kahn Galleries literally around the corner from each other in Lihue's Anchor Cove.

The group of galleries and fine craft shops (not including cooperative galleries and museum shops) that take top honors for regularly exhibiting and consistently supporting local artists are:

• On Oahu, in Honolulu, **The Gallery EAS**, **The Artist Guild** (privately owned), **Ramsey Galleries** (in Chinatown), **Pauahi Nuuanu Gallery** (Chinatown), and the **Queen Emma Gallery** (in the Queen's Medical Center), **The Following Sea** (in Kahala Mall), and **The Little Hawaiian Craft Shop** (in the Royal Hawaiian Shopping Center).

• On Maui, the **Village Galleries**, the **Larry Dotson Gallery** in Lahaina, **Coast Gallery** in Wailea and in Hana and the **Kihei Art Gallery** in Kihei.

• On Kauai, **Stone's Gallery**, the **Kahana Ki'i Gallery** in Koloa, Poipu's **Gallery at Waiohai**, **Kahn's Galleries** in the Coconut Market Place and Anchor Cove, **Kilohana Galleries** in Puhi, the **Kauai Museum** and the **Garden Island Council** in Lihue, **Montage Galleries** in Princeville; **Hawaiian Art Museum** in Kilauea and the **Artisan's**

Hawaiian Calabashes

The beautiful Hawaiian calabash of today is a legacy of Hawaii's craft rather than sculptural tradition. Hawaiian calabashes, made of wood, gourd, coconut, and fiber, have been an important part of Hawaiian culture. *Kou* and *koa*, the "Hawaiian mahogany", are two of the most popular woods that craftspeople carved into bowls. Similar to *koa* but smaller, *koai'e* (also an acacia) is harder with a curly grain and was once used to make fancy paddles.

The rich brown to red wood with wavy lines of the *milo* tree was originally made into *poi* bowls and utensils. Like *milo* trees, the *kamani* tree has medicinal properties and was also used for calabash bowls. Near the sea you'll find the gnarled and crooked *hau* tree, sometimes erect and sometimes growing horizontally, yielding a light, tough wood.

The distinctive dome-shaped canopy of the monkeypod (*ohai*) tree reaches a height of 80 ft. Its light, tough, dark-colored wood is favored for platters and bowls, while its seeds are made into *leis*. Common mango, part of a species of about 500 members, has a yellow wood with streaks of black, orange, green and pink. Macadamia, grown mainly for its nut crop, yields fine-grained, reddish wood for carving and furniture. Slow growing and somewhat rare, the *kolohala* and its beautiful flowering cousin — the royal poinciana—both make colorful wood carving. Beautiful bowls, looking like they were turned on a lathe, existed when Captain Cook arrived. These magnificent wooden bowls are the most treasured objects of Hawaiian crafts today.

Hawaii's tall, inwardly sloping bowls, with lips and walls as thin as possible, were unique in Polynesia. Without metal tools, Hawaiian used hot coals to burn out the interior of the calabashes and then, using stone tools, scooped out the remainder of the interior. Wide bowls carved from tree crotches, with multiple heartwood cores spaced around the circumference, were among the most beautiful. Rounded covers harmoniously completed their spherical forms.

By the 1870s, sadly, Hawaiian bowl makers had disappeared and most *koa* trees too. Lathe-turned bowls were becoming increasing popular, produced by western craftspeople synthesizing Hawaiian and western forms. This tradition is carried on today by master woodturners such as Ron Kent, Daniel DeLuz, Jack Straka, Jerry Kermode, Michael Dunne and others.

These artists carefully select their wood so that it contains "curly", "birdseye", or "fiddleback" grain and iridescent color.

Guild of Kauai in Hanalei.

•On the Big Island, **Studio 7 Gallery** in Holualoa, **Ackerman Gallery** in Kapaau, **Gallery of Great Things** and **The Parker Gallery** in Kamuela, **Blue Ginger Gallery** in Kainaliu, **Hawaiian Handcraft** in Hilo; **Waipio Valley Artworks** in Kukuihaele, **Alapaki's** in Kona, the **Kealakekua's Grass Shack** in Kealakekua, and **The Showcase Gallery** in Keauhou-Kona.

Some artists have formed or joined cooperative galleries and fine craft showcases on Oahu, mainly in Honolulu:

Gateway Gallery (on Nuuanu St. in Chinatown), **Art A La Carte** (in Ward Centre), **Arts of Paradise** (in Waikiki's International Marketplace), and in Windward Kaneohe, **Koolau Gallery**.

Organizations primarily dedicated to exhibiting and/or selling or helping to sell the work of local artists are your best sources for information about art and artists on their islands:

• On Maui, **Hui No'eau Visual Art Center** (in Makawao), the **Maui Crafts Guild** (in Paia), and the **Lahaina Arts Society** (in Lahaina).

- On the Big Island, the **Wailoa Center** (in Hilo), the **West Hawaii Arts Guild** and **Malama Art** (in Kailua-Kona);

- On Oahu, the **Hale Naua III Society of Hawaiian Art**, the **Pacific Handicrafters Guild**, the **Association of Honolulu Artists**, the **Honolulu Printmaking Workshop**, and **Hawaii Craftsmen**.

Craftwork

Fine craftwork is found in only a relatively few locations on each island. At the **Maui Crafts Guild**, for example, two floors of this old wooden storefront are full of quality craft gifts, most of which only rarely turn up at galleries and craft shops elsewhere on the island or other islands. As yet there is no islandwide chain of stores which sells fine crafts like those carried by the Artist Guild and Following Sea on Oahu and Elephant Walk on Kauai.

Shops & Galleries

The shops to find fine wood crafts are mostly the same places that you can find Big Island master craftsman Jack Straka's turned-wood bowls: Hotel Hana-Maui, on Maui; Gallery of Great Things, Volcano Art Center, the Artist Guild, Following Sea, Honolulu Academy of Arts' Academy Shop and Martin & McArthur, on Oahu; on Kauai at Stone's Gallery, the Kokee Museum, the Kauai Museum, Kong Lung Company (in Kilauea), and Ola's (in Hanalei); and on the Big Island at the Kealakekua's Little Grass Shack and Waipio Valley Artworks. Galleries specializing in national and international art are located on all of the islands, but are heavily, and increasingly, concentrated in Maui's Lahaina, where some art retailers have three and four galleries. Some of them carry artwork by the same artists, especially Robert Lyn Nelson, Otsuka, Anthony Casay and the Makk family. These galleries and their featured artists are: **Center Art Galleries**, ranging from Chagall and Norman Rockwell to Anthony Quinn and Chris Lassen; the **Lahaina Galleries** with Robert Lyn Nelson, Raymond Page and Loren Adams, Otsuka's paintings and prints, and well-known artists of Hawaii, including the Makk family's impressionism, Guy Buffet, wildlife sculpture by Bruce Turnbull and Jan Kasprzycki's abstract-expressionist paintings;

Images International Gallery of Hawaii, with Otsuka, Tatsuo Ito, and Raymond Page; **Livingston Gallery** with the Makk family and surrealistic paintings by Jan Kobelansky; *Sunset Galleries* featuring marine artist Dick Kearney and works by the famous southwest artist, R. C. Gorman;

The Dolphin Galleries, featuring marine artist Don McMichael; and **Dyansen Gallery**, Anthony Casay, Erte and occasional French impressionist painters.

Palm fronds put to pretty use.

The place where Kamehameha I ruled from 1813 to his death, **Kamakahonu** and **Ahuena Heiau**, the king's temple, are easy to find, reconstructed at the back of the King Kamehameha Hotel in Kailua-Kona. The rebuilt *heiau*, an authentic *hale* surrounded by canoes and *tikis* and the grounds of the king's home are part of a tour from the hotel. Just down Alii Drive are **Hulihee Palace** and **Mokuaikaua Church** across the street, the first Christian church in Hawaii, built on the foundations of an old *hieau*.

Only a stone platform remains at **Puukohola Heiau National Historic Site**, Kawaihae, where Kamehameha I built his hilltop temple that originally included thatched-roof shelters and carved wooden statutes in addition to the 224-foot-long, 100-foot-wide, 15-foot-high lava walls. Further north, beyond Lapakahi (see below) at the tip of North Kohala, is **Kamehameha's birthplace** and nearby, **Mookini Heiau**, where the king to-be underwent his royal birth rituals. To see the most complete restoration of a *hieau*

Puuhonua O Honaunau.

Mookini Heiau.

(temple) in Hawaii, built as a sanctuary for people who had broken *kapus* and defeated warriors, you have to visit **Puuhonua O Honaunau National Historic Park**, Hanaunau, built during the 16th century. A wall, 1,000-feet long and six-feet wide, had to be scaled in order to enter the refuge for absolution, after swimming through shark infested waters. In addition to a restored *hieau*, a royal fishpond, a royal canoe landing and a stone for playing *konane* (something like checkers), visitors are invited to try *lei*-making, *lauhala* weaving, *poi*-pounding and tying fish nets.

Lapakahi State Historical Park in North Kohala, the Big Island, consists mainly of rock walls and walkways, some old canoe sheds and house sites

and ancient artifacts. It offers an interesting glimpse of a 14th century Hawaiian fishing village. The only other place where you can see such an old village is neither an ancient ruin nor an historic site. **Kamokila Hawaiian Village**, Wailua, Kauai, a recreated Hawaiian village, was built near an old settlement. The various huts showing village life and demonstrations of crafts and agricultural activities are worth the visit.

Lahaina was not only the playground of Maui's ruling chiefs before Kamehameha the Great conquered the islands, but also his early political center, one of the missionaries' two main bases (the other Kailua-Kona) during the whaling era, the main whaling and provisioning port for America in the

Ahuena Heiau.

Pacific, the home of later kings in the Kamehameha dynasty before the capital shifted to Honolulu. It also contains other interesting remnants of the later 19th century after the demise of the whaling era. A National Historic Landmark since 1962, the **Lahaina Restoration Foundation** is doing an excellent job of reclaiming Front Street shops and other buildings and sites.

Parker Power

The only major center of power in Hawaii that does not have missionary roots – **Parker Ranch** – grew out of an adventuresome sailor, John Parker, jumping ship in 1809, later marrying an Hawaiian princess, granddaughter of the king, cleaning up the king's wild cattle problem and winding up with 250,000 acres on the Big Island. The small, rustic, original family home of **Mana** and the opulent **Puuopelu**, home of the current owner, are centerpieces of an historic tour of the ranch that spans 150 years of history. While John Parker was establishing a ranching dynasty on the Big Island, King David Kalakaua was traveling around the world gathering ideas for his new home, **Iolani Palace**, in Honolulu, built in 1882. Only 11 years later, his sister and successor, Liliuokalani, was deposed and imprisoned in her own palace for the next three years. Still undergoing restoration, with many former furnishings and

Inside Bishop Museum.

artifacts retrieved from collectors and museums by Friends of Iolani Palace, the Palace once again evokes its former 19th century elegance.

At the opposite end of the social spectrum in the 19th century, Hawaiians afflicted with the contagious disease of leprosy or suspected of it were banished to **Makanalua Peninsula**, a tongue of lava protruding from 2000-foot cliffs on the north shore of Molokai. In 1873, Father Damien, a Catholic priest from Belgium, arrived in their second settlement on the peninsula, **Kalaupapa**, found a diseased, disorganized and lawless population trying to survive under the worst conditions.

Today, in **Kalaupapa National Historic Monument**, with leprosy (Hansen's Disease) treatable and non-contagious among the remaining voluntary residents, some of them give tours of the settlement to visitors who arrive on mule or on foot down the 1600-foot cliff or arrive on the peninsula by plane. The white concrete **memorial above the USS *Arizona***, the battleship bombed during the Japanese attack on Pearl Harbor, Oahu, December 7 1941, commemorates the loss of lives and US entry into World War II. Across Pearl Harbor, a Visitor Center houses a museum and a theater showing a film about the attack.

Next to the Visitor Center is the Pacific Submarine Museum housing the USS Bowfin submarine, a memorial to the thousands of men who died on sub-

Kauai Museum.

marines during World War II.

Museums & Mission Houses

The Bishop Museum and Planetarium in Honolulu, founded and named in honor of Bernice Pauahi Bishop, the granddaughter of Kamehamcha the Great, offers the foremost collection in existence covering Hawaii's heritage. Beyond the sperm whale skeleton suspended from the ceiling in the Hawaiian Hall, you can trace the history of Hawaii from prehistoric times when Polynesians sailed to Hawaii in their canoes through to the Royal Monarchy, their portraits, clothing and paraphernalia. All important aspects of each

century are depicted on three floors and in a new wing. The cultural, artistic and geological exhibits in the **Kauai Museum**, Lihue, are miniscule compared to the Bishop Museum but not to be missed by visitors to Kauai. Feather helmets and cloaks belonging to the *alii*, wooden and gourd calabashes, and Niihau *leis* are among the highlights of the museum's excellent collections.

The **Thomas A. Jagger Museum**, in Hawaii Volcanoes National Park, on the rim of Kilauea Crater, displays a fascinating collection of videos, volcanic murals, instruments and other information on the Big Island's and the park's volcanic activity.

The **Mission Houses Museum**, in Honolulu, the home shared by the Judds

Hulihee Palace on Hawaii.

Queen Emma's bedroom.

and the Binghams, provides the best glimpse in Hawaii of why and how a few Protestant missionaries could so dominate Hawaii and leave an imprint that lasts to this day on its land holdings, economy, politics, education and so forth. **Lyman Mission House and Museum**, in Hilo, on the the Big Island, another New England-style missionary homestead, is stuffed with a remarkable collection of artifacts that show a more rounded view of both the religious mission and convivial lifestyle of missionaries. **The Grove Farm Homestead**, in Lihue, Kauai, shows how the sons of missionaries created the sugar plantation economy that resulted in Hawaii. The **Museum** in Lahaina, home of Rev Dwight Baldwin, contains the furnishings of this missionary physician, including a Steinway piano, four-poster *koa* bed in the master bedroom, imported china in the dining room and even a toilet in the bathroom, reputedly Hawaii's first.

A Queen Named Emma...

Queen Emma's Summer Palace, in Honolulu, the former home of Queen Emma and King Kamehameha IV, has been converted into a museum that houses a fascinating collection of family furniture and memorabilia, including craft works that you won't see anywhere else except in the Bishop Museum – *kapa* cloth, feather fans (*kahilis*), quilts, calabashes, *koa* cabinets, and other wood

A Maori Hawaiian.

craft. Queen Emma and her husband were guests of Princess Ruth Keelikolani in another early gem, **Hulihee Palace**, Kailua-Kona, on the Big Island, visiting frequently on vacations from the busy court in Honolulu. Rugs, china, glassware, sofas, prints and paintings, *kahilis*, and other family momentos that you see in the Palace today belonged to King David Kalakaua who purchased the palace after Ruth's death.

The **Honolulu Academy of Arts**, in Honolulu, except for special exhibits, offers little of interest pertaining to Hawaii. Its handsome galleries feature an Asian collection, including Japanese prints and Chinese artifacts and a notable collections of Italian Paintings and European impressionist art.

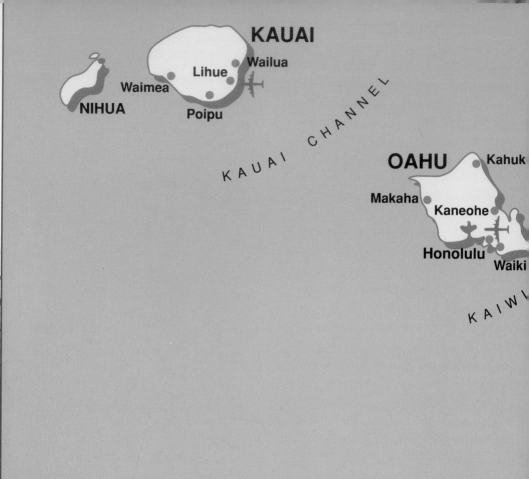

KAUAI

Wailua

Lihue

Waimea

NIHUA

Poipu

KAUAI CHANNEL

OAHU

Kahuk

Makaha

Kaneohe

Honolulu

Waiki

KAIWI

THE HAWAIIAN ISLANDS

N

PACIFIC OCEAN

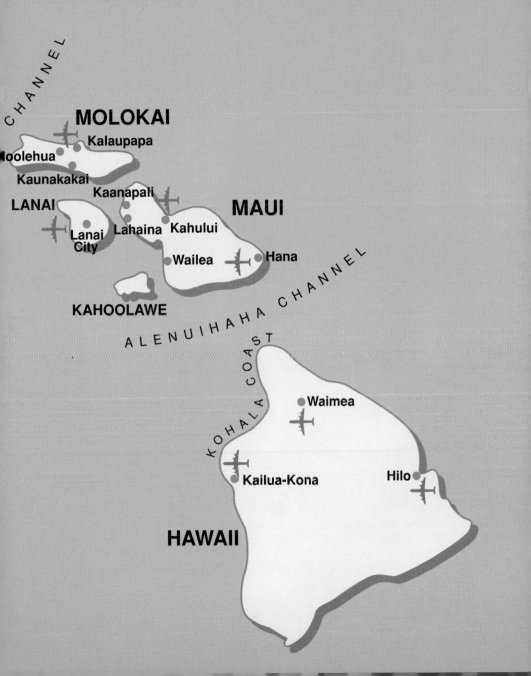

Oahu

Crowds of people – more than a million visitors annuall – make Oahu there vacation destination because it offers so much. Well-heeled tourists no longer arrive with their steamer trunks and servants for month-long getaways. Sidewalks of Waikiki choked with pedestrians and bumper-to-bumper traffic have replaced them. But Oahu is still beautiful along its more than 50 miles of shoreline and parallel Koolau and Waianae mountains. Ringed by more than one hundred beaches and a third of the state's surfing spots, Hawaii's third largest island abounds in natural attractions laced with colorful history.

Honolulu, the nation's 11th largest metropolitan area, would be well worth visiting even if Waikiki didn't exist. Restored old buildings fit more or less harmoniously with the new. When shoreline playgrounds grow a bit tire-

125

Waikiki welcomes daily waves of tourists.

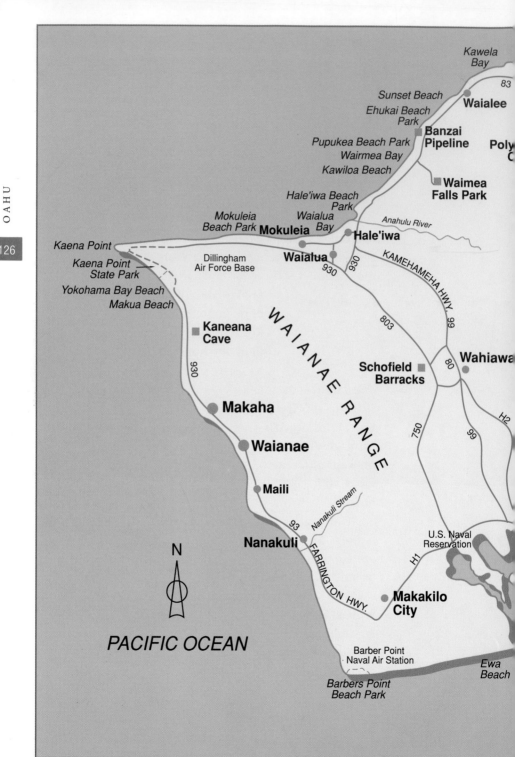

Kawela Bay

83

Sunset Beach

Waialee

Ehukai Beach Park

Banzai Pipeline

Pupukea Beach Park

Poly C

Wairmea Bay

Kawiloa Beach

Waimea Falls Park

Hale'iwa Beach Park

Anahulu River

Mokuleia Beach Park

Waialua Bay

Mokuleia

Hale'iwa

KAMEHAMEHA HWY.

Kaena Point

Waialua

930

930

99

Kaena Point State Park

Dillingham Air Force Base

Yokohama Bay Beach

803

Makua Beach

WAIANAE RANGE

Kaneana Cave

930

Schofield Barracks

80

Wahiawa

Makaha

750

99

H2

Waianae

Maili

Nanakuli Stream

93

Nanakuli

U.S. Naval Reservation

FARRINGTON HWY.

H1

N

Makakilo City

PACIFIC OCEAN

U.S. Naval Reservation

Barber Point Naval Air Station

Ewa Beach

Barbers Point Beach Park

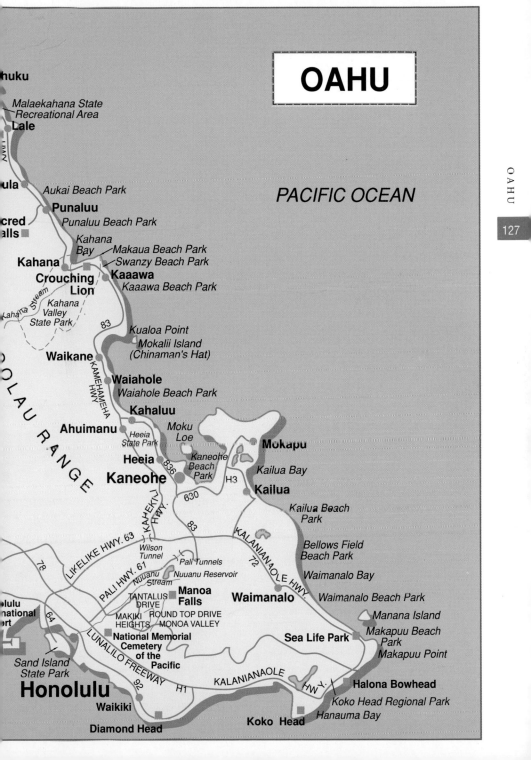

OAHU

PACIFIC OCEAN

huku

*Malaekahana State
Recreational Area*
Lale

ula

Aukai Beach Park
Punaluu

cred
alls

Punaluu Beach Park

*Kahana
Bay* /*Makaua Beach Park*
Kahana `—`*Swanzy Beach Park*
Crouching **Kaaawa**
Lion *Kaaawa Beach Park*

Kahana Stream

*Kahana
Valley
State Park* 83

Waikane

KAMEHAMEHA HWY.

Kualoa Point
*Mokalii Island
(Chinaman's Hat)*

Waiahole
Waiahole Beach Park

Kahaluu

Ahuimanu *Moku
Loe*
*Heeia
State Park*

Heeia 836 *Kaneohe
Beach
Park* **Mokapu**

Kaneohe 630 *Kailua Bay* H3

KAHEKILI HWY.

Kailua

*Kailua Beach
Park*

83 *Bellows Field
Beach Park*

LIKELIKE HWY. 63 *KALANIANAOLE HWY.*

*Wilson
Tunnel* 72

K *O* **OLAU RANGE**

78 *PALI HWY. 61* *Pali Tunnels* *Waimanalo Bay*
*Nuuanu
Stream* *Nuuanu Reservoir* *Waimanalo Beach Park*
**Manoa
Falls**

*TANTALUS
DRIVE* **Waimanalo**
64 **MAKIKI** *ROUND TOP DRIVE*
HEIGHTS *MONOA VALLEY* *Manana Island*
lulu
national **National Memorial** **Sea Life Park** *Makapuu Beach
Park*
rt **Cemetery
of the** *Makapuu Point*
*Sand Island
State Park* **Pacific**

LUNALILO FREEWAY 92 H1 *KALANIANAOLE* **Halona Bowhead**

Honolulu *Koko Head Regional Park*
Waikiki *HWY.* *Hanauma Bay*
Koko Head
Diamond Head

some, Hawaii's early royalty can be glimpsed at **Iolani Palace**, the nation's only palace, a few minutes drive from old-world Chinatown and a moving remembrance of the bombing of Pearl Harbor that triggered U.S. entry into World War II. Outside of Honolulu and Waikiki, the five parts of Oahu might as well be on another island: Diamond Head to Hanauma Bay and Makapuu Beach Park, serene panoramas and great snorkeling and surfing just southeast of Waikiki; the windward or east coast between the Koolaus and the Pacific, beautiful flora and beaches ending at the Polynesian Cultural Center in Laia; the North Shore famous for giant waves out to rocky Kaena Point, the turning point to the Waianae Coast, the most native part of Oahu and Hawaii; and the central area between Koolau and Waianae mountains—pineapple country and Schofield Barracks, setting for *From Here to Eternity*.

From the Airport

The Honolulu International Airport is about five miles west of Waikiki. It's a 20-minute drive to Waikiki from the airport except during rush hour when it can take as long as 45 minutes. If you have a fly/stay package, shuttle services are usually part of the package. Otherwise, for about $9 per person use the **Airport Motor Coach** (926-4747), **Airport Express** (949-5249) or **Gray Line** (834-1033) to get you to your hotel with baggage if you plan to spend your first days in Waikiki or Honolulu. A car is unnecessary for sightseeing in Waikiki and is an expensive nuisance for parking in Honolulu. A taxi from the airport to Waikiki will cost about $20. Rent a car if your accommodations are outside of Waikiki or you plan to sightsee outside Waikiki and Honolulu soon after arriving. Good service and car rental prices are available from **Dollar Rent-A-Car** (800-367-7006) and **Tropical Rent-A-Car** (800-367-5140). Dollar will

Hanauma Bay.

rent with a cash deposit and Tropical requires a credit card. For the lowest rates, always make reservations ahead of time through the 800-number service.

Bus service — **The Bus** — between and within Waikiki and Honolulu and around Oahu is excellent. The fare is only 60 cents. For schedule information, call 531-1611.

Beyond Waikiki, exploring Greater Honolulu and the rest of Oahu on The Bus works well for people with patience who are not in a hurry. The **No. 8** between Waikiki and Ala Moana runs often. A **No. 22** runs from Waikiki to Hanauma Bay and **No. 57** or **58** will take you to Sea Life Park and back around to Ala Moana via Kailua. Take **No. 2** to the Bishop Museum. **No. 52** or **55** to Circle Island from Ala Moana for an all day trip around the island.

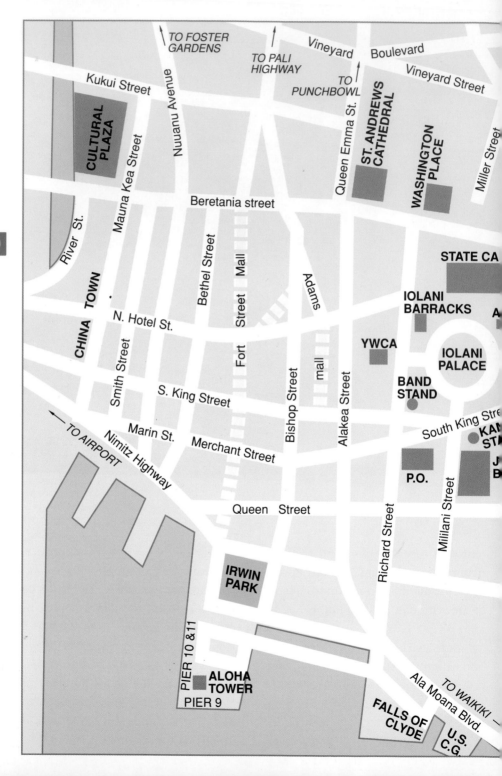

TO FOSTER GARDENS

TO PALI HIGHWAY

Vineyard Boulevard

TO PUNCHBOWL

Vineyard Street

Kukui Street

Nuuanu Avenue

Queen Emma St.

ST. ANDREWS CATHEDRAL

WASHINGTON PLACE

Miller Street

CULTURAL PLAZA

Mauna Kea Street

Beretania street

STATE CA

River St.

Bethel Street

Street Mall

Adams

IOLANI BARRACKS

A

CHINA TOWN

N. Hotel St.

YWCA

IOLANI PALACE

Smith Street

Fort

mall

BAND STAND

S. King Street

Bishop Street

Alakea Street

South King Stre

Marin St.

KAM STA

TO AIRPORT

Nimitz Highway

Merchant Street

P.O.

J B

Queen Street

Richard Street

Mililani Street

IRWIN PARK

PIER 10 & 11

ALOHA TOWER

PIER 9

FALLS OF CLYDE

TO WAIKIKI

Ala Moana Blvd.

U.S. C.G.

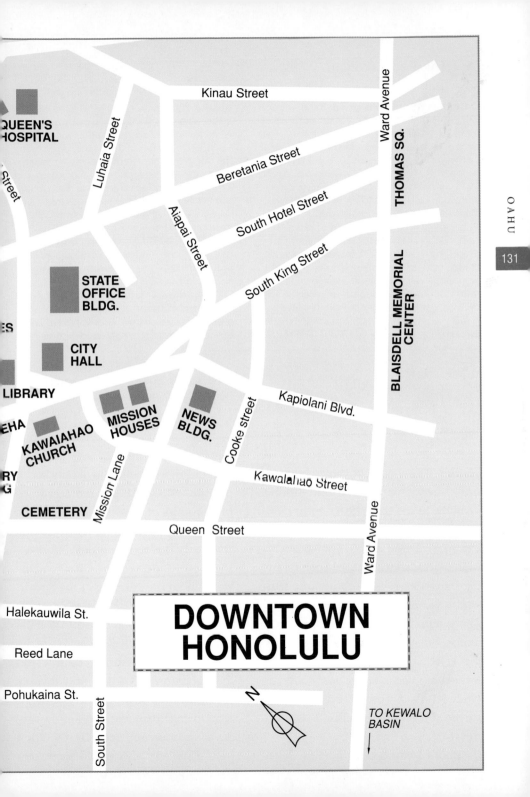

Hokulea Voyages

Celebrated artist-historian, **Herb Kane** — born and living on the Big Island, author and illustrator of *PELE, Goddess of Hawaii's Volcanoes* — has been one of the key persons in Hawaii to spur a cultural revival over the past 20 years. He helped to found the Polynesian Voyaging Society in 1973 committed to building a full-scale voyaging canoe capable of sailing between Hawaii, Tahiti and other Polynesian islands.

Kane was dissatisfied with the drawings and written accounts of these canoes by early Europeans. He researched Polynesian canoes in books, gathered information from museums around the world and from a variety of expert sources from archaeologists to sailors. Kane became part of the team that designed — actually recreating the design of a vessel that is more than a thousand years old — and tested

Hokulea, the *Star of Gladness*. On the canoe's first cruise, a Hawaiian crewman lost his life when the canoe foundered off Kauai.

In 1976, the first of three successful trips by the *Hokulea* confirmed that Polynesian navigators could sail between Tahiti and Hawaii and Tahiti and New Zealand and back. Each round-trip between Tahiti and Hawaii covered 5,500 sailing miles — all without Western navigational instruments. But Kane is not satisfied. He's guiding the building of another voyaging canoe using only traditional construction techniques in order to demonstrate Polynesian knowledge and craftsmanship.

At the **Hawaii Maritime Center** (Pier 7 near the foot of Punchbowl St, 536-6373) a 60-ft replica of a Polynesian double-hulled sailing canoe, the *Hokulea*, is docked for visitors.

Waikiki

Waikiki's waves were perfect for the favorite sport of Hawaiian royalty — surfing. The waves haven't changed, unlike everything else in and around Waikiki. In the early 19th Century, the traditional royal playground was changed forever when Kamehameha built a grass shack on the beach for his favorite wife, Queen Kaahumanu, Hawaii's second most famous celebrity. The magnificent beach's destiny as a deluxe vacation resort and sanctuary for celebrities was set. Later, King Kalakaua's beach house hospitality included Robert Louis Stevenson who stayed for several months to write a novel.

Mark Twain's *Letter from the Sand-* *wich Islands,* however, did not automatically create an explosion of Mainland tourist traffic.

Waikiki's lowlying interior swamp was drained in the 1920s when the Ala Wai Canal was built. The serene beach playground of the alii remained the playground of movie stars and the wealthy until World War II arrived and changed "the good old days" forever. During and after the war, GIs spread the word about the paradise of the Pacific. In the 60s and 70s tourism boomed, hotels and condos sprouted and Waikiki ceased to be an exclusive enclave of the rich and famous, starting its transformation into one of the most densely populated tourist spots in the world.

Up until 1986, Waikiki simply wore down with use and acted as if it didn't matter since tourists would keep coming anyhow. But gone are the pedicabs, profusion of delivery vans, skittering skateboards and even much of the handbills that used to paper Waikiki's less pleasant sidewalks.

In the late 80s, Waikiki decided to rebuild its image and offer more upscale and elegant facilities for American, Japanese and other foreign travelers. A surge of Japanese investment also made a very big difference. At the same time, direct flights to Maui and the Big Island allowed more tourists to bypass Oahu and Waikiki.

However, Waikiki still offers something for everyone, burgers and gourmet food, ultra-luxury suites and the widest assortment of moderate and inexpensive accommodation in Hawaii. (Among the Neighbor Islands, only on Maui's Kehei can the supply of moderately priced accommodations begin to compare with Waikiki.)

Waikiki got its start as a surfing beach in the 16th century, long before missionaries were appalled by the sight of semi-naked bodies balancing artfully on long boards.

Waikiki's surfing tradition continues today albeit in a less regal manner. Perfect summer surf still produces the ultimate wave riding pleasure. Today, however, recreational shoppers in Waikiki now outnumber surfers at least one hundred to one.

Along Kalakaua Avenue, are the International Market Place, Royal Hawaiian Shopping Center, Waikiki Shopping Plaza, Kuhio Mall, hotel gift shops where shopping area browsers, souvenir hunters and serious shoppers fulfill most of their needs from object d'art to knickknacks.

Waikiki is an island resort jampacked with hundreds of hotels, restaurants and bars, shops, galleries, night spots and other businesses crammed into a mere one-and-a-half square miles. Across from three-mile long **Ala Wai Canal**, the 18-hole municipal **Ala Wai Golf Course** is the busiest in the nation — with more than 700 players daily.

Ala Wai Boulevard is a good way to bypass Waikiki for Honolulu and a jogging route to Kapiolani Park.

Kuhio Avenue running through the center of Waikiki includes a sprinkling of recommended accommodations and restaurants but the main action is on Kalakaua Avenue which runs parallel to the beach.

Try to learn the local terms for directions in order to avoid confusion. "Diamond Head" means "east", towards Diamond Head; ewa (pronounced "ay-vah") means "west", towards Pearl Harbor and Ewa Beach. *Mauka* means "towards the mountains" and *makai* means "towards the coast or ocean"

The Beaches of Waikiki

Waikiki Beach is actually a series of beaches covering a $2^1/_2$ mile stretch from Kapahulu, where the breakwater protects the shoreline of Kuhio Beach, to Hilton Hawaiian Village.

Taking in the sun and sea with Diamond Head overlooking.

For calm waves and a sandy ocean bottom, **Kahaloa** and **Ulukoa** beaches in front of the Royal Hawaiian and the Ala Moana Surfrider hotels and **Kahanamoku Beach and Lagoon** in front of the Hilton Hawaiian Village are good spots. Surfers head out beyond the reef at **Gray's Beach** to find break No. 3's in front of the Halekulani and offshore from Royal Moana Beach for breaks named Popular's, Queen's and Canoes.

Waikiki Beach for many people lies along **Slippery Wall**, a retaining wall that fronts Waikiki Beach and **Prince Kuhio Beach** along Kalakaua Avenue creating an almost enclosed salt-water pool with safe year-round swimming. These beaches adjoin **Kapiolani Park**

and **Sans Souci Beach**. Between **San Souci** and **Kahala Beach** are **Kaluahole Beach**, **Diamond Head Beach Park**, **Kuilei Cliffs Beach Park** and **Kaalawai Beach**.

All of these beaches have small pockets of sand, some protected areas for swimming and bodysurfing and are always dangerous in high surf. The beach in front of the Kahala Hilton, at the eastern end of **Kahala Beach**, is a dream!

Waikiki Watersports

Along Waikiki Beach, you can hire catamarans for one-hour rides while beach concessions in front of Fort DeRussy, the

Suggested Itinerary: Ten Days on Oahu

Waikiki combines shopping, walking streets day and night, eating in a variety of restaurants, peeking into a few hotels, enjoying night-time activities and using the beaches for sun and watersports.

Waikiki deserves at least one night and two days. Sightseeing in Historic Honolulu requires at least another day and preferably one night and two days.

After at least three nights and four days spent sightseeing in Waikiki and Historic Honolulu, including days of arrival and departure, touring Greater Honolulu and the rest of the island ideally requires at least an additional six days:

DAY

• 5 a full-day for the Punchbowl, Lower and Upper Tantalus (including at least one short hike and a picnic lunch), a visit to the Contemporary Museum, and sights along Nuuanu Avenue and Valley up to the Pali Lookout;

• 6 a full day for the University of Hawaii, East-West Center, Manoa Valley and Manoa Falls, possibly Paradise Park and, if at all possible, Lyon Arboretum;

• 7 a full day for the USS *Arizona* Memorial and Pearl Harbor, Bishop Museum, and some serious shopping;

•8 at least a full-day from Diamond Head around Makapu Point to the windward coast, down the coast to attend the afternoon, dinner and evening program at the Polynesian Cultural Center in Laie, and return to Waikiki (if possible, check out of Waikiki this morning and check-in for a night in the vicinity of Laie, rather than returning to your hotel in Waikiki at night);

• 9 (from Laie) tour the North Shore to Haleiwa and Mokuleia, and then back to Honolulu-Waikiki through Wahaiwa (which can be done in reverse if you return to Waikiki the night before instead of staying overnight near the North Shore);

• 10 drive up the leeward coast to visit the Sheraton Makaha Resort, and possibly Kaena Point (if you haven't hiked out there from the Mokuleia side).

These ten days on Oahu are so full of sightseeing and other activities there is not much time left for swimming, picnics, beachcombing, snorkeling or diving, horseback riding, tennis, golf or other fun outdoor activities.

One option is to stay longer on Oahu or simply to move on and come back another time.

Sheraton Moana-Surfrider, Outrigger Hotel, Halekulani and Hilton Hawaiian Village are ready to provide surfboards and sails, lessons, equipment, outrigger canoe rides and other services. There are also snorkeling excursions to Hanauma Bay and you can rent masks and snorkels.

For surfing, windsurfing and sailing information, contact the **Haleiwa Surf Center**, a county agency. Kailua also is a good place to learn windsurfing.

Chinatown Oahu.

Japanese tourists contribute dollars to the state economy.

Waikiki Shopping

Most of the people you see flooding Kalakaua and the rest of Waikiki are tourists from around the world. The street reflects a dynamic mix of life at the beach, from tacky fast-food joints and gaudy tourist emporiums to chic French designer boutiques – Tiffany, Gucci and Chanel. Muumuus, aloha shirts, macadamia nuts, mass produced koa *tikis* and other supposedly exotic merchandise still accounts for the bulk of purchases in Waikiki's shops. You can also buy cosmetics, floral-scented Hawaiian perfumes, black coral, guava jelly, other gifts, medicines, deli and sundry impulse needs.

Clothing at discount prices is stocked at **Liberty House** department stores. For comparison shopping, look at the resort wear at **Casa d'Bella II** (2352 Kalakaua) and **Island Fashions** (2520 Kalakaua). Unless you've shopped in Hong Kong, you may look down your nose at discount garment factories. The odds are good, however, that you'll find something you like among the 50,000 choices at the **Hilo Hattie Fashion Center** (700 Nimitz Highway). In addition to a free bus ride from Waikiki, Hilo Hattie's van also will take you to the nearby **Dole Pineapple Cannery**. Before leaving the vicinity of Hilo Hattie, **Crazy Shirts Factory Outlet** is just around the corner (1095 Dillingham Boulevard). The designs of these shirts are the best in Hawaii and make good gifts, especially at those prices.

Open booths at the **International Market Place** around a giant banyan tree are surrounded by tropical planting and people buying all kinds of souvenir jewelry, from plastic to coral, pearls in the oyster and a wide variety of trinkets, *sans* authentic Hawaiian crafts. Upstairs in the back, **Art of Paradise** is a cooperative that features the art of about two dozen local artists. For one of the best places to find excellent Hawaiian crafts, head for the **Crafts Court** in **Kuhio Mall** directly behind the International Market Place.

Right across the street from the International Market Place, three city blocks are covered by three tastefully designed floors and over 120 shops of the **Royal Hawaiian Shopping Center**. **The Little Hawaiian Craft Shop** on the third floor has Hawaii's best display of the state's traditional and contemporary crafts as well as handcrafts from other Pacific islands. The shopping center fronts the entrance to the **Royal Hawaii Hotel** (and the Sheraton Waikiki) so you can tour the "Pink Palace" and perhaps stop for a drink at the hotel's beachside bar. Not far from here, in the early part of the Century Hawaii's most famous "beachboy," Duke Paoa Kahanamoku, used his 114-pound, 16-ft surf board made of *koa* to win world championships.

King's Village, behind the twin-towered Hyatt Regency Waikiki towering 44-stories above Kalakaua Avenue, is supposed to look like a 19th Century European village shopping place, replete with a changing-of-the-guard ceremony shortly after 6 pm. The variety of gift shops makes the visit worthwhile, especially **Kitamura's Oriental Arts, Crafts and Antiques** for its Japanese doll, kimono and obis collection; **Casa Tesoro** for Filipino clothing and handcrafts; and fossilized and crystalized items in the **The Fossil Shop**.

The elegant atrium shopping complex of the Hyatt Regency Waikiki has more than 70 shops on three floors surrounding a 3-tier waterfall. **Harry's Bar** beside the pool is a pleasant meeting place, especially for the fashion show on Wednesday at 4 pm. A competitor for elegance and sophistication of shops is the **Waikiki Shopping Plaza** (2350

Tales of fortune in Chinatown.

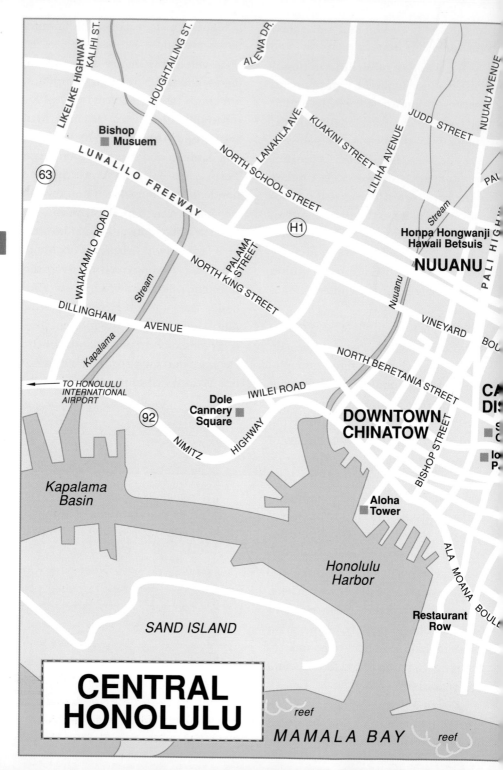

CENTRAL
HONOLULU

MAMALA BAY

reef

reef

SAND ISLAND

Kapalama
Basin

Honolulu
Harbor

Aloha
Tower

Restaurant
Row

Dole
Cannery
Square

DOWNTOWN
CHINATOW

NUUANU

Honpa Hongwanji
Hawaii Betsuis

Bishop
Musuem

LUNALILO FREEWAY

LIKELIKE HIGHWAY

KALIHI ST.

HOUGHTAILING ST.

ALEWA DR.

NUUAU AVENUE

JUDD STREET

LANAKILA AVE.

KUAKINI STREET

LILIHA AVENUE

PAI

NORTH SCHOOL STREET

PALAMA
STREET

NORTH KING STREET

WAIAKAMILO ROAD

Stream

DILLINGHAM

AVENUE

Kapalama

TO HONOLULU
INTERNATIONAL
AIRPORT

NIMITZ

HIGHWAY

IWILEI ROAD

NORTH BERETANIA STREET

VINEYARD

BOU

PALI HIGHW

Stream

Nuuanu

Stream

BISHOP STREET

ALA MOANA BOULE

CA
DIS

S
C

Io
P

63

H1

92

Kalakaua) with its five-story fountain designed by Bruce Hopper. Many of the shops here obviously cater mostly to Japanese tourists. Just about a mile east of the Che Pasta Restaurant on Waialae Avenue is the Kahala Shopping Mall with Jody Nako's **Following Sea**, displaying one of the best collections of local crafts, including: large curly *koa* bowls of Jack Straka; handsome jewelry and other boxes made of Hawaiian woods by another Big Island artist, Greg Pontius; Honolulu's own master woodworker, Ricardo Jepson Dellera (**Dellera's Woodworks**); beautiful bracelets from Erik and Hillery Gunther's **Cloud Forest Woodworks**; fiber sculpture by Maui's Mika McCann; and more. Stop at **Yen King** for a Chinese lunch or dinner feast in any regional style.

Nightlife

Waikiki nightlife and entertainment covers the spectrum of tastes, energies and ethnic backgrounds. Throbbing disco, slow dance, piano bars, big band, guitars and ukeleles, rock and Hawaiian singers, oldies but goodies, very local with no commercial trappings and splashy Las Vegas-style revues.

The young and restless with high-energy action on their minds will head for **Moose McGillicudy's** (310 Lewers Street, 923-0751), the smashing new **Maharaja Restaurant and Disco** in the Waikiki Trade Center (Kuhio Avenue, 922-3030), or the **Hard Rock Cafe**

Headdresses and hulas.

(1837 Kalakaua, 955-7383) on the edge of Waikiki. At the Hyatt Regency's **Trappers** (923-1234), top 40-music and oldies but goodies are popular nightly. **Spats** at the Hyatt Regency (923-1234) is a swanky disco and 30-stories higher up, **Annabelle's** atop the Ilikai (949-3811) sparkles with comparable glitter. **Rumours** at the Ramada Renaissance on Ala Moana (955-4811) is a popular disco for the slightly older crowd.

In the Diamond Head area, **Bobby McGee's Conglomeration** at the Colony East has dinner and dancing every night. The rest of the area is fairly quiet. On the other side of town, at **Restaurant Row** in downtown Honolulu, one of the few places that doesn't fold up at night, **Studebaker** (526-9888) cranks out rock-and-roll.

There are plenty of pleasant places in the vicinity of Ala Moana for gathering around a bar without any music. Try Ward Center for several of them: **Ryan's Parkplace** (523-9132), **Compadres** (523-1307), and **Monterey Bay Canners**. In Waikiki, the **Hulekulani's House Without a Key** guarantees tranquility with mellow background Hawaiian music. At the **Sheraton Moana Surfrider** (922-3111), the **Veranda's** piano and the **Beach Bar's** atmosphere are soothing and romantic complements to cocktails at sunset.

Moving a small notch toward entertainment but still very easy on the ears, Jimmy Borges sings ballads nightly at the **Hilton Hawaiian Village**. Enjoy ukulele music from 9 pm-midnight on Sunday nights at **Buzz's Original Steak House** (2535 Coyne Street, 944-9781).

Since 1981, Don Ho has been performing at the **Hilton Dome** in the Hilton Hawaiian Village with dancers and singers in a Las Vegas-Polynesian-style revue six nights a week, plus cocktail shows Sunday through Friday nights.

Singer-songwriters Robert and Roland Cazimero – the Brothers Cazimero – at the Royal Hawaiian's Monarch Room are one of the most special Hawaiian shows, with old and new music and hula for dinner shows Tuesday to Saturday and cocktail shows on Friday and Saturday nights.

At the **Polynesian Palace** in the Reef Towers Hotel (247 Lewers Street, 923-9861), Al Harrington and his group of dancers and musicians have been pleasing crowds with their revue for many years from Sunday through Friday. On the other end of town, for just as long Danny Kaleikini at the **Kahala Hilton Hotel** has amused and entertained audiences with his revue. For sheer energy, the **Ainahau Showroom's** dancers from Fiji, Samoa, New Zealand and Tahiti have thrilled people at the **Sheraton Princess Kaiulani Hotel**.

Some of the most interesting local theater in Hawaii is performed by amateur groups. Kumu Kahua Theater Company produces plays about Hawaii on the grounds of **St Andrews Cathedral**. John F. Kennedy Theater, **University of Hawaii-Manoa** (948-7655) presents Chinese opera, Kabuki, Noh plays and also American musicals. Consult your local papers for up-to-the-minute listings and schedules for all entertainment events.

Kapiolani Park

Starting with early morning joggers and walkers beating a path around the perimeter, tennis players, soccer teams, kite-flyers, picnickers, and others throughout the day and evening enjoy this 140-acres of greenery donated by King Kalakaua to the people of Honolulu. The San Souci Beach runs along the shorefront, a favorite place for family picnics and friends to gather. Named after the King's wife, the site has had horse and car races, polo matches, and military units parading around Camp McKinley at the turn of the century. Fashionable ladies in long flowing skirts – pa'u riders – once rode horses around this section of crown lands.

Between the hustle of Waikiki and the profile of Diamond Head, the park is an oasis of relaxation, exercise and special entertainment events. Free concerts in the evening by the **Honolulu Symphony** and visiting music groups are heard at the Waikiki Shell. The **Royal Hawaiian Band** plays free concerts nearby on Sunday afternoons.

Lines start at 8 am for the popular 10 am **Kodak Hula Shows** on Tuesdays, Thursdays and Fridays. The 75-minute show is in the bleachers off Monsarrat Avenue near the Waikiki Shell outdoor

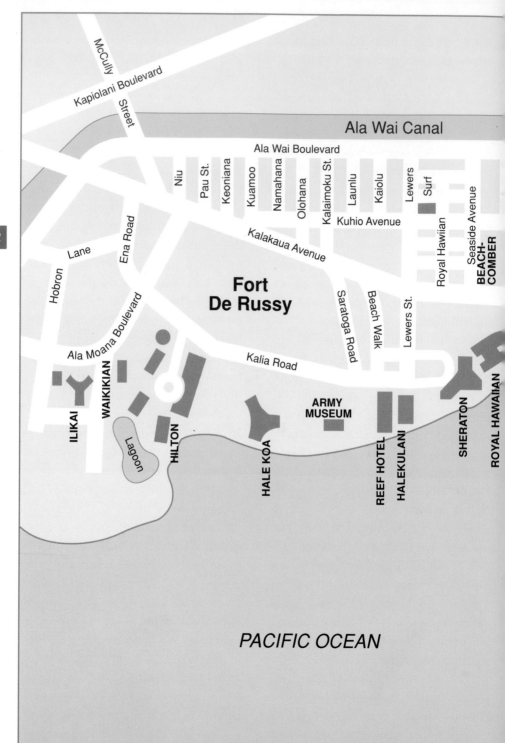

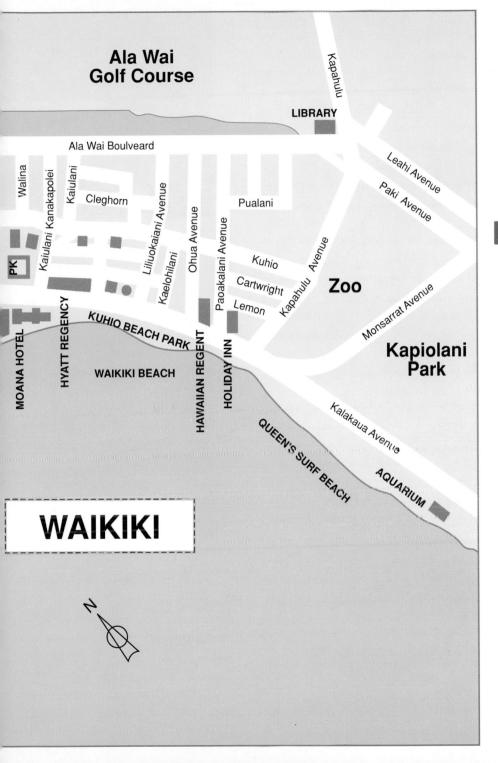

Ala Wai
Golf Course

LIBRARY

Kapahulu

Ala Wai Boulveard

Leahi Avenue

Paki Avenue

Walina

Kaiulani Kanakapolei

Kaiulani

Cleghorn

Liliuokalani Avenue

Ohua Avenue

Pualani

Kaelohilani

Paoakalani Avenue

Kuhio

Cartwright

Lemon

Kapahulu Avenue

Zoo

Monsarrat Avenue

Kapiolani
Park

PK

MOANA HOTEL

HYATT REGENCY

KUHIO BEACH PARK

WAIKIKI BEACH

HAWAIIAN REGENT

HOLIDAY INN

QUEEN'S SURF BEACH

Kalakaua Avenue

AQUARIUM

WAIKIKI

N

amphitheater. Be prepared for thousands of people arriving by the busloads to fill the bleachers to see modern *hula* performed by women wearing traditional *ti*-leaf skirts, cotton *muumuus* and *leis*, and using traditional *hula* instruments. Free hula dance lessons are a big part of the program. Admission is free.

The **Hawaiians by the Sea** exhibit at the **Waikiki Aquarium** shows how Hawaiians built and used fishponds. Other fascinating exhibits show fish, coral and other sea life in the waters of Hawaii, Polynesia and Micronesia. All of the books you might want to see or buy on the flora and fauna of Hawaii are found in the aquarium's bookshop.

Across the street, the **Honolulu Zoo** (151 Kapahulu Avenue, 923-7723) has the plants, trees, flowers and other flora and birdlife that you can see around Hawaii (but may not), in addition to the usual collection of elephants, giraffes, monkeys and so forth that you expect to see in zoos. Open daily 8:30 am-4:30 pm. admission $3 adults, children under 12 free accompanied by an adult, (971-7171). On Tuesday, the **Art Mart** – works of local artists – is also held on the nearby **Zoo fence** from 10 am-4 pm. Much more and better quality art is displayed on Saturdays and Sundays.

Beaches from Waikiki to Mokoleia

The best beaches for swimming are Kahala Hilton, Hanauma Bay Beach

Park (except for being very crowded), Waimanalo Beach Park and Waimanalo Bay State Recreation Area, Bellows Field Beach Park (only open from Friday noon until dark on Sunday), Lanikai Beach, Kailua Beach Park, Kaaawa Beach Park, Kahana Bay Beach Park, and Punaluu Beach Park, Hukilau Beach (private), Laie Beach, Malaeke-

Lobby at the Turtle Bay Hilton.

hana State Recreation Area, Goat Island, Kaihalulu (next to the Turtle Bay Hilton), and Turtle Bay's Kuilima Point.

At more than a dozen beaches on the south, east and north shores of Oahu, swimming is either dangerous or poor — Diamond Head Beach Park, along the five-mile shoreline from Waialae Beach Park to Maunalua Beach Park, at Sandy Beach (Koko Head Beach Park), Makapuu Beach Park, polluted Kaneohe Beach Park and others bordering the Bay, Swanzy Beach Park and Hauula Beach Park. In fall and winter, Kahuku

Golf Course Park beach, Ehukai Beach Park, Sunset Beach, Waimea Beach Park, Pupukea Beach Park, all the way to Haleiwa, Alii Beach Park, and Mokoleia.

Diamond Head to Koko Head

The long way around to the windward coast (instead of over the Pali Highway) passes the **Diamond Head Lighthouse** and through the posh Kahala residential area on Kahala Avenue to the **Kahala Hilton Hotel**.

The huge dormant volcanic rock, **Diamond Head**, a national landmark, is the backdrop for some very expensive and exclusive real estate in Kahala, including the very private **Waialae Country Club** next to the Kahala Hilton Hotel (not available to guests). Follow Kalakaua Avenue to Diamond Head Road and the route to the Diamond Head Tunnel.

According to legend, *Pele's* younger sister, *Hi'iaka*, saw a resemblance in Diamond Head to the yellowfin tuna and named it *Leahi* ("Brow of the *Ahi*"), close to the name Hawaii. Diamond Head was a place of *mana* ("power") for Hawaiians long before Western sailors used it as a landmark. Worthless volcanic glass (calcite crystals) discovered on its slopes by 19th Century English seamen were confused with diamonds; hence the name "Diamond Head", one of those wonderful historic misnomers.

Climb the 760-ft to the top of the State's most famous landmark if you have the energy. Otherwise, on the island side, a tunnel leads into the crater to a small city park, and in 10-minutes of easy walking, a dusty footpath leads to the crater rim. The spectacular view from the summit of Diamond Head is well worth the moderate exertion. The 7/10ths of a mile trail to the summit starts on the other side of the tunnel. Heavily fortified during World War II, old gun emplacements and connecting service tunnels still lace the top. A series of steps and a dark tunnel (bring a flashlight) take you to the summit.

About two miles past Diamond Head, in the ritzy Kahala neighborhood, the plain looking Kahala Hilton is one of Hawaii's most elegant resorts. The

Tourist with ideas of his own.

view of Diamond Head from the hotel is unsurpassed and every other room has a balcony from which to enjoy it, the scenic Pacific beachfront, the beautiful Waialae Golf Course and coral reefs just offshore for snorkeling.

Valet park your car, ask for a walking tour pamphlet at the hotel's desk, plan for a swim on the superb beach, lunch in one of the restaurants and leave refreshed. Catch the dolphins and turtles getting fed at 11 am, 2 or 4 pm and penguins strutting in lagoons. Exquisite sandwiches or Kahuku prawns are served in the open-air **Hala Terrace** (734-2211) for lunch. For an unforgettable but pricey dinner, try the gourmet **Maile** restaurant and stay for dancing after 9 pm in the adjoining lounge.

Roy Yamaguchi's culinary extravaganza in a duplex (bar downstairs and restaurant upstairs) overlooking **Maunalua Bay. Roy's** East-meets-West cuisine is an exemplary combination of French training and Asian influences. Two other redeeming culinary features of bland Hawaii Kai that rank among the better, lesser-known restaurants on Oahu are the **Pacific Broiler** (Koko Marina Shopping Center, near Hanauma Bay, 395-4181) with dishes to satisfy vegetarians or die-hard meat eaters and ex-Kahala chef Martin Wyss' **Swiss Inn**, a paradise especially for veal lovers. In the Koko Marina Shopping Center, stop at the **Aloha Dive Shop** to rent snorkel gear or arrange for an excursion to Hanama Bay.

Koko Head to the Windward Coast

Kealaolu Avenue leads to H-1 (Lunalilo Freeway) which becomes Route 72 (Kalanianaole Highway) out to the slopes of 642 ft **Koko Head** and 1,200-ft **Koko Crater**, an extinct volcano. A one-mile trail leads to the top of Koko Head and another one-mile trail leads from Route 72 to the top of Koko Crater. Both provide fantastic views of Hanauma Bay, Diamond Head and the Koolau Mountains.

Hawaii Kai, built by Henry Kaiser in the 1960s, is a one-of-a-kind-in-Hawaii, huge, uninteresting East Honolulu suburb providing plenty of business for

Hanauma Bay State Underwater Park

Along **Maunalua Bay**, pass up Kawauikui Beach Park, Niu and Paiko beaches, Maunalua Bay Beach Park, and Kokee and Koko Kai Parks, until you reach **Hanauma Bay State Underwater Park**. Arrive early in order to avoid the crowds.

The sea eroded an extinct volcanic crater in the side of Koko Head and created **Hanauma Bay** with a wall open to the sea, a paradise for snorkelers, scuba-divers and swimming. Tall cliffs surround the horse-shoe like bay lined with tall coconut trees. Inevitably, Hanauma Bay is over-run with tourists.

Snorkelling in Hanauma Bay.

The lovely park around the circular bay and the underwater marine reserve filled with colored coral and sealife is usually so crowded that it may be closed a few days a week. Only a limited number of escorted dives are allowed in the bay. Shuttle buses take the thousands of tour- ists from the parking lot at the top of the hill down to the beach.

Arrive as early as possible in the morning or at the end of the day. More or less tamed tropical fish wait to nibble food from the fingers of eager visitors. Snorkel gear is available for rent but

Swell surfs at Sandy Beach.

may not be of the best quality. Rent gear in Waikiki or at the **Aloha Dive Shop** before you arrive at the bay. **Hanauma Bay Snorkeling Excursions** and **Steve's Diving Adventures** have half-day tours to Hanauma Bay and for full-days, lunch is included.

Koko Head & Koko Crater

Hike up the closed road at the entrance to the parking lot for 15 minutes to the 642-ft summit of Ko**ko Head**. Across Kaiwi Channel, Molokai rests 20 miles off shore. A few miles to the northwest is *Kohelepelepe* ("Fringed vagina") — **Koko Crater** — where, according to legend, the pig god (*Kamapua*) was diverted and

seduced by *Pele's* sister (*Kapo*) who created Koko Crater as the illusion of a vagina, which *Kamapua* dove into instead of raping *Pele*.

Across from Hanauma Bay, follow the road next to the Hawaii Job Corp Training Center to an abandoned tramway track that serves as a stairway up to the Crater's 1,208-ft summit. For a guided trail ride to the crater, follow Route 72 to the Hawaii Kai Golf Course and take a left turn on Kealahou Street to **Koko Crater Stables** (395-2628). You can hike from Hanauma Bay two miles to the **Halona Blowhole**, passing the "Toilet Bowl" tidepool along the way that fills and flushes with tidal action. The Halona Blowhole is just below Koko Head Crater. From Kalanianaole Highway a look-

Soapy and frothy.

out reveals Halona Cove (relax and tan but don't swim) and its sea geyser spouting water through a lava tube.

Continuing on Highway 72, the islands of Molokai and Lanai are visible offshore. **Sandy Beach**, one of Oahu's best bodysurfing beaches, must hold some unofficial record for body damage to surfers. Perfect as the east-breaking waves are, they are dangerous, too. When you see red flags, stay out of the water. (No less dangerous is **Wawamalu Beach**.) All but the most experienced bodysurfers should pass and take a left turn up to **Koko Crater Botanic Gardens** (behind Koko Head Stables). The Succulent Society of Hawaii grows several hundred acres of cacti, plumeria and other flowering plants here.

Golfers will appreciate the beautiful view from the **Hawaii Kai Golf Course**. Actually two courses – the **Championship** course (par 72, 6350 yards), and **Hawaii Kai Executive Golf** (par 55, 2433 yards). As you pass the Hawaii Kai Championship Golf Course, the road rounding the island's southeast corner arrives at a spectacular view of the windward coast. **Manana – Rabbit Island** – offshore, a seabird sanctuary, **Mokapu Peninsula** and **Makapuu Beach** lie below the lookout point.

Bodysurfers who avoid or survive Sandy Beach have **Makapuu Beach** to look forward to, the state's most (in)famous bodysurfing beach. Without the protections of a reef, 12-ft waves are common in winter, jamming on exposed rock rather than on beaches. Across from Makapuu Beach is the famous **Sea Life Park**. The park features the 300,000 gallon **Hawaiian Reef Tank** with thousands of sea creatures and the **Hawaii Ocean Theater** showing its trained porpoises, penguins and whales.

This easternmost point on Oahu is the favorite place on the island for hang gliding. Hang gliders catch updrafts along nearby cliffs sailing down the Koolau Range to Makapuu Beach below. Adventurous spirits can contact **Tradewinds Hang Gliding** (396-8557) for lessons and thrills.

Sea Life Park

Within walking distance of Makapuu Beach, **Sea Life Park** offers much more than simply oceanarium entertainment. The park has a genuine marine life research program that provides informative lectures. See the park's new "wolphin" — Kekaimalu — a cross between a bottle-nosed dolphin and a false killer whale.

The **Hawaiian Reef Exhibit**'s 300,000 gallon tank contains a scientifically accurate recreation of a Pacific Reef and its plant and sealife. A spiral ramp wrapped around the tank enables visitors to observe the tank above and below.

Manta rays and shark swim by together with hundreds of multi-colored fish. At the bottom of the tank are creatures swimming around reefs that usu-

ally are not visible to snorkelers and many divers. Take a tour behind the scenes to off-limits areas of Sea Life Park where trainers work with marine life. Ask all of your questions about Hawaiian marine life. The **Sea Life Park Hawaiian Revue**, a Polynesian show on Thursdays and Sundays, is outstanding family entertainment.

On Friday nights, the **Gallery Restaurant** serves Hawaii food (*kalua* pig, *lomilomi* salmon, and *poi*). Near this restaurant, outside the Sea Life complex, is the **Pacific Whaling Museum** which houses a large collection of whaling artifacts and memorabilia. When you add up all of the interesting and enjoyable things to see and do at Sea Life Park, a half-day would be required rather than just two hours.

A friendly leap at Sea Life Park.

Waimanalo

Local Hawaiians use **Kalona Beach** as a more or less permanent campground. **Waimanalo Beach Park** at the end of Waimanalo's 3-1/2 mile long beach and **Waimanalo Bay State Recreation Area** off Route 72 are excellent swimming and picnic places.

Waimanalo, the longest stretch of beach on Oahu and certainly one of the best, takes on the character of the adjoining local town.

Bellows Air Force Base Beach Park, on the northern end of Waimanalo, is even prettier, white sand bordered by ironwood trees, but only open to the public on Fridays noon to 6 am on Mondays. The beach is about two miles from the base's gate. Excellent swimming and bodysurfing, picnic tables, rest rooms, cold water showers and shade trees make this one of Oahu's best camping spots (requires a county permit).

In front of double-spiked Olomana Peak is beautiful **Olomana Golf Links** (par 72, 6449 yards, 259-7926). Anyone with a taste for Mexican food will want to eat **BYO** at **Bueno Nalo** in Waimanalo. Unfortunately it is only open for dinner, from 5-9 pm, to 10 pm on Sundays, and closed on Mondays.

Kailua

Route 72 intersects Route 63 to **Kailua,** which contains one of the best beaches

on the island for swimming and windsurfing, **Kailua Beach**. This wide, sandy beach and pretty park (divided by Kaelepulu Canal) leads on the south end, around the hill and rocks, to **Lanikai Beach.** Marvelous, uncrowded Lanikai Beach and its blue-green water extends along more than a mile of residences, with plenty of street parking on Mokulua Drive and access ways to the beach.

The dormitory town of Kailua is a beachside commuter suburb of Hono-

Pali Lookout for a lush view of Oahu.

lulu, with one of the most dramatic drives in the world to and from work over Pali Highway through the Koolau Mountains.

Helped by calm winds and onshore waves, beginners and advanced windsurfers will be well cared for by **Windsurfing Hawaii** (156-C Hamakua Drive, 261-3539). Rent a board and sail for for four hours or for the whole day at a fraction more.

Kailua Road out of Kailua becomes Pali Highway (Route 61) through the Koolau Mountains and the **Pali Tunnel** to to Nuuanu Valley.

For those taking a short morning or afternoon trip, take the well-marked turnout for the **Nuuanu Pali Lookout**. This spectacular view of Kailua and Kaneohe is one of the two best night views on Oahu (and the other is Honolulu from Tantalus Drive).

A giggle of girls.

Accommodations & Dining

The only accommodations in the area between Diamond Head and Kailua are among the least expensive and most comfortable in the Greater Honolulu area. **Hawaiian Family Inns** consist of three (perhaps more now) homes in Hawaii Kai renting out rooms with a private entrance and, in some instances, kitchen privileges (395-3710, 395-3710, or 395-8153). Patrick O'Malley's very attractive six **Kailua Beachside Cottages** are located next to Kailua Beach Park. Many other rental units handled by Patrick provide all amenities. For these units on the beach, just a short walk to Lanikai beach, it's worth the 30-minute drive over the Pali to visit Honolulu and Waikiki.

You can eat well at chef Alfred Mueller's **L'Auberge Swiss** (117 Hekili St., 263-4663) – the best continental-style restaurant on the windward coast on Tuesdays through Saturdays from 6-10 pm and Sundays from 5:30-9:00 pm Lunch or dinner at **Buzz's Original Steakhouse** (413 Kawailoa Road, 261-4661), right across the street from Kailua Beach (adjacent to Kaelepulu Canal) also makes a perfect ending for a visit to Kailua-Lanikai.

Kaneohe to Kahuku

Follow Kaneohe Bay Drive to Kam High-

Byodo-In Temple.

way and the northern section of town to **Heeia Pier**. At **Heeia Kea Boat Harbor** (235-2888), board the glass-bottom *Coral Queen* for an hour-long trip over fascinating coral formations and decoratively colored fish flashing through the flowery cup and gorgonian coral. (Hopefully the Bay will not be too murky with silt. Erosion from Waiahole and Waikane has flowed in Kaneohe Bay, polluting the only barrier reef left in Hawaii.)

The **Windward Mall** Shopping Center in Kaneohe, like Ala Moana Shopping Center, provides most of the inexpensive and really tasty eating that you'll need in this part of the island. **Yummy Korean BBQ, Deli Express, Taco Shop, Cinnabon**'s cinnamon rolls,

Harpo's excellent deep-dish pizza, **Patti's Chinese Kitchen**, and **Little Tokyo** offer plenty of variety and filling portions.

Be prepared for **Route 83** to change its name from Kamehameha Highway to Kahekili Highway past its intersection with Likelike Highway heading over the Koolaus to Honolulu. Two beautiful valleys along Route 83 are not to be missed: **Haiku Valley** and the **Valley of the Temples**. Route 83 to the northeast of Likelike Highway is the way to get to beautiful **Haiku Gardens** (46-316 Haiku Road) with acres of exotic plants, streams and a picturesque lily pond, the **Valley of the Temples** and the Buddhist **Byodo-In Temple** .

A former favorite get-away-place

for ancient Hawaiians, in the mid-1800s the 16-acre site known today as **Haiku Gardens** was given to an Englishman by Hawaiian *alii*. Acres of exotic plants, streams and picturesque lily and tropical fish ponds, a bamboo grove and huge banyan tree are the foreground for spectacular Koolau cliffs rising up from the dense foliage. On Saturdays, a thatched-roof hut tucked into the tropical vegetation is the scene of a procession of weddings. Wander around the tropical trees and plants which now surround a **Chart House** restaurant (247-6671) overlooking *pali* cliffs. The menu of steak, seafood and prime rib is the same as Chart Houses everywhere.

The **Valley of the Temples Memorial Park** (47-200 Kahekili Highway, 239-8811) is in a perfect setting for a universal faith cemetery. Waterfalls cascading from the Koolau's *pali* in the background can be counted on for rainbows and rain keeps the dense foliage a rich moist green. Set in a classic Japanese Garden with swans and peacocks, the centerpiece of the park is the ornate Buddhist **Byodo-In Temple** ("Temple of Equality"), an impressive replica of the famous 900-year-old Byodo-In Temple of Kyoto. After making an offering, strike the 3-ton brass bell to produce meditative vibrations in tune with the Amida Buddha. From the pagoda ("Meditation House") at the top of the hill is the best view of the grounds. There is an admission charge.

On Saturdays and Sundays, from 10 am-3 pm, art enthusiasts can have

one of the rarest treats in Hawaii: a visit to the serene and beautiful gardens, gallery and home of **Hiroshi Tagami and Michael Powell**. Tagami's oils inspired by tropical Hawaii and the surrounding Kahaluu area are exhibited worldwide. Powell has been painting for only a few years and already is highly regarded on Oahu and among private

Japanese archway and a crescent moon over Oahu.

collectors. Tagami and Powell both ex-
ude a remarkable sense of warmth,
peace, gentleness and genuine interest
in their guests. Their gallery, arranged
within interconnected Japanese-style
buildings and rooms with the gentle
sound of water flowing in small court-

yards, contain sculptures, pottery and a
varying amount of their art.

An aviary in one corner of the garden, much smaller than it was years
ago, is filled with many varieties of rare
and colorful songbirds. The garden is
planted with hundreds of daylily hy-

brids, unusual bamboo varieties, bread-fruit trees, fruit and macadamia nut trees, and other plants. This garden and lawn go steeply down a ravine at the rear of the property for at least a hundred yards, with a cemented path winding through the result of 20 years of planting hundreds of varieties of rare and unusual plants from Central and South America, Asia and other tropical and subtropical locations. Walk the gardens before visiting the galleries in order to enhance the latter experience.

In a lush 725-acre setting about a mile from the junction of route 83 and Kahekili Highway is **Senator Fong's Plantation and Gardens**. Eisenhower Valley contains the visitors center; Kennedy Valley, 15 varieties of sugarcane; Johnson Plateau, fruit and nut orchards and 75 varieties of edible trees and plants; Nixon Valley, traditional ethnic gardens (Japanese, Chinese, Filipino, and Hawaiian); and Ford Plateau, a pine garden. After a three-mile, 40-minute guided mini-bus tour of Senator Fong's Plantation and Gardens, you can return to Honolulu on the Likelike Highway (Route 63) via the Wilson Tunnel, or continue along Kaneohe Bay past fertile Waiahole and Waikane Valleys. Unfortunately, erosion from these verdant areas has flowed into Kaneohe Bay, polluting the only barrier reef left in Hawaii.

If you're tempted to see old-time Oahu, turn up **Waiahole Valley Road** and drive into a valley full of papaya, taro, bananas and very modest Hawai-

ian homes until it becomes a dirt track. This area, so near to exploding Kailua and Kaneohe, is in the path of development by Hawaiian leaseholders of agricultural land. Fruit stands along the area's roadways offer fresh fruit at bargain prices.

Just outside Kaneohe bay, Route 83 passes **Kualoa County Regional Park** best known for conical **Mokolii Island** ("Little Dragon" otherwise known as Chinaman's Hat Island) which at low tide can be reached by walking (in old

Chinaman's Hat.

sneakers because of sharp coral) about 500 yards. Pele's sister, *Hiiaha*, is supposed to have killed a dragon, cut off its tail and cast it into the sea, which created Little Dragon.

A picturesque white sand beach bordered by palm trees, Kualoa is a deservedly favorite spot for local picnics and swimming. A most sacred place on Oahu, the park is in the National Register of Historic Places. Chiefs' children were taught beside the beach, and ancient canoes lowered their sails out of respect. The historic importance of Kualoa is reflected in its choice as the beach from which the double-hulled canoe, H*okulea*, was launched in 1976.

The **Molii Fishpond**, built over 700 years ago and still in use, can be seen from Kualoa Regional Park. Look for a circular lava wall at the end of the parking lot built to protect this fishpond

Windward Oahu at Kahana Beach.

which used to be stocked with mullet and milkfish. According to legend, guardian water spirits called *moo* inhabited fishponds and appeared as beautiful mermaids.

Route 83 passes the ruins of an old sugar mill, one of the first on the island and, four miles from Kualoa, the mountain ridge rock formation resembling a crouching lion. **The Crouching Lion Restaurant** (bar and souvenir shop, 237-8511) has been an inn since 1927 and serves a decent lunch to busloads of tourists.

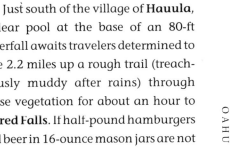

Valley State Park, a five-mile trail past old Hawaiian farms winds deep into Kahana Valley.

Just south of the village of **Hauula**, a clear pool at the base of an 80-ft waterfall awaits travelers determined to hike 2.2 miles up a rough trail (treacherously muddy after rains) through dense vegetation for about an hour to **Sacred Falls**. If half-pound hamburgers and beer in 16-ounce mason jars are not to your liking, skip **Paniolo Cafe** and move on to **Pat's at Punaluu** for Kahuku shrimp curry and guava-glazed lamb, and three meals a day. The shoreline condominiums here are sheltered by a reef in front of **Halehaha Beach**, in windward Hauula. The 30-40 units for rent in this building start at $60, with a swimming pool, sauna and gym. About halfway between Paniolo and Pat's, a tradition for budget travelers, Margaret Neal's **Countryside Cabins** are simply announced by an easily missed white sign that says "cabins" – reasonably-priced, clean but rustic studios in one of Oahu's prettiest coastal areas.

Pounders Beach (appropriately named for its pounding surf) is privately-owned but open to the public and has no facilities. The mile-long beach in the armpit of **Laie Point**, reached by a stairway down the rocks through a right-of-way half-way up the peninsula, is one of the loveliest in Hawaii. Midway down the beach, look for an opening in the coral for extended, protected swimming and snorkeling. Shady trees make picnicking perfect on

Large schools of delicious *akule* ("big-eyed scad") fish visit **Kahana Bay**, about 15 miles north of Kaneohe. Hawaiians living in the valley built shrines on bluffs surrounding the bay and fishponds. Kahana Bay County Park has camping (county permit), picnic, and other facilities, good swimming and bodysurfing. Across the road in **Kahana**

this beach.

One of the island's prettiest parks, **Malaekahana State Recreation Area** is located on **Kalani Point**. For campers, this beach should be the choice destination along the windward coast, insulated from the highway by shady trees, with the joyful bonus of wading over to **Mokuauia Island (Goat Island)**. The channel over to Goat Island is shallow on calm days and waist high on others. The white-sand beach on the leeward side of this bird refuge is a dream South Pacific-getaway. On this bird refuge you may sight a wedge-tailed shearwater, brown booby, black noddy, brown noddy, the strange looking masked-faced booby and the elegant gray-backed turn, or even a laysan albatross.

Highway 83 continues through the village of Kahuku and past **Kahuku Sugar Mill**. After operating for about 90 years until 1971, it reopened as a shopping mall with self-guided tours (10 am-6 pm) of the first room in the old mill. Since this is the midpoint of our suggested circle-the-island-tour, a visit to the **Country Kitchen Restaurant** (293-2414) makes sense. The interior is much nicer than the outside suggests – carpeting, antiques lamps and Victorian touches are pleasant; the menu offers all three meals any time of day, 8 am-9 pm daily. The restaurant's specialty – old-fashioned calico bean soup – is worth the drive.

A big mid-day decision is whether to eat lunch at the Country Kitchen or wait a few minutes longer for famous home-grown shrimp at **Amorient Aquafarm**, a roadside stand on Highway 83 next to their own 175-acre shrimp and fish farm. Open 10 am-5:30 pm Takeaways are a pleasant alternative

North Shore

At Oahu's windy northerly point, the Hawaiian Electric Company built one of the largest **wind farms** in the United States. Down below, the shoreline between **Kuilima** ("to hold hands") **Point** and Haleiwa is the most famous surfing coastline in the world. At the northern end of this spectacular coastline, the **Turtle Bay Hilton and Country Club** benefits from its isolation, the only hotel and resort on the north shore.

The resort has one of the most beautiful beaches on Oahu, in Kuilima Cove, where you can swim year-round; there is also golf, tennis, horseback riding, scuba diving and snorkeling and a wide range of hotel and condominium accommodation as well as restaurants. The Turtle Bay Hilton is an ideal base for a few days of exploring the North Shore and attending the Polynesian Cultural Center.

Beaches along the north shore – Sunset and **Waimea Bay** – provide great surfing performances in winter months. Huge breakers crash onto the 2-mile long Sunset Beach, almost safe for swimming close to shore in summer (but do not assume too much) and wild in win-

Giant trays of waterlily leaves at Waimea Falls Park.

ter. If there's an important surfing contest going on, go early in the morning to avoid huge traffic jams.

A shallow reef offshore forces waves to crest forward and quickly toward the infamous Banzai Pipeline. Park along the roadway near Sunset Beach Elementary School and you'll be across the road from the Pipeline. Waimea Bay below Sunset has Hawaii's biggest waves, reaching 30 ft, but blissfully calm in the summer.

Waimea Falls Park lies in historic Waimea Valley which has yielded many exceptional archaeological finds. Get on and off the tram through **Waimea Arboretum and Botanical Gardens**, actually 34 gardens with more than 5,000 species of plants, full of tropical birds, peacocks and parrots, roaming about this 1800-acre paradise. The Park also contains plenty of hiking trails, short guided tours, a tram ride to the 55-ft falls where you can swim, and numerous very pleasant picnic spots. Picnic items can be purchased at the park's **Country Store**. Five times a day, daring men dive from a 60-ft high cliff into water at the base of the falls.

In the Upper Meadow rimmed with rock walls and lush greenery, demonstrations of early *hula* (*kahiko*) are danced by men of the *Halau 'O Waimea*. The park contains old grass huts and a reconstruction of one of the oldest *hieau* in Hawaii, dedicated to *Lono*, the god honored at the annual *Makahiki* festival in October.

The Proud Peacock (638-8531) in the park, open daily for lunch and dinner, serves meals overlooking tropical trees and plants stretching up to the falls. Above the park is Oahu's most famous temple and largest sacrificial *hieau*, **Puu o Mahuka Heiau** ("Hill of Escape"). Next to the supermarket between these two beaches, take Pupukea Road up the hill to an HVB marker near Puu o Mahuka Heiau. Once used for human sacrifices and now a pile of rocks registered as a National Historic Landmark, spectacular views of the north shore unfold from this ancient temple. Three separate enclosures have all been reduced to rubble but remain spiritually significant.

Haleiwa

Kam Highway continues to **Haleiwa**, a former sugar plantation town that, at the turn of the century, was a fashionable beach resort at the end of the railroad line from Honolulu.

In the early 1900s, trains used to come around Kaena Point from Honolulu and deposit guests at the Haleiwa Hotel (1899 to 1928).

New shopping facilities and restaurants have been added to the village landscape and now **Ko Olima**, a massive resort as large as Waikiki, is under construction between Haleiwa and **Waialua**, another old plantation town and the Waianae Mountains to the southwest.

Amazingly Haleiwa ("house of the frigate bird") is the only town or village along Oahu's entire coastline that preserves any quaint rural charm which today is combined with boutiques, gift shops and art galleries and an arty atmosphere.

The down-home country atmosphere is still preserved in neighboring Waialua, an old plantation town where **R Fujioka & Sons Ltd.**– a grocery store next to twin gas pumps – has been in business for fifty years and the local bank is now the **Sugar Bar and Restaurant**.

The center of youth and surfing culture since the 1960s, Haleiwa is jammed with crowds of tourists and locals on weekends. These people are getting out of Honolulu and combining – in one place – breakfast, lunch, walking and sightseeing, shopping, people-watching and beaches and swimming.

Haleiwa has small quantities of each. Haleiwa Beach is safe for swimming all year. Just outside of Haleiwa, on Haleiwa Road, **Kaiaka State Recreation Area** is a beautiful setting for picnics. However, this beach's bottom is too rocky for comfortable swimming.

Haleiwa Alii Beach Park is the heart of the town — watch the surf and surfers, walk the jetty, see where some of best surfboards are made. Drop in on Ing Jausel's **Oogenesis Boutique** to see original hand-painted designs, whale-artist **Wyland**'s marine art gallery, or **Fettig Art Gallery** which specializes in Fettig's own local scenes.

The Polynesian Cultural Center

Entertainment at the 42-acre Polynesian Cultural Center.

Laie is the center of the Mormon Church in Hawaii, the **Brigham Young University-Hawaii Campus**, site of the **Mormon Temple**, and the famous **Polynesian Cultural Center** (PCC). The Mormons established their Hawaiian Temple in 1919 and the Brigham Young University campus in 1955. Starting in 1963, the Church of Jesus Christ of the Latter Day Saints packaged Polynesia into a highly successful theme park that really is a unique educational experience worth its stiff price. Students from BYU staff the PCC. Comforting is the thought that proceeds from this non-profit operation benefit the Laie BYU.

The core of the 42-acre PCC is its seven recreated villages: six Polynesian and one Melanesian — Hawaii, Samoa, Tonga, the Marquesas, Fiji, New Zealand and Tahiti. Each village displays excellent craftsmanship in construction and handicrafts native to the particular cultural homeland. Guides native to each island explain the cultural background of the homeland, talk about the foods and handcrafts exhibited.

Walk, take a shuttle tram or tour the area by canoe over artesian-fed waterways. Most of the people working in the villages are students at nearby Brigham Young University who actually are from the islands that they represent in the villages while wearing traditional dress.

See how *kapa* (bark cloth) is made from the bark of mulberry trees; Tongan women demonstrate their version of preparing tapa cloth, ngatu; Tahitian girls making shell *leis* and grass skirts; learn how *poi* is made; see a 50-ft *Maori* war canoe from New Zealand carved from a single log and their sacred house of learning with beautiful, intricately carved *Maori* panels; Marquesans weaving palm-leaf baskets near the tattooing hut; traditional war dances of Fijian men; and many other fascinating exhibits. *Music Polynesia* presents the historical evolution of Polynesian music, dance and singing.

This is Polynesia, the very exciting and moving evening 90-minute dinner show of music, dance and historical drama, begins at 7:30. An all-you-can-eat dinner is served at the center's **Gateway Restaurant**. After the buffet dinner, a 70-ft by 130-ft wide screen in a new theater shows a 40-minute adventure film about the Pacific region.

You can buy different packages of entertainment and meals in addition to the seven Polynesian villages, craft, hula and other demonstrations from 12:30-9 pm. Book round-trip transportation or better still, incorporate an all afternoon and evening trip to the PCC with an all morning excursion from Honolulu to Laie. The closest accommodations to the PCC is the **Laniloa Lodge**.

Eating & Dining Choices

The most popular local breakfast spots are **Cafe Haleiwa** across from the post office or the **Coffee Gallery** in the North Shore Center. For the best shaved ice on the island, get in line at **M. Matsumoto Grocery Store**. Try shave ice with ice cream and azuki beans and just in case, also order a strawberry.

For lunch and dinner, there are several very good choices. **Jameson's By the Sea** serves stuffed shrimp, *mahi mahi*, catch of the day and a variety of other tasty lunch and dinner fare. The deck facing the ocean is the place to be at any time of day. There are several eating places are in the **Haleiwa Shopping Plaza**.

Accommodation in Haleiwa

Haleiwa has no hotels but Alice Tracy's 12 cottages, **Ke Iki Hale**, are outstanding but expensive. Ke **Iki Beach** is edged with coconut palms and ironwoods. At the front door of modest one and two-bedroom cottages on the beach and duplex one-bedrooms behind them, white sand and calm swimming waters prevail in summer and high surf crashes on rocks in winter. Weekly rates are the best deal. In Mokoleia, condos like the **Mokoleia Beach Colony** offer very nice units facing the ocean with minimum stays of a week — a bargain compared to hotel rates.

Mokuleia

Mokuleia Beach Park offers excellent swimming (except in winter), miles of beachcombing along a secluded coast and some of the best unofficial camping in Hawaii. At the traffic circle outside of Waialua, head west on Farrington Highway (Route 930) for more than seven miles to Mokuleia, past the polo field and across from **Dillingham Airstrip**. The **Hawaii Soaring Club** offers 20-minute rides in three-seat sailplanes (with members of the club), 10:30 am-5 pm.

Farrington Highway continues for a few miles until it becomes an unpaved track that is passable but rough in dry weather. Instead, walk along the jeep trail for about two miles to Kaena Point, Oahu's northwest tip. Views of the Waianae and the rugged coast are spectacular.

Route 930-80 from Mokoleia and Route 82 from Haleiwa rise through endless rows of pineapples up the 1,000-ft Leilehua Plateau toward **Wahiawa**, and splits again into Kam Highway and Kaukonahua Highway (Route 99). James Dole started his first cannery for pineapples in 1899 and not far from Wahiawa, the **Dole Pineapple Pavilion** demonstrates the canning process 9 am-6 pm daily. A little further toward Wahiawa, **Del Monte** displays 20 kinds of bromelaids. Across Route 99 from Schofield Barracks, made infamous in James Jones' From Here to Eternity,

Kemoo Farm on the shore of Lake Wilson provides lunch and dinner (except Monday) hearty enough to satisfy GIs, locals and tourists.

Mid-Town Honolulu

Along Ala Moana Boulevard between Ward Avenue and the Ala Wai Canal are three of Honolulu's best shopping complexes — **Ala Moana Shopping Center**, **Ward Centre** and **Ward Warehouse** — which can supply everything that you didn't find or bother to look for in Waikiki. From the Ala Moana Shopping Center, **The Bus** takes you around Oahu and across the street, cruises depart from **Kewalo Basin** day and night around the Waikiki-Honolulu shoreline.

At the intersection of Ala Moana and Ward, Kewalo Basin (Fisherman's Wharf) is the place to charter sport fishing boats. Up to six people can charter a boat, with tackle, lures and other essentials (except lunch) provided. Around 5:15, about a dozen twilight and sunset-dinner cruises set out from Kewalo Basin (or from Pier 7 near the Aloha Tower) for a two-hour round-trip to Diamond Head. At 7:45 and 8:45 pm, these same cruises become "starlight cruises." Some of the island's better restaurants are located in Kewalo Basin, in the shopping centers along Ala Moana and on Kapiolani Boulevard. Once a swampland like the rest of Waikiki, **Ala Moana Park** across from the shopping center is the most popular public beach and picnic area

for residents of Greater Honolulu.

Gigantic Ala Moana ("Ocean Way") Center claims to be the largest shopping center in the world. This three-level shopping center is just a short bus ride (#8, #19, and #20) or drive (plenty of parking) west of Waikiki. Open seven days a week until 9 pm, on weekends most stores close by 5:30 pm. The more than 200 shops cover just about every shopping and gift need.

Across Ala Moana, Ala Moana Park and its calm swimming beach is always busy with locals picnicking and playing. **Magic Island** park, on a man-made peninsula that forms one side of the channel to the Ala Wai Yacht Harbor, offers an excellent view of Waikiki.

Upscale **Ward Center** contains expensive boutiques, art galleries, restaurants and cafes, sweet shops and the like. Just down the street, across from Kewalo Basin, plain-Jane **Ward Warehouse** has more than a hundred shops and restaurants, with many tourist gift items. Both places are open 10 am-9 pm, until 5 pm on Saturdays and 4 pm on Sundays.

Take Piikoi west of Ala Moana Shopping Center to Mott-Smith (just past Wilder) which joins Makiki Heights Drive, then Round Top Drive, turning into **Tantalus Drive** at its highest point. On the way up Makiki Heights Drive, stop at the **Contemporary Arts Museum** (526-1322). Its collection is housed in a beautiful historic structure on 3 $\frac{1}{2}$ acres with extensive Japanese-style gardens.

Browsing for Art & Crafts

Besides Chinatown, Hawaiiana art and craft hunting in mid-town Honolulu is one way to get to know off-the-beaten path areas of the city. Drive *mauka* on Ward Avenue a few blocks to Kapiolani Boulevard, then head toward Waikiki on Kapiolani Boulevard, turn left on Keeaumoku, midway down the Ala Moana Shopping Center on your right and take the immediate next right on Makaloa to a stub of a wide driveway on your left called Makaloa Square. Your destination at the end of this short side street, making all of this intricate navigating worth it, is one of Hawaii's best places to see local art and buy very lovely and tasteful gifts in all price ranges: Charlene Tashima's **Gallery EAS**.

On Waimanu Street, one block south of Kapiolani Boulevard, is **Bob McWilliam's Pottery Studio**.

The sculptural form and glazes of Bob's functional pottery is unsurpassed on Oahu.

Drive mauka up Piikoi to **Creative Fibers** where you can find more Polynesian silk-screened fabrics by Colleen Kimura (Tutuvi). It's only a few blocks to **The Honolulu Hat Company** to look at *Kona lauhala* in a dozen forms of hats that Rebecca Sullivan has "imported" from the Big Island. Next to **Kimura's Lauhala Shop** in Holualoa on the Big Island, this is one of the only places in Hawaii left that sells high

quality, made-in Hawaii *lauhala* hats.

Stay on South King Street heading *ewa* to the **Hula Supply Center**, a few blocks from **Flowers by Jr. and Lou**, in Moiliili, where you can find bamboo nose flutes, *hula* implements, *pahu* drums and gourds, red and yellow feathered gourds and other interesting Hawaiiana gift items.

Mission Houses Museum.

Historic Downtown Honolulu

Mission Houses Museum consists of three restored missionary buildings, one white wooden structure shipped from Boston around the Horn (1820), a four-bedroom house, the oldest wooden structure in Hawaii and two coral ones (1831 and 1841) — the Chamberlain Depository and the printing house which contains a replica of the first press to print the Hawaiian language.

Iolani Palace.

The three restored buildings are a museum open for guided tours by members of the Hawaiian Mission Children's Society (9:30 am-3 pm). The museum sponsors an excellent **walking tour of the historic central district** on Mondays and Fridays only. A special **Living History Program** on Saturdays is presented every hour from 10 am-3 pm Costumed actors play the roles of missionaries and others involved with the mission and visitors can join in the conversations.

Sample a 19th century meal at the

Lunalilo, Hawaii's first elected king (1873), is buried in a tomb outside this coral stone church.

Across King Street, the **Mission Memorial Building** honors early church leaders and nearby **Honolulu Hale** (City Hall), built in 1929 of adobe in Spanish-Moorish style, has free daily concerts at noon in the courtyard. West along King Street is the completely refurbished **Hawaii State Library**.

Following South King Street toward downtown Honolulu, beautiful **Iolani Palace** is on the right, the royal residence until the overthrow of Queen Liliuokalani. A 45-minute guided tour of the Palace is very worthwhile. Also on the grounds are the fort-like Iolani Barracks, built (originally near the present state capitol) to house the Royal Household Guards.

Beyond its fence of golf-tipped spears, a palm-lined promenade leads to Victorian Iolani ("bird of heaven") Palace, the only royal palace in the US. Built in Italian Renaissance style in 1882 by King Kalakaua, the building's architecture reflects the king's world tour, hitherto unprecedented for a head of state. Downstairs in the Throne Room, Queen Liliuokalani was tried for treason and upstairs, in the guest bedroom, she was subsequently imprisoned for nine months. Under the new territorial government, for more than 50 years the legislature met in the Throne Room and the Senate convened in the dining room.

Founded by King Kamehameha V, the **Royal Hawaiian Band** gives con-

Mission Houses' annual Thanksgiving program and see one of the best collections of gift items in Hawaii at the **Christmas Fair** in early December.

Just across the alley, towering above the graves of missionaries and their families, **Kawaiahao Church** welcomes visitors at Sunday services conducted at 10:30 am in English and Hawaiian.

certs at noon on Fridays on the band-stand in front of the palace. The **Bandstand** was constructed for King Kalakaua's coronation in 1883. Picnics on the grassy lawn in this historic and scenic place is one of downtown's traditionally happy moments.

The State Capitol Building (S. Beretania St., between Punchbowl and Richards St) replaced Iolani Palace as the Capitol. Built on an Hawaiian grave-yard, the building and grounds are full of Hawaiian symbolism and is unique among state capitols in its attempt to incorporate symbolic themes in its architecture: pillars resembling palm trees, House and Senate chambers resembling volcanoes rising from the sea, and other features. Statues of Queen Liliuokalani and Father Damien stand near the entrance. The statue of Queen Liliiukalani clutches the Kumulipu, Hawaii's treasured creation myth, the failed Constitution of 1893 and music for *Aloha Oe*, written by the Queen.

The State Judiciary Building (*Aliiolane Hale*) at King and Mililani streets, built in 1874 as a palace for Kamehameha V, was used by David Kalakaua for receptions but was never used as a royal residence. The restored interior is worth seeing but most visitors come to see the black and gold statue of Kamehameha I in front of the building. This statue is a replica of the original lost at sea en route from Italy, later recovered and now standing in the Kohala town of Kapaa on the Big Island near the king's birthplace.

At the corner of Queen Emma Street and South Beretania Street, beyond **Washington Place**, the governor's official mansion, is **St Andrew's Cathedral** with its stained glass windows illustrating events from Hawaii's past.

Good planning or luck will get you to the best modern and ancient hula competition of the year, at the *Neal Blaisdell Center* – the international **King Kamehameha Hula Competition** on the third weekend in June. Across Thomas Square, the **Honolulu Academy of Arts** brings the art of East and West together in a beautiful building with sunny courtyards. Built around six courtyards and including 37 gallery rooms, the museum has a very fine permanent exhibition of paintings and other art works from Europe and Asia (Italian Renaissance and French Impressionists, rare collections of Oriental art including Japanese wood block prints, lacquerware, 13th Century art), and 19th Century American painters, and some contemporary Hawaiian painters. Open Tuesdays through Saturdays, 10 am-4:30 pm, and Sundays 1-5 pm, 45-minute guided tours at 11 am Tuesdays-Saturdays, 2 pm on Saturdays and 1 p.m on Sundays.

Foot-weary visitors can rest in the courtyard of the YWCA across from the Iolani Palace on Richard Street. Otherwise, from the Cathedral continue walking on **Fort Street Mall**, a pedestrian shopping mall that runs for seven blocks to the waterfront. An alternative direction from the mall is to turn right on

Maritime Museum.

Hotel Street and walk four blocks to Maunakea in Chinatown.

Hawaii Maritime Center

From the historic district, the longer walking tour proceeds down the mall to the harbor end, across Nimitz Highway and through Irwin Park, to **Pier 9** and the 10-story **Aloha Tower** overlooking the water, part of the **Hawaii Maritime Center Museum**, then returns to Merchant Street and follows it to Chinatown. Between 8 am and 9 pm, ride to the 10th floor observatory in Aloha Tower for a panoramic view of the harbor.

At Pier 7, purchase a ticket at the Hawaii Maritime Center to see the re-stored, four-masted *Falls of Clyde*, a 266-ft square rigger more than a Century old, the *Hokulea*, a 60-ft replica of a Polynesian double-hulled canoe and the **Kalakaua Boathouse**.

Opened on King Kalakaua's birthday, the Hawaii Maritime Center commemorates the king's sponsorship of surfing competitions, canoe races, *hula* dance and Hawaiian music performed at his nearby boathouse. **The Kalakaua Boathouse Museum** displays Hawaiian and Western maritime contributions to Hawaii.

Merchant Street

Returning to the five-block long **Mer-**

chant Street, well-preserved late 19th and early 20th Century buildings mark the old downtown section of Honolulu where wealth from agriculture, whaling and commerce produced a range of appealing architectural styles.

Around the corner, on Bishop Street near Queen Street, the **Alexander & Baldwin Building** (1929) mixes Chinese and Hawaiian themes and art in its exterior and interior design. Across Bishop Street, once the city's most beautiful road connecting mountains and harbor, the restored **Kamehameha V Post Office** (1871) was the first structure in Hawaii to be built of concrete. The **Honolulu Magazine** occupies the **Yokohama Specie Bank** building (1910) at the corner of Merchant and Bethel, across the street from the Spanish colonial-style **Honolulu Police Station Building** (1930). The brick and stucco **Royal Saloon** (1890) at Nuuanu now is **Murphy's Bar and Grill**.

Chinatown

The lower end of Maunakea Street in Chinatown has a group of antique shops that draws collectors — **Robyn Buntin of Honolulu** (No.900A) for Japanese art, Oriental antiques and unusual jewelry; **Aloha Antiques and Collectibles** (No.926) for everything from Chinese jade to *poi* pounders; antique Japanese swords at **Bushido** (No.936), and Japanese antique treasures at nearby **Garakuta-Do**. Another

place to look for oriental antiques is **The Art Treasure Gallery**.

For *haku leis*, Hilo *maile leis*, rich orange *ilima, akulikuli,* purple *ola'a*, gingers and a large assortment of other simple and elaborate *leis*, there is plenty of comparison shopping clustered on Maunakea Street in Chinatown: **Leis by Sharon** at the corner of Maunakea and Beretania; **Violet's Lei Stand, Jenny's Lei Shop, Aloha Leis and Flowers**, and **Pauahi Leis and Flowers** down to Pauahi Street; and **Cindy's Lei Shop** next door to famous **Wo Fat's Restaurant** on Hotel Street, across from the big new Maunakea Marketplace that stretches around Hotel to Maunakea Street.

A new Chinatown is slowly developing within the old Chinatown in an architecturally compatible way. The largest new retail complex in Chinatown and downtown Honolulu, **Maunakea Marketplace** (Maunakea, Hotel, and Pauahi streets) has 70 shops, restaurants, an open-air market, and an ethnic food court. At the top of Maunakea Street, across King Street, the **Chinese Cultural Plaza** has more shops and restaurants.

In nearby herbalist stores you'll see century-old remedies such as ginseng root, dried seahorses and snake skins. If you're ready for a taste treat, **Sung Chong Yuen Chinese Pastry Shop** on Maunakea (between King and Hotel) has delectable almond cookies, gin dui, moon cakes filled with lotus root paste, colorful candied fruits and vegetables,

Where else but Chinatown for sweet meats and roast duck.

and crack seed (preserved fruits).

Dating back to 1904, the open-sided **Oahu Market** at the corner of King and Kekaulike (one block from River St) is filled with stalls selling fruits and vegetables, Chinese roast pork, ducks and hog heads and fresh fish. **China Sea Tattoo** (on Smith St. between King and Hotel), Hawaii's oldest tattoo shop, can show you Hawaiian-style, oriental, classic, and modern tatooing.

Since 1930, **Lai Fong's** (1118 Nuuanu between Hotel and Pauahi) has specialized in Chinese fabrics and tailormade clothing, but their store is also filled with teak and rosewood furniture, hand-painted screens, oriental antiques, jade and ivory jewelry and much more. This is the place to order a silk brocade cheong sam (Chinese-style dress).

If possible, save your visit to Chinatown for a Tuesday when the **Chinese Chamber of Commerce** conducts a 2 -2$^1/_2$ hour guided tour, starting at 9:30 am and ending with lunch at **Wo Fat's restaurant**, all for $7, including lunch. (**Hawaii Heritage Center**, 1026 Nuuanu Avenue, also sponsors a three-hour tour on Mondays, Wednesdays and Fridays at 9:30 am for the same price.) This tour visits Chee Kung Tong, one of Chinatown's many clubhouses and meeting halls, on the third floor of the **Chinatown Cultural Plaza** on Beretania Street, which also houses the Sun Yat-sen Hall, several good places to eat (including the excellent **Won Kee Fine Chinese Cuisine**), import shops, and more. The **Hawaii Heritage Center**, a nonprofit organization, also sponsors a guided walking tour. Both tours include a brief history of Chinatown. Otherwise, buy *Exploring Honolulu's Chinatown* by Frances Carter and take your own tour.

An "art galleries row" is developing on Nuuanu and neighboring streets in Honolulu's historic Chinatown. First walk on Merchant Street in order to visit **Ramsay Galleries** and see Ramsay's incomparable quill pen and India ink drawings. Her images of architecturally and historically significant buildings, drawn on location without any drafting aids or preliminary sketches, crafted with microscopically fine lines and dots, really captures the essence of each building's look and character.

Located in the old Han Sing Building, which housed the first Chinese printing press in Hawaii, **Ramsay Galleries** on Smith Street always presents an interesting show. Ramsay herself opened a cafe next door where art lovers and others can relax on a warm day or in the evening over wine or beer.

William Waterfall is one of the foremost photographers of the world's scenic attractions. In addition to brilliant photography, he has brought back marvelous craft work from his travels in Thailand, Bali and other parts of the Pacific Basin which he exhibits at his small but exceptionally attractive gallery, *Global Images*.

Almost next door, in a building that housed a Japanese restaurant for 75 years, the **Pegge Hopper Gallery's** main floor and mezzanine give you a complete view of this fabulous painter's past and recent work. Pegge Hopper, like Madge Tennent (see below), is fascinated with the beauty, mass, and strength of Hawaiian women, their features, personalities, and attitudes. Her life-sized, strong Hawaiian women — tender and stern, knowing and innocent, languid in flowing muumuus — have created one of the major success stories of artists in Hawaii.

These paintings, with marvelous simplicity of line, form and color, adorn collectors' walls throughout the world. In order to see Pegge's originals, visit her gallery on Nuuanu Street in Honolulu's Chinatown, but you'll find prints and posters of her Polynesian maidens lounging on pillows, surrounded by cats, nibbling dim sum, in many galleries and frameshops around the islands.

Across from the Hopper and Waterfall galleries is the **Hawaii Theatre** (No.1922). Once Hawaii's largest and best performing arts center, this gem is undergoing restoration. Adjacent to the theater, **Chinatown Gateway Plaza**, a high-rise apartment building with shops, is fronted by a plaza with two traditional carved Chinese lions marking the entrance to Chinatown.

Gateway Gallery, a multi-artist-owned gallery showing only local artists has extended its gallery into the adjoining commercial space, selling artwear and other types of artwork. A one-of-a-kind gallery in Honolulu, **Pauahi Nuuanu Gallery**, on the corner of Pauahi and Nuuanu, displays contemporary Hawaiian sculpture with traditional motifs by two of the best sculptors in Hawaii, Richard Morgan Howell and Henry Kila Hopfe, as well as Julee Smythe's beautiful basketry. Just down the street, oil painter Bill Walsh shows his work at **Bakkus** (Gallery of Fine Arts and Fashion).

Park either in the public garage on Merchant Street (take a right on Bethel Street and another on Merchant Street to the garage entrance immediately on your right) or in the metered lot (bring lots of quarters) at Smith Street and Hotel Street. Across Nuuanu Stream (along Kukui St) from the **Chinese Cultural Plaza** is **Izumo Taisha Shrine**, a replica of a Shinto temple in Japan, erected in 1923.

Across Vineyard Boulevard is the oldest and most frequented Chinese temple in Honolulu, the **Kuan Yin Temple**. Dedicated to the Chinese Goddess of Mercy the temple houses a beautiful statue of Kuan Yin surrounded by the aroma of burning joss sticks.

The 65-year old pineapple cannery has been turned into **Dole Cannery Square** (650 Iwilei Road, off King or Nimitz Highway), with restaurants and food bars, multi-level shops and souvenir stands sellings lots of gifts with Dole's logo on them.

After a 10-minute film showing the historic role of the pineapple industry in Hawaii, a 45-minute tour of the cannery is accompanied by plenty of pineapple samples and juice (canned). The Cannery's **Hawaii Children's Museum** and its hands-on gadgets will be the highlight of the Cannery for children of all ages.

Nuuanu Valley

From Honolulu or Waikiki, at the base of the Koolaus, you're only minutes away from some of the most enjoyable natural beauty in all of the islands. Up Pali Highway at **Nuuanu Pali Overlook** is a breathtaking view of the windward Pali side of the island. Here Kamehameha's warriors and guns forced an army of King Puiwa's Oahuan defenders over a 1,000 ft precipice.

Nuuanu Stream flows through a dense rain forest through Nuuanu Valley ("cool heights"), Honolulu's first suburb. Take a right turn near Nuuanu Park to the wood-shuttered **Summer Palace** that Queen Emma, Kamehameha IV's wife, built in cleared rain forest. Emma's grandfather, John Young, was one of those who fired Kamehameha's cannon in 1795 to change Oahu's history forever.

Queen Emma's retreat from the monarchial court and heat of Honolulu is surrounded by a wide verandah supported by Doric columns. Inside, knowledgeable Daughters of Hawaii lead you from room to room explaining the materials and design and history and stories connected with the furnishings. Emma named her son after a prince of England. His cradle, shaped like a wooden canoe, is one of the memorable items and keepsakes that fill the house. Plan to stop at the **gift shop** for Hawaiian books and a variety of tasteful art, craft and gift items.

On the way down the valley, travelers who want to sample Hawaiian food should stop at the **People's Cafe** (1310 Pali Hwy), which serves an authentic, delicious, one-of-a-kind "squid" *luau* dinner (octopus in a coconut milk-taro stew). Get there before 7 pm any day except Sunday.

Further down Nuuanu Avenue, past the **Chinese Buddhist Association of Hawaii** (42 Kawananakoa Place) which displays several statues of Buddha in an

The delicate Cattleya orchid at Foster Botanical Garden.

elaborate edifice, is the **Royal Mausoleum** where the Kamehameha and Kalakaua dynasties are buried. Open 8 am-4:30 pm weekdays, Kuhio Day (March 26) and Kamehameha Day (June 11). Continue past the **Sanju Pagoda**, **Kyoto-Kinkakaku-ji**, and **Tenrikyo Mission** on Nuuanu, a remarkably delicate woodframe temple; **Honolulu Memorial Park**, a Japanese cemetery with an ancestral monument; **Honolulu Myohoji Temple**; and **Soto Mission of Hawaii**, an austere-looking Zen Buddhist temple with an ornate interior. From Kaukini proceed to Pali Highway and the **Honpa Hongwanji Mission Temple**, the cathedral of the Jodo Shi Buddhist sect in Hawaii.

Crossing Nuuanu Stream on Hotel Street and then right on College Walk brings you to the **Izumo Taishakyo Mission**, a Shinto Shrine. **Foster Botanical Garden** is across North Vineland Boulevard. About 15 acres growing thousands of species of trees, flowers, and plants, including many rare specimens from Asia, can be seen 9 am-4 pm daily. Obtain a brochure from the office for a self-guided tour or take a free guided tour on Monday, Tuesday and Wednesday at 1 pm

Manoa Valley

About 2 miles from Waikiki, the **University of Hawaii**'s campus consists of mostly undistinguished architecture in a magnificent valley setting and a campus full of tropical plants and trees. Stop at the University Relations Office for a map of the campus and the locations and names of this vegetation.

Bachman Hall's Charlot fresco, Bilger's murals by Juliette May Fraser and several other buildings exhibiting the works of well-known Hawaiian artists are worth seeing in addition to two art galleries. The University's John F. Kennedy Theater was designed and equipped to provide outstanding performances of Eastern and Western theater.

At the **East-West Center**, off Dole Street and East-West Road, adjoining the University of Hawaii — Manoa's campus, lovely shady trees around picturesque ponds, especially encircling Jefferson Hall, provide a serene place for strolling. The Center is a separate institution bringing students, faculty, researchers and visitors together from Asia, the Pacific and North America. The architecture of this building is worth a tour. Free guided tours start from Thomas Jefferson Hall at 1:30 pm on Wednesdays.

Manoa Road leads past the University of Hawaii into Manoa Valley. Pass **Punahou School**, built of lava rock in 1841, a prestigious preparatory school that provided outstanding private education to children of missionary and wealthy families. A restoration of the **Little Grass Shack** that **Robert Louis Stevenson** supposedly lived in down in Waikiki sits on a sideroad halfway up the valley.

Paradise Park is located deep in a rain forest of *hau* trees, bamboo groves and other luxurious foliage at the end of Manoa Road. Amidst 13-acres of lush tropical plants in a very wet place (160-inches of annual rainfall), more than 50 species of exotic and rare birds fly among the incredible array of blooms. Simply wander and look at the flowers, trees and plants or, from the amphitheater in a giant birdcage, watch a variety of tropical birds trained to perform circus-like tricks such as, believe it or not, ride a bike on a highwire. Open daily 9:30 am-5:30 pm Inquire (988-2141) about a free shuttle-bus service from Waikiki.

Three times a month (the first Friday, third Wednesday, and third Saturday), the 124-acre Lyon Arboretum, operated as a research garden by the University of Hawaii, opens to the public for guided tours. The hundreds of species of taro, gardens with countless forms of flora, and lush wild areas form a stunning combination. The tours are well worth a reservation made before you ever leave the Mainland.

Otherwise, the gardens are open weekdays 9 am-3 pm and 9 am-12 noon on Saturdays. Don't forget to bring some mosquito repellent. Behind Paradise Park and Lyon Arboretum, from an undeveloped parking area, there's a one-mile trail (that can be quite muddy) through *kukui* trees across several streams to a series of pools known as Manoa Falls. Freshwater swimming is permitted and picnics are marvelous.

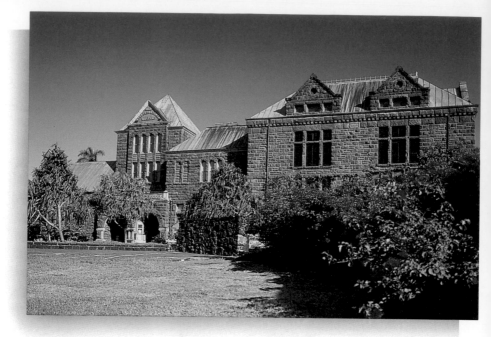

The Bishop Museum.

Bishop Museum

The **Bishop Museum** was named in honor or Bernice Pauahi Bishop, granddaughter of Kamehameha the Great, married to a banker, politician and philanthropist, who collected Hawaiian art and artifacts. The museum, founded by her husband, Charles Bishop, in her memory in 1889, has two main galleries, a demonstration and performance hall, and a Science Center and planetarium set on ten acres. The museum tour is very worthwhile for explanations of the meaning of many of the exhibits which reflect Hawaiian beliefs.

Follow Nuuanu to the H-1 Freeway heading west, take exit 20A (Route 63, Likelike Highway), head to the far right lane, exit on N School Street, make your first right turn to Bernice Street, then another right to the museum.

The fascinating **Kilolani Planetarium** show explains how the Polynesians sailed to Hawaii over a thousand years ago. At 7 pm on Fridays and Saturdays, the planetarium is open for skyshows. Other shows are scheduled weekdays at 11 am and 2 pm

The Bishop Museum contains the largest collection in the world of Pacific anthropology, artifacts, geological origins and immigration heritage, interconnected Polynesian cultural traditions, natural history, photography, literature, specimens and other items. The romanesque central building dating from Queen Victoria's era is made of lava rock and has a magnificent koa wood interior. There is no better place anywhere to grasp the various stages of Hawaiian history and culture, from pre-European chieftainships through 19th century European influences culminating in the Honolulu monarchy mimicking Windsor and other European courts, to the era of immigration from Portugal, China, Japan and the Philippines. In this overwhelming collection of exhibits, at least see the Hawaiian Court, the first floor of the main hall's display of old Hawaii's artifacts and the *koa* wood collection.

The awesome collection of exhibits (more than 20 million items) pertaining to the culture and natural history of the South Pacific is merely the visible side of the world's foremost research program in this region. Hawaiian Hall's exhibits show Hawaiian culture in its different phases, with feather cloaks, outrigger canoes, calabashes, weapons of war, the evolution of plant and marine life, and more for as much time as your itinerary can spare. Open 9 am-5 pm, Mondays through Saturdays and the first Sunday of each month. Ticket price includes admission to the planetarium and exhibitions at the **Atherton Halau.**

Hawaiian *hula* dance is demonstrated daily at 1 pm in the **Atherton Hulau** ("long house" where *hula* and other Hawaiian arts are taught). Traditional crafts also are demonstrated 9 am-3 pm, open Mondays through Sat-

urdays and the fourth Sunday of each month, 9 am-5 pm. The museum's **Shop Pacifica** has one of the best collections of books on the Pacific region available in Hawaii in addition to collections of wooden items, jewelry, and other gift items worth browsing through.

Glenn Okuma, coconut leaf weaver, who has been weaving Hawaiian coconut baskets with traditional techniques for over 15 years, sells some of his more unique pieces at the museum, such as the one-piece hat or basket that uses only one side of a frond. Glenn's baskets, open- and closed-top hats, sun visors and small animals, fish, birds, and crickets also are for sale at the Kukio Mall in Waikiki, where he demonstrates in the evenings, 7-9:30 pm, Mondays through Saturdays.

Makiki Heights/Tantalus Drive

Combine a drive up to Tantalus Mountain and a visit to the **Contemporary Arts Museum.** Tantalus Drive starts only 10 minutes from the Ala Moana Shopping Center, leading to a wonderful network of wilderness hiking trails and spectacular views of Diamond Head-Waikiki and Honolulu. Just take Piikoi (*ewa* of Ala Moana Shopping Center) to Mott-Smith (just past Wilder) which joins Makiki Heights Drive, then Round Top Drive, turning into Tantalus Drive at its highest point.

Pu'u Ohia Trail winds through

eucalyptus trees, bamboo, ginger, giant fern, paper bark, koa, wild fruit trees (passion fruit, guava, apples), and Norfolk pine to connect with the **Aihualama Trail**, the **Pauoa Flats Trail**, and the **Moana Falls Trail**. On these beautiful trails, you can see many of the trees and native plants that have shaped the content of Hawaiian art, craft and traditions, such as *maile, ohia, kukui* and, in spots, even taro. (Be sure to take ample mosquito repellent on these and other trails.)

The Contemporary Museum on the way up **Makiki Heights Drive** is housed in a beautiful historic structure on 3 1/2 acres with extensive Japanese-style gardens. The museum regularly exhibits works by a very select group of Hawaii's contemporary artists. Other, larger exhibits are scheduled at the downtown **News Building**, the museum's former location (Kapiolani Boulevard at the corner of South Street).

Unlike the Academy of Arts' and the Bishop Museums' traditional exhibits of art, which rarely change, exhibits in the Contemporary Museum's six galleries are changed regularly and frequently. The museum makes an effort to balance the shows "imported" from the Mainland and around the world with local contemporary art exhibits, sometimes around a theme.

Punchbowl

Afterwards, head for H-I and drive to the Ward Avenue exit, turn right on Ward Avenue and then left on Prospect Street, around to Puowaina Drive and the 112-acre **Punchbowl — The National Memorial Cemetery of the Pacific**. This crater of an extinct volcano below Tantalus, called *Puowaina* (Hill of Sacrifice) by Hawaiians, contains the graves of over 30,000 US servicemen and civilians, some of the casualties of three wars — World War II, the Korean War and the Vietnam War. Pacific War service people recorded as missing or lost during these wars are listed here. (The administration building is the place to visit for information regarding grave sites.) The crater's rim has a dramatic panorama of Honolulu. Open every day 8 am-5:30 pm, from September 30 through March 1 and until 6:30 pm the rest of the year.

The **Tennent Art Foundation Gallery** (open Tuesdays-Saturdays, 10 am-noon, and Sundays 2-4 pm) displays some 45 original works of Madge Tennent. This immensely creative and talented artist became internationally famous with her unique style of painting Hawaiians. For fully half a century, the much-imitated Madge Tennent (1889-1972) captured the strength, grace, and spiritual qualities of Hawaiian women, imbuing them with sublimely human qualities that transcend Hawaii. Indeed, she made these idealized *wahine* figures universal.

Without equivocation, Tennent believed Hawaiians to be "the most beautiful people in the world." Her underly-

Arizona Memorial.

ing artistic purpose was to share, in simple terms, what she saw and felt about these people. Her artistic mentors were Picasso, Gaugin and especially Renoir. Swirling masses of brilliantly hued color and the play of light in her mural-sized paintings – applied with palette knife strokes – showing a development over decades of experimentation and discovery can be seen clearly at the Gallery.

•If you prefer to start your tour with the Punchbowl and work your way back to the University of Hawaii, here is a suggested itinerary:

From the Punchbowl, return to H-1 and drive further west, take exit 20A (Route. 63, Likelike Highway), head to the far right lane, exit on N School Street, make you first right turn to Bernice Street, then another right to the Bishop Museum. Return to H-1, drive east to Exit 24 B (University Avenue), follow University Avenue to the second traffic light, Dole Avenue and make a left to the East-West Center. Pick up a self-guiding map at the John Burns Center (or plan to join the free tour weekdays at 1:30 pm) Take Moana Road through Manoa Valley, past the Punahou School, to Paradise Park, Lyon Arboretum and Manoa hiking trails.

Pearl Harbor

The **USS Arizona Memorial** at Pearl Harbor commemorates the more than

Pineapple, an industry of less importance to Oahu.

2,000 navy, army and marine personnel and civilians who died in the December 7 1941 Japanese attack on Pearl Harbor. About 1,200 of these casualties were on board the USS Arizona..

Take Kam Highway past the Honolulu Airport, Hickam Air Force Base and the main gate to Pearl Harbor. Follow Route 90 to the Halawa Gaye and make a left turn to the **USS Arizona Memorial**. Be prepared to wait up to three hours on an especially crowded day to get a shuttle to the memorial's Visitor Center. Mornings are better than afternoons. The tour itself takes 1-1/2 hours. The commercial cruises from Kewalo Basin to Pearl Harbor are not allowed to let you off on the memorial.

Arriving between 8 am and 3 pm,

the National Park Service will issue a free ticket and a group number. The **Visitor Center** houses a museum and theater and you will be called by group to watch a 20-minute documentary of the Battle of Pearl Harbor and its aftermath. Afterwards (7:45 am-3 pm), a US.Navy launch will take you from the Visitor Center to the memorial, a 184-ft long floating concrete bridge which spans the width of the sunken USS Arizona.

Next to the Memorial Visitor Center, the **Pacific Submarine Museum** and its **Bowfin** submarine are a memorial to the 52 submarines and thousands of men who died in them during World War II. Open 8 am-4:30 pm, there is an admission charge.

Get back on Route 90 for a drive to the Leeward Coast. An alternative is to take H-2 inland through pineapple and sugarcane fields, past Wahiawa and Schofield Barracks, home of the 25th Infantry Division, to **Del Monte's Pineapple Variety Garden**, which illustrates the pineapple's evolution and the **Dole Pineapple Plantation** where you can purchase pineapple in pieces or whole. This route heads for Waialua and Haleiwa on the North Shore.

Waianae Coast

Instead of driving directly on Route H-1, take Route 90 past Pearl Harbor to Route 76 (Fort Weaver Road) to the picturesque sugar mill town of **Ewa**. Highway 90 (and H-1) becomes Farrington Highway (Route 93 as it heads up the West Coast beneath the dry Waianae Range).

Pass a string of beaches (Barbers Point, Kahe, Hawaiian Electric, Nanakuli, Ulehawa, Maili , Lualualei) until Pokai Beach Park, south of Waianae Town for year-round swimming (or surfing). Turn right (inland) at Waianae Valley Road for a drive up to the sentry post where you can get permission to drive on to **Kolekole Pass** for spectacular views over both sides of the Waianae Range. The now defunct Oahu Railroad passed through hot and dusty leeward Oahu, along the Waianae Mountains, looping around **Kaena Point** from 1895 to 1947. Today Farrington Highway runs from Honolulu to Kahe Point, passing

few restaurants, shops, or hostelries. Most residents are locals. On Kaena Point, according to legend souls awaited assignment to heaven or hell, finally exiting from Ghosts' Leap among the black lava rocks.

In winter, beaches lose sand to erosion. In summer, beaches return. The coastline is rustic and rough. Without the contrasting **Sheraton Makaha Resort** hidden in a verdant oasis in Makaha Valley, few tourists would make their way out the dry and rocky leeward coast toward Kaena Point. On the leeward coast, except from October through April, swimming is good at Nanakuli (except on weekends), Makaha, Keauu, Makua and Yokohama (*Keawaula*) beach parks. Notwithstanding stories to the contrary, at any time of year, without precautions, you're more likely to drown than get mugged along the Waianae coast.

A safe beach and anchorage, Pokai Bay Beach Park backed by mountains is a pretty place for a picnic lunch. Robert "Bunky" and Gail Bakutis are two of the best known residents of Waianae and the Pokai Bay area. Both have won numerous awards for their *raku*-fired forms. They welcome visitors by appointment to their beachfront studio, **Pokai Pottery**, on Pokai Bay Street off Farrington Highway (Hwy. 93). Much less well known is Olivia Ling's **Oko'a Pottery**, making wheel thrown Hawaiian pottery similar to pre-European contact forms and styles. From Farrington Highway in Waianae town, turn right on Lualualei to Halona Road and, near the end of the Lualualei Reservoir, take a left on Pohakea Place to Oko'a Pottery.

Call for an appointment with **Herman** or **Freda Gomes** (695-9192) in Waianae who make calabash gourds, nose flutes, gourd rattles, sticks and other implements used by traditional hula dancers. On weekends you'll probably find them at home teaching students how to grow, find, or use local materials (kamani seeds, pods, coconut, etc.) to make traditional implements. North of Lahilahi Point, from Farrington turn *mauka* on Jade to Lahaina, then left and the first right to the Gomes' residence at 84-239 Ikuone Place.

Makaha Beach is famous for its surfing competitions. Follow Makaha Valley Road inland past condos and high rise buildings clinging to the walls of the valley. Ten miles up the valley stands Mt. Kaala (4,025 ft), the highest peak on the island. Two ridges form the northern and southern sides of the valley, ending at Puu Keauu (2,650 ft) and Puu Kawiwi (2,975 ft). Most of the upper valley remains wild, arid and rocky. In its midst, a few miles above the Sheraton, stands 17th century Kaneaki *Hieau* dedicated to Lono, god of agriculture. Two grass huts, two prayer towers and an altar for human sacrifice stand next to the Makaha stream flowing down from the top of the mountain. Stop at the **Sheraton Makaha Resort** for permission to visit the *heiau*, restored by Bishop Museum on behalf of the resort.

The valley's walls soar dramatically up to jagged peaks above the Sheraton Makaha Resort. The Sheraton's renovated bungalows and Polynesian-style buildings sit in an oasis of bougainvilleas, hibiscus, and plumeria. Off-season rates of $80 a day for a double room with a car are still possible, possibly even less expensive in good packages. The Sheraton's cottages are particularly attractive inside and out. The resort is several miles from the ocean but the resort has a full watersports program second to none in Hawaii. In addition to tennis courts and horseback riding, jog-

Windsurfing off Oahu.

ging and hiking trails reach upper parts of the valley. The jewels of the resort are two beautiful golf courses: a 7,200 ft West course and another 6,400-ft course.

The **Kaala Room** serves elegant dinners in a somewhat formal atmosphere. The view down the valley to the ocean, especially during a legendary Waianae sunset, is one of the most unforgettable parts of the Makaha experience. Open Sundays through Thursdays, 6-9 pm, and Fridays and Saturdays until 10 pm **EJ's** serves a mix of inexpensive Italian, Mexican and local food for lunch and dinner.

Oceanside lanais of the **Makaha Beach Cabanas** with wonderful surf views front Spartan rooms that are still expensive. The views from **Makaha Shores** are just as expensive and from the upper floors, the views are even better. On the north side of broad Makaha Valley, **Makaha Valley Towers** line precipitous cliffs in watered patches of lawn, with great views from upper floors.

Big Island

Formed by five volcanoes – **Mauna Loa, Mauna Kea, Hualalei, Kilauea** and **Kohala** – the Big Island's variety of faces is shaped by these mountains, the way that they flow together to meet the sea. Extremes of landscapes and seemingly contrary personalities occur within short distances from north to south and east to west. Each distinctive side of the Big Island's landscape provokes different emotions and opens new sightseeing experiences for visitors. First time visitors can look forward to some occasionally stunning surprises. The coastal route around the island is about 225 miles and broken in only two places: at the northern tip of Kohala and in Puna where local highways have been wiped out by lava flows. You can drive around the island in a day, but 11-hour "circle island tours" are available. A more leisurely and sensible pace requires a car and a flexible plan.

189

Big Island's landscape is shaped by its volcanoes and the way its lava flows.

Getting Around

The Big Island has

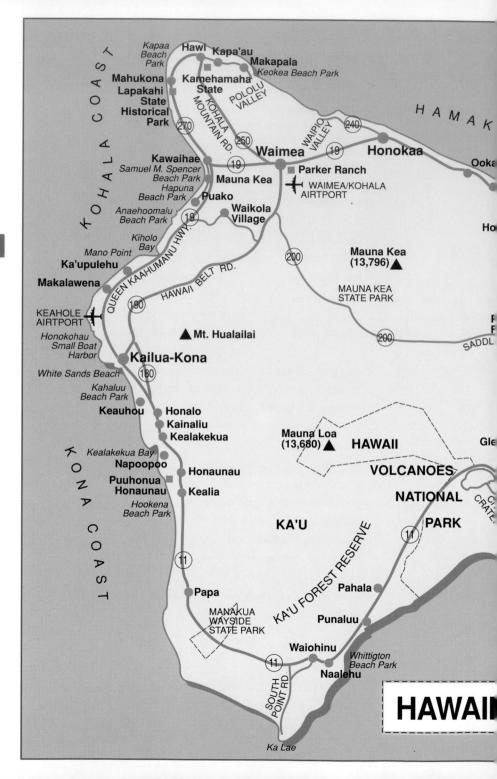

KOHALA COAST

Kapaa Beach Park
Hawi Kapa'au
Makapala
Keokea Beach Park
Mahukona
Lapakahi State Historical Park
Kamehameha State
POLOLU VALLEY
270
KOHALA MOUNTAIN RD.
250
WAIPIO VALLEY
240
Waimea 19 Honokaa
19
Kawaihae
Samuel M. Spencer Beach Park
Mauna Kea
Hapuna Beach Park
Puako
Anaehoomalu Beach Park
Waikola Village
19
Parker Ranch
WAIMEA/KOHALA AIRTPORT

HAMAK

Ooka

Ho

Kiholo Bay
Mano Point
Ka'upulehu
Makalawena
QUEEN KAAHUMANU HWY.
HAWAII BELT RD.
190
200
Mauna Kea (13,796) ▲
MAUNA KEA STATE PARK

KEAHOLE AIRTPORT
Honokohau Small Boat Harbor
▲ Mt. Hualailai
Kailua-Kona
White Sands Beach
180
Kahaluu Beach Park
Keauhou
Honalo
Kainaliu
Kealakekua
200
SADDL

KONA COAST
Kealakekua Bay
Napoopoo
Puuhonua Honaunau
Hookena Beach Park
Honaunau
Kealia
Mauna Loa (13,680) ▲ HAWAII
VOLCANOES
NATIONAL
PARK
Gle
C
CRATE

KA'U
11
KA'U FOREST RESERVE
11
Papa
MANAKUA WAYSIDE STATE PARK
Pahala
Punaluu
Waiohinu
Whittigton Beach Park
Naalehu
11
SOUTH POINT RD.
Ka Lae

HAWAII

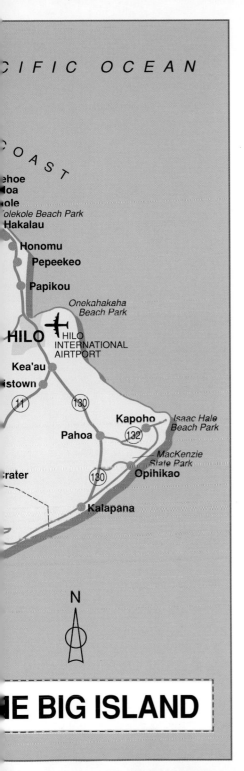

two main airports – **Hilo International Airport** (General Lyman Field); and **Keahole Airport** outside of Kailua-Kona on the east or leeward side of the island. Flights from the Mainland all fly into Keahole Airport. Inter-island flights go to both airports as well as little **Kamuela Airport** in Waimea.

A flight into the Hilo Airport makes sense if you plan to see Hilo and perhaps use it as a base for short trips north to see the Hamakua Coast and west for sight-seeing in Puna and Hawaii Volcanoes National Park. A flight into Keahole Airport gets you with eight miles of Kailua-Kona and 10-15 miles of North Kona and South Kohala resorts.

Transportation

Rent a car because you'll need one in Hilo and anywhere else on the island. **Dollar** (800-367-7006) at the airport offers competitive rates. Reserve in advance over their 800-line in order to save money. Be prepared to pay drop-off charges in Kona if you plan to leave the Big Island from there.

Tour-bus companies offer standardized rates. **Jack's Tours Inc** (Kona, 329-2555, Hilo 961-6666) offers a circle island tour; likewise, **Akamai Tours** (329-7324). **Gray Line Hawaii** (Kona: 329-9337; Hilo: 935-2835), **Hawaii Resorts Transportation** (885-7484) and other companies provide round the island, half-day and full-day tours. Ask about van tours of Waipio and Kona, and

Mauna Kea. Hawaii Resorts Transportation also offers horseback tours of Waipio. **Hele-On Buses** travel between Kailua-Kona and Hilo twice a day. Otherwise there is no island-wide transportation.

Planning Your Stay

The Big Island is larger than all of the other islands combined. To plan an itinerary, divide the Big Island into seven main parts:

• the Kohala Coast and its resorts and public beaches combined with Waimea-Kamuela;

• Waimea and North Kohala combined with the Kohala Coast and the Hamakua Coast;

• the Hamakua Coast and Waipio Valley combined with Waimea;

• Hilo and the Puna District combined with Hawaii Volcanoes National Park;

• Hawaii Volcanoes National Park and Kailua-Kona and South Kona.

• The Kau District, a seventh touring area, can be seen when driving between South Kona and Hawaii Volcanoes National Park.

    If time is short (and even if it's not), seriously consider *flightseeing* – a thrilling helicopter tour, second to none in Hawaii.

Hilo

Frequent rain or drizzle, especially in

winters, should be regarded as part of the city's natural blessings and charm. Spend a little time in Hilo and the rain feels like it fits the setting perfectly. Granted, at certain times, the 130-200 inches of annual rainfall ceases to be fun for visitors. Residents don't seem to mind.

The tranquility of Lili'uokalani Gardens.

The capital of the Orchid Island is a tropical city and very different from any other place in Hawaii. Commercially grown orchids and anthuriums are the city's chief crop

The few sightseeing attractions in Hilo appeal to very particular tastes – **Banyan Drive**, lined with banyan trees named mostly for old-time sports, theatrical and other celebrities; lovely formal Japanese public gardens near Banyan Drive, **Liliuokalani Gardens**, created around a Japanese teahouse; and small **Suisan Fish Market**, also

Drive With Care!!

One main road – Highway 11 – runs from Kailua-Kona to Hilo. From Hilo, Highway 19 circles the island to Kailua-Kona. From Kailua-Kona, the Hawaii Belt Road (Route 190) extends along the side of Mt. Hualalei to Kamuela. Thus the main road system on the Big Island and the alternative roads are fairly simple to figure out.

From Kailua-Kona to Hilo, the drive takes about 2-$^1/_2$ hours, with a great deal of twisting and turning down and up hills and in and out of gullies from ten miles out of Kamuela to the northern outskirts of Hilo. Under normal driving conditions, allow at least 1-$^1/_4$ hours from Kamuela to Hilo.

Try to keep your gas tank at least half-full around the Big Island because gas stations are scarce between towns and tend to close early. Before driving on the wet east side, Hamakua to Hilo and Hilo to Volcano and return, be sure that your windshield-wipers are working. When it rains, it frequently pours.

There are a few stretches of road that nervous and other drivers need to know about and perhaps should avoid.

The Saddle Road runs from near Hilo to intersect with Highway 190. Route 250 runs along the Kohala Mountains to the northern tip of Kohala and returns south at Route 270 to join Highway 19 near Kawaihae. The Saddle Road gets narrow at times. With tight turns, too, in foggy and wet weather, driving the road can be scary.

The Honokaa-Hilo road, Highway 19, is preferable to the Saddle Road, but also is narrow, winds through gullies, with blind turns, heavy truck traffic and can get really hair-raising at night when it's raining and visibility is poor.

The road between Captain Cook and South Point includes a 20-mile section of winding, narrow road with no shoulder on the southbound side.

Especially at night or when visibility is poor, you'll definitely wish that you were somewhere else.

Sticky situations.

near Banyan Drive, where fishermen and traders engage in multi-lingual bargaining each morning starting around 8am Commercial flower gardens south and north of central Hilo are 'musts' for visitors. For anyone interested in the history of the island, **Lyman Mission House and Museum** should not be missed.

When you feel the urge to go swimming or snorkeling in Hilo, pretty **Leileiwi Beach Park**, perhaps your first look at a black sand beach, lies east of Hilo Bay. Black-sand **Richardson's Beach**, behind **Richardson Ocean Park Center**, off Kalanianaole Avenue and Leileiwi are your best choices for swimming, bodysurfing, snorkeling and even surfing and unofficial camping under the ironwoods. Precisely because Hilo occupies its own unique time and space, resistant to trendy change, the pace of life continues to be early 20th century and the values expressed in human relationships remain genuine and unhip. Residents love the city, wouldn't leave for anything and don't mind saying so. Just ask anyone who lives in Hilo. No matter that in 1935, 1942 and 1984, Madame *Pele* seemed on the verge of melting Hilo or that, as recently as 1960, the waterfront and 281 structures were wiped out by a gargantuan *tsunami*.

East Hawaii Cultural Center

A walking tour through the heart of

historic Hilo covers a 24-block area with over 200 buildings of historical interest, including many in Pacific art deco-style. The self-guided walking tour starts at **Kalakaua Park**, named in honor of King David Kalakaua. The first destination is the Old Police Station which houses the **East Hawaii Cultural Center**'s "Old Police Station Gallery." The Center sponsors workshops that draw on local craftspersons with outstanding skills and experience, like *lauhala* weaving and coconut frond basket and hat weaving. Dramatized hula presentations for the center about *Pele*, *Ili'iaku* and other legends can also be watched.

Up Waianuenue Street two enormous stones stand in front of the Hawaii Public Library – the **Pinao Stone**, once the entrance pillar to an ancient temple and the 2-$\frac{1}{2}$ ton **Naha Stone** that legend says Kamehameha turned over as a young boy, proving to the royal Naha clan that he had the strength to conquer and unify the islands.

The **Lyman House Memorial Museum** was established by members of the Lyman family in 1932, 100 years after their arrival as missionaries in Hilo. The listed Mission House was built in 1839 and later restored to its original appearance and furnishings.

The museum's Island Heritage Gallery contains: an extensive collection of Hawaiian artifacts, crafts, and art; pre-contact exhibits including *pili* grass and *kapa* structures, ethnic artifacts that came with Japanese, Chinese, Filipino,

Special Events

Celebrated during April in Hilo, the *Merry Monarch Festival* is the island's premier local event.

The month of June has a flurry of special events. *Kamehameha Day*, June 11, generates parades and festivities in Kailua-Kona, Kamuela and Hilo.

In Kamuela, an honorary princess wears the traditional *pau*, a full skirt worn by female horseback riders. In Kapaau (North Kohala), the statue of King Kamehameha is draped in *leis*. Nearby Hawi, the birthplace of Kamehameha, has additional celebrations.

Hilo hosts annual orchid shows in June and July. One of the Hawaii's most important historic sites, *Puuhonua O Honaunau National Historical Park* celebrates an *Annual Cultural Festival* at the end of June or sometimes in early July. From late June to September, *O-Bon festivals* in Hilo are bigger than anywhere else in the islands except in Honolulu. *Waimea's Memorial Day*, *July 4* and *Labor Day Rodeos*, and the *Waikoloan Rodeo* in the middle of February, are popular.

The *Annual Big Island Bonsai Show* in July is followed by the *Annual Hawaii Anthurium Association Show* in August. The Mauna Kea Beach

Aloha Week parade.

Korean and other immigrant groups and an impressive Hawaiian land shell collection (one-of-a-kind in the world). The Earth Heritage Gallery includes a huge mineral collection (the largest in the Pacific) and an interpretive exhibit of volcano lore and geology.

Wailoa River State Park

Backtrack on Kilauea Avenue to the **Wailoa River State Recreation Area** covering 150 acres of Hilo Bay shoreline as a *tsunamic* buffer as well as a park. After the havoc caused by the 1960 tidal wave, a plateau was built in the cleared disaster area for commercial and government buildings, the Wailoa park and its Wailoa River/Waiakea Fishpond.

The building that looks like a volcano (with a *tsunami* monument standing next to it) on Piopio Street, just behind the State Office Building, is the **Wailoa Center**.

Managed by energetic and committed Pudding Lassiter, the Center offers a continuing free exhibit on the natural history and culture of the island, art exhibits that change every month, and a permanent exhibit on *tsunamis*.

Hotel's magnificent golf course is the site of the *Annual Pro-Am Golf Tournament* in July. Fishing tournaments also start in July with the *Kona Ahi Jackpot Fishing Tournament* building up to the *Kona Hawaiian Billfish Tournament* in August, both centered around Kailua-Kona. Besides parades and parties, for spectators the most exciting part of these fishing tournaments is weigh-in time at Kailua Pier at the the end of each day.

Aloha Week produces a major island-wide celebration late in September and in early October, just before the *Annual West Hawaii Makahiki Festival* in Keauhou-Kona. For a week in late October and early November, the *Kona Coffee Festival* combines pageants, beauty contests, coffee tasting and dozens of special activities throughout Kailua-Kona.

October also is the month for the island's

Ironman Triathlon.

most famous event, the **Ironman World Triathlon**, a competition which combines a 2.4 mile rough-water swim from Kailua Pier, a 112-mile bicycle race and a 26-mile run up and down the Kona-Kohala Coast.

Hilo Gardens

Kauai may be the "Garden Isle," but over 2,500 species of plants and flowers flourish in the Big Island's landscape, 95 percent found only in Hawaii. There are many commercial nursery operations to see here.

South Of Hilo

Across Highway 11 from Nani Mau, **Panaewa Rainforest Zoo** features rainforest creatures in a natural setting, like

African pigmy hippopotamuses, rainforest tigers, endangered Hawaiian birds (Nene Goose and Hawaiian Stilt), among others. Open daily, 9am-4:30pm, admission free.

Puna

Scenic Puna's coastal landscapes, mainly formed by lava eruptions, the pounding of ocean waves and erosion and its black sand beaches, reveal the impacts of the Big Island.

Blacknetting over anthurium nurseries seen as you approach Pahoa, a

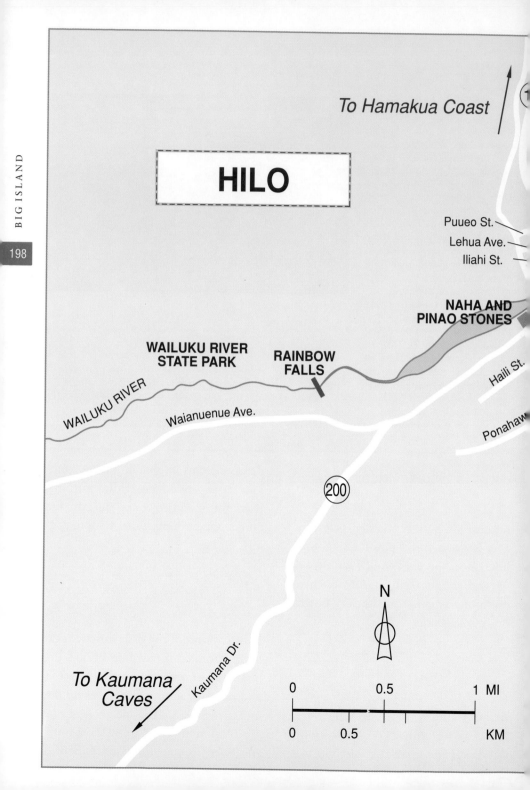

To Hamakua Coast

HILO

Puueo St.
Lehua Ave.
Iliahi St.

NAHA AND
PINAO STONES

WAILUKU RIVER
STATE PARK

RAINBOW
FALLS

Haili St.

WAILUKU RIVER

Waianuenue Ave.

Ponahaw

200

N

To Kaumana
Caves

Kaumana Dr.

0   0.5   1 MI

0   0.5   KM

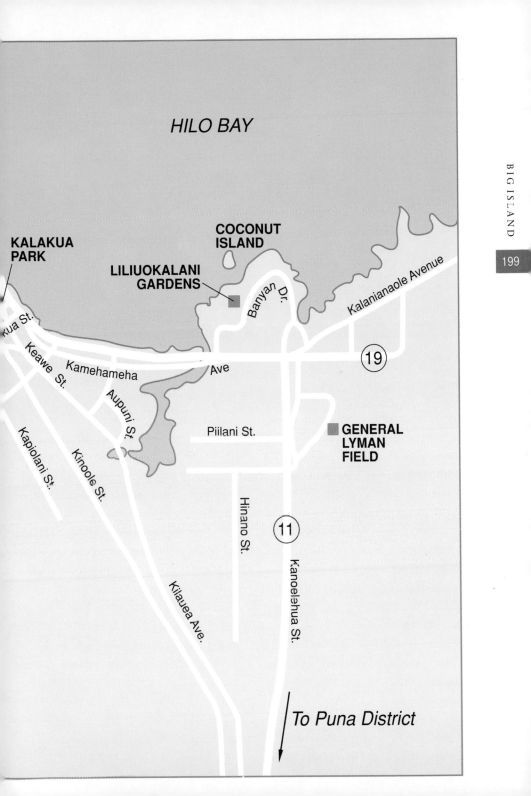

HILO BAY

**KALAKUA
PARK**

**COCONUT
ISLAND**

**LILIUOKALANI
GARDENS**

Banyan Dr.

Kalanianaole Avenue

kua St.

Keawe St.

Kamehameha

Ave

⑲

Aupuni St.

Piilani St.

**GENERAL
LYMAN
FIELD**

Kapiolani St.

Kinoole St.

Hinano St.

⑪

Kanoelehua St.

Kilauea Ave.

To Puna District

Orchids at Hilo.

former lumber and then sugar town, announce the anthurium (and papaya) capital of Hawaii and the world.

Puna is home of *Pele* whose handiwork is everywhere – in the glistening jet-black sands of coastal beaches, a forest of lava tree molds, a huge 420-ft-high cinder cone where a village once stood, papayas, tropical flowers and orchids thriving in rich volcanic soil and the incredible Hawaii Volcanoes National Park itself.

Pahoa is quaint and ramshackle, colorful and drab, always on the verge of bursting forth with energy as a little tourist location.

From Pahao, three miles on Route 132 leads to a beautiful stretch of tree-lined road and the **Lava Tree State Monument**.

The *pahoehoe* lava that poured through this *ohia* forest in 1790 left hardened tree-shaped shells after cooling that today stand in the midst of lovely new *lehua* trees.

From Keaau, take Highway 130 for 11 miles to **Pahao**. Stop even for a few minutes to walk along the raised wooden sidewalks in front of false-front shops in Pahoa. Turn on Highway 132 along an especially lovely tree-lined road for three miles to Lava Tree State Park. An eruption in 1790 immersed a grove of *ohia* trees and then hardened around the skeletons, forming this fascinating fossil forest perpetually unchanged in the midst of lovely new *ohia* growth.

Even if the ends of Routes 130 and

Fern Forest.

137 are blocked by lava, the best part of Puna is the natural beauty of its **southeast coast along Route 137** (which so many tourists mistakenly overlook). Route 132 ends in 10 miles at **Cape Kumukahi** ("First Beginning"). Along the way HVB Warriors mark the lava flows of 1955 and 1960. At **Cape Kumukahi**, the 1960 lava flow that swept through this entire region parted around and spared the **Lighthouse**, adding another 500 yards of land to the point. Drive down the paved road to the Lighthouse, two miles from the intersection of Routes 132 and 137

Take a right turn on **Pohoiki Road** just past Lava Tree and you'll pass the controversial **geothermal power station** which may or may not be in operation depending on politics and economic feasibility. Pohoiki Road brings you to the coast at **Isaac Hale Beach Park**. The main attraction of Isaac Hale is a volcanically-heated fresh water pond. Bordered by black lava sea cliffs, camping (with precautions) is preferable in the ironwood grove at beautiful **MacKenzie State Park**.

The 1960 Puna eruption, on the east rift of Kilauea, 28 miles from the Kilauea Caldera, destroyed 70 buildings in **Kapoho** and added 500 acres to Puna. The former sugar town of Kapoho that used to border both sides of Route 137 no longer exists, covered by lava erupting for 31 days from the cinder cone beside Route 137 (Opihikao Road).

Kahuwai, one of the best kept secrets on the Puna coast, is a former center for canoe building and residence of *alii*. The beautiful black sand beach formed by the 1960 Kapoho lava flow is tucked between two low sea cliffs on the rugged shoreline pounded year-round by surf. The area has many sites of historical and archaeological interest.

At the end of 1990, crescent-shaped Kaimu Black Sand Beach in the small residential community of Kalapana, a former Hawaiian fishing village, was inundated by lava flow from Kilauea. Palm trees that rimmed the waters edge also were destroyed. A new black sand beach formed afterwards, even larger than the original but new lava flows threaten the area. Lava flows also destroyed **Kalapana Black Sand Beach** (8 mile from Kaimu) and the **Painted Church (Star of the Sea)** which fronts on the park.

When an *a'a* lava flow enters the ocean, water penetrating the hot center of the flow causes steam explosions at the shoreline and forms clouds of liquid lava drops that become black (or red as at Hana on Maui) volcanic glass sand as they chill on contact with water. Ocean currents carry this sand to sheltered spots along the shoreline forming beaches.

Tropical Rainforests

Hakalau Forest National Wildlife Refuge at the 2,500-6,500-ft levels on the slopes of Mauna Kea above the north side of Hilo aims to protect four species

Pahoa – The Anthurium Capital

A native of Columbia, South America, the first anthurium plants arrived in Hawaii from London over 100 years ago. The long-lasting "flower" on this colorful perrential is actually a leaf (spathe). The actual flowers are the microscopic bumps on the cylindrical protrusion (spadix) rising from the base of the white, pink, salmon, red, orange or other colored leaf.

With proper care, anthuriums will last 3-4 weeks as cut flowers. By mail a 5-6 inch starter seedling costs about $4 with postage and will bloom in 1-2 years. A dozen cut ones of 5 inches with leafs should cost less than $20 sent by air.

While in Pahoa visit the **Hawaiian Greenhouse** or **Hawaiian Anthuriums of Pahoa**.

A Hawaiian beauty – the Anthurium.

More than 100 genera and 2,000 species of anthuriums in the Araceae family (a "cousin" of philodendrons) can be seen at these two greenhouses.

of Hawaiian rain forest birds, including the *i'o* (Hawaiian hawk) and the *koloa* (Hawaiian duck).

Saddle Road

From Hilo, drive up Waianuenue Avenue to visit **Rainbow Falls.** Come between 9am and 10am in the morning and see rainbows forming over mango trees in the mist.

Saddle Road first passes through thick rainforest, then fern and *ohia lehua* forest until the 3,000-ft level when the landscape changes dramatically to a vast lava flow. Mid-way up from either the Kona or Hilo side is the turnoff for the **Mauna Kea Summit Road,** paved until the **Ellison Onizuka Center for International Astronomy** at the 9,200-ft level. From this base camp for scientists and astronomers, a gravel road winds across and up the steep mountain nearly 7 miles to the 14,000-ft level.

At Mauna Kea's summit, location of the world's foremost collection of optical and infrared telescopes, you will find the **WM Keck Observatory**'s instruments. The best way to see Mauna Kea's observatory complex, view a magnificent sunset and see the clear night

The Merry Monarch Festival

Begun in 1963 as a promotional event for Hilo and the Big Island, the *Merry Monarch Festival* celebrates *hula*. Now the state's premier annual *hula* competition, the festival is recognised internationally as a cultural and competitive event. The last king of Hawaii, David Kalakaua – the Merry Monarch – rejuvenated the *hula, and many mele* (chants) are dedicated to him for reviving the study and practice of *hula* after it was banned by missionaries as "vulgar."

This week-long celebration in Hilo includes parades, craft fairs, local entertainment and like mardi gras, countless private and open parties. *Hula* competitions are held on Thursday, Friday and Saturday nights with modern and ancient *hula* and *Miss Aloha Hula* is selected. Over 30 *hula halau* (schools teaching *hula*) participate, each led by their *kumu hulas* (teachers).

A chanter summons the dancers dressed in bright, beautiful costumes, wearing fragrant *leis*. With swirling motions, the dancers tell spiritual stories to ritual chants, accompanied by intricate choreography – each dancer's movements express specific meanings. Each *halau* presents judges with a written explanation of their performance, its choreography and costuming. The festival's competition brought about several *hula halau* on and off the Big Island. Hilo's *Hula Halau O Ka Ua Kani Lehua*, under the direction of Johnny Lum Ho, has been one of the most successful over the years. It also has placed the Big Island in the spotlight as the focal point of *halau* enrichment and development. Princess Abigail Kekaulike Kawananakoa, great grand-niece of King Kalakaua, who presides over the festival each year, selected the Big Island as the location (at Napoopoo) for Hawaii's archive of literary translations of Hawaiian works for *halau* to study. Most other major *hula* competitions are in Honolulu.

---

sky full of stars through a portable telescope is with Monte Wright's **Paradise Safaris** or **Waipio Valley Shuttle/ Mauna Kea Summit Tours**. It is a 5-6 hour customized van tour by the owners of Waipio Shuttle, with pick-ups and drop-offs in the Honokaa-Waimea area.

Five miles west of the Mauna Kea Observatory Road (20 miles from Highway 190), at 6,500 ft in the midst of rolling grasslands, seven fully-furnished cabins (with hot showers as well as cooking utensils) in **Mauna Kea State Park – "Pohakuloa"** – can be rented from the State Dept. of Natural Resources.

Among the four **Hawaiian Eyes-Big Island Bicycle Tours**, **Mauna Kea Iki** makes a 2 $^1/_2$ hour, ten-mile descent down a 3000-ft slope of Mauna Kea. A Saddle Road trip covers 27 miles and a 4000-ft descent from 9am-3pm (lunch provided). Other Hawaiian Eyes bike trips worth noting are 4 hours in the Kohala Mountains leisurely covering 15 miles with a 3000-ft descent and an all day **Chain of Craters Road** bike trip that covers 27 miles and a 4000-ft descent. Pickup points are in Waimea (and Hilo) and the tours include a mountain bike and helmet, windbreaker and red T-shirt, a mountain bike lesson, guides and a support van and plenty of picture-taking opportunities.

Hawaii Tropical Botanical Garden

At Dan Lutkenhouse's **Hawaii Tropical Botanical Garden**, at last count 14 kinds of ginger, 94 varieties of bromeliads, orchid gardens and one of the largest assortments of other tropical plants grow in a beautiful natural environment.

After visiting the HTBG, follow this scenic route north along Onomea Bay back to Highway 19. Hilo is only 4.5 miles away. The last minibus departs for the garden at 4:30pm.

South of the Garden, on the left, a quarter-mile from the registration house, Barbara and Paul Gephart operate **Hawaiian Artifacts**, a showroom and a workshop where Paul produces bowls, trays, fish and other wood craft from *koa*, *milo*, mango, guava and a dozen other woods. They display a nice variety of jewelry made from wood, plant and palm seeds, coconut and seashells. The Gepharts' seashell collection from around the Pacific Basin will interest both collectors and gift buyers.

Honomu

Further north on the Hamakua Coast – the lower north and east slopes of Mauna Kea – deep, lush gulches and their waterfalls are very dramatic and beautiful. Drive 10 miles north of Hilo on Highway 19 to the turnoff on your left for Route 220 to **Honomu**.

Akaka Falls to Honokaa

Follow Route 220 past sugar cane fields for another 3 miles to **Akaka Falls State Park**. Besides several stunning falls, the 65-acre park in the jungle-like gulch contains tropical plants from all over the world. A 40-minute circular walk through the parkwill immerse one in gingers, orchids, ferns, bamboo groves, heliconia and plants and flowers in shadows, mist, bright light, rainbows and other delights. Walk along winding trails, cross wooden footbridges over streams, dip through tunnels of orchids and bougainvillea to a breathtaking overlook to view Kahana Falls cascading more than 400 ft.

The stream from Akaka Falls runs four miles toward the ocean and empties at **Kolekole Beach Park** under the first bridge on Highway 19 north of Honomu, a popular local picnic area with camping facilities (county permit required). A much better spot for picnics or just a rest stop is **Laupahoehoe Point**, a beautiful peninsula just 11 miles from Honakaa. Along the way, several very deep gulches with roaring waterfalls can be seen most completely by parking on the Hilo side of each bridge and walking to the center. **Papa'Aloa** just south of Laupahoehoe, is a picturesque village thick with tropical growth and palm trees.

Kalopa State Park, one of the least visited natural areas on the Big Island, is easily accessible two miles south of Honokaa and another two miles up a good secondary road. The 100-acre park provides a rare opportunity to explore one or more of the lush gulches along

Akaka Falls.

the Hamakua Coast. Best of all, in addition to tent camping with a state permit, several **cabins** are available (call 961-7200).

A series of well-marked nature trails identify a tremendous variety of flora. Walk through groves of acacia, *koa,* *kopiko, pilo* and *hapuu* along the **Native Forest Nature Trail**.

Honokaa

Honokaa, the major town on the

Waipio Valley

You have to pass Honokaa in order to turn north on Route 240 to **Waipio,** the Big Island's largest and the least accessible valley of the Kohala Mountains on the north shore. Waipio is six-miles deep and one-mile wide at the black sand beach across its mouth. This broad, deep gash in the Kohala Mountains is surrounded on three sides by steep cliffs and covered with incredible vegetation on the valley floor. **Hiilawe Falls** plunges 1,300 ft.

Long before Westerners knew that the Sandwich Islands existed, more than 40,000 Hawaiians lived in fertile Waipio Valley beneath 3,500-ft cliffs, where they fished, grew taro and worshipped their gods. The dim remains of a 15-acre fish pond and ruins of ancient terraces at the back of the long valley attest to its population and history as a place of plentiful food and sometimes too much water – from rain, waterfalls, the river and periodic *tsunamis.* The population of Waipio dwindled from around 5,000 at the time Captain Cook arrived in Kealakekua to about 1,300 in the 1820s, and down to about 150 a hundred years later.

Today, amidst taro, coconuts, avocados, bananas and a large assortment of other wild fruits, nuts and flora, Waipio has 60-100 residents, a mixture of farmers of Hawaiian, Japanese and Chinese ancestry and *haoles* looking for seclusion and self-sufficient life-styles.

Many Hawaiian *alii* were buried in

Hamakua Coast, has only 2,500 residents. It still feels like the 1920s. Main street Honokaa consists of false-front buildings and local stores with a smattering of shops catering to tourists.

Hanokaa has one of the world's largest macadamia nut growing areas. Hawaii's macadamia nut industry, currently depressed, started here.

Macadamia, nutty little nuggets and a hugely satisfying industry.

Waipio where a section of the beach is called *Lua o milu*, doorway to the land of the dead. Great chiefs lived in the valley long before Kamehameha made it his base of spiritual power. According to legend, a priest from this valley gave Kamehameha custody of *Ku*, his war god, before he set off to conquer the islands.

This legendary gateway to the other world was favored by *Wakea*, creator of all the islands; prankster demigod *Maui*'s head was smashed against the rocks by the great god *Kanaloa*, making blood-

cal experiences of any kind who spend an overnight in Waipio Valley admit to leaving with an eerie feeling that the place has *mana*.

From near the black-sand beach fronting Waipio Valley, hikers in good condition can climb a switchback trail over the Pali and through more than a dozen gulches to **Waimanu Valley** 7 miles away–smaller, greener and wilder than Waipio. Like in Waipio Valley, the black-sand beachfront is an excellent place to camp and relax.

There are several ways to get around sacred Waipio Valley, but there is only one route down from the cliffside: a narrow, steep, twisting road into the valley from **Waipio Lookout** at the end of Route 240 past **Kukuihaele**. Peter and Maka'ala Tobin of **Waipio Valley Wagon Tours** bring visitors into the valley for a three-hour excursion twice a day in a covered wagon pulled by mules. **Waipio Shuttle**, the oldest of several tour operators with four-wheel vehicles, offers a 1-$^1/_2$ hour-tour of Waipio.

Tom Araki's hotel fits perfectly in this remarkable valley. Since the '60s, Tom has offered kerosene lamps, communal (cold) showers, no-frills but cheap accommodation in Waipio Valley. Bring your own food.

There is no refrigerator at the "Waipio Hilton." Three of the five rooms have double beds. Sheets and pillow cases are provided. Make reservations several weeks in advance.

Linda Beech's treehouse 30 ft up a

colored earth forever in the upper valley; inseparable lovers *Hiilawe* and *Kakalaoa*, who were turned into a 1,300-ft beautiful waterfall and a large boulder set below, rather than be parted by the god *Lono* (looking for a bride), have not yielded an inch, even to 55-ft *tsunami* waves. No wonder that even visitors who are very skeptical about mysti-

monkeypod next to a 1,000-ft-high waterfall sleeps three and has a kitchen.

Ahualoa to Waimea

Most visitors skirt **Ahualoa** missing one of the most beautiful rainforest hideaways on the Big Island around old Mamalahoa Highway between Honokaa and the top of the hill, about five miles away.

Mamalahoa Highway, which today looks like and is simply a sideroad, winds up the mountainside 11 miles to rejoin Highway 19, about 6 miles from Waimea Center, after crossing beautiful rolling pastureland.

On the way into Waimea, discover one of the Big Island's most enjoyable hikes – a 2-hour **Waipio Ridge Walk** along the **Kohala Ditch** twisting through ginger and bamboo groves. The breathtaking surprise after two miles is the beginning of a cliffside trail cut into the side of and overlooking a 1,000-ft-deep canyon streaked by numerous waterfalls.

Kamuela

From the South Kohala Coast, it's only a 10-mile drive up to Waimea on the plateau between the Kohala Mountains to the north and the western slopes of Mauna Kea.

Parker Ranch dominates the region in every respect. However, **Kamuela** (the Hawaiianized version of Samuel, one of John Parker's grandsons) has developed its own life style and combination of rustic and sophisticated personality which evolves more or less independently of the Ranch.

The **Parker Ranch Shopping Center** is one of two main shopping facilities. Across the street is the newer **Waimea Center**.

The Ranch's Kahilu Theater across from the Parker Ranch Visitor Center brings about a dozen top theatrical, dance and concert events to Kamuela each season.

In addition to sightseeing at the Parker Ranch, off-the-beaten-track **Mana Road** – up the slopes of Mauna Kea, the Kohala Ditch route to Waipio, North Kohala, Mauna Kea's summit – includes some of the best walking, hiking and picnicking in Hawaii.

Parker Ranch

The museum at **Parker Ranch Visitor Center**, first stop on a tour of the Ranch, was started by Thelma Parker Smart. Seeing the 15-minute film covering the ranch and its history is a good way to start.

The **John Palmer Parker Museum** depicts the history and genealogy of six generations of Parker Ranch owners, displaying old family-photos, furnishings, special and day-to-day clothing, old saddles and other riding paraphernalia and other interesting items. One

Parker Ranch

John Palmer Parker, a frustrated and adventuresome sailor from Newton, Massachusetts, jumped ship in Hawaii in 1809 and created a dynasty that changed the history of the Big Island forever. Palmer had the good fortune or sense to marry the King's granddaughter in 1816, Princess Keliikipikaneokaloahaka (or Kipikane for short) and become the first *haole* to join the royal family.

On his second trip to Hawaii, Captain George Vancouver brought cattle as a gift for the King which, with royal protection, grew rapidly in numbers and consumption of vegetation on Mauna Kea's slopes. In exchange for drastically reducing the herd, in 1847 Parker received two acres of land from Kamehameha III on the slopes of Mauna Kea that became the nucleus of the vast Parker Ranch. His noble-born wife was entitled to 640 additional acres.

While rounding up the best and killing the rest, Parker selected his own herd. With over 250,000 acres spreading across North Kona, South Kohala, Waimea and North Kohala, Parker Ranch today is the largest cattle ranch in the United States, with one of the largest Hereford herds in the world.

Parker imported cowboys from Mexico and South America – *paniolos* (a Hawaiian version of *Españoles*) – to work as ranch hands. Ranch hands today are a mixture of Hawaiians, Japanese, Chinese, Filipino and Caucasian-Americans. In several rodeos held during the summer (Memorial Day, Fourth of July and Labor Day), these *paniolos* show that they can hold their own with Mainland cowboys.

room is dedicated to Duke Kahanamoku, the Hawaiian olympian and sheriff of Oahu for 25 years credited with introducing surfing to Australia.

Shuttle buses take visitors around the ranch to see **Puukalani Stable** and the adjoining horse-drawn carriage museum and two Parker Family historic homes: **Puuopelu** and **Mana**.

Around Kamuela

East on Route 19, a few minutes past the Parker Ranch Center, is a "church row" that includes the **Imiola Congregational Church** built in 1857 by Rev. Lorenzo Lyons (who also built the Hokolua Church in Puako). Like Mana, the walls and even ceilings are made of rich *koa* wood. Under the pink pews, the wood is also *koa*.

Kamuela Museum, located on Route 19 (Kawaihae Road) just below its intersection with Route 250, is privately-owned by Albert and Harriet Solomon. It has one of the most eclectic collections of objects from around the world. A conversation with Harriet, a descendent of John Palmer Parker, is worth the visit to the museum. For more than 50 years, the Solomons have collected everything from ancient Hawaiian artifacts to old China and lithographs, stuffed mooseheads and lizards, sombreros and priests' vestments. Admission charged.

North Kohala Coastline

En route to the birthplace and home of Kamehameha, the shoreline of North Kohala is etched with historical sites and beach parks that tourists rarely visit. Like Anaehoomalu and Hapuna beaches, spacious **Spencer Beach Park** at the base of the Kohala Mountains is another wide swath of white-sand beach. Swimming is excellent and camping

Birthing stones of Kamehameha.

(with a county permit) is very popular, with restrooms, showers and tennis courts.

Puukohola *Hieau*, a National Historic Site next to Spencer Park off Route 27, was originally built in 1500 on a 224-by-100-ft platform. This sacred site was rebuilt and rededicated in 1791 by King Kamehameha in honor of the war god *Ku*. Reconstruction of the *hieau* resulted from a prophecy that this action would lead to control of the islands. Thousands of workers built the structure under Kamehameha's personal super-

north of Kawaihae offer marvelous views of Maui across the Alenuihaha Channel, unusual privacy for campers and good fishing (redeye, threadfin, mullet, and other fish), but little more than that. Neither park is good for swimming. Mahukona Beach was part of a shipping destination in the early part of the 20th century when a railway line brought sugar to inter-island steamers. Shaded by *hau* trees, local people fish from the pier. Not until cliff-rimmed **Keokea Beach Park** rimmed by *hala* and palm trees, six miles past Hawi, there is a beach park worth stopping at along this part of the North Kohala Coast. Camping at all of these parks requires county permits.

Lapakahi State Historical Park, a 600-year-old, partially restored Hawaiian fishing village, stands on isolated, rugged terrain about 12 miles from Kawaihae. A sheltered canoe-landing and a fresh water well were the original reasons for its existence. When water ran out, the village was abandoned. Open daily for self and guided tours, canoe sheds, a fishing shrine, a demonstration of Hawaiian salt-making, exhibits of games (that children of all ages are encouraged to try), numerous house sites, stone tools and utensils and other interesting artifacts are displayed along trails around the site. From December through April, you may even see migrating whales near the shore.

Upolu Point, a desolate place, is the closest point to Maui. At mile-marker 20, a sideroad (Route 271) off Route 270

vision. After inviting his main rival to the rededication ceremony, Kamehameha ordered him killed and then offered him to *Ku* as a sacrifice. Kamehameha went on to conquer the Big Island and all of Hawaii.

Mahukona Beach Park and **Kapaa Beach Park**, 13 and 14 miles respectively along the Kohala Coast

loops around the northern tip of the island and passes tiny **Upolu Airport** where only propeller planes occasionally stop.

Originally built for human sacrifices, the remains of 20-ft stone walls surrounding **Mookini Heiau National Historic Site** are reached by a left turn on a bumpy unpaved road at the end of Upolu Airfield's runway.

Surf pounds against steep cliffs below windswept fields around this sacred site, home of all-powerful gods. The remaining foundation of the **Mookini *Heiau* National Historic Site** is an irregular triangle measuring 125 by 250 ft, with 30-ft high and 15-ft thick walls. Offerings (not human, of course) are still to be seen on the altar.

Legend has it that this remote *hieau* was built in a single night from rocks passed along a chain of 18,000 men all the way from a Pololu Valley 14 miles way.

Interestingly, responsibility for maintaining this historic site is divided between the National Park service, the State of Hawaii and the Mookini family of Kohala – traditional stewards of the *heiau* for at least seven centuries.

Kamehameha's birthplace – **Kamehameha Akahi Aina Hanau** – .is a few hundred yards away. Inside the low stone wall around this historic place are some boulders believed to be the actual birthing stones on which Kamehameha, unifier of the Hawaiian kingdom, was born around 1752.

Dense rainforest covers deep val-

leys, gorges and ravines on the eastern, rainy side of the Kohala Mountains. More waterfalls pour off these mountains than anywhere else in Hawaii except on Kauai.

On the Western side of the mountains, dry *pili* fields of former cattle ranching country dotted with *kiawe* trees fall steeply to a beautiful rugged shoreline.

Cutting across the Kohala Range at 3-4,000 ft, Route **250** runs from Highway 19 near Kamuela to Hawi at the northern tip of the peninsula. All along this winding road, a succession of spectacular views frame the western shoreline.

Hawi, a former plantation town and the Big Island's northernmost town, is full of rustic and derelict charm. Before the Kohala Sugar Company pulled out in the early 1970s, the town could boast of four movie theaters.

Today there are none. Colorful old houses and falsefront stores in Hawi also resemble Makawao and Paia on Maui, or a bustling version of Kauai's comparatively quiet Hanapepe.

Between Hawi and Kapaau, only a few miles apart, the humidity increases perceptibly as you move through pandanus forests, hidden taro patches and the invisible line dividing wet and dry sides of the island.

The original gilt and bronze statue of Kamehameha the Great stands across the street, along the road to the **Pololu Valley Lookout**. (The statue of Kamehameha in downtown Honolulu is a replica.)

From **Pololu Valley Lookout**, the valley floor and a black sand beach are visible 300-ft below. Looking down the fantastic coastline – Hawaii's *pali* of hidden valleys, gorges and luxurious foliage – the only access to the shoreline is a dirt trail down to **Pololu Beach**. Pololu is five valleys and 12 miles from Waipio Valley.

The trail down to Pololu is an easy 15-minute walk past thick *lauhala* growth.

Like other Hamakua Coast valleys, once inhabited with taro-growing Hawaiians, very little evidence of habitation exists today even if you hike back into Pololu Valley. Trails to Waipio do exist in a state of disrepair and hiking is possible but not recommended.

South Kohala Coast

The desolation of the area in which Laurance Rockefeller chose to build the **Mauna Kea Beach Hotel** in 1965 shows very clearly on the drive from Keahole Airport north to a string of North Kona and South Kohala Coast resorts.

Route 19 (Queen Kaahumanu Highway) north from Kailua-Kona first passes industrial and warehouse areas, Keahole Airport and then nothing but huge flows of old *a'a* and *pahoehoe* lava bordered here and there by bushes blooming pink and purple.

Wisps of grass breaking through the inky lava turn green past the 70 mile-marker.

Kona Village Resort

The **Kona Village Resort**, built on the site of an ancient fishing village, 15 miles north of Kailua and 7 miles north of the airport, consists of 125 "plush primitive" thatched-roofed huts (*hales*), fashioned after seven different styles of Polynesian island accommodations.

The *hales* contain no television sets, radios, air conditioners, or even keys for the doors. Two miles down a road through lava from the Village, a gatehouse at Highway 19 lets no one in without approval by guests or management.

A perfect white-sand cove rimmed with palm trees completes this secluded tropical world.

Many royal fishponds and burial caves, *heiau* and petroglyphs are hidden (although clearly marked) on the grounds of all major resorts on the coast. Also invisible along the coastline is a trail – the **Ala Kahakai** – of smooth rocks built by ancient Hawaiians to ease the trip across island over rough lava rocks.

Beaches along the coast were frequented by Hawaiian *alii* at play, surfing like their counterparts at Waikiki. Later, cattle were run on the trail to docks at Kawaihae and donkey caravans carried salt to and from Kailua. This trail also passes along the edge of Kona Village Resort, past ponds, tide pools and lava tubes filled with clear water.

Mauna Lani, where golf's a breeze.

Waikoloan Resort

The **Waikoloan Resort** features the 1,241-room **Hyatt Regency Waikoloa** on 62 acres landscaped with protected lagoons for swimming instead of a beach. Oriental art fills the grounds and lines a mile-long walkway that parallels the monorail and canal route.

Anaehoomalu Beach, a long crescent of palm-fringed white sand and one of the Hawaii's most beautiful beaches, adjoins the 543-room **Royal Waikoloan**. Drive into the resort and, just before the Royal Waikoloan, make a left turn to the beach and also a nearby field of **petroglyphs**. This beach and two adjoining 18-hole golf courses

(and a third one available up in Waikoloa, eight miles away) are some of the outstanding attractions of the hotel. The **Waikaloa Kings** (18 holes, par 72, 6,594 yards) and **Beach Golf Course** (18 holes, par 70, 6,500 yards) are two of the coast's most beautiful and challenging golf courses.

Mauna Lani Bay Resort

The resort is set in a historic area known as **Kalahuipua**, along the **King's Trail**. Kamehameha I built a small village and canoe landing at Keawanui Bay. Samuel Parker, grandson of the founder of the Parker Ranch, purchased the site for $1,500 at the turn of the century. In

Puako Petroglyphs.

the mid-1930s, Francis I'i Brown, with Hawaiian ancestry and a state legislator for over 20 years, bought the acreage and built a cottage on it. He restored and restocked native fishponds and replanted native trees, selling the 1,359 acres to the Mauna Lani in 1972.

A little more contemporary and European in design and atmosphere are the **Mauna Lani Bay Hotel and Bungalows**.

Nearby, more than 3,000 petroglyphs are preserved in the **Puako Petroglyph Archaeological Preserve**.

Puako & Hapuna

Between Hapuna and the Mauna Lani Resort, Puako is a residential community along three miles of Puako Bay. Rev. Lorenzo Lyons, composer of "Ha-

Petroglyphs

Petroglyph etchings.

Ancient doodling? Graffiti? Casual chipping away at vast areas of *pahoehoe* lava baking in the intense Hawaiian sun? None of these attempts to decipher Hawaiian petroglyphs comes even close to the truth. Much more plausible is the similarity between the cultural and religious life of the earliest Polynesian immigrants and that of the Marquesas. Ordinary people, not artists, seem to have made the linear and triangular figures – warriors, canoes, paddles, spears and other objects. The drawings were made as part of ritual or prayer and speak of spiritual phenomena – *mana*.

Why **Puako**? Why should Puako be so very rich in petroglyphs? Hawaiians will tell you that Puako exudes very powerful *mana* – the elemental power of the universe. Ancient Hawaiians could feel the *mana* at Puako, in full view of awesome snow-capped Mauna Kea. Puako petroglyphs also seem to be dedicated to the ancestors of ancient Hawaiians.

With some caution, because so little is known about petroglyphs, researchers believe that certain petroglyphic sites elsewhere seem to have been chosen to express experiences of fertility and birth.

The *mana* of nearby **Anaehoomalu**, for example, may be dedicated to children from birth through growing up. But not from the perspective that contemporary Hawaiians or *haoles* look at the world and life in it. Ancient Hawaiians had their own way of viewing the cosmos which leave us mystified because they left behind no written or oral history to explain their drawings.

---

waii Aloha," the state's unofficial anthem, built a very picturesque church, **Hokuloa Church**, along Puako Road. The shoreline remains a mix of super-luxury estates and unpretentious beach cottages. Tidepools and snorkeling along this coast are excellent.

Hapuna Beach State Park, crowded on weekends, is one of the nicest beaches in Hawaii. Only three miles from Kawaihae, this wide white-sand beach is bordered by *kiawe*, *hala* and coconut trees. Above the beach, six very basic screened A-frame shelters sleeping four people each can be rented for a nominal fee from the Division of State Parks.

Mauna Kea Resort

Mauna Kea, one of the original

Skiing on Mauna Kea.

Rockresorts is renowned for its collection of art and antiques that line corridors, walkways and landings of the hotel. The Mauna Kea's understated elegance is the perfect setting for superb Pacific and Asian art selections and traditional Hawaiian quilts. Art tours are conducted twice a week for guests and outsiders.

For spectacular ocean views, only Mauna Lani's two golf courses can match Robert Trent Jones' **Mauna Kea Golf Course** – one of the toughest oceanside courses in the world – and the new course. The grounds include 13 tennis courts.

The Mauna Kea rises elegantly and unpretentiously above one of the loveliest white sand beaches in Hawaii. The south end of the beach, furthest from the hotel, is open to the public with a couple of dozen parking spaces set aside for public use at the end of the roadway that passes by the hotel and the golf club house. Occasionally in the winter, waves get brisk and choppy but otherwise the water is perfect for swimming from one end of the bay to the other.

North Kona Coast

With dependably dry weather, the Kailua-Kona area is the center of cruises, fishing and at a few decent-to-excellent beaches, swimming, snorkeling, surfing and other watersports.

The heart of Kailua-Kona is around the King Kam and nearby **Kailua Pier**, near the intersection of Alii Drive and

The Eye of the Universe

Perched on a cinder cone at Mauna Kea's 13,600-ft level, with glistening white observatory bubbles protruding from the mountain's snow-covered crest, astronomers contemplate the cosmos.

In a joint effort called CARA – the California Association for Research in Astronomy – the University of California and the California Institute of Technology built a formidable observatory near Mauna Kea's summit to find answers to the universe. CARA, a nonprofit corporation, received major funding from the W.M. Keck Foundation and so is called the **Keck Observatory**.

Pristine skies washed by a remarkably undisturbed overhead airstream above Mauna Kea arch over the world's best site for conducting astronomical research. The inactive 13,796-ft volcano stands above most atmospheric water vapor, which absorbs valuable infrared light. Proximity to the equator also ideally positions Mauna Kea for viewing the astronomically rich center of the Galaxy.

This combination of optimum astronomical viewing conditions over Mauna Kea is found nowhere else on earth. The tradeoff is often hostile summit conditions. Gale force winds and freezing temperature sometimes blast Mauna Kea's summit.

Altitude makes oxygen scarce while scientists are breathing intensely cold and dry air. Before observing at the summit, astronomers must acclimatize by spending the night at **Hale Pohaku**, a dormitory facility at the 9,300-ft level.

Fortunately, CARA's astronomers have the option of remote observing through electronic linkage between Keck Observatory and its more comfortable headquarters 10,000-ft below in Kamuela.

Keck Observatory.

Time Machine

Nearly four centuries after Galileo first studied the heavens through a telescope, the Keck Telescope is on the verge of making the greatest leap forward in telescopic history. Light traveling from distant objects in the universe enables viewers to travel back in time. A galaxy billions of light years away means that the light started to travel towards earth billions of years ago.

Hualalai Road. **Hale Halawai**, a small oceanfront park with no beach, is an ideal place for watching the sunset. Visit the Pier at weigh-in time, 4-5pm, especially during summer billfish tournament time, when big game fish are hauled off charter boats. The Pier is another favorite spot for sunset watchers.

Kamakahonu Beach and Hale Halawai are decent snorkeling spots. Much better snorkeling can be found at

Thus, the deeper into the universe that a telescope can reach, the further back in time it can see. The Keck Telescope on top of Mauna Kea will be the world's largest and most powerful "time machine". Like other telescopes, it will gather celestial light and separate the light into its component colors. But that is where the comparison stops. Gathering this spectrum of colors from much deeper in the universe than any other telescope requires larger and larger glass mirrors. Enlarging conventional telescope mirrors eventually results in their deformity. The mirrors lose the precise curvature needed to focus starlight from the furthest reaches of time.

The unique design of the Keck Telescope's mirror solved this scientific problem. A honeycomb of 36 hexagonal mirror segments function as one mirror 33 ft across. These many thin segments also make a lighter and less expensive telescope. Sensors positioned along seams between hexagonal mirror segments – 168 of them – transmit to computers electronic signals which report all adjustments required to make the 36 mirrors act as if they were a single, continuous piece of glass. From Waimea ranchlands or at the Mauna Kea's wind-swept summit, such an intricate cosmology machine almost three miles up the mountain is indeed a wonder.

After flawlessly creating 36 precision mirror segments, the trick for the Keck Telescope's designers was to invent an operating and support system capable of making them work in unison to within a millionth of an inch, night after night, with zero maintenance.

The eight-storey 270-ton Keck Telescope compensates for changing wind loads. The space-frame structure onto which the mirror segments are mounted must hold its shape to within $1/_{25}$th of an inch. To maintain focus, computers reposition each segment within the frame by less than a millionth-of-an-inch.

The Keck Telescope will play an important role in unraveling the mysteries of dark knots of gas and dust scattered along the arms of the Milky Way (birthing clouds) which, shrink and eventually spin into new stars hidden from view, but transparent to infra-red light. Faint light from distant clusters of galaxies on the fringes of the Milky Way transmits clues about the formation and chemistry of our universe. Infra-red penetrates regions where new stars and orbiting planets are born and then passes through interstellar dust clouds en route to the Keck Telescope.

The Keck's huge collecting mirror – 17 times larger than the Hubble Space Telescope's collecting area – collects photons for spectroscopic analysis of the composition of faint objects in these distant galaxies, picking up brilliantly luminous quasars, serving as galactic searchlights and illuminating gas clouds and other objects. What does it mean to see ever closer to the edge of the big bang explosion that many scientists think created the universe between 15 and 20 billion years ago? Keck's sight could take astronomers 12 billion and more light-years from Mauna Kea. In just one light-year, starlight travels about 6 trillion miles. What is 12 million (light-years) x six million (miles)?

According to Dr Edward Stone, Cal Tech astronomer, former lead scientist afor the Voyager spacecraft mission and chairman of the board of CARA, it is "about three-fourths of the way to the edge of the Big Bang, when galaxies slowly began to form." Someday, Stone says, even bigger telescopes spawned by Keck will be capable of seeing back to "...the point where there was nothing at all."

Old Airport **Beach** north of town, which is the reason why you'll find many glass-bottomed boats there. **Honokohau Beach** also has some good snorkeling spots but sightings of sharks in the area have made some snorkelers nervous.

King Kam Hotel

Throughout the lobby of King Kam Hotel, Hawaiian history is displayed telling the story of Hawaii's founding and

Kailua at the Oceanfront Lookout.

transformation. This is a good place to start touring Kailua-Kona, before entering the maze of restaurants and boutiques in town.

The King Kam Hotel also has kumu hula Ulalia Berman leading her free "Hula Experience" tours on Mondays and Wednesdays at 10am. Ulalia leads visitors around the compound of houses, gardens and fishponds that once were the residence of Kamehameha. On the grounds of the hotel, the Bishop Museum and Amfac Hotels restored the **Ahuena *Heiau***, dedicated to Lono, god of fertility and **Kamakahonu** ("Eye of the Turtle"), the final residence of Kamehameha the Great in 1819. Carved *kia aku*, temple images, an oracle tower, *Hale Nana Mahina*, a thatched hut for meditation and other structures represent about one-third of the original *heiau*.

Across from the Ahuena *Heiau*, at Kailua Pier and the seawall that borders the first half mile of Alii Drive, the **Ironman Triathalon** begins each October bringing together thousands of the world's finest athletes to run and bike along the coast highway to Kawaihae and back after their swim off off the pier.

The seawall along Alii Drive is a marvelous place from which to watch fishing charters and other boats sail past, especially when billfish are in season. Billfish – swordfish, sailfish, marlin, and *a'u* – with swordlike snouts and dorsal fins and especially blue, striped and black marlin, are the leading gamefish in Kona waters and reason enough for Kailua-Kona to be a tourist destination. *Ahi*, *mahimahi*, *aku*, or *ono*, other gamefish in Kona's waters further explain boating activity around **Honokohau Harbor**, about two miles north of Kailua-Kona. Several dozen charter boat companies do business there. Cruises above and below water from Kailua-Kona have something for everyone. The 65-ft submarine **Atlantis** takes passengers 80-100 ft below Kona Bay to explore an underwater world. For about an hour view underwater marine life through a glass-bottom boat with **Captain Bean's Cruises**. Sing old songs of Hawaii while cruising in an authentic Polynesian war canoe to Kealakekua Bay for swimming and snorkeling.

The first whales off the Big Island are sighted in November and whale-watching cruises begin in December. The best whale-watching experience is with research biologist **Dan McSweeney** who has been researching whales for over 15 years along the Kona coast.

Mokuaikaua Church & Hulihee Palace

Long before anyone was fishing for 1800-lb Black Marlin, missionaries built a handsome coral-and-stone church, **Mokuaikaua Church**, across the street from the two-storey **Hulihee Palace**, along a seawall made of the same material. Originally built in 1823, the church was rebuilt in 1838 by Governor John Adams.

The historic center of Kailua-Kona, the Mokuaikaua Church and Hulihee Palace, are just a few short blocks from the King Kam along Alii Drive. The 112-ft steeple of the church has been the town's landmark for over 150 years. The lava stone walls and their mortar of crushed coral are still holding up well. Inside, pews, railings, pulpit and other beautiful woodwork are made from rich *koa*. The Daughters of Hawaii do an impeccable job looking after the church.

Hulihee Palace across Alii Drive along the seawall, built at the same time as the church, was a favorite summer getaway place for King Kalakaua. The interior furnishings are marvelous examples of *koa* craftsmanship – the huge dining table, Queen Kapiolani's four-poster bed and other pieces that were actually auctioned off by Prince Kuhio and later retrieved by the Daughters of Hawaii.

A royal vacation home until 1916, the palace today is a museum full of Hawaiian furniture and other effects run by the Daughters of Hawaii, all of whom are at least part Hawaiian. The **gift shop** in the Palace displays some of the nicest selections of Hawaiian woodwork that you'll find in town, in addition to locally made jewelry and Hawaiiana books.

Alii Drive

Shopping dominates Kailua-Kona with

galleries and craft shops. Tourist traffic fluctuates greatly during the year.

Past the Hilton, Alii Drive becomes a narrow street that winds along the shoreline to **White Sands Beach** (also known as Magic Sands or Disappearing Sands), where the sand occasionally washes away in the winter time. Bodysurfing is good here and surfers congregate a little further north toward Kailua at **Banyans**.

Excellent snorkeling spots with fewer crowds and much more tropical fish can be found at popular **Kahaluu Beach Park**. On the rocky shore of Kahaluu Bay is **St. Peter's**, the Little Blue Church, merely a small chapel with a blue tin roof (1880) built on the site of an old *heiau*. Walk inside the church to enjoy its spare simplicity.

Keauhou Shopping Village adjoins Kam III Road which connects Alii Drive and Highway 11. Oriented to an interior court area, with surrounding parking, it's more pleasant to walk around than other local shopping centers and caters primarily to locals rather than tourists.

Holualoa and Kona Coffee Country

From Kailua-Kona you can take two routes up to the **Mamalahoa Highway** (Route 180) to **Holualoa**. **Palani Road** (Route 190) takes you to the north end of the coffee country road – Route 180. This is not the most direct way from Kailua-Kona to tiny Holualoa, 4.5 miles above Kailua, but traveling 5 miles past lush ginger and Christmas berries along Mamalahoa Highway from Palani Junction is a perfect way to absorb the special feeling of Kona Coffee Country before arriving in Holualoa.

The western slopes of Mauna Loa and the Hualalai mountains provide perfect growing conditions for coffee trees. Trees grow in about 2,500 acres of rocky, porous, rich soil between the 800- and 2,000-ft-levels where sunshine, rainfall and temperature blend perfectly for coffee plants that annually produce about 2 million pounds of this world-famous aromatic coffee.

Waiono Meadows, about a mile from town towards Palani Junction on the *mauka* side of Route 180, offers one, two or four-hour trail rides up Mt Hualalai for beginners and seasoned riders.

The four-hour ride includes fishing for rainbow trout in a reservoir. Trails meander through an 1,800-acre working cattle ranch and beautiful groves of ohia trees.

Holualoa

Hualalai Road is the most direct route to the quaint and thriving small art community of Holualoa, a good road that twists and turns its way up Mt. Hualalai.

Many local artists work in studios and homes up narrow dirt driveways

Kona Coffee

Mother Nature and *Pele* must have intended it this way. Volcanoes and volcanic soil are ideal growing conditions for the Kona plants to be found above the 1,200-ft level, especially the 1500-2500-ft levels. Mauna Kea, Mauna Loa and Hualalai mountains block morning clouds and protect the coffee plants from prevailing trade winds in the Holualoa, Kaonaliu and Kealakekua areas; the climate is calm and balmy; midday cloud-cover slipping around Mauna Loa shields the coffee plants from the direct sun during the hottest time of day and good volcanic soil is watered by ample rainfall.

From an accidental beginning, Kona coffee had the right lineage for a coffee of eventual distinction. Coffee has been growing in Kona since 1828, mainly on small family farms.

The first Protestant missionaries had the good sense to bring slips of arabica coffee, originally from Brazil, over to the Big Island from Governor Boki's Manoa home on Oahu. Had they made the fatal mistake of bringing over "the other kind" of coffee (*robusta*), the awful result would have been much higher yields of vastly inferior, rubbery-tasting coffee, with a much higher caffeine content. And the entire history of the Kona Coast would have been vastly different.

Never mind that this prized coffee was first grown as ornamentals at the mission station in Kaawaloa, near where Captain Cook's monument stands. Coffee beans processed and brewed into gourmet coffee seemingly had a special destiny in Kona and not elsewhere in Hawaii. While coffee plants growing elsewhere in the Hawaiian Islands were replaced by more profitable sugar crops after Hawaii's annexation in 1900, rocky volcanic terrain and growing conditions in Kona clearly favored small farms growing coffee.

Kona coffee was "discovered" and boosted early by some of the Big Island's most famous visitors. In 1866, Mark Twain wrote: "The ride through the district of Kona to Kealakekua Bay took us through the famous coffee section. I think Kona has a richer flavor than any other, be it grown where it may and call it by what name you please."

Very rich and exotic *arabica* cousins, like Jamaica Mountain Blue and Celebese Kalossi from Indonesia, also grew on tropical islands, but Kona coffee had a distinct advantage. Kona coffee became a coffee celebrity while Ethiopia's Mocha Harrar and Kenya AA almost inevitably remained obscure coffees. Only Kona's much-publicized *arabica* cousin from Columbia is much more well-known and widely used.

None of the *arabica* family of coffees offer the rich, sweet, intense taste, body, character and aroma of Kona.

that squirm off the network of mountainside roads between Kailua-Kona and Coffee Country. Holualoa is a unique, compact little artists' town.

While driving south on Highway 11, stop at **Mrs Fields' Macadamia Nut Factory**, the **Honwanji Buddhist Temple**, the **Central Kona Union Church**, the **Lanakila and Christ Churches** and, down Napoopoo Road, the **Royal Kona Coffee Mill and Museum** (8am-4:30pm daily) for a taste-test of *Royal Kona Blend Coffee*.

Less than a mile south of Kealakekua on Highway 11, the historic Greenwell Store of the Greenwell Ranch coffee operation houses the **Kona Historical Society Museum**.

Built in the mid-1800s by HN Greenwell, the masonry uses native stone joined with lime made from burned coral. The museum's reference library and archive contains photographs, manuscripts, maps and a few artifacts of old Kona that can be examined 9am-3pm on weekdays.

Kealakekua Bay

Near the town of Captain Cook, Route 11 along the slopes of Hualalai intersects with **Napoopoo Road** to **Kealakekua Bay**. This zig-zagging road passes the Royal Kona Coffee Mill and the **Mauna Kea Mill and Museum**.

At the bottom of the hill is **Napoopoo**, a former fishing village and Kealakekua ("Road of the God") Bay at road's end. The bay is a **Marine Life Conservation District** with a fine beach and fantastic snorkeling out of **Napoopoo Beach Park**.

In a picturesque setting with cliffs surrounding the harbor, Napoopoo Beach Park has good swimming and excellent diving. Diving is even better near the Captain Cook monument, about a mile across the bay. (Don't swim over in the early evening when sharks come to feed.)

Near the parking lot is the well-preserved **Hikiau** *Heiau*, dedicated to the god *Lono*, carved into the *pali* with a marvelous view of the bay. From this vantage point, priests could see the prophesied arrival of *Lono*'s "floating island." The prophecy of *Lono* returning on his "floating island," which led to Captain Cook's welcome and later death, is centered here. At the northern end of the bay is a 27-ft white marble obelisk, the **Captain Cook Monument**, where Cook was felled in 1779.

Since Kealakekua Bay is a Marine Life Conservation District, be pre-

pared for hoards of visitors who come to see spectacular underwater sights and also the historic place across the bay where Captain Cook met his tragic death.

For just a day-trip to Kealakekua, consider taking a boat cruise for snorkeling and to tour the bay for close-up views of the Captain Cook Monu-

Captin Cook Memorial, Kona Coast.

ment standing on an isolated distant shore.

There are plenty of good choices for cruises to Kealakekua Bay from Kailua-Kona or Keauhou Bay. **Hawaiian Cruises'** glass-bottom boats make a four-hour cruise every day. The 96-ft **Captain Cook VII** leaves Kailua Pier daily at 8:45am, with time for swimming and snorkeling in Kealakekua Bay in addition to a local history lesson. Cruise from Keauhou Bay near the Kona Surf Hotel to Kealakekua Bay for snorkeling aboard the **Fair Wind**, a 50-ft trimaran.

Puuhonua o Honaunau

Four miles along a rough and bumpy coastal road from Kealakekua Bay is **Puuhonua o Honaunau National Historical Park**. Just a half-mile down this road, turn right onto a lava-bed road for **Keei Beach**. This narrow salt-and-pepper beach has hardly enough room to pitch a tent, the swimming is decent, but the main attraction is a channel through the coral to an underwater sea grotto. **Puuhonua o Honaunau Park** itself has excellent diving spots.

The temple, on a 20-acre finger of lava, is surrounded by the sea on three sides. Once inside the 1,000-ft long, 10-ft high, 17-ft wide lava walls on the fourth or land side, *kapu*-breakers were safe from pursuers no matter what they did and *kahuna* (priests) would perform necessary rituals to absolve them from all wrong. Within the refuge, two *heiau*, one built in 1550 and one dating from around 1650, a temple and a mausoleum for more than 23 *alii*

until 1818, have been restored and reconstructed along with several thatched huts, idols and canoes. For more than 200 years, starting with Kamehameha's great-grandfather, Keawe, *alii* were buried on this site, reinforcing its *mana*.

Even Queen Kaahumanu sought sanctuary here as a 16-year-old bride who disobeyed Kamehameha openly and fled to the temple for protection against his wrath. When Hawaii's old religion was destroyed, which Queen Kaahumanu was instrumental in bringing about, the temple was abandoned and gradually fell apart until restoration in 1961, including new carvings of temple gods. You'll see a *konane* board (for Hawaiian checkers), thatched-roofed *hales* and tall *tikis* guarding the water's edge. There is an admission charge. Pick up a brochure from the Visitors Center – open 7:30am-5:30pm daily (but the park doesn't close until midnight).

Honaunau to Milolii

Continuing up Route 160, on the same side of the road, watch for the very inconspicuous sign next to the road pointing to the left for **St. Benedict's Painted Church**. The latticework front and Gothic-style belfry of this small church siting on a knoll above the road is very picturesque, especially on a sunny morning. Inside, 60 years ago biblical scenes were painted on the walls, the vaulted nave behind the altar **Father Veighe**, an inspired missionary-artist from Belgium whose art work here and in Puna (Star of the Sea Painted Church in Kalapana) has been seen by thousands of visitors. The Renaissance-style murals of biblical scenes were painted

by this Belgian priest to show his congregation what Europe's cathedrals looked like.

Full of coconut trees, **Hookena Beach Park** offers some good diving spots near the cliffs south of this lovely black sand beach. About 21 miles from Kailua, the park is a two-mile sidetrip from Route 11.

If you have time, and it's no later than mid-afternoon, drive ten miles south of Pu'uhonua O Honaunau (33 miles from Kailua) on narrow winding Route 11 through bleak stretches of lava (1919, 1936 and 1950 flows) and thick patches of macadamia orchids to the **Milolii** turn-off. Five miles down a paved road is a picturesque fishing village with some of the best tidepools in Hawaii. For divers, Milolii also abounds with fasci-

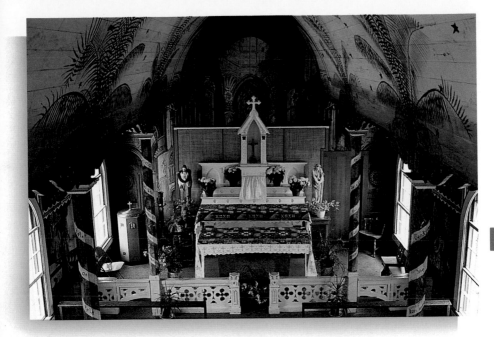

St Benedict Church.

nating marine life. **Warning: don't swim outside of the reef.**

Kau & South Point

Avoid driving to the Kau District, South Point and Volcano-Puna at night – the driving is dangerous and you'll miss some fascinating scenery and other attractions along the way. Route 11 southbound is narrow, twisting and turning past sharp drop-offs with no shoulder on the makai side. Drive carefully! You will cross fingers of the 1950 Mauna Loa lava flow while driving 14 miles south from Hookena.

Drive past ranch grazing lands and a huge macadamia nut orchard to a wonderful picnic or rest stop before heading to *Ka Lae* (The Point) – **Manuka State Wayside Park** – 12 miles before South Point Road. This lovely botanic park on rolling terrain at the 2,000-ft level is located on your left about eight miles past the Milolii turnoff. All plants are identified in the park and trails winding through trim, colorful gardens and an arboretum are very pleasant. Camping in shelters is allowed (with a permit).

The best kept secret in this area is the **Road to the Sea**, two beaches (Humuhumu Point and Awili Point) at the end of a seven-mile long cinder road. The road leads to several cinder cones and these green-tinted black sand beaches. Drive slowly and then park

Captain Cook & Kamehameha

In the 13th century, for reasons not fully understood, a second wave of Polynesian migration, this time directly from Tahiti, discovered the southern tip of the Big Island. Marquesans had traveled back and forth to their home islands and lived in the archipelago for five centuries before these Tahitian warriors arrived and conquered the island of Hawaii.

Pa'ao, a Tahitian priest, built a heiau at Waha'ula ("Temple of the Red Mouth") dedicated to Ku the war god. To strengthen the god's mana, he introducing the idea of human sacrifice into the hitherto benign Hawaiian religion. These human sacrificial temples known as luakini spread through the islands. (The restored Waha'ula Heiau and a museum sit at the Park Visitor Center (Marker 27) at the end of Chain of Craters Road in Volcanoes National Park, now cut off from Route 130 by Kilauea's lava flow.)

Pa'ao returned to his homeland to bring back a chief (Pili) potent enough to rejuvenate Hawaii's lineage of ali'i. This dynasty lasted until Kamehameha the Great. Comings and goings between Hawaii and Tahiti inexplicably ceased for 500 years before Capt. Cook arrived. In other words, Hawaiians were isolated even from the rest of the Polynesian world for the five centuries preceding Capt Cook's fateful sighting of the West Coast of the Big Island. In the perspective of these five centuries, the timing of Cook's arrival – the year, the month, even the day – in 1778, is uncanny, once again seeming to confirm for Hawaiians the prevailing notion that "nothing is accidental."

According to Hawaiian legend, Lono, god of the Harvest Festival, Makahiki, left the island of Hawaii after mistakenly killing his wife for infidelity, promising to return one day on a "floating island." Precisely during the annual celebration of Makahiki, Capt Cook's ships fatefully sailed into Kealakekua Bay and were proclaimed by kahuna on shore to be "floating islands." Indeed, the masts of Cook's ships, with sails furled, looked remarkably like Lono's idol displayed at the Makahiki celebration – a tall crosspole draped with white tapa (cloth) banners. Cook almost instantly became "Lono returned," worshipped as a god until the moment when circumstances stripped him of his godliness and caused his death.

Kamehameha, the prophesied future king of Hawaii, was born only a quarter of a mile from Paao's Ku Temple, the Mookini Heiau, at the northern tip of Kohala. Just at the time of Cook's first landfall, the goal of Kamehameha's warring relatives on various Hawaiian islands was a multi-island kingdom under one ruler. The massive, six-ft-six, "savage looking" Kamehameha, in his mid-twenties, was one of the ali'i who boarded Cook's ship Resolution for an overnight visit. The ship's weaponry, cannons and muskets, understandably made a big impression on Kamehameha, especially in the context of ongoing inter-island warfare. Months later, he felt their power when he was fired on and injured during the time that Cook was killed in Kealakekua Bay.

---

above the last slope. Trails offer hiking possibilities for panoramic views.

Vast tracts of lava rubble in South Kona give way to high forests on the slopes of Mauna Loa becoming green pasturelands edged by black sand beaches in the Kau District. The narrow road to South Point branches off Highway 11 six miles west of Naalehu. Experts dispute when the first ancient Polynesians arrived here. Few people live here now.

South Point Road passes through about 12 miles of grassland, roaming cattle and horses and the Kamoa Wind Farm, to the southernmost point in Hawaii and the nation. Where the first Polynesians probably made landfall, fishermen have built platforms along seacliffs for their haul of ulua (tuna) and

Eleven years later, in 1790, "fate" sent Isaac Davis and John Young, two captured Americans with gunnery skills, and the captured ship *Fair America* with its potent cannons, to enable Kamehameha to subdue *Kahekii* (who some say was Kamehameha's real father), ruler of Maui, Molokai, Lanai, Oahu and, through his half-brother, *Kaeo*, in control of Kauai. (During your visit to the Waipio Lookout, try to visualize a sea-battle between Kamehameha and *Kahekii*, with cannon mounted on double-hulled canoes, off the coast of serene Waipio Valley.)

Pa'ao , a man of great spiritual power, lands on the Big Island with a radically new war god, *Ku*. 500 years later, the unifier of Hawaii, born virtually under *Ku*'s shadow, as a young *ali'i* greets the first outsider to arrive in five centuries. Cook brings to the island implements of destruction borne from and perfected in Western Society's perpetual warfare. Cook arrives during *Makahiki* festival time two years in a row, the second time at the sacred shrine of *Lono*, *Hikiau Heiau*, in Kealakekua Bay. A sudden storm forces Cook to return for ship repairs to Kealakekua a third – and last – time to his death.

Thirty-one years later, Kamehameha the Great's artillery and superior numbers finally secure control over all the islands, including Kauai, which took 15 of those years and several abortive invasion attempts to subdue. Without Cook's ill-fated visit, and Kamehameha's Western arsenal of weapons and advisors, his goal of conquering and unifying the Hawaiian islands probably would have been thwarted.

ahi. Rocks below hold old canoe moorings still in use today. Remnants of an ancient *heiau* foundation remain near a light tower. From the **Kaulana Boat Ramp** at South Point, it's 2-1/2 rough miles along the waterline to reach **Green Sand Beach**. Hiking round-trip takes two hours. This volcanic sand beach acquires a greenish tint from olivines eroding from the cinder hill, **Puu Mahana**, behind the beach. Avoid climbing down the cinder cone since it crumbles easily underfoot.

The South Point area possesses a combination of *mana* from its Polynesian discovery and habitation and a pervasive sense of remoteness. The countryside and its small country towns convey the feeling of an earlier, quieter and more peaceful era. Returning to the Belt Road, pass through **Waiohinu**, past a **monkeypod tree** growing from the roots of one planted by Mark Twain in 1866 which was downed by high winds in 1957.

Six miles past the turnoff to South Point is **Naalehu**, the nation's southernmost town, situated against a backdrop of very scenic hills. It is a former plantation town with a touch of cosmopolitan feeling.

Wittington Beach Park has more wonderful tidepools and very good snorkeling, about three miles north of Naalehu. Some coconut and ironwood trees dot the lava-rimmed shoreline. Getting to a comfortable swimming area over the lava rocks at Wittington is tricky. Instead, simply enjoy the beach's wonderful tidepools.

For easy access to safe swimming in a beautiful black sand beach area, head past Wittington Beach Park to lovely **Punaluu Beach Park** and one-third of a mile further south to the more secluded and very pretty **Ninole Cove Park**, both part of **Seamountain Resort** in Ninole.

Punaluu Black Sand Beach in the

Exploring nature at the Volcanoes National Park can at times be dampened by a small dizzle.

Kau District is the most well-known black-sand beaches in Hawaii that is still accessible.

Hawaii Volcanoes National Park

Approaching the Park on Route 11 from South Point, about a mile after crossing the Park boundary you reach a trailhead and also a very worthwhile sidetrip – the two-mile **Kau Desert Trail** (no longer "Footprints Trail"), where Halemaumau's eruption in 1790 portentously buried Keoua's army en route to battle The Kamehameha for control of the island. The **Mauna Loa Strip Road** leads to incinerated **Tree Molds**, that are fossil monuments to molten lava flow and to the **Bird Park** nature trail.

At Keoua 80 men were lost to toxic

A little further along the same road is Kipuka Puaulu or Bird Park, a forested area and bird sanctuary with more than 20 species of trees and a one-mile long self-guided nature trail running through it. One of the loveliest spots on the Big Island, this sanctuary for birds and plant life a few miles up Mauna Loa Road contains one of the finest and most varied examples of native Hawaiian forest. In the *koa*, *ohia* and *mamani* trees, you may be fortunate enough to see rare honeycreepers (*apapane* and *i'iwi*).

The most challenging and strenuous hike in the park is along the 18-mile **Mauna Loa Trail**, a 3-4 day hike to the top of the mountain. (The 15-mile hike up Mauna Kea actually is less rigorous but has to be completed in one day since no camping is permitted along the way.) A 10-mile hike on narrow, winding Mauna Loa Strip Road leads to a lookout at the 6,000 ft level.

Back on Route 11, keep your eye out for the turn-off to the **Kilauea Visitor Center** (containing a museum, souvenir shop and information desk. Next to the visitor center, the original Volcano House (1877) houses the **Volcano Art Center** displaying one of the finest collections of local art in Hawaii.

If your time for visiting Hawaii Volcanoes National Park is limited, at the very least explore the summit of Kilauea Volcano along **Crater Rim Drive** (11-mile loop). The first stop is **National Park Headquarters and Visitor Center**.

Allow about 3 hours for stops at **Sulfur Banks**, **Steam Vents**, **Thurston**

fumes and gases as they ended up a human sacrifice at Puukohala *Heiau*. It's a two-hour round-trip hike to the footprints left in molten lava by these troops and their families .

Continuing on Route 11 past the turn-off to **Namakani Paio Campground** is the **Mauna Loa Strip Road** to the **Tree Molds**. Lava flowing through an *ohia* forest encircled and ignited tree trunks, leaving holes in the ground, some of them quite deep – a reverse of Lava Tree State Park to the east in Puna.

Hawaii Volcanoes National Park

Hawaii Volcanoes National Park occupies a large part of the southeastern slope of the most massive mountain on earth, **Mauna Loa** (13,679 ft). This immense mountain is 60-miles long and 30- miles wide. Measured from its base 18,000 ft under the Pacific Ocean, Mauna Loa is taller than Mount Everest. Its entire girth consists of 10,000 cubic miles of iron-hard lava. The central feature of the mountain's park is **Kilauea's Caldera** encircled by **Crater Rim Drive**. After *Pele* was flooded out of Kauai by her sister, the sea goddess, *Namalaokahai*, for seducing her husband and was ravished by the Pig God, *Kamapua*, she made her home in **Halemaumau Crater** in the Kilauea Caldera. For at least a thousand years, Hawaiians appeased *Pele* with sacrificial offerings of pigs, dogs, humans and sacred *ohelo* berries. In the early 1820s, after the *kapus* were abandoned, chieftess Kapiolani climbed down into the crater, defied *Pele* and claimed the crater for *Jehovah*, her newly adopted Christian God.

In 1881, a lava flow enveloped areas within undeveloped Hilo's city limits. Until the 1920s, Kilauea was a burning lake of fire. After that, lava flows subsided and hardened, except for periodic outbursts from the mountain's sides such as in 1942 when a heavy flow came within 12 miles of Hilo.

The world's most active volcano, Kilauea last spewed fountains of lava thousands of ft in 1959-1960 and pushed lava through underground tunnels to consume the village of Kapoho, 30 miles away. (In 1975, Hawaii's strongest earthquake in recorded history sunk the Puna coast by almost three ft and caused a *tsunami*.) While Kilauea blew up again in 1983-84, Mauna Loa also erupted once more in 1984 after nine quiescent years, the first simultaneous eruption of Kilauea and Mauna Loa in 65 years.

In 1986, lava destroyed homes in Kapaahu and Kalapana Gardens, crossed Highway 130 several times, destroyed ancient **Punaluu Heiau**, historic Queen's Bath and poured into the sea. Lava flow from Kilauea in 1990 destroyed most of the remaining homes in Kapaahu and many homes in Kalapana Gardens. Lava continues to flow incessantly from Kilauea.

Hissing and smoulding, Pele's reminder that there's life below the volcanoes.

Lava Tube, Kilauea Iki Crater, Halemaumau Overlook, the Jaggar Museum and possibly a walk along Devastation Trail.

A self-guided tour of the natural history museum and a free lecture and film presented by the Park Service at the **Kilauea Visitor Center** (every hour on the hour starting at 9am) provides all the background on volcanic geology and volcanism that most people need to enjoy sightseeing in the park. In addition to driving **Crater Rim Road** and down the **Chain of Craters Road**, easy walks from the Rim Road and hikes on backcountry trails reveal fascinating aspects of the park.

From the Visitor Center, start driving on spectacular Crater Rim Road, an 11-mile loop around **Kilauea Crater** that passes lava flows, steam vents, sulphur smells, deep rifts in the volcano floor and exciting vistas of Kilauea and **Halemaumau Craters** (which also contain hiking trails). Halemaumau Firepit, a crater within Kilauea, is supposedly the current home of *Pele*. Nearby is **Kilauea Iki Crater**, with a short hiking trail and **Keanakakoi Crater**.

Clockwise on Crater Rim Drive your first stop would be **Thurston Lava Tube**, a fascinating 450-ft tunnel created by cooling lava that you can walk through. **Devastation Trail** is about a one mile hike through a former *ohia* forest killed by the 1959 eruption of Kilauea Iki.

Driving counterclockwise to the **Thomas A Jagger Museum**, in a former volcano observatory on the crater rim is a great view of Halemaumau Crater. In the museum, exhibits on the history and volcanology of Mauna Loa and Kilauea provide a much better understanding of what you're about to see (or have just seen).

Get an update on Chain of Craters Road from the Volcano Update (tel: 967-7977), a 24-hour recorded message. Large parts of the lower section of Chain of Craters Road are closed due to lava flows. Find out if the trail near Puuloa is open to the **petroglyphs**; and if the **Wahaula Heiau** can still be seen (behind the remains of the Wahaula Visitor's Center destroyed by the 1989 lava flow). **Star of the Sea Painted Church** was moved in 1990. Crater Rim is circled by the 11.6-mile **Crater Rim Trail** for ambitious hikers. Incredible views of steaming Halemaumau are revealed along the 3-mile **Halemaumau Trail** that crosses the crater floor. Many visitors walk along **Devastation Trail**.

The park maintains three drive-in campsites. Tent camping with a permit from Park Headquarters and 10 cabins for up to four people, arranged with Volcano house, are available at Namakani Paio, near the Hawaii Volcano Observatory. **Kipule Nene** is a secluded campsite near the rim of Kilauea off Chain of Craters Road. See if beautiful **Kamoamoa**, an oceanside campsite near Kalapana, still exists after the lava flows of 1990-91. For information on all campsites in the park, contact Hawaii Volcanoes National Park, HI 96718, 967-7311.

Legend has it that *Maui* — half man/half god — and his brothers used a magical fishhook and bird bait to haul the Hawaiian Islands off the ocean floor. Maui's brothers disobeyed his warnings not to look back and thus, only the tips of the islands rose above the seas. Most of Maui's two volcanoes are submerged, joined by lava flows at the isthmus of Central Maui.

West Maui's volcano, peaking at Puu Kukui (5788 ft), was the first of two volcanoes to appear on what became the Hawaiian archipelago's second largest island (729 sq miles). Compared to wrinkled and deeply eroded West Maui, the massive volcano Haleakala of East Maui looks smooth, ascending from a very broad base to its huge crater at the 10,023-ft summit. Haleakala's slopes contain a whole world of farms, ranches, villages and towns crisscrossed by small roads branching off Route 37.

Maui

Ulupalakua landscape.

237

Artists living and working on Haleakala's slopes share a profound sense of the volcano's role as a spiritual and natural refuge, especially for artists who cluster around the Makawao-Haiku-Kula area. Its natural beauty, its climate and the legendary energy emanating from within the volcano all contribute to the powerful attraction. Like volcanic Mauna Loa-Kilauea 80 miles away on the Big Island, which has produced an artists' colony at Volcano Village, Haleakala acts as a magnet for artistic talent that thrives on proximity to *Pele* (see box story).

No sooner had Maui's Chief Kahekili lost his battle for control of the island to Kamehameha than the conqueror from the Big Island started transforming Lahaina into a political center for the Hawaiian islands. Queens Kaahumanu and Keopuolani made Lahaina their home base, followed by Kamehameha II and Kamehameha III who made Lahaina the capital of unified Hawaii until the 1840s.

As a whaling port full of sinful activities, Lahaina became a magnet for proselytising Protestant missionaries who sired dynasties in agriculture and real estate – the Baldwins and the Alexanders, who later joined forces as Alexander and Baldwin. Their sugar and pineapple plantations and cattle ranching changed the face of Maui's landscape and population. Chinese, Japanese and Portuguese laborers followed by Filipinos soon outnumbered Hawaiians and *haoles*.

Marginal cane fields were not replaced by hotels, condominiums and golf courses on West Maui until 30 years ago when Amfac started Kaanapali. Kapalua sprang out of West Maui's pineapple fields in the 1970s. On the lower slopes of Haleakala, the land is still owned by descendants of the American sea captain James Makee who, in the early 19th century, established Rose Ranch, today's Ulupalakua Ranch. The family sold this immensely valuable coastal land to developers and retreated up the mountain without road access.

Mauians sum up their pride for the island with *Maui no ka oi* — "Maui is the best". Maui certainly is the fastest growing Hawaiian island. A major enlargement of Kahului Airport will accommodate greatly increasing volumes of domestic and international traffic. Attracting more tourists than any other island, Maui's boom in tourism and real estate values is a mixed blessing.

Historically, in the past 30 years, most tourist development has been concentrated in Wailea and Kihei, Lahaina, Kaanapali and Kapalua – a small fraction of the island. A large part of both sides of the island is inaccessible – the rugged mountains of West Hawaii are virtually impassable;.

The lowland in the Central Maui isthmus adjoining the twin cities of Kahului and Wailuku is largely planted with sugarcane and huge Haleakala dominates eastern Maui.

The island's biggest new development is in Wailea Resort on eastern

T-shirts have become a small industry thanks to tourists.

Maui. The new eight-storey Grand Hyatt Wailea on 39 acres of beachfront south of the Maui Inter-Continental Hotel added nearly 800 rooms and 20,000 square ft of shops to Wailea. Next door is the new eight-storey Four Seasons Resort on 15 acres of beachfront de-signed as "a palace by the sea". More such developments, including condo-miniums, came onstream in 1991.

The central, west and eastern parts of Maui include Kahului-Wailuku (cen-tral Maui); Lahaina, Kaanapali and Kapalua and around the north shore

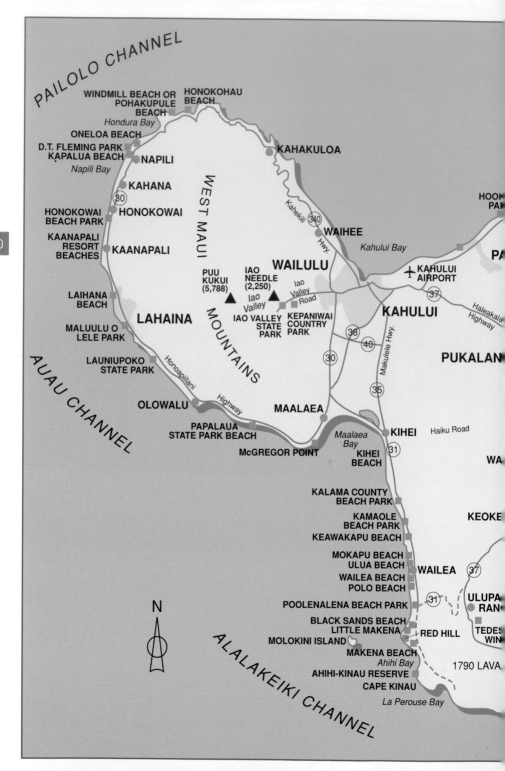

PAILOLO CHANNEL

WINDMILL BEACH OR
POHAKUPULE
BEACH
Hondura Bay
ONELOA BEACH
D.T. FLEMING PARK
KAPALUA BEACH
Napili Bay
KAHANA
80
HONOKOWAI
BEACH PARK
KAANAPALI
RESORT
BEACHES
LAIHANA
BEACH
MALUULU O
LELE PARK
LAUNIUPOKO
STATE PARK
OLOWALU

HONOKOHAU
BEACH

NAPILI

HONOKOWAI

KAANAPALI

LAHAINA

KAHAKULOA

WEST MAUI

Kahekili 340

WAIHEE

Kahului Bay

WAILULU

PUU
KUKUI
(5,788)
IAO
NEEDLE
(2,250)
Iao
Valley
IAO VALLEY
STATE
PARK
KEPANIWAI
COUNTRY
PARK

Iao
Valley
Road

KAHULUI
AIRPORT

KAHULUI

37

*Haleakala
Highway*

PUKALAN

MOUNTAINS

Honoapiilani

Highway

MAALAEA

38
40

30

35

Makulele Hwy.

PAPALAUA
STATE PARK BEACH
McGREGOR POINT

*Maalaea
Bay*
KIHEI
BEACH

KIHEI

31

Haiku Road

WA

KALAMA COUNTY
BEACH PARK
KAMAOLE
BEACH PARK
KEAWAKAPU BEACH
MOKAPU BEACH
ULUA BEACH
WAILEA BEACH
POLO BEACH
POOLENALENA BEACH PARK
BLACK SANDS BEACH
LITTLE MAKENA
MOLOKINI ISLAND
MAKENA BEACH
Ahihi Bay
AHIHI-KINAU RESERVE
CAPE KINAU

KEOKE

WAILEA

37

31

ULUPA
RAN

TEDES
WIN

RED HILL

1790 LAVA

La Perouse Bay

HOOK
PAI

PA

AUAU CHANNEL

N

ALALAKEIKI CHANNEL

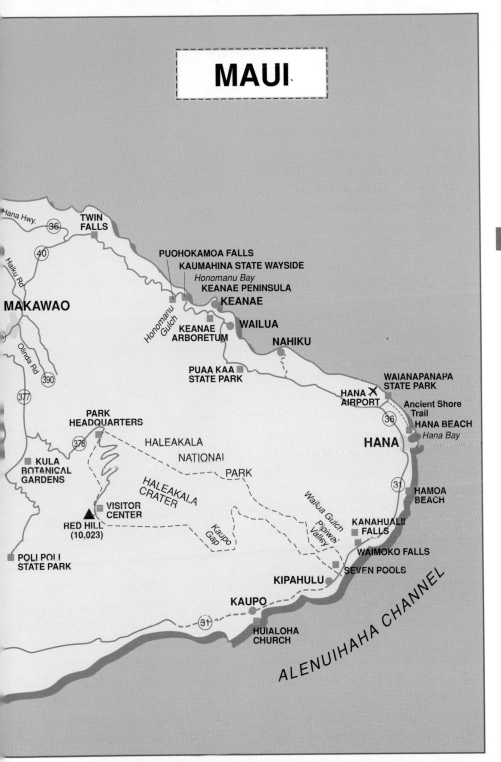

MAUI

Hana Hwy.

36

40

Haiku Rd

TWIN
FALLS

PUOHOKAMOA FALLS
KAUMAHINA STATE WAYSIDE
Honomanu Bay
KEANAE PENINSULA
KEANAE

MAKAWAO

Honomanu Gulch

KEANAE
ARBORETUM

WAILUA

NAHIKU

Olinda Rd

390

377

PUAA KAA
STATE PARK

WAIANAPANAPA
STATE PARK

HANA
AIRPORT

Ancient Shore
Trail

36

HANA BEACH
Hana Bay

HANA

PARK
HEADQUARTERS

378

HALEAKALA

NATIONAL

KULA
BOTANICAL
GARDENS

HALEAKALA
CRATER

PARK

Waikua Gulch

VISITOR
CENTER

RED HILL
(10,023)

Kaupo
Gap

Pipiwai
Valley

KANAHUALII
FALLS

HAMOA
BEACH

31

POLI POLI
STATE PARK

WAIMOKO FALLS

SEVEN POOLS

KIPAHULU

KAUPO

31

HUIALOHA
CHURCH

ALENUIHAHA CHANNEL

(west Maui); and the southern shore through Kihei, Wailea and Makena to La Perouse Bay; the northeast shore from Paia to Hana and Kipahulu, for the adventurous ending up in Ulupalakua; Upcountry on the slopes of Haleakala, extending to Ulupalakua and Haleakala the magnificent volcano itself (all on eastern Maui) .

The recommended itineraries circle the east (counterclockwise to Wailea and clockwise to Hana) and west (counterclockwise to Lahaina and beyond) parts of Maui. Circling east or west Maui in one day is possible but inadvisable.

Even the most limited touring of Maui requires various combinations of seven or eight half and full-day trips. Kahului Airport in central Maui will probably be your landing place, but not your starting point for touring. However, Wailuku (for rare urban charm) and Iao Valley's scenic surprises are certainly worth visiting before leaving central Maui.

Kaanapali and Lahaina on West Maui are usually the first stopping places, no matter how many times a visitor comes to the island. Besides sightseeing and buying twice as much as you remember in Lahaina, a few restaurants and snorkel cruises from there are "musts". The only special surprises on this side of the island are reserved for travelers who continue past Kapalua to the beaches of the north shore and through a short stretch of rough dirt road in "Old Maui" to Kahakuloa and

then on to Kahului.

With several major new hotels and golf courses, Wailea and Makena will be even more interesting southern destinations for some travelers. Resort development thus far stops at Makena (Maui Prince) and nature's beauty takes over again, continuing past Makena to isolated La Perouse Bay. A vacation on

Convoy of windsurfers.

Maui is incomplete without spending some time on at least one of the still fantastic white-sand beaches of Wailea and Makena. Besides golf, the other great lure on this developed eastern end of the island are a half dozen outstanding (and expensive) hotel restaurants.

From Kahului, the road to Hana swings past Paia and beneath Upcountry (Haleakala). Continuing on Routes 37, 377 and 378, you arrive at Haleakala Crater. Haleakala, *House of the Sun*, at the center of east Maui pushes through thick clouds and is encircled by the other destinations — on the west, the Wailea Resort and ten miles of Makena, Wailea and Kihei beaches; on the north side by Paia and the otherwise mostly undeveloped coast reached by the most beautiful and tortuous drive in Hawaii, Hana Highway; and on the east side, isolated and glorious Hana, extending on Route 31 to Ulupalakua Ranch past Oheo Gulch (Seven Pools) near the final resting place selected by Charles Lindbergh in the Palalapa Hoomau churchyard (Kipahulu).

East Maui

For years there were only two hotels, some expensive condos and a number of appropriately extravagant homes in Wailea and Makena. Mauians waited patiently and perhaps apprehensively for the inevitable explosion of further development in one of the best resort areas in the Pacific region. Thousands of acres shielded Ulupalakua Ranch on the slopes of Haleakala from the prospect of towering cranes and bulldozers. In the 1980s, Alexander and Baldwin created Wailea on *Kiawe*-covered land they owned on the dry side of the island, soon followed by the adjoining Makena Resort.

Since 1988, the ground has trembled with the rise of new hotels and condominiums and the multi-million dollar refurbishing of hotels and restaurants.

Wailea lacks the sightseeing and shopping attractions of Lahaina, but its restaurants are better than ever – a newly refurbished **La Perouse** Restaurant at the Inter-Continental, **Raffles** at Stouffers, the Maui Prince's three very fine restaurants, the Grand Hyatt's five new restaurants and **Seasons** at the Four Seasons. Still, a lot of people in Wailea go to Lahaina for nightlife.

Wailea physically is closer to Upcountry but there is no travel advantage to Upcountry over Kaanapali. Wailea also is much closer in distance to Hana than any other populated part of Maui, but actually no closer than Kaanapali because Highway 36, the Highway to Hana, is the preferred route.

Three golf courses — Wailea Blue, Wailea Orange and the new Makena golf course — in addition to the previously existing Makena course are within 15 minutes' drive from any Wailea or Makena hotel. Kaanapali-Kapalua have six of the best courses in Hawaii within 30 minutes of any guest.

Wailea's luxury hotels are priced about the same as Kaanapali and Kapalua. Not far away are **Poolenalena Beach Park**, **Makena Beach**, **Black Sands Beach** as well as **Ahini-Kinau Reserve** — 2,000 acres of land and ocean with wonderful tidepools and coral reefs. The 1790 lava flow created Cape Kinau between Ahini Bay and **La Perouse Bay** is reached by a *very* poor road. Be prepared to explore the lava flows and thumb-shaped La Perouse Peninsula on foot, with snorkeling equipment, water and snacks.

Have breakfast at the **Wailea Golf Course Restaurant** or lunch at the **Makena Resort Golf Course Restaurant**, both of which have some of the best views on the Wailea/Makena Coast.

Shop at **Wailea Shopping Village** which has a **Maui's Best** for *Kula* onions, protea wreaths, hand-painted silk scarves, Hawaiian quilt pillowcases, natural fiber baskets, bamboo nose flutes, koa cutting boards and many more crafts and gift items.

Makena

Not that long ago, Makena was a fishing community and upcountry relatives came down from Kula, almost directly above on Haleakala's slopes, to trade vegetables for fish and to socialize. Later, old Makena Road, a remnant of the 16th century King's Highway encircling the island, became the province of refugee hippie surfers and their girlfriends from the mainland. Today, three golf courses envelop the luxurious **Maui Prince Hotel's** Makena resort. At least for the time being, Makena's magnificent **Oneloa Beach**, three-quarters of a mile long and 100-ft-wide, precariously stays undeveloped, hidden behind dense thickets of *kiawe* and *panini* bushes.

The **Makena Resort** adjoins the **Puu Olai** volcanic vent echoing crescent Moolokini, the offshore underwater volcano. **Big (Oneloa)** and **Little Makena** beaches hidden from the road are part of this partially hidden world,

along with **La Perouse Bay** further to the east, formed by lava flow from Haleakala's last eruption (*circa* 1790), now a marine preserve.

From Makena, take the *Hoapili* or **King's Trail** of ancient Hawaiians who used to travel the southern shore to Hana — **Makena Stables** provide rides. Follow this rough trail down to **Ahini-Kinau Nature Reserve** and **La Perouse Bay**. Witness the final phase of the struggle to preserve Hawaii's cultural and natural environment. Catch glimpses of scarce wildlife – axis deer, wild turkeys, ring-necked pheasants, chukar, California valley quail and the Hawaii owl. In winter, pause on a grassy knoll and watch humpback whales perform in choppy channels between nearby islands. Walks or trail rides later in the day almost always will encounter a magical Maui sunset lighting up the ocean and the islands of Lanai, Kahoolawe and Molokini.

Molokini Island

According to Hawaiian legend, *Pele's* dream-lover, *Lohi-au*, married a *mo'o* (dragon), incurring Pele's terrible wrath. The volatile fire goddess swiftly cut the *mo'o* in half – one-half became **Puu Olai** hill in Makena and the other half we know as Molokini.

Five blue miles from the white sands of Wailea and Makena, crescent-shaped Molokini Island surrounds the largest concentration of tropical fish in all of

Molokini Island, off Wailea and Kihei, a crescent rising from the ocean.

Hawaii. The 150-ft volcanic tuff cone (Maui's only one) opens to the north with a protective semi-circle embracing more than 200 species of fish, many varieties of seaweed, reef coral and a vast array of other sea creatures unwittingly enjoying the protection of

Molokini Shoal Marine Life Conservation District.

Only accessible by boat, Molokini can be reached in 20 minutes on the *Kai Kanani*, a sleek 46-ft sailing catamaran that departs from Makena. Arrangements for this wonderful morning

Beach boutique.

snorkeling can be made at the **Maui Prince's** Ocean Activities desk. Continental breakfast is served on the cruise which also provides snorkel gear, lunch and sodas. Non-snorkellers can arrange for a champagne sunset dinner sail which leaves from Maalaea Harbor on Mondays, Wednesday, and Fridays. Sail at 7:30am or noon on the 60-ft *Lavengro* out of Maalaea Harbor for Molokini Crater, with continental breakfast and a buffet lunch or on the *Trilogy* for a half-day excursion.

Kihei

While Wailea and Makena were evolving as planned developments, condo-

miniums were springing up like weeds west of Wailea along the Kihei Coast. Maalaea/Kihei became a six-mile stretch of increasingly haphazard development, mostly condos, cottage hostelries and a few hotels, with shopping centers in Kihei every few blocks — its main disadvantage.

Kehei's advantages over other locations of Maui consists of a combination of less expensive accommodation, ample sunshine and easy access to some very good beaches in Kihei (**Kamaole Beach Parks I, II and III** and **Keawakapu Beach**), in Wailea (**Mokapu, Ulua, Wailea,** and **Polo**) and in Makena (**Big and Little Makena, Black Sands Beach,** and **Poolenalena**). Kihei is also closer to Lahaina and west Maui then

Maui's resort coastline of great beaches.

any place in Upcountry.

Moderately-priced condominiums are plentiful. Some of the beaches and beachfront parks are among the most attractive on Maui and in Hawaii and usually no further than across the road from these accommodations. Some of these condominiums, like **Nani Kai Hale**, have minimum stay requirements of seven days in season. Ask about off-season discounts, rental car and airport pick up packages and air conditioning if it's important to you.

West Maui

Highway 30 (Honoapiilani Highway) circles west Maui. Full of contrasts, on the north side is **Kahakuloa**, a pictur-esque fishing village. Along the south coast, where affluent vacationers con-gregate, two well-planned resorts – 750-acre **Kapalua Resort** and 500-acre **Kaanapali Resort** – 10-miles apart, con-nected by condominiums and homes along the bays of Piilani.

Lahaina is the shopping capital of Maui, especially for art. In the heart of the waterfront shopping district is the historical and cultural center of the town and the oceanfront strip, where sailing charters, cruises, snorkeling and scuba excursions and other watersports take off. Lahaina's only shopping competi-tion comes from Kaanapali's **Whaler's Village**, a large open-air oceanfront shopping center which includes a unique

Old Lahaina town by the sea.

whaling museum.

Kapalua Resort has a few gourmet restaurants and chic boutiques, Napili has a few more small stores, boutiques and restaurants. Outside of Lahaina, rest and relaxation are the vacationers' primary activities in addition to golf.

Lahaina

Kamehameha conquered Maui and established a seat of power in Lahaina in 1795. The state's first capital, Lahaina proved very attractive to Hawaiian royalty. Out of 21 spouses, the king's favorite wife, Kaahumanu and his sacred wife, Keopuolani, were Mauians, which certainly says a lot for Maui's native charm.

Drawing on a long history of the native, whaler and foreigner's infatuation with the town, Lahaina's modern character has emerged from a potent mix of purposeful whaler debauchery and missionary soul-saving. Missionaries arrived in Lahaina in 1823 only to find it had become the "hellhole of the Pacific". The whalers' dream of uninhibited Polynesian women swimming out to meet their ships understandably was the Congregationalists' vile nightmare. Mission homes were actually cannon-balled in conflicts that ensued.

The early 19th century whaling capital of the world, Lahaina became the capital of the Hawaiian islands in 1843 when Kamehameha III moved the royal seat from Honolulu. Battles be-

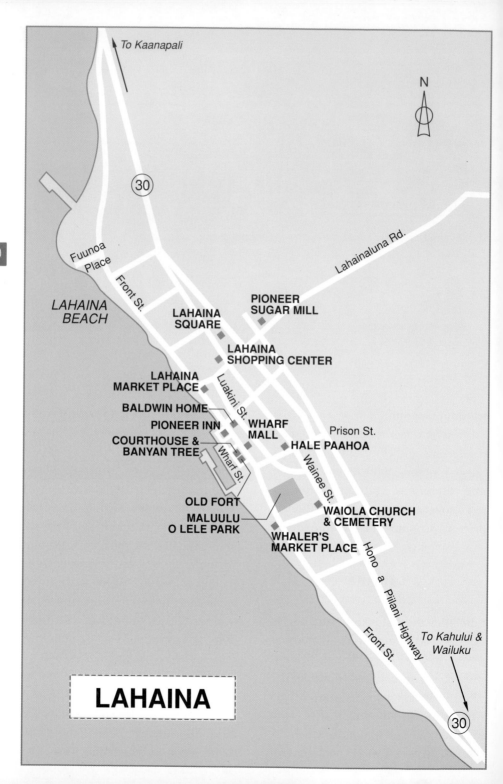

LAHAINA

At work on scrimshaw.

tween whalers and missionaries over sin and degradation were over soon thereafter when refined oil replaced whale oil. In the aftermath, the waterfront town of Lahaina was left with not much more than the charm of its ramshackle storefronts intact and between November and early May, increasing numbers of whales happily cavorting offshore. After Lahaina lost its economic purpose and fell into disrepair, locals and the Federal Government had the uncommon good sense in 1966 to declare 37 acres of the town's ramshackle buildings a national historic landmark. The **Lahaina Restoration Foundation** began several decades of successful restoration.

The vacation hub of the Valley Isle,

Lahaina preserves itself as a living museum of the whaling era which, not accidentally, benefits local shopping, especially contemporary marine art sales. The eclectic vitality along Front Street is magnetic. Even visitors who find the honky-tonk hard to take after a while keep coming back for more.

Since the 1970s, the town's legacy of whaling and whales has turned Lahaina into Maui's number one tourist attraction. Following the development of the Kaanapali resort from 1970-1989, Lahaina's population increased by 400 per cent (actually only a few thousand people). Commercial space doubled from 1987-1990, heralding the beginning of another phase of Lahaina's growth as one of Hawaii's premier tour-

Scrimshaw, an old and caring art.

ist destinations.

When the much-needed Lahaina by-pass is built in the 1990s, relieving gridlock conditions on Honoapiilani Highway and in Lahaina, another spurt of tourist-oriented commercial development will probably be launched.

Kaanapali plans to add 3,200 more resort units covering hundreds of acres on both sides of Honoapiilani Highway, thousands of residential units, new shopping centers, unique water-oriented entertainment ("Living Reef") and Hawaiiana ("Hawaiian Sea Village and Living Arts") complexes, a 600-acre Olowalu resort complex, Maui Ocean Center and much more.

Structures from the early 1900s remaining on Front Street protected as National Historic Landmarks salvage Lahaina's charm from tacky souvenir shops (interspersed with some high quality craft shops and many art galleries).

Unfortunately, many late-1800s buildings were destroyed in the fire of 1917, so "old" today refers to missionary buildings from the 1830s or buildings built in the 1920s.

Historic remnants of maritime, whaling, missionary and royal family history (the **Old Fort**, the **Waiola Church** and **Cemetery**, the **Courthouse**, the **Baldwin House Museum**, the **Lahainaluna School**) restored by the Lahaina Restoration Foundation are open to the public.

Pick up a *Lahaina Historical Guide* at the visitors center kiosk or a County of

Carthaginian rests at a Lahaina pier.

Maui Historic Commission brochure ("*Lahaina: A Walking Tour of Historic and Cultural Sites*") at the **Baldwin House Museum** on Front Street. Rev. Dwight Baldwin's whitewashed home contains the furnishings of the physician and his family from the 1830s to the 1860s.

Old and new wings of the landmark **Pioneer Inn** near the sprawling old **Banyan Tree** provide the least expensive accommodations in town.

The Inn's **Old Whaler's Grog Shop** facing the *Carthaginian II* is a perfect place to watch Lahaina's sunsets. *Carthaginian II* is a replica of the 19th century brig on which missionaries from New England sailed to Hawaii. The **Whale Report Center** next to it provides up-to-date information about the

best places to spot whales. In addition to whale-watching, Lahaina is most identified with art galleries. In front of the Banyan tree is the **Lahaina Courthouse** (1859). The Lahaina Art Society occupies the former jail in the Courthouse — the **Old Jail Gallery** and holds the Saturday Banyan Tree Fair, where artists display their art for sale. In two decades, Lahaina has grown into one of the top art gallery centers in the United States. Most of its galleries are along Front Street and a few are on intersecting Lahainaluna Road and Dickenson Street.

The **Village Galleries'** main gallery, located just down the street from Lahaina Coolers, exhibits more than 50 local artists at any one time at two

Après-canoe fun on the beach.

Village Gallery locations in Lahaina (120 Dickenson Street and The Cannery), and at the Embassy Grand Suites in Kaanapali. Genuine *aloha* is offered by friendly and extremely knowledgeable people working at the galleries for many years.

The Cannery on Honoapolani Highway also includes **Maui on My Mind**, with its fine handcraft (fiber blankets, ceramics, wind chimes, koa wood) and paintings of local artists.

Simplify your quest for the right art or crafts at the **Art Informational Desk of Maui** on Lahainaluna Road to find out about the latest exhibits. Most galleries are open Friday night ("art night" in Lahaina).

The **Maui Marine Art Expo** held annually Feb-Mar at the Maui Inter-Continental in Wailea, organized by Coast Galleries, has its competitive counterpart in Lahaina Galleries' **Ocean Arts Festival**, Jan-Mar. Ever since Yankee whalers began carving teeth, bones and baleen of whales, Lahaina has been the world's largest scrimshaw source.

Good examples are found at **Lahaina Scrimshaw** along with artifacts, ornaments and jewelry from the Pacific next door at the **South Sea Trading Post**. **The Wo Hing Temple**, a museum depicting Chinese contributions to the island, is another Lahaina Restoration Foundation project, originally constructed by Chinese plantation laborers.

The **Lahaina Whaling Museum**

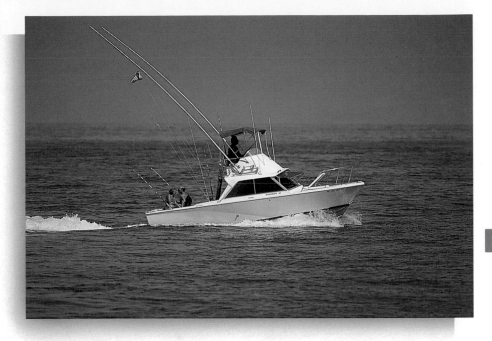

Out marlin fishing.

displays old photographs and a wide variety of whaling artifacts and paraphernalia. Established by the owner of Crazy Shirts, it's free and open 9am-10pm daily.

Lahaina Printsellers stocks antique maps and engravings in all of its branches.

Kaanapali to Kapalua

The **Kaanapali Resort**, four miles north of Lahaina, contains six hotels, a shopping center, the Whalers Village Museum and Shopping Complex and three 18-hole golf courses. Only a few of the hotels and condos or their grounds in the Kaanapali Resort are attractions in

themselves. The **Sheraton Maui Hotel**, the first hotel in Kaanapali was built on **Black Rock** (*Puu KeKaa*) peninsula, from which divers jump at sundown into the ocean as part of a torchlighting ceremony. **Whaler's Village Shopping Complex** and two **Royal Kaanapali championship golf courses** are neighbors.

The **Hyatt Regency Maui** and the even more lavishly decorated **Westin Maui** are replete with multimillion dollar Asian and South Pacific sculpture, art and artifacts, like outdoor museums. The much less ostentatious **Kaanapali Alii** condominium is surrounded by beautifully landscaped grounds.

Kaanapali Beach Hotel is the smallest and least expensive accommodation in Kaanapali. Modestly-furnished rooms varying mainly in views are perfectly adequate.

The best value in Kaanapali are condominiums within walking distance of beaches, golf links and tennis courts, with kitchens, perhaps more than one bath and bedroom, priced on the basis of size and not number of occupants. None is better than the **Maui Eldorado Resort**, next to the 11-court **Royal Lahaina Tennis Ranch**, with three swimming pools to supplement the beach across the golf course.

Al fresco dining in the Hyatt Regency Maui's **Swan Court** is almost a theatrical event, with tiered seating overlooking lush landscaping, waterfalls, flamingos, swans and penguins, antiques and sculpture etc. The menu is enormous in every category but you pay dearly to dine in this stunning environment.

Between Kaanapali and Kapalua is Maui's largest concentration of hotels and condominiums (even though Kihei usually is accorded the dubious honor of being the "condominium capital of Maui").

Along Honoapiilani Highway which circles west Maui, there are six bays between Kaanapali and the turn back to Kahului. Kaanapali's beach extends to Honokowai and then beaches periodically reappear on an otherwise rocky coastline until lovely beaches surface at Napili and Kapalua.

Travelers who want to stay near Lahaina and Kaanapali without paying Kaanapali prices should look for accommodation in Honokowai and Napili, next door to Kapalua. The Maui Sands or the Honokowai Palms in Honokowai are your best moderate-priced deals.

Low-rise accommodation around **Napili Bay**, just south of Kapalua Bay, range from expensive to luxury. One of the area's best values, **Coconut Inn**, is about a quarter mile from the beach. Napili condos share the same view of Molokai across the channel as Kapalua Bay, the same cool trade winds of northwest Maui. Rooms at the **Mahina Surf**, **Napili Point** and especially the **Napili Kai Beach Club** are comparably tasteful. The difference between rooms in Napili and Kapalua Bay lies in luxury and amenities like air conditioning in addition to wooden ceiling fans and big marble baths. However, Kapalua's two great golf courses are available to non-guests.

Kapalua Bay's remoteness adds appropriately to its exclusivity and quiet splendor. A new **Ritz-Carlton** is going up on the Resort, the chain's second hotel in the Neighbor Islands. Adjoining the 200-unit **Kapalua Bay**'s 18 acres, 143 condos of **Kapalua Villas** spread over a wide expanse of manicured green hillside sloping to the sea and three marvelous beaches, surrounded by three of Hawaii's finest 18-hole golf courses. Nowhere on Maui at sea level are the ocean views better. The Villas and Kapalua Bay deluxe hideaways have the added advantage of sharing on the premises two of Maui's best restaurants — the **Plantation Veranda** and the **Bay Club**.

Kapalua's most distinctive shops for browsing include **Distant Drums**, a veritable small museum of Pacific artifacts such as Balinese handcrafts, masks and primitive objects from the South Pacific, and South American artifacts.

Lovely coral and shells for collectors and others are displayed at **By the Bay**. Highway 30 leads to a cluster of lovely "hidden" beaches surrounded by cliffs between Kapalua and Honokohau Bay where it becomes Route 340. Along this northwestern shore, the road climbs and follows the curvature of high sandstone cliffs before turning into a dirt road full of ruts and potholes to picturesque **Kahakuloa**. Nearby, look for one of Maui's best hiking trails into the mountains. (Route 340 is reminiscent of Route 31 past Kipahulu where for seven miles the pavement gives way to dirt as the road rises along seaside cliffs). Many car rental agencies forbid driving their cars around either the west Maui mountains or the southeast coast. A series of valleys along the very scenic north shore create a mini-*pali* of spine-backed ridges rising toward Puu Kukui (5,788 ft).

Past lush gulches heading towards the plantation town of Waihee, surrounded by canefields covering the slopes of foothills, the road improves again on its way to Kahului. Route 340 passes remnants of great *heiaus* – Halekii and Pihana Kalani – dating back 300-400 years.

Central Maui

The trip from the Kahului Airport to Lahaina or Kihei does not inspire visitors to return and explore the central area of the Valley Isle. Ranging from uninteresting to downright ugly, only the heavily-advertised **Maui Tropical Botanical Garden** lures back large numbers of visitors, with its 45-minute **Tropical Express** train-ride through 50 of the plantation's 120 acres: a *paniolo* barbecue, hayride and other entertainment is offered three nights a week 5:30-8:30pm.

Kahului

Kahului, frequently bypassed by vacationers, offers a number of worthwhile attractions for people with special interests — for birdwatchers, the former royal fishpond, **Kanaha Pond Wildlife Sanctuary**, sheltering the rare Hawaiian stilt; for history buffs, a photo-mural exhibit, working scale-model of a sugar factory, artifacts of the sugar plantation era and a museum shop with unique items at the **Alexander & Baldwin Sugar Museum** (free for children); for Hawaiian fine and performing arts enthusiasts, the new **Maui Community Art and Cultural Center;** and for children of all ages, mainly farm animals and large variety of native Hawaiian plants at the **Maui Zoological and Botanical Garden** (admission free) off Kaahumanu Avenue.

Kahului's three large shopping centers look unexceptional. Few tourists would expect to find excellent espresso and croissants, deliciously fresh onion soup (with Maui onions) or a first-rate picnic basket emporium and walls full of local art, in the **Kaahumanu Shopping Center** at **CD Rush's Café**. **Maui's Best** has a tempting display of Island Princess macadamia nut brittle, fudge, white chocolate-coated Kona coffee beans and other sweets and aromas which you have to pass in order to get to a very large and wide selection of quality Maui craft items.

Another of downtown Kahului's delightful surprises are the croissants, cappucino, exotic teas, excellent pesto pasta salad, quiches, cheesecakes, bagels and other goodies at **Sir Wilfred's** in the otherwise drab **Maui Mall**.

Wailuku

Cross the bridge over Wailuku Gulch to more interesting and attractive Wailuku, administrative center of Maui sitting in the foothills of the west Maui mountains. Kahului's Kaahumanu Avenue turns seamlessly into Wailuku's Main Street, which leads to High Street, "downtown" Wailuku. Three miles from Wailuku, at the end of Iao Valley Road (an extension of Main St), is **Iao Valley State Park** with its famous **Iao Needle**, a 1,200-ft green-carpeted cinder cone (actually 2,250-ft above sea level). The road ends dramatically at the vertical

crater walls of the **Puu Kukui** volcano.

The oldest church on Maui — the more than 150-year-old picturesque **Kaahumanu Congregational Church** — sets the historic tone for Wailuku. Opposite the newer federal, state and county administrative buildings on High Street, between Main and Aupini streets, and behind the **Kaahumanu Church**, is the **Wailuku Historic District**. The old Bailey House, *Hale Hoikeike* (**Maui Historical Society Museum**) contains pre- and post-missionary era displays and one on the history and techniques of making *tapa* cloth, the Polynesian bark cloth that Hawaiians developed to its fullest extent. The museum's Hawaiian quilt exhibit is quite exceptional.

The home of Edward and Caroline Bailey was once the first Hawaiian girls' boarding school on the island (in 1833, the Central Female Boarding Seminary). *Hale Hoikeike* tells the story of two major eras of Hawaiian history. Downstairs are displays of pre-contact Polynesian life and artifacts and upstairs are scenes from the missionary era. Former missionary and teacher (as well as artist, architect, musician, botanist and writer) Edward Bailey epitomized the missionary-sugar plantation connection, becoming the first manager of the **Wailuku Sugar Company**. A small adjoining building houses Bailey's paintings that show early Wailuku. The small **Hale Hoikeike Gift Shop** is one of the best places on the island to find a variety of Hawaiian crafts, from *tapa* purses to *lauhala*.

Iao Needle.

Before driving into Iao Valley, a right at Market Street leads to **Happy Valley**, the former red-light district that retains its weathered charm.

Iao Valley State Park and nearby Wailuku are metaphors for contemporary Maui's connection to its past his-tory – scenes of bloody inter-island war-fare in the 18th century are today peace-ful places reflecting three major histori-cal events and periods:

• the arrival of American Protes-tant missionaries from New England in 1820 (just a year after the overthrow of

Heritage Garden.

traditional Hawaiian religion by Queen Kaahumanu after King Kamehameha's death in 1819);

• the development of sugar plantations by the sons of missionaries (Alexander & Baldwin, Inc.) beginning in the 1850s (and also pineapple plantations in the 1900s);

• importation of Chinese, Portuguese, Japanese, Puerto Rican, Korean, Spanish, and Filipino laborers, creating Hawaii's multi-ethnic society with its very strong Japanese cultural influence.

Massive **Pihana** and **Halekii Heiaus**, one above another, sitting on a sand dune above Wailuku are monuments of precontact Hawaii whose sites offer spectacular views of the valley. The landmark white stone **Kaahumanu Church**, the fourth built on the same site, named after remarkable Queen Kaahumanu and the oldest church on Maui, embodies the story of early missionary history. Simple wooden and tin-roofed houses on the back streets of today's Wailuku reflect the plantation era.

Iao Valley

Except in foul weather, the beautifully landscaped oriental gardens, with pavilions for Japanese, Chinese and other ethnic groups in Iao Valley's **Kepaniwai Park** and **Heritage Gardens** provide a very restful stopping point, perhaps for a picnic, swimming or wading in the pools. Heavy rainfall in the valley 2250-ft above sea level ensures incredible growth for all flora and plenty of wild fruit in season for hikers. The end of the road in Iao Valley State Park holds the spire of moss-green lava rock called Iao Needle rising 1,200 ft against the background of green cliffs that are twice as high.

Up Country

Take the Hana Highway (36) and then Haleakala Highway (37) to the town of **Makawao**, a mere speck on the western slopes of Haleakala. The Upcountry area between **Pukalani** to the southwest of Makawao, **Paia** downslope to the northwest, **Haiku** to the north and **Kula** to the southeast is the heart and "motherload" of "New Age" lifestyles, the largest concentration of artists on Maui. It is a lush world oriented towards its own historical fabric and local lifestyles.

Views are marvelous from **Pukalani** ("hole in the heavens"), the first town above Kahului en route to Makawao or Haleakala; northward on Route 400 winding down the lush slopes to **Pauwela**; directly above Makawao from the eucalyptus-lined roadways and fields of beautiful **Olinda**; westward down to the valley and over to the eastern side of west Maui; or southward along Route 37 to **Ulupalakua Ranch**, Maui's largest (30,000 acres). Ulupalakua raises about 5,000 heads of Hereford and Angus cattle.

Routes 37 and 377 are a botanical tour of Upcountry's proteas at the **Maui Agricultural Research Center**, where the first protea were planted in the mid-1960s. Between 7:30am and 3:30pm, stop at the office on Copp Road off Route 37 to sign in before touring the center. Just up Copp Road is **Maui Sunburst Farm** growing 16-acres of protea varieties waiting to be picked and shipped to the Mainland.

Continuing towards Ulupalakua, the entrance to **Kula Botanical Gardens** is on the left just past the intersection with Route 377. The gardens grow native and exotic trees and plants, including protea. **Sunrise Protea Farm** on Route 377 offers another wide selection of proteas for export.

Upcountry extends over to Ulupalakua Ranch on the Kula side of Mt. Haleakala and was first planted with a thousand acres of sugar by former US Navy Capt James Makee. King Kalakaua (the "Merry Monarch") was a guest in the white wooden Ulupalakua building with green trim that used to be owned by the Baldwin family. Cattle, sheep and even elk graze on green rolling Ulupalakua hillsides above Wailea and Kihei, combining some of Maui's most beautiful landscapes and best views.

Upcountry is as much a state of mind and spirit as it is an amazing variety of physically and climatically different areas that flow seamlessly into one another. It is part thick forests, part huge and remote mountain ranches

Bicycle touring is a great way to see Maui.

and pasturelands, swathes of wild flowers tumbling across hillsides, flower and vegetable nurseries thriving on rich Kula earth and climate, **Poli Poli State Park**, a thriving winery and magnificent and mysterious Haleakala itself.

Makawao

A rural area first farmed by Portuguese immigrants, **Makawao** acquired a slightly western flavor from third and fourth-generation *Paniolos*, cowboys working in surrounding ranches, like **Haleakala Ranch** up Olinda Road. Makawao is headquarters of the 20,000-acre Haleakala Ranch, but it is not a cowboy or a *paniolo* town. Rather,

Makawao is a small mountain town near large cattle and horse ranching areas which holds a "Wild West" rodeo on the Fourth of July. Except for Waimea-North Kohala on the Big Island (which is covered by the 250,000-acre-Parker Ranch), Makawao is unlike anyplace in all the islands.

Before World War II, the only local businesses of note in Makawao were **Komoda's Store and Bakery** (with its famous cream puffs) which opened in the 1930s, and **Kitada's Kau Kau Korner**, serving really inexpensive meals since 1947. The **Hui No'eau**, an afternoon painting group of wealthy patrons was already in existence before the war and was transformed into the local art center in the mid-1970s when artists began to congregate in the Makawao and Upcountry.

As a sign of the times, in 1973 the largest stove store in Hawaii, **Silversword Stoves**, opened on Baldwin Avenue to take the chill off Upcountry nights. Nearby at the **Makawao Steak House**, the town's main claim to culinary fame, serves real prime rib, fresh fish and fettucine. Gayle St. Johns' **Collections**, across from Komodo's, was an early business pioneer catering to the surrounding area's refugees from the mainland, selling casual, hip and not too fancy stuff (an eclectic mix of soaps, candles, baskets, clothing, hand tooled leather accessories, and jewelry).

Kitada's on Baldwin Avenue still serves wonderful *saimin*, plate lunches and chicken *hekka* in a run-down looking storefront, as it has for generations. Open 6am-1:30am daily except Sundays, Kitada's is Old Makawao just as new Makawao is the "yupcountry" **Casanova Italian Restaurant and Deli**, since 1986 has served some of the best pasta and pesto on Maui, it also operates the one and only nightclub in Upcountry. (Try the linguine al pesto, ziti marinara, tagliatelle with tiger prawns, or spinach ricotta lasagne for lunch.)

Casanova's arrival in Makawao seemed to mark a turning point for the town. David Warren moved his art studio to a small frame building on Baldwin Avenue, across from the recently refurbished and first-rate Makawao Steak House. Boutique newcomer **Maui Moorea Legends** opened down the street

from Collections. Cheryl Holmes' **Coconut Classics** introduced a Hawaiiana mixture of things for gifts. And a laid-back refugee from New York opened **Country Cupboard**, a fast-food shop and gift emporium with a chalkboard menu on the corner of Makawao and Baldwin.

These boutiques and shops all share the same cozy comfort that makes Makawao's historic clapboard buildings and the charming town so enjoyable. Quaintness and touches of seediness somehow still remain mostly undisturbed in Makawao while it undergoes a transition from *paniolo* (cowboy) town to upscale marketplace and getaway for more or less permanent residents, in addition to tourists passing through. Upgrading in Makawao typically means a fresh coat of paint.

New and old art galleries on Baldwin Avenue stay in character — all visibly different and unconventional. **Klein Fein and Nielson) Gallery** on Baldwin Avenue fills a simple, tiny two-room structure with excellent art and disarmingly honest opinions about local art and artists. The **David Warren Gallery** and **Stan Ort's Gallery** are casual and friendly studios unlikely to intimidate browsers or provoke an aesthetic controversy.

Look for the artists in Beverly Gannon's **Haliimaile General Store**. From being a short-lived deli in the old general store, once a market for pineapple plantation workers, her innocent restaurant experiment took off to become one of Maui's most successful and best kept secrets of gourmet dining.

Hui No'eau Visual Arts Center

For more than 50 years, the nonprofit **Hui No'eau Visual Arts Center** in Makawao has been a magnet for the Upcountry's artists. Four decades after Ethel Baldwin first called together prospective members of what later became the Hui No'eau, the organization took over her grand Mediterranean-style Kaluanui estate in 1976, with its old pines and European-style garden. Today its nine acres are a historic landmark and the center of art exhibits and education in Upcountry.

With almost 700 members from Hawaii and all over North America, the Hui No'eau continues its historic role as a serene hotbed of art activity.

Over the years, Hui No'eau's classes in ceramics, weaving, papermaking with fibers, composition, *raku*, calligraphy, drawing, printmaking and basketry have brought in some of the Hawaii's finest artists — John Young, Jean Charlot, Helen Gilbert, Hiroki Morinoue, Chiu Leong among others. The Hui sponsors the juried **Art Maui** show in spring, the island's major art event of the year and an outstanding juried membership show in September. The annual **Christmas Craft Fair** in the beginning of December displays a wonderful assortment of gift possibilities.

Kula & Olinda

Upcountry is a cool, lush, laid-back mountain retreat. The B&B's in **Kula** and nearby **Olinda** are among the best anywhere in Hawaii and are an important part of the "Upcountry experience."

Jody Baldwin's **Kilohana B&B** is in a perfect location from which to drive up Haleakala at sunrise or anytime. From the 3,600-ft level of Kula's slopes, the porch and spacious garden look out over a panoramic view of green pastures dotted with cattle to the west Maui mountains, Maalaea Bay and the Kihei Coast, Lanai offshore, with equally magnificent sunsets and dawns. Jody's new cottage in the front yard offers privacy and tasteful comfort.

A few miles in the opposite direction from the Mt Haleakala road is the **Kula Botanical Gardens** on Highway 37 at the 10-mile marker. Nearby **Kilohana** is also one of the closest places to stay for a visit to **Tedeschi Vineyards** on the Ulupalakua Ranch.

Another outstanding Upcountry B&B, with marvelous views and surroundings, is Stewart & Shaun **McKay's B&B**. At the top of Olinda Road, 4,000-ft up the slopes of Haleakala, the McKay's manor house sits in the midst of a 12-acre protea flower farm. Beautiful, winding **Olinda Road**, five miles above Makawao, is one of the loveliest drives in Hawaii. Over the driveway, a Scottish coat of arms confirms what you already know about Stewart – his heart and soul mix Scotland and Upcountry, which happen to be remarkably compatible.

In the midst of a pineapple farm, the **Gildersleeves' B&B** pole house has three attractively furnished guest bedrooms with private baths.

Highway 377 leads to the **Poli Poli Springs Recreation Area** and the **Kula Forest Reserve**. After a rugged but beautiful drive through towering trees on Waipoli Road off Highway 377, which definitely requires a four-wheel drive vehicle, a four-mile hike leads to spectacular views from the 6000-ft level on slopes over Ulupalakua. If you decide to drive to Poli Poli by yourself, consider staying overnight or for several days at the Park's three-bedroom cabin, which has to be reserved well in advance with the Division of Parks.

Kula Lodge's five rustic chalet-style cabins are next to Route 37, a few miles before the turn-off to Route 377 (Kekaulike Avenue) up Haleakala. The Lodge's restaurant (open daily for breakfast, lunch, and dinner) looks out onto a wooded slope with protea gardens just below. Downstairs is the **Curtis Wilson Cost Gallery**. A Californian artist residing in Kula, Cost works in all sizes and media but favors transparent and opaque watercolors. Kula's idyllic rural highland countryside lends itself perfectly to his style of art. Further along the way to Ulupalakua Ranch is the **Kula Botanical Gardens** with its native koas, kukui trees, Norfolk Island pine, bamboo orchids, proteas and native and imported flora. Besides the amazing flora, the gardens are a perfect spot for a picnic lunch.

Kula is famous for its protea, one of the most amazing and beautiful varieties of flowers, with huge blossoms in 1,400 varieties. These botanical wonders are grown by Upcountry farmers like John Hiroshima (**Sunrise Market and Protea Farm**). Like just about everyone else you'll meet along Highways 377 and 378, John thinks that Kula is "God's Country". Kula's serene rolling meadows and ranch country are dotted with cows and groves of *koa* and mango; roadways twist through eucalyptus and Norfolk pine past old clapboard, tin-roofed homes and elegant contemporary dwellings, seen through brilliant sunshine or fog and rain are reminiscent of the peace and beauty of the English lake country. The special experience of Upcountry touring should include a visit to Sunrise Market or another of Kula's small farms. David and Lisa Morrison have only been in the protea business a few years and moved from Indiana to take up farming at Upcountry **Proteas Farm** (down from the Kula Lodge). Other local farmers also welcome visits (with just a little advance notice to be polite) — Masaru and Celestine Uradomo's **onion farm** and Ray Nishiyama's **Maui Carnations**.

Hiking Haleakala

With 32 miles of hiking trails, two campsites and three 12-person cabins inside

Hiking in Haleakala Crater.

Haleakala Crater (guests selected by National Park Service lottery three months in advance), there are ample opportunities for exploring the mountain's awesome moonscape. The **National Park Service** offers guided tours three days a week. **Pony Express Tours** leads half and full-day horseback trips through the crater.

Trails outside and inside the crater offer completely different hiking experiences. With over eight miles of spectacular views of Maui and the Neighbor Islands, **Skyline Trail** (6-$^1/_2$ miles) starting at 9,750 ft near the top of Haleakala, descends about 3,000 ft to **Haleakala Ridge Trail** (1.6 miles), which descends about another 1,000 ft.

Sliding Sands Trail, a ten mile hike within the crater, starts near the Visitors Center and descends steeply for 3,000 ft to Kapalaoa cabin and on to Paliku cabin and the campground a few hundred yards away. **Halemauu Trail** joins Sliding Sands Trail near Paliku cabin after descending 1,400 ft and passing Holua cabin and campground along a 10-mile trek from the road above Park Headquarters. Sliding Sands Trail and Halemauu Trail can be combined with **Kaupo Trail** — a descent of 10,000 ft and 18 miles (one-way) through Kaupo Gap to Kaupo. Drivers have to meet hikers here. Starting the drive to Kaupo from Ulupalakua results in a shorter trip and a road that is in better condition than the one from Hana.

An adventurous and memorable

way to reach Haleakala Crater is an overnight horseback trip up Kaupo Trail through Kaupo Gap with Charlie Aki.

Hikers should plan to spend a morning in the **Waikamoi Preserve** on the Hana side of Maui, which requires a permit and membership of the Nature Conservancy of Hawaii. Additional miles of hiking trails through **Polipoli Spring State Recreation Area** on the southwestern slopes of Haleakala in the Kula Forest Reserve pass through exotic forests intentionally imported at the beginning of the 20th century. Careful reforestation has made Polipoli Spring a place of great beauty.

Another very memorable alternative is a half or full-day tour of the crater with **Thompson Riding Stables** or **Pony Express Tours**. Good weather or bad, streams of **Cruiser Bob**'s helmeted bicycle enthusiasts 9-90 years old cycle down the 38-mile stretch from Haleakala's summit to Paia — a three-hours journey, with a welcome breakfast break at Kula Lodge (cyclers eat a continental breakfast in Paia before starting). Essentially the same bicycle tour is provided by **Maui Downhill**.

Ulupalakua Ranch

Alfred Franco's **Grandma's Coffee House** on Route 37 is off-the-beaten-path except for locals who know just where to find a delicious cup of *cappucino* after a stroll on idyllic **Thompson Road** (two miles long) with great views of Ulupalakua Ranch and Wailea below. Alfred Franco is a fourth-generation Upcountry resident, one of 68 grandchildren of the Grandma after whom the coffee shop is named. Grandma used to pick, process and roast her own coffee. She is over 90 years old. If you have time to see more of Kula's picturesque landscape on foot, drive Highway 37 to **Kokee**, park on **Polipoli Road** and walk for about 40 minutes parallel with Highway 37, through a built-up area up along the hillside.

Beyond Kula, high above the Wailea coast, Maui's largest ranch – Ulupalakua – covers 30,000 acres of Haleakala's southwest flank. Continue past the ranch headquarters to a lava rock building (former jail of the original Rose Ranch), today the tasting room and gift shop of Hawaii's only winery, **Tedeschi Vineyards and Winery**. Tedeschi makes good wine from purchased pineapples and more recently, an even better wine from Carnelian grapes grown at the 2,000-ft level. Taste Tedeschi's *Blanc de Noir* Hawaiian champagne, *Maui Blush* or *Maui Nouveau*. Open 9-5pm daily.

Ulupalakua's natural beauty comes through best at elevations over 3,500 ft. For such views, ride upslope on the Ranch's grassy trails with *Thompson Riding Stables* for at least a half-day.

Paia

The last stop for gas before reaching the fabled stretch of Hana Highway, **Paia**'s location has given the town a big boost from its former plantation headquarters status. Former plantation town, windsurfers' mecca next to Hookipa Bay and psychedelics' paradise in the 1960s, Paia has some of the peculiar ingredients essential for success as a hip Hawaiian shopping town. Add to Paia's delightful recipe for success a thriving and amazingly diverse community of fine craftspeople, ancient mom-and-pop stores dispensing *aloha* and tourist-oriented boutiques selling mostly apparel.

Born as a plantation community in the 1880s around an Alexander & Baldwin sugar mill, the **Alexander & Baldwin Sugar Museum** (9:30am-4pm, children under 6 free) is just down the road from the mill. The museum tells the story of 5-8,000 Hawaiians and immigrants from Japan and the Philippines populating Paia earlier in the century. Their separate communities, camps or villages in upper Paia clustered around the mill and each maintained their native language, customs, traditions, foods and festivals.

A half-mile down the road, lower Paia's stores, services and dining places survived a major fire in July 1930, the prolonged impact of a nearby marine camp during World War II, the dreadful *tsunumi* of April 1946, the post-War exodus of workers from camp communities to Kahului housing and an influx of hippies in the 1960s and 1970s while Paia itself was becoming a ghost town.

The tiny town's two main cross streets (Hana Highway and Baldwin Avenue) are lined with wooden storefronts that by statute cannot be altered. These preserved storefronts are colorfully painted and inscribed with hip names for casual clothing, imaginative surf and beach wear and an astonishing assortment of local arts and crafts, antiques, jewelry, objects fanciful and functional and occasionally plain junk. Eddie Flotte has painted Paia's buildings, landscapes and people for years and plans to continue doing so as long as the town's old character lives on. Look out for for Eddie-the-street-artist in a folding chair on some sidewalk in Paia or the vicinity. Visitors often "discover" Paia while heading to **Mama's Fish House** on the Hanaside of town for *opakapaka* in champagne or smoked fish mousse. Right in the middle of Paia, the Fish House draws discriminating diners from far afield on Maui.

The **Maui Crafts Guild** is reason enough for visiting Paia, representing over 50 of Maui's best artists spanning a wide spectrum of creations. Stop at **Dillon's Restaurant** in **Paia** for a breakfast of French toast with Kahlua before the three-hour trip to Hana.

Hana

Fill the gas tank, check the tires and windshield wipers. Drive slowly and carefully, especially around narrow, blind curves and stay on your side of the road. Picnics just around the corner on Baldwin Avenue is the best place to pick up a picnic lunch including local fruit, Maui potato chips and macadamia nut bread. Plan to stay overnight, making a reservation for accommodation well in advance. The magnificent scenery on the 51-mile road to Hana – carved into lava cliffs and winding through overhanging tropical foliage – across streams gushing down gullies, is the perfect entranceway to this primeval and remote resting place.

Highway 36 is no longer pitted and potholed for 30 nerve-racking miles. Nevertheless, it still takes a minimum of 3 hours to drive through 617 curves and across 56 one-lane bridges, stopping at some of the scenic viewpoints, lovely waterfalls, gardens and sundry other turn-offs/detours and attractions.

Past Pauwela, the straight and easy road starts curving through an incredible variety of vegetation. **Twin Falls** has a swimming hole and both **Waikamoi Ridge** and **Puohokamoa Falls** have lovely picnic areas. At **Kaumahina State Wayside**, viewpoints look off 3,000-ft cliffs to the black sand beach of **Honomanu Bay**, reached by a side-road along the gulch which drops to sea-level.

Above Keane Peninsula, visit the beautiful tropical gardens of **Keane Arboretum** and stop at **Keane Overlook** to view taro patches below before taking a sideroad onto the peninsula to an old Catholic church built of lava rock cemented with coral. After another detour to the farming and fishing village of **Wailua**, pull over at **Uncle Harry's Fruit Stand and Living Museum** for local fruit, hand crafted wood souvenirs made by Uncle Harry's family and to "talk-story".

Past Koolau Lookout, at **Puaa Kaa Park**, picturesque **Waikane Falls** and another waterfall flow into pools perfect for a refreshing dip before a picnic. Stunning views of the coast open from bluffs near the picturesque village of **Nahiku.** A few miles before Hana, **Waianapanapa Cave**, actually a lava tube, leads to a black sand beach in **Waianapanapa State Park.** One of Hawaii's largest remaining *hala* groves (also called pandunus) grows in this wildly beautiful area. *Hala* trees are male or female. The female *hala* bears fruit and the males have fragrant flowers; the female is soft inside and the male hard throughout, used for making bowls and other items requiring tough wood. The leaves (*lauhala*) are used for weaving and Hawaiians have used many parts of the tree for some practical and artistic purpose.

The Hana-Waianapanapa Coastal Trail, part of the ancient King's Highway, follows the coastline between Waianapanapa State Park and Hana Bay for three zig-zagging miles over volcanic rock past a *heiau*, blowhole and sundry caves.

Resorting Away

Look out on the right side of the road into Hana for nearby **Helani Gardens**, one of Hawaii's loveliest tropical bo-

Haleakala

Riding in the crater.

Haleakala is enormous. The 19-square-miles covered by Haleakala, its valleys, rain forests, gulches and other land forms, lie within a magnificent circumference of well over 150 miles that narrows to 21 miles at its crater. The incredibly scenic, waterfall-laced 54-mile road to Hana from Kahului passes through less than a third of this distance around "the house of the sun"

The lower slopes of Haleakala (Upcountry) are a splendid, pastoral mixture of vegetable, fruit and flower farming, sugarcane and pineapple fields yielding to rolling hills and pastureland, cattle and horses grazing amidst eucalyptus groves and wild flowers blooming on small tracts and huge ranch lands.

Cool air blows through the mornings and evenings, before and after comfortably warm days and the rich volcanic soil is perfect for growing almost anything. Sweet Kula onions are one delicious result.

Haleakala National Park, its **Kipahulu Valley** the rugged and remote area of virgin forest of **Waikamoi Preserve** is home to about one-third of Hawaii's endangered birds. Living within a magnificent canopy of *koa* and *ohia* trees, species include: the Maui honeycreeper and the crested honeycreeper – two of an at least thirty-seven species family, the Maui parrotbill, the scarlet and black *i'iwi*, the *'apapane* and others. Kipahulu Valley, reached from Hana, is better known for its beautiful **Oheo Gulch** (or the "Seven Sacred Pools").

Formed by two great valleys joined by erosion (Koolau and Kaupo), volcanic eruptions covered the area with lava and cinder cones. The largest dormant volcano in the world, Haleakala last erupted in 1790. At the **Haleakala Observatory Visitors Center,** two miles up the mountain, you learn that Hawaiians used the crater for centuries as a highway across the island.

From Kahului Airport area, the trip to the summit to view a (hopefully) spectacular sunrise, takes about 2 hours (from Makawao about 1-$^1/_2$ hours) covering 36 miles and rising 10,000 ft above sea level. First dial the **National Weather**

tanical gardens. Howard Cooper's 60 acres of carefully labelled plants is obviously a labor of love assisted by Hana's generous supply of rainfall.

Adapting to Hana's tranquil *aloha* spirit usually requires some time, assist-

ance from the hosts of accommodations and opportunities to "talk-story" with old-timers. All the hostelry in Hana, whether expensive or modest, will help you to slow down or they wouldn't exist in Hana in the first place. Hana may not

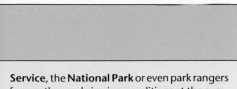

Service, the **National Park** or even park rangers for weather and viewing conditions at the summit. Driving up 10 miles of switchbacks, the early morning's destination is the **Puu Ulaula Overlook**, a glass-enclosed observation shelter sitting above a parking lot on a cinder cone next to **Science City**, a solar and lunar observatory of the University of Hawaii.

The crater floor – a wasteland 3000 ft below the rim filled with cinder cones and small craters – is more likely to be visible from **Leleiwi Overlook** (8,800 ft) and **Kalahaku Overlook** (9,325 ft), although you can only park at these overlooks on the way down. The purple, brown, yellow, black and other colors of the crater actually might be more vivid in the afternoon, but there is no telling

Northern and eastern Maui are generously watered by rain-clouds delivered by northeasterly tradewinds to the slopes of Haleakala. Emptied of their rain, the clouds leave southwestern Maui with the blessing of almost continuous sun. Within the huge crater itself (seven-miles long and two-miles wide), several micro-climates prevail. Nearly 200 inches of rain was recorded near Paliku cabin and as little as 12 inches on the southwestern side of the crater. The answer to how much rain-gear to bring on a crater hike depends on what part of it you are planning to hike. To be safe, assume that where you're going in the crater gets windy, wet and cold.

Day temperature in the crater is consistently between 55 and 75°F. and falls to freezing or below at night. The intensity of ultraviolet radiation at the bottom of the crater, 6,700 ft average altitude, necessitates a good sun-block while exploring this magnificent scene of volcanic desolation.

have many vacation units for rent, but the ones available are some of the best vacation values that you'll find in a remote South Pacific paradise.

An alternative to driving to Hana is a 15-minute flight from Kahului Airport on *Aloha Island Air* to **Hana Airport** (248-8208). **Dollar Car Rental** (248-8237) will send a car to pick you up. **Hana-Maui Resort** or **Hana Kai-Maui Resort Condominiums** will be there with a minibus if you're a guest.

Plenty of tourist literature about Hana is available starting with the State Visitor Information Kiosk in Kahului Airport and at the Maui Visitors Bureau. Don't miss five very special Hana area highlights:

• **Red Sand Beach** and cove, reached by a tricky footpath from the parking area at the end of Uakea Road, behind the Hana School and Hana Community Center;

• **Waianapanapa State Park**'s scenic ancient Hawaiian coastal trail to Hana over volcanic rock (requiring very sturdy shoes), which passes within a stone's throw of the State's 12 housekeeping cabins in a forest of *hala* trees;

• the very scenic, twisting road to **Oheo Gulch** ("Seven Sacred Pools") and the hike up the gulch to **Makahiku Falls**, or especially, for the more physically fit, the 1-1/2 miles through an exotic bamboo forest to **Waimoku Falls**;

• **Hana Ranch** trail rides along Hana's scenic coastline or to hidden waterfalls or four-wheel-drive ranch safari tours through unspoiled countryside to see their modern ranching system;

• by arrangement with the **Hotel Hana-Maui**, visit the otherwise inaccessible 15th Century **Piilanihale**, Hawaii's largest *heiau* (340' x 415' terraced

A popular stop on the Hana Highway.

stone platform) surrounded by bread-fruit and *hala* trees.

If you're a guest of the Hana-Maui, ask them to pack a picnic lunch for excursions to any of these locations.

The **Hana Cultural Center** (*Hale O Waiwai 'O Hana* or "Hana's House of Treasures") on Uakea Road displays artifacts from the area and handicrafts of local residents (10:30-5pm Mon-Sat, 10am-noon Sundays).

At the end of Uakea Road starts the path to beautiful and secluded Red Sand Beach.

The cluttered **Hasegawa's General Store**, one of Hawaii's famous institutions was burned down in 1990 and may be replaced by a new structure. Hopefully this delightful shopping land-mark will be around when you get there.

Stay for at least one night in Hana in order to experience some of these attractions. If you are traveling within a tight budget, try to reserve one of the fully furnished, not fancy but perfectly adequate housekeeping cabins that sleep up to six people next to Waianapanapa State Park – and stay several nights!

On the way into Hana, behind a Japanese gate on the left guarded by two stone lions, is the charming **Heavenly Hana Inn**. Around a common area designed in Japanese motif are four 2-bedroom garden suites, one in each corner of the building, with private bath and kitchenette and screened in *lanai*.

Other comfortable alternatives

Red Sand Beach at Hana.

managed by the Inn include a beach cottage on Hana Bay and **the red barn**, which is not a barn at all but a very roomy and homey cottage, next to Hasegawa's.

Hana Plantation Houses have a wide variety of attractive units — the **Lani Makaalae Studio** is very private with its own entrance to a tropical bath garden and jacuzzi tub/shower built into a deck under plumeria trees; **Lani Too**, a two-bedroom cottage in Japanese-Balinese style; and three other units on a beautifully landscaped five-acre site. Situated on a secluded black sand beach, a mile from the center of Hana, are the **Waikoloa Beach Houses** – two-bedroom cottages with the interior built of exotic woods and a separate, private

sleeping room with outdoor private bath and no kitchen.

The 19 private oceanview studios and one-bedroom apartments of the **Hana Kai-Maui Resort** condominiums on Uakea Road are only a few steps from a stony ocean beach. The *lanais* with lovely ocean views more than compensate for the plain rooms and lack of air-conditioning.

The **Hotel Hana-Maui**, an exclusive luxury retreat, was completely refurbished a few years ago to enhance its charm and elegance. In its garden setting, low-rise bungalows framed by orchids and plumeria reflect the Hawaii of a half-century ago combined with plenty of contemporary pampering and activity choices.

Cattle ranch on the rolling landscape of Hana.

Guided jeep tours to the rain forests, snorkeling off **Hamoa Beach**, horseback riding or hiking along mountain trails and other activities take advantage of **Hana Ranch** and Hana's lush surroundings. Three meals are included in the extravagant price. The hotel shut-tles its guests over to lovely Hamoa Beach, west of Hana town, which anyone can use, except for the hotel's private facilities.

The Hotel Hana-Maui has its own stables for all types of rides, from sun-up to sundown. Otherwise contact **Adven-**

excellent variety of meat, chicken, fish, vegetable and salad servings, 11am-3pm Above the Hana-Maui, Fusae Nakamura's **Aloha Cottages'**, six simple, cozy two-bedroom units seem to have grown up together with surrounding papaya and banana trees.

For your vacation pleasure, Stan and Suzanne Collins of **Hana Bay Vacation Rentals** have gathered many home, cabin and apartment choices in secluded shoreline or hillside locations.

Kipahulu/Oheo Gulch

South of Hana, private lands and roads conceal many *heiau* that Hawaiians must have built in tropical terrain reminiscent of temples proliferating in Guatemalan jungles.

A terrible winding road through gorgeous terrain brings too many tourists to large parking lots near the "Seven Sacred Pools" that are neither "sacred" nor "seven." Water cascades down **Oheo Gulch** through a few dozen pools to the ocean along a path of rocky ledges perfect for picnics and swimming. About a mile beyond Oheo Gulch, the area's famous part-time resident, Charles Lindbergh, returned with his wife, Ann Morrow Lindbergh, to spend his last days near one of Hawaii's most precious and beautiful valleys, **Kipahulu**. He was too far gone to trek into the wilds beyond Kipahulu Falls, but being near them for a few days was, as he put it, "better than a month in New York."

tures on Horseback about their half-day excursions. Besides the ultra-expensive **Hana Maui**, the only places to eat in Hana are **Tutu's** for salads, sandwiches and plate lunches and the **Hana Ranch Restaurant**, on the hill across the Post Office. From the take-out window, breakfast and lunch are inexpensive; inside, the buffet lunch offers an

Molokai's two extinct volcanoes — **Mauna Loa** (1,381 ft) on the dry west and **Kama-kou** (4,970 ft) in the eastern tropical rainforest — define the main profile of this long, narrow, mountainous island. The island derives its name from a large prairie on its west side (*molo*, "barren" *kai*, "sea"). The north or windward shore's magnificent ravines, shaped by 245 inches of rain, terminate at immense cliffs along the seacoast (claimed to be the highest in the world). These secluded valleys, forested mountains and beaches form the essence of Molokai.

Ancient Molokai was a spiritual sanctuary whose *kahunas* were regarded with special reverence and feared by *kahunas* on other islands, nobility and commoners alike. Molokai's *mana* was the strongest in the archipelago. Today the island is still a retreat for its roughly 6,000 residents, including the largest percentage of pure-blooded

Kaulapapa, for scenic views.

Molokai

277

Molokai, the friendly isle.

Hawaiians in the islands. Protected largely from tourism development by its Hawaiian heritage, real estate activity and prices have nevertheless been booming in recent years, especially on the island's gorgeous southeastern shore.

By-passed by Cook and "discovered" by a British vessel in 1786, American protestants established a mission on Molokai in 1836. Before that, Kamehameha I had conquered the island with an army so large that the king's war canoes were said to have stretched for about four miles. In 1946, Halawa Bay was struck by a *tsunami* that filled the valley slowly enough for people to escape, then receded and took most of the homes and possessions of several hundred residents.

The pineapple kingdoms of Dole and Del Monte no longer could compete with pineapple production in Asia and pulled out of Molokai between 1975 and 1983. In the 1970s, Molokai Ranch sold about 14,000 acres of the west end of the island for resort development, currently underway. Recently, a New Zealand cattle raising company bought acreage on the ranch to raise one of the largest herds in Hawaii, second only to Parker Ranch.

The island's slower pace, the friendliness of its people and many historical sites — ancient fishponds and *heiau* of all ages — some very interesting and beautiful hiking trails and legendary valleys, make Molokai a very appealing destination for adventurous travelers.

The one settlement on the island that qualifies as a town, Kaunakakai, doesn't have a traffic light, no shopping malls, fast food, or touristy glitz. Weathered one-storey shops cater mainly to locals and welcome visitors. In addition to hiking opportunities, Molokai has some of the best bike riding in Hawaii, especially west of Kaunakakai.

Several very different sightseeing experiences are packed into Molokai's small area: a mule-ride down the cliffside trail to Makanalua Peninsula, site of **Kalaupapa**, Molokai's famous "leper colony", a safari through Molokai Ranch's wildlife preserve; and a horsedrawn Molokai Wagon Ride to visit the island's largest *heiau*, **Iliiliopae**, a mango grove and a beach for demonstrations of throwing Hawaiian fishing nets, husking coconuts and traditional arts and crafts.

The island's **Makahiki Festival** in January, in Kaunakakai Park, draws thousands to hear some of Hawaii's best musicians and singers, see top *hula hulau* performances and attend *luau* feasts open to everyone with competitions in Hawaiian games (*ulu maika*, lawn bowling, *o'o ihe*, spear hurling, *kukuni*, foot races, *pohaku*, rock throwing, and *haka moa*, wrestling in a circle with one foot tied).

Hoolehua Airport

Aloha Island Air and **Panorama Air** fly 9-to-18-seat Dash-7 turboprops to Molokai from Oahu and Maui with connections to all islands. **Hawaiian Air** runs 50-seat DH-7 aircraft. These flights land at **Hoolehua Airport**, near the center of the island, and shuttle vans will take you to your hotel or condo. From Hoolehua, **Pacific Aviation International** offers an exciting 40-minute North Shore flight over Kalaupapa Peninsula, one of the best helicopter values in Hawaii. You could arrange to take this flightseeing excursion or a flight to Kalaupapa (see below) directly from the airport after landing.

The 118-ft **Maui Princess** ferry from Lahaina takes about 1-$1/_4$ hours one-way to Molokai and is excellent for a round-trip or one-way sightseeing — flying in from Honolulu or one of the neighbor islands and leaving Molokai by ferry to Maui. Between December and May, when the trip gets a bit rough, you may spot some humpback whales. A day-trip is barely enough time to see the best of Molokai, especially including a round-trip by ferry.

There is another small landing strip on **Makanalua Peninsula** that exclusively services Kalaupapa. You can fly directly from Honolulu or the Neighbor Islands on **Aloha Island Air**.

Ground Transportation

There are no buses or public transportation on Molokai. Cab service — **Teem Cab** or **Molokai Taxi** — includes tours of several itineraries on the island. Half-

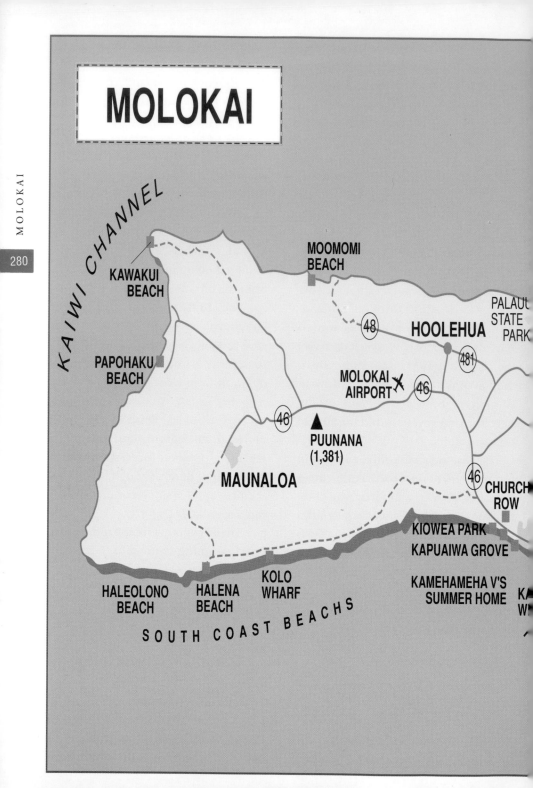

MOLOKAI

KAIWI CHANNEL

KAWAKUI
BEACH

MOOMOMI
BEACH

PALAU
STATE
PARK

48   HOOLEHUA

481

PAPOHAKU
BEACH

MOLOKAI
AIRPORT

46

46

PUUNANA
(1,381)

MAUNALOA

46   CHURCH
ROW

KIOWEA PARK
KAPUAIWA GROVE

HALEOLONO
BEACH

HALENA
BEACH

KOLO
WHARF

KAMEHAMEHA V'S
SUMMER HOME

KA
W

SOUTH COAST BEACHS

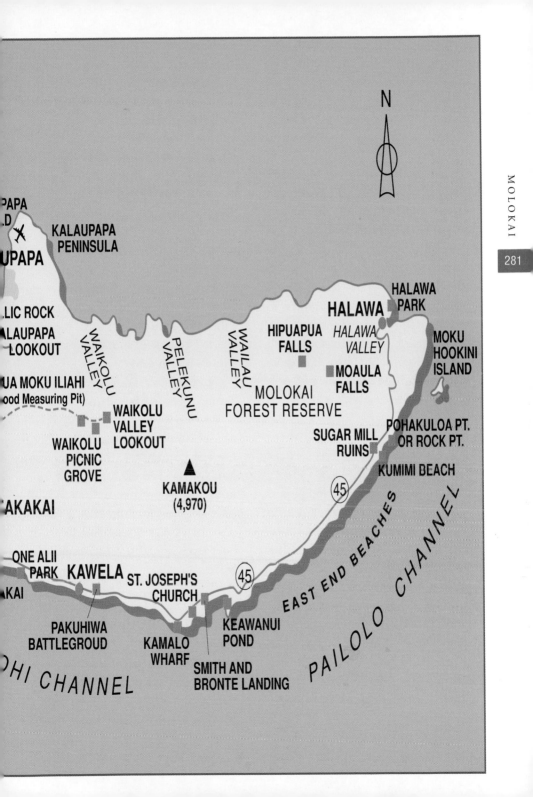

and full-day tours can be arranged through **Gray Line Molokai** and **Robert's Hawaii**. Most tours include the Kalaupapa Lookout but be sure to take a tour that also includes the beautiful east coast to Halawa Valley Overlook.

For four-wheel drive sightseeing off the beaten track, such as the **Waikoulu Lookout** and **Moomomi Beach**, call **Molokai Taxi**. **Damien Molokai Tours** will also fly sightseers in and out of Kalaupapa Peninsula and arrange for a ground tour.

For most people, the best plan is to rent a car at the airport so that you can drive yourself to all parts of the island. **Dollar Car Rental** has four-wheel drive vehicles to rent at twice the cost of a compact rental.

Central Molokai

Ala Malama, the two-block long main street running through **Kaunakakai**, is bordered by general stores, restaurants, a post office and court house and the fabled **Kanemitsu Bakery**. Famous for its bread (raisin nut, cheese, onion cheese, French Molokai and others), the bakery's thousands of loaves may be sold out before you stroll in at breakfast time. Mexican butternut and macadamia nut cookies and banana hotcakes are also specialties. Order your choices in advance!

Several other choices for enjoyable eating in Kaunakakai and the vicinity will not stretch your budget: fried *akule* and other fresh fish at the **MidNite Inn**, a sandwich or other health food items at **Outpost Natural Food** and Chinese food at the **Hop Inn**.

At the end of the street, deep-sea fishing boats and the ferry leave from the concrete, one-half mile long **Kaunakakai Wharf**. The foundation of **Kamehameha V's summer home** is just to the west of the approach to the wharf, but there's not much to see. At the wharf, you can arrange for snorkeling or whale-watching excursions (**Whistling Swan Charters**) or other day-long sailing trips, for example, to Lanai. Rent snorkeling gear from **Molokai Fish and Dive**.

Just west of Kaunakakai, six tiny clapboard churches and a mission school — **Church Row** — are lined up on one side of Route 46. Noon on Sunday in front of Church Row is the only traffic jam on the island. **Kapuaiwa**, originally a grove of about 1,000 coconut palms planted for Prince Lot, a Molokai resident (Kalae homestead land) and later Kamehameha V, is considered sacred.

Kualapuu to Hoolehua

Maunaloa Highway heading north passes through **Kualapuu**, Del Monte's former pineapple plantation town for 50 years before the company pulled out in the early 1980s. From the road, you can see a huge **rubber-lined reservoir**,

Taking it easy at Kaunakakai.

said to be the largest man-made rubber-lined reservoir in the world, originally built in the 1960s to irrigate the pineapple fields. Nearby is the nine-hole **Ironwood Golf Course**.

On Route 470, between Kualapuu and Palaau State Park (two miles away),

is a restoration of the **R.W. Meyer Sugar Mill**. The only surviving 19th century sugar mill in Hawaii (circa 1878), listed on the National Register of Historic places, the mill displays memorabilia of German immigrant, Rudolph Meyer. Meyer married a Hawaiian chieftess,

Dorcas Kalama Waha, settled on Molokai, and raised 11 children. In the mid-19th century, he bought up large tracts of land after King Kamehameha's *Great Mahale* in 1848.

Rudolph Meyer's land was purchased in the 1870s by King Kamehameha V who subsequently sold **Molokai Ranch** to some Honolulu businessmen for an unsuccessful sugar plantation. Bought by Charles Cooke, he converted the land back into a ranch in the early 1900s. The mill is open Mon-Sat 10am-noon, Sundays 1-5pm.

The town of **Hoolehu** along with neighboring **Palaau** were declared Hawaiian Homestead Land in the 1920s. People of Hawaiian ancestry could lease lots on this land at very little cost.

However, the terrain was so dry that local Hawaiians in turn leased this land to Del Monte and Libby to develop pineapple plantations. These companies imported Japanese and Filipino workers to plant and harvest pineapple crops.

At **Purdy's All Natural Macadamia Nut Farm** located in **Hoolehua Homesteads**, you'll get a personal tour from Tuddie Purdy (or his mother) covering everything there is to know about growing and processing the nuts. Before leaving, be sure to taste honey from macadamia blossoms and get some samples of delicious toasted and raw nuts made without any preservatives. Chances are that you'll buy some nuts and honey to take with you. Also in Hoolehua, stop at **The Spice Farm** or

Bill's Farm at **Molokai Agricultural Park** to pick up some delicious Molokai bananas (the sweetest you've ever tasted), Hawaiian watermelon and fresh spices.

There is good swimming, snorkeling and unofficial camping at **Moomomi Beach**.

Palaau State Park

One of the better places on the island for

Phallic-shaped stone at Palaau Park, where women would
visit in the old days to awaken their fertility.

camping (if the camp grounds have
been cleaned and repaired), **Palaau
State Park** contains trails through thick
ironwoods to the **Phallic Stone**
(*Kauleonanahoa*). In the old days, women
would come to the stone in order to
awaken their fertility. Even if you don't
take a trip down to Kalaupapa itself,
drive to the Overlook, about 10 miles
from Kaunakakai on Highways 460 and
470. Park at the end of the parking lot in

Palaau State Park.

It's only a short walk through the
pine and cypress to **Kalaupapa Lookout**, a spectacular viewpoint from high
cliffs over Makanalua Peninsula and
Kalaupapa.

The reasons why Kalaupapa was
chosen as the place of exile and incar-
ceration for lepers are clear from this
view. To your right are the 3,300-ft
seacliffs rising from Umilehi Point.

Kalaupapa

Makanalua Peninsula, an isolated stretch of lava covering 12 square miles, surrounded by seas on three sides and sheer cliffs on the fourth side, became a prison for lepers starting in January 1866. Dumped off ships near the peninsula, lepers who survived the sea lived and died in unimaginable conditions in the most inaccessible place on the islands that the Hawaiian government could find — **Kalaupapa**. Originally living in **Kalawao** on the rugged east coast (now **Kalawao Park**), the settlement moved to Kalaupapa in 1888. Fifteen years earlier, **Father Damien** arrived to look after the victims of Hansen's disease. One year after the move, he himself died of leprosy.

In the 1940s, the introduction of sulfone drugs arrested and stopped the spread of Hansen's disease. With the disease no longer contagious, the residents were free to leave Kalaupapa or voluntarily remain at the settlement, which had been declared a National Historic Park. From a population of about 1,200 at the beginning of the century, the settlement today numbers fewer than 100.

Kalaupapa is a deeply moving experience that is definitely not for everyone. Minors under 16 are not allowed to enter the peninsula. Everyone else must have a permit which is obtained by tour operators, all of whom are former patients. Advance reservations for any of

Sea cliffs rising to 3,300 feet were used as the natural demarcation
for leper colonies.

Father Damien

Among the diseases brought to Hawaii by *haoles* and others, against which Hawaiians had no defenses, none was more frightening than leprosy. The first case occurred in the 1840s and the disfiguring and deadly disease proved to be so contagious that King Kamehameha V began banishing its victims to Molokai's Makanalua Peninsula.

Provided with no supplies or building materials, victims of this disease were dumped from a ship with their meager belongings. Survivors of the treacherous waters lived in primitive huts built from scraps of wood and eating pitifully small amounts of foraged food.

Father Damien de Veuster, a Catholic Priest from Belgium, arrived in the midst of this human suffering and rampant lawlessness in 1873. Sleeping under a tree until all residents of Kalaupapa had shelter, he converted St. Philomena chapel, built earlier by a visiting priest, into a hospital and also built another church. In April 1889, Father Damien died of Hansen's disease.

Father Damien's grave.

the tours are essential. You can bring a camera (photos of residents are not allowed) and binoculars.

The **Rare Adventures/Molokai Mule Ride** adds excitement to the trip down the $3^1/_8$ -mile mountainside trail, 1,600 ft down through 26 switchbacks. Hiking down or up is not too difficult if you're in good physical condition. Otherwise it's tough coming back up. Riding or hiking down takes about $1^1/_2$ hours. Hikers have to start ahead of the mules, by 8:30am at Kalae Stables. Mule

The north shore of Molokai.

riders return to the stables by 4pm. The cost of a "hike-in" includes a pass to enter the peninsula, a picnic lunch and a guided tour of the settlement.

The best tour deal in Hawaii is flying into Kalaupapa round-trip with Richard Marks **Damien Molokai Tours**. Richard provides as much information and insight as you could possibly want. Tours of the settlement includes a visit to Kalawao, the early settlement in a beautiful setting with a spectacular view of the north coast, where Father Damien's St Philomena Church has been faithfully restored and the gravesites of Father Damien (his remains have been moved to Belgium) and Mother Marianne Siloama Church, medical facilities, houses, graveyards and other places.

Another way of seeing the north coast is aboard Captain Glenn Davis' powerboat, *Hokupa'a Ocean Adventures*, a four-hour trip from Halawa Bay to the waters off Waialua and Kalaupapa and back.

Waikolu Valley Lookout & Kamakou Preserve

Sandalwood Measuring Pit is a nine-mile drive along Highway 460. It is a depression in the ground about the size of a sailing ship's hull used in the late 19th century by local Hawaiian chiefs to measure the amount of sandalwood stripped from local forests that were being shipped to *haole* traders. In about two more miles is **Waikolu Valley Lookout**, a spectacular viewpoint over a 3,000-ft gorge. Just past the lookout is the gate to **Kamakou Preserve**, a 2,774-acre forest and bird conservation area established by the **Nature Conservancy**.

The Nature Conservancy owns a total of about 3,000 acres of mountain rainforest at the **Moomomi Dunes** near the west end of the island and in **Pelekunu Valley/Kamakou Preserve** along the north coast. You can hike in the preserve or drive in with a four-wheel drive vehicle. Be sure to get maps and information first. Tours can be arranged by contacting the Nature Conservancy. Hunting (wild boar) trails run through the preserve. No camping is permitted but there is camping in the park at Waikolu Lookout (with a permit from the Department of Forestry and Wildlife in Kaunakakai).

Western Molokai

Most of the west side of Molokai is owned or leased by the company that purchased Molokai Ranch. This arid, high tableland, largely used for grazing, growing cattle feed and on hold for inevitable future development, contains the **Kalaukoi Resort**, the former Dole company town of **Maunaloa** and its few interesting shops and a fringe of "hidden" beaches, some very scenic, that are mostly difficult to reach, which makes them all the more appealing to adventurous travelers.

Kaluakoi Resort

The biggest and best hotel and only resort on the island, the 117-room **Kaluakoi Hotel and Golf Club** on 29 acres started out in 1977 as the Sheraton Molokai. Situated 15 miles from the airport, the hotel is part of the 6,700-acre Kaluakoi Resort. At this resort, your own car is essential for sightseeing.

The hotel's very nicely decorated rooms are in 32 one and two-storey villas around the grounds. The hotel has a small swimming pool, four lighted tennis courts, two restaurants and a lounge and the 18-hole championship **Kaluakoi Golf Course** . This picture-perfect golf course designed by Ted Robinson (par 72, 6,618 yards) has five holes that run along the beach.

A breeze constantly blows at **Kepuhi**

Kaluakoi Resort.

Beach in front of Kaluakoi Resort. The half-mile usually empty beach has shower rooms. Swim with caution, especially in winter when waves get rough.

Plan for dinner by the open glass doors at the **Ohia Lodge** in Kaluakoi Hotel. In addition to daytime activities, live bands play top 40 music for dancing from 6:30 to 9:30 every evening.

The new **Kaluakoi Villas** consist of 100 condominium units, studios and one-bedroom suites, with oceanfront *lanais*, beautifully decorated with all amenities. Next door, the *Ke Nani Kai* condominium has 55 one and 2-bedroom units (with full kitchens and *lanais*) looking across the seaside golf course and the beach. There's a very large pool, jacuzzi and two tennis courts.

Paniolo Hale also adjacent to the Kaluakoi has 77 studios, one and two-bedroom units with full kitchens, pool, paddling pool and tennis court and of course access to the golf course.

The minimum stay is three nights for all resort condominiums.

Molokai Ranch Wildlife Safari

The **Molokai Ranch Wildlife Safari**, a $1^1/_2$-hour trip through the Molokai Ranch Wildlife Park, departs from the Kaluakoi Resort in open-windowed vans driving over rough rutted roads to view hundreds of animals from Africa and Asia (giraffes, impala, Indian black

Papohaku Beach.

buck, oryx, greater kudu, Barbary sheep, sable antelope, axis deer and zebras, among others). The Ranch breeds these animals for zoos around the world.

Beaches

The island's best beaches are scattered around the west side. The white sands of **Poolau Beach**, about a half mile north-west of Kaluakoi Hotel, are an excellent place for camping and surfing. Obtain a county camping permit at the County Parks Division in Kaunakakai.

The loveliest beach on the west coast is **Kawakui**, about 20 miles from Kaunakakai, down a dirt road off Route 46 to the end of a point north of the Kaluakoi Hotel. Swimming and snorkeling in the cove are good and camping is wonderful, with a permit required only on weekends from Molokai Ranch. **Papohaku Beach**, two miles south of the Kaluakoi Hotel, is a marvelous, scenic beach extending for three miles, with restrooms and showers, camping by county permit and good swimming with caution! About $1\frac{1}{2}$ miles past Papohaku is **Pohakuloa Beach** in a cove with excellent swimming and an outdoor shower.

Maunaloa

When Dole abandoned its pineapple fields and left **Maunaloa** in 1975, the near-empty town about a mile from the ocean went through a ghost-town period before a modest revival began around some artisans' shops such as Jonathan and Daphne Socher's **Big Wind Kite Factory**. In addition to selling beautiful kites, they offer a kite factory tour and free kite-flying lessons for their unique aerobatic kites that can fly at 100-mph speeds.

The **Plantation Gallery** next door was opened by the Sochers to sell imports from Bali and the works of other island artisans, such as deer-horn scrimshaw, wood carvings and jewelry. Sculpture, bowls and wood carving from native wood are sold by the **Tao Woodcarver**, including hand-carved bowls and boxes of Hawaiian woods, *raku* pottery, pillowcase quilts and other items. **Dolly Hale** sells delightful handmade Hawaiian dolls from her cottage shop across the street.

For lunch or a snack in Maunaloa, try *saimin* or marlin burgers at **JoJo's Cafe**.

Before you get to the built-up part of Maunaloa, a dirt road off to the right leads several miles to a Molokai Ranch gate and then continues another two miles to where it forks. The right fork and then an immediate left takes you a few hundred yards to the end, which is not far from **Halena Beach**. From here the **Molokai to Oahu Canoe Race** starts, in October for men and September for women, 25 tough miles across the Kaiwi Channel.

Haleolono Point is a mile to the west. For another alternative, instead of taking the right fork, go straight ahead for two miles to **Kolo Wharf**, with fish ponds and small sand beaches around it. Along the shore and then inland from Kolo Wharf, the road runs seven miles before joining the main road west of Kaunakakai. You can camp at Halena and South Coast beaches on Molokai Ranch property after paying a nominal fee.

East Molokai

About 30 miles along Route 45, you get into increasingly lush, mountainous and historic terrain — some of the most beautiful and interesting touring in Hawaii. Be aware that in many places you are treading on sacred ground and explore with exceptional awareness and respect.

Several of the best hotel choices on the *makai* side of the highway are within a few miles of Kaunakakai. The **Hotel Molokai** has charm, from its lobby through its grounds and swinging benches on *lanais*. Rent an upper floor room with high ceilings overlooking the ocean.

Just before Kamalo, little remains of **Kawela**, a "city of refuge" like the more famous, restored one on the Big Island. In this same area west of Kamalo, **Pakuhiwa Battlefield**, Kamehameha the Great landed with a huge force of war canoes to conquer Molokai.

On their way from California to Honolulu to complete the world's first

The peaceful surrounds of Halawa Congregational Church.

transpacific flight in 1927, Earnest Smith and Emile Bronte made an emergency landing on the *makai* side of the road at **Kamalo**, just past the lagoon in a stand of *kiawe* trees. A roadside marker – **Smith and Bronte Monument** – notes the event and their survival.

Nearby, the tiny white clapboard **St Joseph's Catholic Church** is another church built by Father Damien in 1876. His statue stands beside it. A few miles down the road, Father Damien, pastor to the whole island, also built **Our Lady of Sorrows Church**, now restored behind a tall wooden cross standing on its lawn. Another statue of Father Damien is on the pavilion near the church.

Just east of Kamalo, on the *mauka* side of the road, is **Iliiliopae *Heiau***, one of Hawaii's largest and most sacred temples.

This *heiau* once covered more than

Fishponds of Molokai

Molokai is renowned in Hawaii for its remarkably advanced fishponds, which may have existed as early as the 13th century. A network of these legendary fishponds may have numbered more than 60 starting in the 1500s, some more than half a mile long, and producing fattened fish for royal tables. Built on the shallow southeastern shores, the ponds were formed of stone or coral in just the right spots for tides to keep the waters in the ponds circulating, but not too strong to wreck the fishponds' walls. Small openings in the walls let small fish in with the water and kept fattened fish from leaving.

From a coconut grove about a half-mile before One Alii Beach Park, you can see **Alii Fishpond**. Or else drive up the road to Cavella Plantations, a residential development, in order to look down on the fish pond below. Some of these ponds bordering the southern shoreline, like **Kalokoeli Fishpond**, have been restored and are still in use today. Two of them along Route 45 — **Keawanui** and **Ualapue** — are part of a national historic landmark.

five acres, consisting of four terraces, 150-ft wide and 50-ft tall. Legend says that the stones used to build this *heiau* were carried from Wailau Valley and fitted together in one night. Human sacrifices were performed at this *heiau*. It is said that this *heiau* was a school of sorcery for *kahuna* from other islands. Since this is a sacred site, see it either with the wagon tour or with permission from Pearl Petro .

The **Waialua hiking trail** starts at the Iliiliopae *Heiau* and crosses the entire island to beautiful **Wailau Valley**. This difficult trail gets tougher as it gains elevation and takes six-to-eight hours through rainforest and crosses private property. At the *pali*, it's up to you to decide whether to climb down a very poorly marked and treacherous trail 3,000 ft to the bottom.

Past **Wavecrest Condominium** at mile-marker 13, the vegetation becomes very lush, the road narrows and the roadside becomes thick with banana and palm trees. In front of **Pukoo Lagoon**, the **Neighborhood Store** marks the last food or drink before Halawa Valley.

Across from the Store, there are two perfect beaches in a cove with the best swimming on the entire coast.

This is not a public beach but you can swim if you are respectful of the private land. Across the cove is the private local Manae Canoe Club. (Don't be surprised if someone providing security for the Club pays a visit to ask your intentions.) This is an area of very traditional community life where taro is still grown in the valleys and old ways are taught to young people from throughout Hawaii.

Swimming and camping at **Waialua Beach** are excellent. On Route 45, starting near the 18-mile marker, you'll pass several small white-sand beaches — **Kumimi Beach, Pohakuloa Point**, and others — that offer very good snorkeling and surfing if you're careful, and excellent fishing. Just before Kumimi Beach, near the 20-mile marker, stands the ruins of the island's first sugar mill. Offshore you can see **Moku Hookini Island** and Maui and Lanai beyond it.

As the sinuous road climbs up the rocky coastline past **Murphy's Beach**, the road passes through grasslands of 14,000-acre **Puu O Hoku Ranch**. Along a beautiful winding road, around a hairpin turn, is the spectacular surprise of **Halawa Valley Overlook**. Across the half-mile valley, surf pounds on the shore of the Valley's beach. Near the mouth of the Bay, a fisherman named Glenn operates a powerboat tour to Wailau Valley and the edge of Kalaupapa.

The east end of the island was once the most densely populated part of the island. The settlement of Halawa Valley may have been as early as the 7th century. Since the huge tidal wave of 1946, which destroyed homes and crops but miraculously didn't kill anyone, no one has lived in Halawa Valley.

A two-mile trail leads to twin **Moaula Falls**. Park in a free space along the dirt road to Halawa Stream next to the small green house that was formerly a church.

The hike to Moaula Falls takes about 90 minutes each way. Cross both forks of the stream and find a trail up the hillside that runs at right angles to the stream. Orange marks on trees mark the trail until you come to the white plastic pipe along the main (horse) trail also marked by white arrows.

A 250-ft cascade of water from Moaula Falls forms a pool of cold water that provides a delightful swim. A third of a mile north, a fork through some heavy bush leads to **Hipuapua Falls** which falls 500 ft down the *pali* to another refreshing little swimming hole.

Molokai Wagon Ride

One of the newest tours on Molokai is a horse-drawn wagon-ride to the Iliiliopae *Heiau*, where a guide explains the historical background. Then the wagon continues to the **Mapulehu Mango Grove**, the largest in Hawaii and perhaps even the world, in Mapulehu, at the 15-1/2 mile-marker on the *makai* side. The grove contains over 2,000 mango trees of many varieties. Purchase some fruit or juices here from a stand next to the ocean and a beach from which you can snorkel and picnic.

Afterwards, the wagon heads to the beach for a Molokai-style barbecue, which means a wonderful party with Hawaiian music, traditional Hawaiian net throwing and fishing, coconut-husking and other activities (somewhat like the Paradise Cove *luau* on Oahu). The 2¹/₂ -trip includes lots of delicious food (kiawe-grilled fish or chicken, taro baked in coconut milk, purple sweet potatoes, Hawaiian chili peppers and salad) at the barbecue.

Ka Hula Piko.

Under orders from Kalani-opuu, whose invasion of Maui had failed, Kame-hameha's troops massacred the population of Lanai. Years later he returned for summer vacations and fishing at Kaunolu. In the early 1800s, missionaries spent enough time on the island to permanently influence its cultural values. In the 1850s, Mormons arrived *en masse* to establish a "City of Joseph." Their leader in the 1860s, Walter Gibson, bought up prime Lanai land, was excommunicated in a period of turmoil and the Mormons left for Laie to establish their church on Oahu's northern shore.

Gibson's heir and her husband tried to establish a sugar plantation near Keomuku, which portentously failed — their water pumps drew saltwater and the sugar cane died. Later, these landholdings were expanded and converted to

Manele Bay, Lanai.

Lanai, Kahoolawe & Niihau

Peaceful sands at shipwreck Beach, Lanai.

ranching and then sold to the Baldwin family of Maui. In 1921, the Baldwins sold most of the island to Jim Dole who spent millions to develop Lanai as a pineapple plantation. Water was pumped in from the wet mountains of the east side and from underground to create ideal growing conditions in the sun-drenched **Palawai Basin**.

This small island in the middle of the archipelago, which for more than a century seemed to be trading hands and futures, recently changed its destiny and identity another time. In 1951, the last of Lanai's cattle were removed and the pastures planted in pineapple. In 1990, Lanai took its first steps from a pineapple plantation to a resort island. Look closely today and you'll see that the island's topography and history give it many personalities — a tropical beach at **Hulopoe Bay**, "upcountry" in **Koele**, winding horse and jeep trails in the mountains and lawn bowling against a backdrop of Cook Pines and lush resort acreage.

The Hulopoe Bay and **Manele Bay** coast was rated by *Scuba Magazine* as "one of the ten best spots in the world" for diving. Today a beautiful new resort edges the sweeping curve of white sand along this majestic coast. Even King Kamehameha the Great came to Lanai for fishing and perhaps whalewatching from November through April. Recently Lanai became a golfer's paradise with two superb championship courses by Greg Norman and Ted Robinson at Koele and one by Jack Nicklaus at Manele overlooking the Pacific Ocean crashing 100 ft below.

With the opening of **Manele Bay Hotel** in May 1991, joining the **Lodge** at **Koele**, Hawaii's sixth largest island offers two world-class resorts. Developed by Castle & Cooke, both resorts are operated by Rockresorts. Lanai today is the biggest "undiscovered" secret in Hawaii, a getaway vacation offering a wealth of vacation possibilities for outdoor activities, touring, and dining.

These modest-sized luxury resorts open up the secluded pleasures and natural beauty of "Old Hawaii" on Lanai. The island has only 30 miles of paved roads and a few thousand residents. Lanai is home to a mixture of Hawaiians, Filipinos, Japanese, Koreans, Chinese and Caucasians, almost all of whom live in Lanai City. Lanaians are known for their *aloha* spirit and warm welcome. Besides exotic flora and spectacular vistas, wild game abound in the mountains; hence the Lodge at Koele in Lanai's central highlands patterned after an elegant country lodge providing access to the island's sporting life.

Hulopoe Beach for years has been a destination for snorkeling trips from Maui. Campers obtained permits from the Koele Company to use only three campsites and enjoy a great view of Haleakala, Lanai's finest beach, restrooms and showers. Visitors to Hulopoe Beach – only eight miles from Lanai City frequent its two grocery stores and eat wholesome, inexpensive meals at the **Hotel Lanai**.

Manele Bay, a perfect small boat harbor in a cliff-lined inlet, has been a well-known gathering place for crews of small craft happy to have a gorgeous, comparatively uninhabited beach nearby.

Until construction of the **Rockresorts**, these two back-to-back bays — Manele and Hulopoe — have been the primary visible attractions on Lanai. Few visitors to Hawaii knew about the seven-mile ridge above Lanai City, situated at 1,645 ft, that provides spectacu-

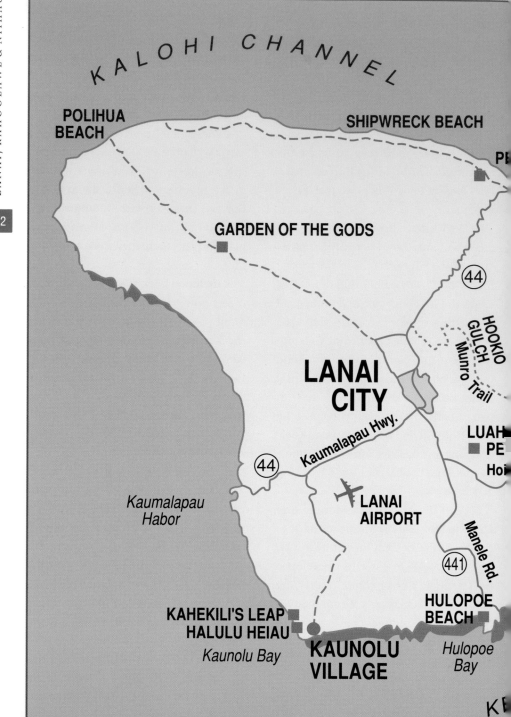

KALOHI CHANNEL

POLIHUA
BEACH

SHIPWRECK BEACH

PE

GARDEN OF THE GODS

44

HOOKIO
GULCH

Munro Trail

LANAI
CITY

LUAH

PE

Hoi

Kaumalapau Hwy.

44

Kaumalapau
Habor

LANAI
AIRPORT

Manele Rd.

441

KAHEKILI'S LEAP
HALULU HEIAU

Kaunolu Bay

KAUNOLU
VILLAGE

HULOPOE
BEACH

Hulopoe
Bay

KE

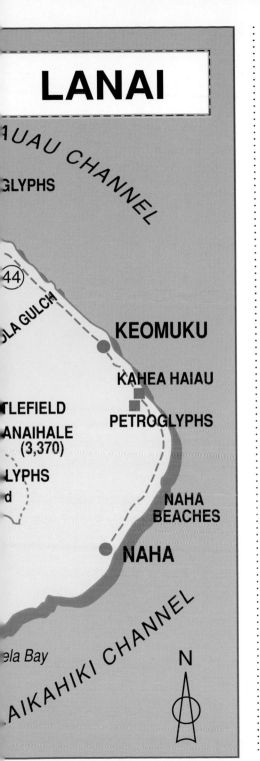

lar views along the Munro Trail. This tough trail bears the name of an unusual New Zealander, George C. Munro, who in the early 1900s imported seeds of Cook and Norfolk pines from his home country and sowed them in the mountains along with other plants.

Lanai remains a treasure trove of nature's gifts and future tourism development will preserve these invaluable assets. About six miles northwest of Lanai City at **Kanepuu**, Hawaii's last remaining dryland forest contains 48 native species including the endangered native Lanai sandalwood, Hawaiian gardenia, *olopua* (native olive), *lama* (native persimmon), vines of fragrant *huehue*, *maile*, and other blossoms. Castle and Cooke granted **The Nature Conservancy of Hawaii** 462 acres at Kanepuu as part of the company's plan to preserve and enhance the island's natural environment.

Getting Around Lanai

Planes land at **Lanai Airport** just four miles from Lanai City. The island is serviced by **Hawaiian Airlines** and **Aloha Island Air** with more than 80 scheduled flights weekly from Honolulu and Maui. The Lodge at Koele, Manele Bay and the Hotel Lanai will pick you up. The only vehicle that you need or can use on Lanai is a 4-wheel drive. **Oshiro's Service Station** and **Lanai City Service Inc.** will gladly rent one to you. An equally good idea is to let Oshiro's

Lanai City.

provide a guided tour of two-to-four hours to the island's off-the-beaten track coastal and mountain areas. The entire island consists of "hidden" destinations that few tourists have seen.

Lanai City

A plantation town, founded in 1924 by the Dole Company, Lanai City is laid out in a neat grid of tree-lined streets. Residents obviously take pride in their homes and gardens.

Houses are painted all colors of the rainbow, surrounded by colorful flower beds, vegetable gardens, flowering shrubs and other growth to relieve the monotony of the houses. At the center of

the town is a village green with its towering Norfolk Island pine trees surrounded by a cluster of country stores, churches, a bakery and old fashioned soda fountain.

Built in the 1920s for guests of the Dole Company, the white wood frame **Hotel Lanai** sits atop a grassy knoll surrounded by Norfolk pines. The knotty pine dining rooms with fireplaces, fit the temperate climate. The big verandah and its bar are the town's meeting place. Ten small rooms in two wings of the building, all with bathroom and shower, feel quite homey and comfortable.

The wrought iron headboards and wooden dressers in the rooms, wicker furniture on the porch and other fea-

Lodging comfortably at Lanai.

tures of the hotel haven't changed much in the last 70 years. Sunset from the porch is a grand sight while "talking story" and having drinks at the end of the day. It can get chilly and foggy at night, even in the summertime.

The dining room of the Hotel Lanai is decorated with photographs of island scenes. A fireplace at one end of the room is welcome on cool winter days. With banana pancakes and homemade soups and sandwiches, here is your best choice for an inexpensive breakfast and lunch. Hours: 7:30-9am, 11:30am-1:30pm and 6:30-8:30pm

Dahang's Bakery serves fresh bread and pastry in the morning and otherwise is a budget luncheonette of the burgers-and-french-fries variety. **S & T**

Property Inc next door is a 1950s-style soda fountain complete with swivel chairs and burgers (good ones, too). If you don't mind video machines flushing on and off, this is the place for a budget breakfast or lunch.

Lanai City is not much of a tourist attraction. The look-alike houses in this plantation center will be spruced up over time but will look essentially the same. The main sights of Lanai lie outside of Lanai City.

South from Lanai City

The most likely direction for leaving Lanai City is south on Route 441 to Manele Bay and Hulopoe Bay. Start

Petroglyphs at Luahiwa.

with the fascinating **Luahiwa Petro-glyphs**, about a mile off Manele Road (Route 441).

These petroglyphs are some of the best in the islands, comparable to Puako on the Big Island. (Get clear, specific directions in Lanai City before setting out.)

The Lodge is only 20 minutes from its sister resort at **Manele Bay**. The 250-room Manele Bay's contemporary architecture and decor offers a complete resort experience on Lanai. The weather on the beautiful white sands of Hulopoe

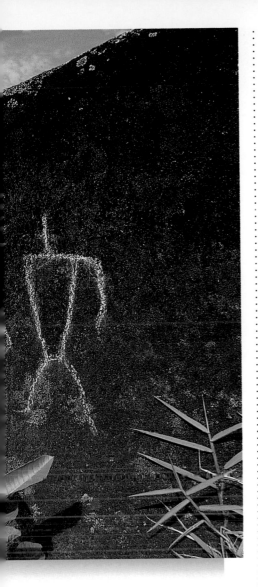

The turn-off to **Kaunolu Bay** is a paved road to the left just past the airport road which soon becomes a very rough road through pineapple fields to Kamehameha the Great's summer home and an ancient fishing community. This national landmark contains the ruins of over eighty houses, stone shelters and graves.

Northeast of Lanai City

Leave Lanai City on Route 44 to the northeast for an adventurous drive on a paved road through arid countryside to Shipwreck Beach. When the pavement ends and divides into two, take the road to the left through kiawe trees to **Shipwreck Beach.**

A dirt track parallels the coast for plenty of coastal hiking or 4-wheel driving. Protected by coral reefs but swept by strong currents, hulks of ships driven into the reefs are still visible.

About 8 miles of beachcombing should satisfy anyone's desires. Stay out of the water in this area — it's dangerous!

To the north of the point where the dirt road ends is a group of **petroglyphs** carved on a pile of brown boulders near the beach. To the south is the ghost town of **Keomuku**, a sugar town abandoned in 1903 and mostly covered with vegetation.

A remaining wooden church is being restored. Ten miles past the remains of **Kahea Heiau** and the **Club Lanai** compound, is the beginning of a string

Beach and at Manele Bay is clear, dry and sunny. Gentle waves provide excellent snorkeling.

Kaumalapau Harbor six miles to the southwest at the end of Route 44, a good two-lane highway, is worth visiting mainly to see the 1,000-ft *pali* on either side and for the detour to **Kaunolu Village**.

In the garden of the gods.

of salt-and-pepper beaches along the road to the village of **Naha**. Enjoy views

Kaunolu Bay

At the end of a long dry gulch, a rocky beach used to provide a canoe anchorage for the village. A well-laid wall is the only remains of a canoe shed. Inland, the remains of **Halulu Heiau** has a commanding view of the area. Taking the trail to the right from the end of the road you get to ruins of Kamehameha's summer house where he escaped from the heat of Lahaina. Here and there the area is still dotted with artifacts and petroglyphs.

After exploring the area's historic sites, look for the opening in the sea cliff — **Kahikili's Leap** — named after a Lanai chief. Visualize Kamehameha'' warriors proving their courage by executing death-defying leaps into 12-ft of water by clearing a rock protruding 15 ft. Off the right is a less famous but even higher leap, above **Kolokolo Cave**.

of Molokai, Maui and Kahoolawe all along the way.

Heading northwest, you reach the **Garden of the Gods**, an unusual conglomeration of lava and multicolored boulders near Kanepuu, with a strange sculptural beauty, by a graded and then ungraded pineapple road. (The boulders may be hard to find if overgrown with vegetation.) Continue on this rugged jeep trail to **Polihua Beach**, a wide, white-sand strand with good swimming and outstanding fishing.

About a mile north of Lanai City in Koele, the **Munro Trail** begins off Route 44. For adventurous visitors, the trail is a "must" to see magnificent views on the way up to **Lanaihale** (3,370 ft), the highest point on Lanai, where you can

Munro Trail

Originally an access trail into the forests of Lanai, this jeep trail is an easy-to-follow foot-trail of 8.8 miles over the highest point on Lanai, **Lanaihale** (3,370 ft). Allow at least eight hours to hike this trail. The trail starts 1.5 miles north of Lanai City along Highway 44. Leave your car at any point and walk or drive if you have a four-wheel drive.

From grasslands and through gullies reforested with eucalyptus, the trail starts climbing at Maunalei Gulch for three miles to **Hookio Gulch** where Lanai defenders were massacred about 215 years ago by invading Hawaiian Island forces. Just before the summit (4.7 miles), watch for a sign marking the **North Hauola Trail** which leads (in 45-minutes of hiking) to spectacular views from the edge of **Hauola Gulch**.

From the top of Lanaihale the trail heads down to the south end of the island into pineapple fields. Views of Maui, Kahoolawe and Hawaii are outstanding on a clear day.

Along the Munro Trail.

see every island except Kauai. Along the way, you'll pass deep gulches — Hoohio, Hauola and Maunalei — on the rugged east slope.

Kahoolawe – Uninhabited Island

US Naval bombardments no longer light up the island of Kahoolawe, an uninhabited target island owned by the US Government that has been the focus of controversy in Hawaii for several decades.

Only seven miles off the east coast of Maui, this barren island is inhabited exclusively by wild goats. Even the goats barely have enough to eat and drink from scrubby vegetation and dry streambeds deprived of water (and cool breezes) by Haleakala.

However, the island supported ranches before World War II and studies have shown that the land in fact is fertile.

Ancient Hawaiians lived on the island until the 13th century, out left when the climate shifted and forced evacuation to other islands.

A penal colony for men in the 1830s, King Kamehameha III leased the island to cattle ranchers in the 1870s until it was taken over and destroyed by bombing, goats and lack of water management.

Bleak Kahoolawe is intensely hot and hotly contested. Native Hawaiians want it back and since 1976, a group

Niihau, a forbidding place.

Kahoolawe, largely uninhabited.

called **Protect Kahoolawe Ohana** has periodically occupied the island to protest against the bombing and claim the island on behalf of the Hawaiian people. Named after one of the four major Hawaiian gods, Kanaloa, since ancient times the island has had sacred religious significance for those traveling to Tahiti.

Ancient temples and fishing shrines on the island have survived years of bombings and the Ohana wants to preserve these historic sites and use the island for cultural and educational purposes.

Ironically, in 1981 the island was designated a National Historic Site even while it was bombed by the Federal Government.

Niihau – Forbidden Island

After more than a century of isolation from the outside world, Hawaii's mystery island is open for tightly controlled helicopter tours (see Box).

Tours start at Port Allen, the Hyatt Regency Kauai and Lihue Airport for a 15-minute helicopter ride to the formerly closed island.

From the time of Captain Cook's first visit, Niihau's Hawaiian natives raised yams for sale or barter to whalers and trading ships.

Bought by Elizabeth Sinclair from King Kamehameha V in 1864, in the Western Hemisphere only the Kalaupapa leper colony and Niihau have

Tours Open Forbidden Island

Niihau , only 17 miles southeast of Kauai, seems like an island lost somewhere in the South Seas that somehow escaped foreign traffic and intrusions. It was no accident, however, that the island has no automobiles or paved roads, mostly no electricity, no telephones or television sets, no cinemas, shops or eating places. About 225 full-blooded Hawaiians living on the island still speak their native tongue. Owned since 1864 by the Robinson family, visitors to Niihau have been banned for over 125 years.

The veil of secrecy started to be pulled from Niihau in 1987 when **Niihau Helicopters**, owned by the Robinsons, landed tourists on the northern coast, far from the island's only village. No contact was allowed with residents.

New tours started in January 1991 which permit (not encouraged or arranged) spontaneous contact with residents. The village of **Puuwai** is still off-limits. In other words, if some residents happen to be nine miles from Puuwai, in the same remote parts of the island where the helicopter lands, they are permitted to meet and talk with visitors.

There are tours originating on Kauai which provide contact cost with the natives and include a circle-island flight, two landings, a picnic lunch and snorkeling gear for several hours on the golden sands of **Puukole Beach**. Tours with no contact cost less. No video cameras or liquor are allowed on both types of tour.

The way that meetings between tourists and Niihau's residents actually happen is fascinating but fits the strange history of the island. The pilot of the helicopter, Tom Mishler, informs village elders as to whether his craft is carrying "good people." With this encouragement, some Niihau residents and elders may come to the beach to show visitors rare and valuable Niihau shell necklaces and how the necklaces are made.

been quarantined so completely from the outside world.

Purchased for $10,000 in gold, the island's ownership is in its fifth generation. A sea captain's widow from New Zealand, Elizabeth Sinclair and her descendants created a sheep and cattle ranch covering the island's grassy meadows dotted with lakes, including the largest lake in Hawaii. Hawaiians schooled and employed by the ranch purchase their food and goods from the company store.

Only one type of private business was ever permitted on the island — making intricate, beautiful shell *leis*. The tiny, multi-colored shells are collected every October when work stops for beachcombing and Niihau shell *lei*-making.

Two kinds of shells are collected — tiny pink and brown *Kahelelani* shells and *Momi*, small, lustrous shells that range in color from white to brown.

The population of the island is dwindling. About 30 youngsters attend the island's school.

Youngsters attending school on Kauai or at the Kamehameha School in Honolulu usually move into the outside world when they are ready for work and starting families.

They leave behind a island ranch that feeds about 1,200 head of cattle and 12,000 Merino sheep on scrub grass that is also home to wild pigs, turkeys and pheasants. Most of all, they separate from families who have preserved and shared their Hawaiian heritage for centuries.

Unparalleled in natural beauty among the islands, Kauai is mostly rural, inaccessible and developing slowly along its circular coastline. In recent years, however, the pace of commercial development has visibly quickened. Sugarcane still prevails across the green landscape even though, like pineapples, the crop is doomed to extinction.

In all stages of growth and harvesting, sugar has dominated Kauai's landscape since its first harvest in 1835. We still see gargantuan cane trucks stacked to overflowing with raw stalks roaring down narrow coastal roadways, heading for one of four smoking sugar mills, past a succession of bland strip-shopping centers — transplanted symbols of American suburbia engulfing and merging Kauai's once quiet and separate villages.

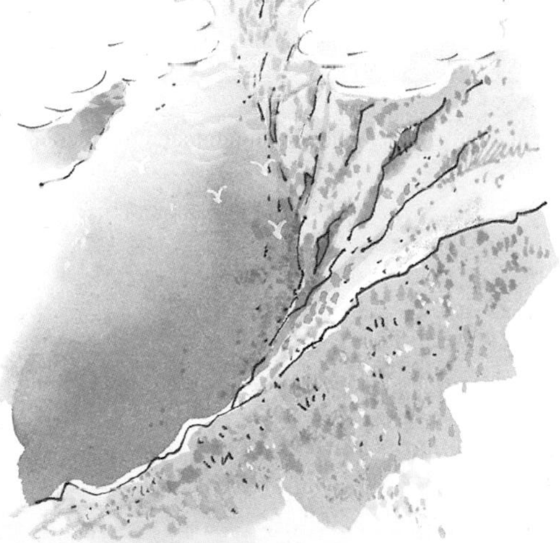

Kauai's separateness

Cruising the Na Pali Coast.

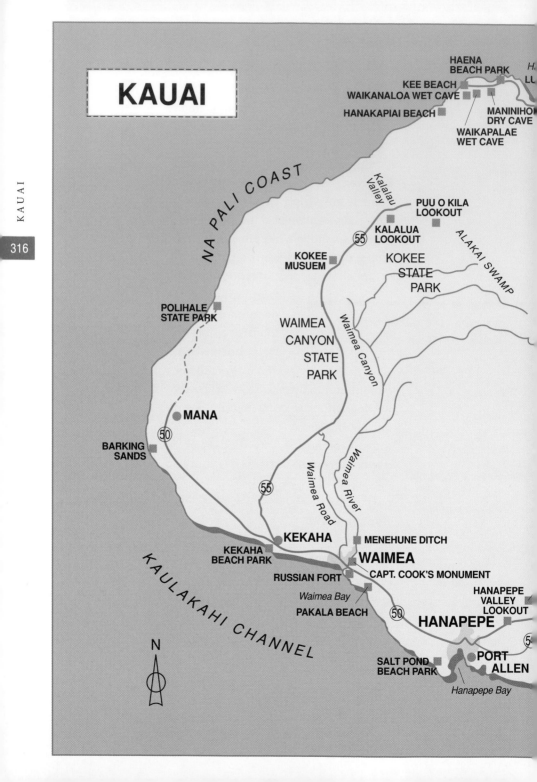

KAUAI

316

KAUAI

HAENA
BEACH PARK

H.
LL

KEE BEACH
WAIKANALOA WET CAVE

HANAKAPIAI BEACH

MANINIHO
DRY CAVE

WAIKAPALAE
WET CAVE

NA PALI COAST

Kalalau Valley

PUU O KILA
LOOKOUT

55

KALALUA
LOOKOUT

ALAKAI SWAMP

KOKEE
MUSUEM

KOKEE
STATE
PARK

POLIHALE
STATE PARK

WAIMEA
CANYON
STATE
PARK

Waimea Canyon

MANA

50

BARKING
SANDS

55

Waimea Road

Waimea River

KEKAHA

MENEHUNE DITCH

KEKAHA
BEACH PARK

WAIMEA

RUSSIAN FORT

CAPT. COOK'S MONUMENT

HANAPEPE
VALLEY
LOOKOUT

Waimea Bay

PAKALA BEACH

50

HANAPEPE

5

KAULAKAHI CHANNEL

N

SALT POND
BEACH PARK

PORT
ALLEN

Hanapepe Bay

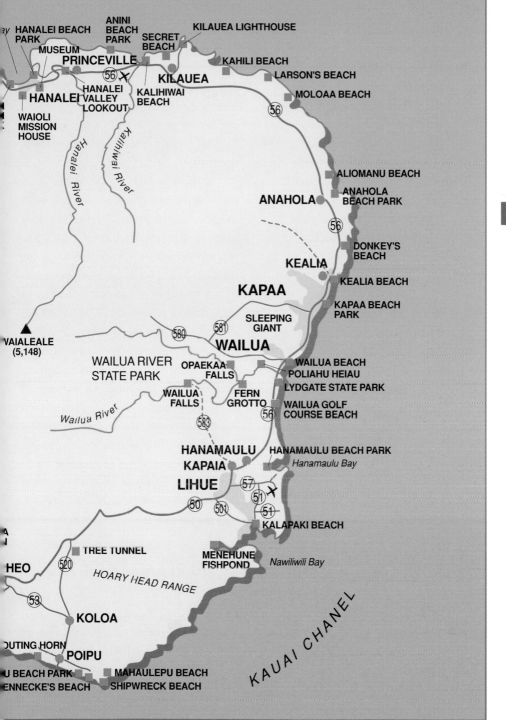

from other Hawaiian islands, geographically and even more so in spirit, intermingles with its beauty as the essence of its emotional attraction for visitors. Kauai has had "New Age " residents long before there *was* a "new age"

Early apostles of free-spirited living were especially drawn to this garden isle in the 1960s and 1970s because of its spiritual closeness to Polynesia and the strength of surviving residues of native Hawaiian culture. Of course, an important lure has been the stunning beauty of tropical landscapes and backcountry wilderness, gorgeous beaches on three completely different coastlines and picturesque (not pretty) rural towns that devoid of chic boutiques.

Westernmost of the major islands, Kauai strives most zealously to resist conquest by tourists and development advocates. On the magnificently verdant Garden Isle, issues involving protection of wilderness resources, general environmental preservation and slow-growth versus luring more tourist dollars, engender volatile and bitter political disputes before, during and after each mayoralty campaign. "Don't kill the goose that laid the golden egg" is one version of a perennially acrimonious debate largely between Kauai's beneficiaries of development and residents.

Even King Kamehameha I must have wondered why Kauai was spared conquest for so long. Having subdued the kingdoms of Maui, Oahu and Hawaii, rough seas in the channel between Oahu and Kauai doomed his first at-

tempt in 1796 at invasion of Kauai. Waiting on Oahu's shores for suitable weather six years later, Kamehameha's army was stricken by a dreadful disease (perhaps cholera or typhoid). Kauai's King Kaumuali wisely did not stretch his luck or divine blessings for a third time but struck a deal with Kamehameha that at least preserved Kauai's semi-autonomy.

Remote and roadless **Mt Waialeale**, the now extinct volcano that gave birth to Kauai, stands in cloud-veiled splendor at the center of this circular island. Catching moist winds continuously in its creased slopes, Mt Waialeale distributes over 500 inches of rainfall annually to lush northern regions – its cloud-enshrouded crater feeds streams, waterfalls and rivers winding through lush valleys growing wild bananas, guavas and mangoes. Jagged green mountains gouged by spectacular canyons spawn countless waterfalls and streams. Drenched on the windward slopes, Mt Waialeale protectively shields glistening beaches along its leeward southern flanks from more than refreshing dabbles of rainfall.

Getting Around the Island

In about 20 minutes from Honolulu, covering 110 miles, your plane lands at the new Richard A. Kawakami Terminal, opened in 1987. This airport continues to be expanded and upgraded into the mid-1990s. Nostalgically, many

A friendly face and a warm welcome to the Garden Isle.

visitors and locals remember the previous terminal, only one-fifth the size, that had the feeling of a distant tropical island.

From the terminal, you can get bus or limousine service to all hotels. Check with Gray Line Kauai (245-3344), Kauai Island Tours (245-4777), Robert's Hawaii Tours (245-9558) or Trans-Hawaiian Kauai (245-5108). Or take a taxi (Aloha Taxi, 245-4609). Otherwise, most people will rent a car. The difference in cost between major and small local companies is negligible, especially if you make reservations beforehand.

You'll need a rental car for active sightseeing on Kauai — exploring natural wonders in **Waimea Canyon**, **Kokee State Park**; and the treasured "**hidden beaches**" of east and north shores; **Poipu** and its remote beaches down a maze of canefield roads; the **National Tropical Botanical Garden**; and other places on and off-the-beaten-track. Each of these areas merit full or nearly-full-day trips even though each area is covered by half-day van tours.

East Kauai

Originally (1837) the centerpiece of a plan to create a sugar plantation, Governor Kaikioewa's failed dream for Lihue was fulfilled by Bostonians Pierce and Bishop. Lihue grew into a port, business, industrial and county seat. Lihue is the midpoint in Kauai's uncomplicated

Westin Kauai and its superb golf scenery.

coastal road system: **Highway 56** runs north to rainy, lush Princeville-Hanalei-Kee Beach; **Highway 50** runs south to the sunny beaches of Poipu, reached by the **Highway 52** leg through Koloa; and Highway 50 continues west along the sunshine coast to Waimea and remote Polihale State Park.

Lihue is only 60 miles from Oahu and yet in many respects its 6,000 residents live light-years from Honolulu. The town's name means "cool chill" but the prevailing atmosphere is friendly, warm and unhurried.

heritage and exhibits on local wildlife and geology. The **Kauai Museum** also has one of Hawaii's better museum gift shops. .

In recent years Lihue has become known as the place where the 800-acre "fantasy" **Westin Kauai resort** spreads across a network of artificial lagoons — **Kauai Lagoons** — and waterways. This water-filled wonderland connects six island-wildlife habitats (for kangaroos, zebras, gazelles, birds, monkeys and flamingos), hotel buildings, no less than 16 restaurants, two excellent golf courses, seven tennis courses, the largest swimming pool in Hawaii, a European health spa, a stadium and other natural and artificial sightseeing attractions.

Even the hotel's disco, the **Paddling Club,** has five levels of Kauai's thickest plush carpet and the state's biggest video screen. For a disco that would not dream of reducing the noise level, you'll have to join DJ Aunt Betty at **Club Jetty**, a few blocks away out on the wharf where luxury cruise liners dock.

From a viewpoint 12-stories up at **Prince Bill's Restaurant**, you can survey the richly appointed 847-room **Westin Kauai**, its marble horses bathed by spraying fountains as they prance through a reflecting pool and other regal aspects of this Versaille-in-the-tropics. This viewpoint serves a marvelous champagne Sunday brunch.

At the Westin Kauai you have a choice of – and pay as dearly for – transport by 35-passenger Venetian mahogany launches, canopied outrig-

Twin stacks of the **Lihue Sugar Company**'s mill share the center of town with a non-descript shopping center next to a little square of state and county office buildings. Adjacent to the shopping center, a distinctive black lava rock structure houses fascinating artifacts which embody the story of Kauai's ethnic history, missionary past, art and

Luxury is not lacking at the Westin.

ger canoes, or carriages drawn through eight-miles of carriage paths by Clydesdales, Belgians, or Percherons.

Resort restaurants at the Westin Kauai reached by these modes of transportation include: elegant dining (jackets required) in the **Masters**, where the menu is based on a Michelin four-star restaurant and the wine cellar shelters over 300 labels; the **Inn on the Cliffs**, where you'll savour seafood and pasta while enjoying a broad ocean view; and less formal and pricey, **The Terrace**, in the **Kauai Lagoon's Golf and Racquet**

trees once grew), most visitors to Kauai probably would bypass Lihue. Pity! A great public beach (adjoining but not belonging to the Westin Kauai) and one of the best swimming and bodysurfing beaches on the island — **Kalapaki Beach** — is just five minutes from the center of town. Unless you decide to stay at the Westin Kauai, Lihue itself is not your best choice for a touring base, except for budget accommodations like the **Hale Lihue Motel** or the slightly higher priced **Garden Island Inn**.

However, Lihue has the largest concentration of excellent and inexpensive restaurants in Hawaii. Huge steaming bowls of golden broth are served at **Hamura Saimin** and an amazing variety of tasty, inexpensive Japanese, American and Chinese specialties, Homemade bread and fresh pies are served at the **Barbecue Inn**.

Within a few blocks of one another are **Tip Top Restaurant Bakery** (macadamia nut pancakes for breakfast), **Dani's** (American-Hawaiian-Japanese meals, and sashimi, ramen) and **Restaurant Kiibo** (authentic Japanese food dished out a bargain prices).

One of Kauai's greatest delights, a *maile lei* with an anise-like scent or a rare *mokihana lei* with a sweet, spicy fragrance, should be ordered ahead at **Fujimoto Flowers**. Alternatively, call **Irmalee Pomroy** in nearby Kapaa, one of Hawaii's finest *lei*-makers, to prepare a fresh ginger, royal *ilima* or other *lei* to bless your tour of the Garden Isle.

Locals frequent nearby **Hana-**

Club, with views over the swimming pool to the **Haupo Mountains**; and **Duke's Canoe Club**, where steaks, ribs and seafood are served in the hotel's boathouse on the sands of **Kalapaki Beach**.

If not for the Lihue Airport and now the extravagant Westin Kauai resort on **Nawiliwili Harbor** (where the *wiliwili*

Menehunes

Kauai, the oldest Hawaiian island, is believed to be the first one populated by Polynesians. Kauai was *Pele*'s first home until her sister drove her away.

Hawaiian legends tell of dwarf-like aborigines called *Mu* and *Menehune*, two tribes that lived on the island before Polynesians arrived. Only two or three-ft tall with hairy, muscular bodies, *Menehune* were nocturnal creatures and fabulous stonemasons. Many unusual stoneworks around the island are attributed to these hard-working little people.

The most famous example of their stonework is the **Menehune Ditch** outside of Waimea where, legend says *Ola*, high chief of Waimea, ordered it built. According to archaeologists, this mysterious stone wall encasing an aqueduct was built with non-Polynesian masonry techniques and not with stone tools used later by Hawaiians!

Legend also has it that a fishpond near Lihue call **Alakoko** was built for a young prince and princess by *Menehunes*. No one was supposed to watch them at work. An aqueduct along **Huleia Stream** was built overnight, stones passed from person to person in a line that supposedly stretched 25 miles. However, the royal couple broke their word, peeked and were turned into stone — twin pillars that today sit on a ridge above the pond.

After finishing their stonework tasks on Kauai, the *Menehunes* were gathered together by their king who was determined to save them from assimilation by Polynesians. An island descended from the heavens and the *Menehunes* floated away on it, some say, to outer islands where stone gods have been found that are unlike any elsewhere in Hawaii.

---

maulu **County Beach Park**, almost unknown to tourists, where campers (with permits) can find showers. Beautifully landscaped with stone pagodas and pebbled paths around a pond filled with flashing carp, **Hanamauku Restaurant and Tea House** is just two miles north on Highway 56. Take one of their plate lunches down to the park or, in the evening, enjoy the Miyaki family's hospitality for a special Eastern banquet while sitting on the floor in an *ozashiki* (tea-house) at a long, low table looking out into the lovely lighted garden.

On the way out of Lihue, Julie Yakamura's **Kapaia Stitchery** carries an unusual assortment of needlework articles sold only in her store – handmade batiks, silkscreened and handpainted fabrics, one-of-a-kind needlepoint canvases and custom-made *aloha*

shirts. Open 10am-4:30pm, Mon-Sat.

Wailua

According to legend, the area where the **Wailua River** meets **Wailua Bay** was claimed by Hawaii's royalty (*alii*) as their private territory. Their *mana* (spiritual power) was great, surpassed only by the gods. After beaching their double-hulled canoes at the river's headwaters, they planted *kapu* sticks to keep commoners out (on pain of death), and the banks became sacred ground.

In between sunning and surfing on the superb beach, playing along the river's grottoes and waterfalls in the tropical forest, building temples and residences, the chiefs dug freshwater lagoons to fatten their fish catches and

Falling water and natural surroundings.

planted magnificent groves of coconut trees.

In the 1840s, Deborah Kapule, widow of Kauai's last king, lived here and tended fish in her ponds, torchlit for regal evening meals of mullet. A coconut grove on this property planted years later by a German doctor with visions of starting a plantation became a major tourist attraction. The **Coconut Coast** from Wailua to Kapaa takes its name from the remains of these towering coconut groves. The venerable **Coco Palms Resort**'s thatched roofed cottages around

Queen Kapule's former fishponds ("lagoons") are particularly attractive. Around sunset each day, a ceremonial tradition of lighting torches in the coconut grove is carried on by the Coco Palms.

Before arriving at Wailua, a really pretty beach lies hidden behind the **Wailua Golf Course** reached by a dirt road along the southern end of the links off Highway 56. Lengthy **Wailua Beach** provides many enjoyable places for swimming, picnicking and unofficial camping.

The remains of an ancient place of sanctuary for *kapu*-breakers and one of many *heiaus* along the river, are found in **Lydgate State Park** at Leho Drive just south of the Wailua River. Along a rugged stretch of coast fringed by magnificent ironwoods, even children can swim safely and snorkel in clean water fronting Lydgate Park's white-sand beach.

At the remains of **Holoholoku Heiau**, once a site for human sacrifice, about a mile up the **Wailua River**, are two **royal birthing stones** believed to possess great *mana* to aid childbirth. Royal mothers traveled here to give birth. One of the most popular and beautiful tourist attractions in Hawaii, the **Fern Grotto**, a huge rock amphitheater draped by ferns under a cascade of water, is three miles up Wailua River, reachable only by a 20-minute boatride.

Enroute to the Fern Grotto, onboard entertainers crack seemingly endless corny jokes and musicians play the "Hawaiian Wedding Song". A steady stream of escorted brides and grooms in privately-rented boats come to exchange vows in the famous green cathedral. The $1^1/_2$-hour trip to Fern Grotto on Hawaii's only navigable river is a worthwhile experience for those who stay in the right frame of mind and keep their eyes on the spectacular green beauty of the river and amphitheater. Contact **Smith's Boat Tours** or **Waialeale Boat Tours** for reservations.

Smith's Tropical Paradise, a 30-acre botanical garden, is filled with a marked collection of Kauai's ordinary, rare and exotic foliage. Skip plywood facsimiles of Japanese, Philippine and Polynesian villages but the botanical garden is worth seeing. There is a guided tram-tour from 8:30am to 4:30pm.

The *luau*/musical show in the evening is as good as any that you'll see on the island with the exception of the incomparably spirited and unpretentious *luau* at the **Tahiti Nui** in Hanalei. The *luau* at the **Sheraton Coconut Beach** is a competitor for food but not for Polynesian show entertainment.

Several miles up Route 580, **Wailua State Park** protects the river and across the road, is lovely **Opaekaa Falls and Lookout**. Across the road at the Lookout, a Hawaiian family has put together **Kamokila Hawaiian Village**.

The road down to **Kamokila Hawaiian Village** on the left just before getting to the falls leads to a village on an island above the **Wailua River**. Restored thatched homes, a sleeping house, eating house with utensils, a herbalist's house, taro patches, ancient implements, demonstrations of *poi*-pounding and preparation of medicinal plants, all are part of the guided tour. Hula dancing and other Hawaiian entertainment is scheduled at regular intervals. Three miles further up the river, **Keahua Arboretum** is an ideal place to picnic and swim.

Take Route 580 to the **University of Hawaii Agricultural Experiment Station**, drive about 2 miles to the **Keahua Stream** where the trailhead starts just past the stream. The **Keahua Trail** is about a half-mile long through a forest reserve maintained by the Division of Forestry. Marked posts identify many varieties of native and exotic plants and trees.

From the Keahua Trail, a panorama of the coastline opens to the east and the **Makaleha Mountains** to the northwest. The trail through the Arboretum is half a mile long. The well-maintained and extremely beautiful **Kuilau Ridge Trail** leads from the Arboretum a little over two miles through a gorgeous area with waterfalls to a ridge where you have a choice of picnic sites with panoramic views. Allow two hours each way.

Kapaa and Waipouli

Coco Palms Resort with its 45- acres of coconut trees and a lagoon is renowned for its nightly torchlight ceremony. On the *makai* side of Route 56, the **Sheraton Coconut Beach** with lovely grounds and a popular nightly *luau* is the northern anchor of **Coconut Plantation Resort**. **Kapaa Village** stretched along Route 56 begins just north of the Plantation. Coconut Plantation, about a mile north of Wailua and Coco Palms, includes other hotels, condos and the **Market Place**. The more than 70 shops in the Market Place include **Waves of One Sea and Elephant Walk** (Hawaiian gift items), island art at **Kahn Gallery**, scrimshaw at the **Ye Olde Ship Store** and hand-printed clothing at **Tahiti Imports**

Further north, **Sleeping Giant** mountain behind Coco Palms shelters an undulating valley and beautiful forest reserve trails on the perimeter reached by Routes 581 or 58. **Nonou Mountain Trail** (east side) begins off Haleilio Road, 1.2 miles from the junction of routes 56 and 580 and climbs 1,250 ft to its summit. The **west side trail** starts on Route 581 and joins the **east side trail** at a picnic area about 250 ft below the summit in the **Nonou Forest Reserve**.

Pick up some fresh local pineapples (which can also be packed and delivered to the airport), papayas, mangoes, bananas or other fruit at the roadside **Farm Fresh Fruit Stand**. In the nearby **Kauai Village Shopping Center**, artist Jacqueline Sibthorpe's **Art to Wear** is full of attractive hand-painted clothing.

East Kauai's champion breakfast eatery is the **Kountry Kitchen**. Authentic Hawaiian food at the absolutely no-

Wood Carvers

Michael Sussman uses beautiful *koa* and spruce to build some of the finest ukuleles and guitars anywhere. Recently, he has even dared to make *koa* violins. His Anahola Valley studio — hard to find but worth looking for — stacks of *koa* and other wood dry and harden before Sussman carves them into different parts of instruments.

Kapaa's **Robert Hamada** carves hardwoods grown and cured on Kauai (*kauila, kamani, kou, hau, milo,* and camphor).

Trees of different ages growing in varying conditions at different elevations produce different colors and qualities of wood that Sussman, Hamada and other wood artists use. Hamada's favourites are *milo* trunks and *hau*. The search for superb wood and grains, such as a *hau* or camphor tree, suitable for turning into bowls and free-form sculpture never ends for these dedicated wood artists.

A self-taught woodworker for over 50 years, Hamada has become expert in identifying and harvesting valuable trees with special properties, like 100-year-old *hau* trees with grains of deep blacks and mauves.

He follows in the footsteps of his father who trained as a carpenter and smith in Japan and carved beautiful stone markers for Japanese cemeteries and the great stone bowls used for pounding.

Hamada knows exactly where the best trees for woodturning remain around Kauai, especially scarce *koa* and valuable *milo*. Tree owners contact him when valuable trees are ready to be cut and sold. Nearly 70, he still logs and cuts his own trees to turn in his workshop — a beautiful, secluded location at the foot of Sleeping Giant.

frills **Aloha Diner** in the **Waipouli Complex** means *lomi-lomi* salmon, *kalua* pig, *poke ahi*, among others. **Norberto's El Cafe** in the Roxy Theatre building serves some of the best Mexican food you'll find in Hawaii (open for dinner only).

Nearby, the excellent **Restaurant Kintaro** also serves dinner only, Mon-Sat, 5:30-9:30pm. Under the same ownership, **DS Collection Gallery** next door carries exceptional block prints, ceramics and other fine Japanese and made-in-Hawaii art and craft work. For seafood, you won't be disappointed with the **Kapaa Fish and Chowder House** .

Anahola to Kilauea

Anahola's claim to fame used to be especially sweet and luscious pineapples, now scarce.

Wonderful watermelons and papayas still grow in Anahola. **Duane's Ono-Char Burger**, a busy roadside stand, brings additional glory to liitle Anahola. Health-conscious travelers will be pleased with Duane's avocado burger piled with alfalfa sprouts, cheddar cheese and lettuce and covered with teriyaki sauce.

On the way into Kilauea, on Kolo Road just off Highway 56, the **Hawaiian Art Museum and Bookstore** features selections of Hawaiian music and books for adults and children that you won't find elsewhere except at Aloha International's other, newer shop in Kapaa, **Kauai Village Museum and Gift Shop**.

Kilauea boasts the title of "Guava Capital of the World," thanks to **Guava Kai Plantation**'s 480-acres under cultivation.

Hidden Beaches of East Kauai

The hidden strands of East Kauai start on the oceanfront of the **Wailua Golf Course**. Locals, especially surfers who enjoy good breaks off its reef, refer to the waters off this part of Wailua as "cemetery". A dirt road on the southern Lihue end of the golf course leads to a pretty beach that offers miles for swimming, snorkeling and unofficial camping.

Bypass **Kapaa Beach Park**. Much better choices of beaches are further north along Highway 56 — **Kealia Beach** and hideaway **Donkey's Beach**, a favorite for unofficial camping in the midst of towering ironwoods, reached by hiking a half-mile down a cane road on the right just before the 12-mile marker.

Anahola Beach Park is a ribbon of sand on the near side of Anahola Bay. On the far side of Anahola Bay is **Aliomanu Beach** which offers safe swimming. These beaches are reached from Route 56 by Anahola Road and Aliomanu Road, respectively.

A leisurely drive northward through sparkling green countryside leads to the turn-off for two of Kauai's loveliest hidden beaches. From Koolau Road, turn on Moloaa Road to the end for **Moloaa Beach** tucked into Moloaa Bay. A little over a mile past the turnoff to Moloaa Road, turn right onto a cane road, then left for 1¹/₂ miles, down two dirt roads to secluded **Larson's Beach**, one of the most appealing places in Hawaii for unofficial camping. This long, narrow, winding white sand beach protected by a reef is excellent for swimming and snorkeling (except in October-April and also at both ends of the beach, where there are bad rip currents).

Between Larson's Beach and Kilauea Bay, another stretch of glorious white sand, **Waiakalua Iki Beach**, nestles at the mouth of Waiakalua Iki Gulch. Bordered by rolling, tree-covered hills, tucked into a cove with its own lagoon, secluded **Kahili Beach** (or what locals call **Quarry Beach**) on Kilauea Bay is reached from Kilauea Road. Just before Kilauea Road

Sailing along the calmer beaches of Kauai.

veers up toward the lighthouse, a narrow dirt road to the right leads 1¹/₂ miles to **Kahili Beach** tucked in a small cove. This dirt road circles **Mokolea Point**'s **Crater Hill**, now part of the **Kilauea National Wildlife Refuge**, adjoining the 78-year old **Kilauea Lighthouse**, a national historic landmark, in retirement since 1976.

Secret Beach, visible to the north from the Lighthouse, and accessed from around the corner, has become the most popular unofficial camping spot among the north coast's string of hidden beaches despite its beautiful, wide, white sand with trees shading its edge. It is accessed by a steep dirt path which can be slippery after rain, through heavy growth. The walk down takes about 15 minutes.

Further north along the coast, the skeleton of a bridge over the Kalihiwai River is a grim reminder of the 1946 tidal wave that devastated this area. Take Kalihiwai Road on the Kilauea side of the river to the peaceful lagoon under the bridge and the green hills, high rock walls and ironwood trees surrounding **Kalihiwai Beach**. Unofficial camping under the ironwoods is easy since the road leads directly to the beach.

Protected by a reef, the smooth-as-glass ocean in front of **Anini Beach Park** is a children's playground, especially busy on weekends. More privacy can be found following dirt roads off Anini Road that lead to more secluded Anini beaches.

Daily tours operate 9am-5pm. A collection of restaurants, bakeries and shops off Lighthouse Road, in and adjacent to the **Kong Lung Center**, provide delightful and refreshing breaks. The **Kong Lung Company**, Kauai's 110-year-old plantation general store, displays some of the finest, most tasteful crafts and antiques from around the world that you'll see in Hawaii. Next door, the **Kahale Kau Trading Company** sells Asian art of the same caliber.

Two outstanding bakeries — **The Bread Also Rises** and **Jacques** — in Kilauea dispense unsurpassed choices of baked goods.

The *al fresco* **Casa di Amici** serves delicious Italian food, pesto and alfredo sauces and tasty pasta dishes like pasta with walnuts in a Romano cheese cream sauce.

Kilauea Lighthouse, two miles from Kilauea on a promontory above the crashing sea, is an ideal viewpoint for watching seabirds, dolphins, seals and from December to May, humpback whales.

Onlookers perched on a high bluff above the sea at the Lighthouse can see: great frigate birds sail on air cushions below, the courtship dance of the Laysan albatross (November-June) and colonies of wedge-tailed shearwaters and other marine birds.

In spring and summer, the comical red-footed booby make somersaults and dances wearing their red dancing shoes and most importantly nest and raise their young.

Princeville

On a royal vacation in 1860, Kamehameha IV, Queen Emma and their son, Prince Albert, visited the rolling plateau overlooking Hanalei Bay. That regal event inspired its naming as **Princeville**. First a sugar plantation and

The Princeville, luxury set close to the beauty
of nature and the ocean.

then Kauai's largest cattle ranch, the 11,000-acre Princeville resort today is built around several championship golf courses, with thousands of acres of development still on the drawing boards.

The new 252-room **Sheraton Mirage Princeville**, practically rebuilt on its old site, is one of the most elegant hotels in Hawaii in one of the most beautiful settings of any resort in Hawaii or the world. For visitors who want more space and privacy for less money, the resort includes a variety of first-rate condominiums like the **Hanalei Bay**

Resort, **Puu Poa**, with a secluded beach a short way down the hill, **Pali Ke Kua** and **The Cliffs**.

Hanalei

Just minutes away, **Hanalei** is situated on the bay below Princeville and over a narrow one-lane bridge across the **Hanalei River** that unintentionally serves as a blessed barrier to large, heavy tour buses and construction trucks. Cross the Hanalei River on Highway 56 over Hanalei Bridge, a steel bridge pre-fabricated in New York, erected in 1912 and now on the National Register of Historic Landmarks.

Village, river and the beautiful valley along its bank take their name from Hanalei ("crescent bay") Bay. The **Hanalei Lookout** at the top of the hill before descending into the valley is one of the most spectacular and tranquil vistas in Hawaii — terraced taro patches surround the Hanalei River as it weaves its way nine miles toward three magnificent mountains and a 3,500-ft *pali* over which more than a dozen waterfalls cascade. Waterfall activity along the Waioli Ridge in back of Hanalei, the birthplace of rainbows, has a backdrop of four mountain peaks ending at the Makana Ridge, start of the **Na Pali**.

Hanalei's marshland was converted into irrigated farmland by Polynesians and even earlier voyagers. (According to legend, the last *Menehunes* lived here.) Until the mid-1800s, the Valley's fields

were cultivated by Hawaiians. Chinese rice growers replaced them until the mid-20th century when rice became unprofitable to grow. Since then, taro has returned as the prevailing crop and today Hanalei Valley grows the largest taro patch in Hawaii.

Each taro crop takes about 8-18 months to grow. Verdant taro fields are

Hawaiian sunset at Hanalei.

the most visible reminder on Kauai of ancient Hawaii when the first settlers came to the Valley 1,400 years ago. Many taro growers in the valley cultivate their crops under the watchful eye of the US Fish & Wildlife Service whose mission is to protect wildlife. Preserved as a **National Wildlife Refuge**, the valley is home to the Hawaiian duck, Hawaiian stilt and the endangered Hawaiian gallinule.

For decades Hanalei has been the center of counter-culture on Kauai and a gathering place for escapists of all types. Hanalei's hodge-podge of ramshackle and new buildings, including general stores, restaurants, museums, boutiques, galleries and shops, appropriately reflect Hanalei's nonconformist charm and mystique. A notable departure from this unplanned pattern is the **Old Hanalei School**, recently refurbished for tourist-oriented shops and restaurants. Registered with the National Register, this building was moved to its present site by the Wilcox family, wealthy descendants of local missionaries and sugar growers who restored **Waioli Mission House Museum** (see below) and **Kilohana** near Lihue, both family properties.

The **Artisans' Guild of Kauai**, upstairs in the **Old Ching Young Store**, showcases local painters and craftspeople. *Maile* and *pikake leis* are sold in the same building at **Pua & Kawika's Flowers & Gifts**. **Ola's** on Kuhio Highway sells a striking variety of woodwork, ceramics and other gifts. Next door to the relatively new **Ching Young Village Shopping Center**, the **Native Hawaiian Trading and Cultural Center** contains a collection of small shops, selling everything from artifacts and jewelry to sundries and knick-knacks, and the tiny **Hale Lea Museum**.

Hanalei comes together day or night at the family-owned and friendly **Tahiti Nui** on Highway 56, the prime local gathering place, down-to-earth, casual and fun with its weather-beaten exterior and thatched-wall interior. Nighttime entertainment is mostly spontane-

Na Pali Trail— Kalalau

Occupied a thousand years ago by *kuaaina* (backcountry folk), villages surrounded by sacred temples and elaborate terraced farms lived peacefully between high cliffs surrounding each valley along the Na Pali Coast. Taro farmers and their families worked Kalalau Valley until the 1920s, one of the last undeveloped and untamed parts of the Hawaiian Islands.

Walking the trail to Kalalau non-stop takes a long, 9-hour day. This strenuous hike requires good boots, a backpack, waterproof tent, a small stove and light blanket or sleeping bag. Be prepared to boil or chemically treat all water. The trail should be hiked in two parts, with a break at **Hanokoa** on the way in and **Hanakapiai** on the way out and another overnight at **Kalalau Beach**. (Don't try to return from Hanakapiai in the dark!) Erosion caused by rain can make the 11-mile trail hazardous between October and May and also during June rains. From May to September, the water is calm enough to land on Kalalau Beach in a canoe.

It only takes an hour to walk the two miles from Kee Beach to **Hanakapiai Beach** where you can enjoy a picnic lunch, swim in the pools in the stream or, between May and September, cautiously swim in the ocean.

On a lovely trail through narrow, sheltered **Hanakapiai Valley**, once thickly settled, continue to **Hanalapiai Falls**, an easy hike (2 miles) for about an hour. (You pass the turn-off to the Falls on the main trail down to the beach.) Notice the abandoned taro patches, stone walls and house foundations, and a large stone chimney that is all that remains of a small coffee mill.

ous, mainly Hawaiian songs. Owner Auntie Louise Marston sometimes chimes in with her renditions of Tahitian songs and *hula*. The *luau* on Wednesday and Friday nights is deservedly popular and reservations are essential. Chef Jeff Bolman prepares consistently good lunches and dinners that are even better. A relaxed, beach-shack atmosphere

Guava and mango trees bear succulent fruit here. Follow the main stream and you can't go far wrong. (If the stream is flooding, don't continue!) Hanalapiai Falls cascades about 300 feet to pools below. Find safe pools to swim in away from the pool at the base of the falls where rocks may fall on unsuspecting people below.

Rainy **Hanakoa** is four miles and two small valleys away from Hanakapiai. At a leisurely pace, the hike should take less than three hours along frequent switchbacks past breath-taking drop-offs. If it's not raining in Hanakoa, many pools in the stream offer delightful places to swim. There are ample camping sites sheltered on old agricultural terraces. Remember that constant rain impacts on cliffs that hold parts of the trail to **Hanakoa Falls**, which may cause slides. Clear pools for swimming at these falls are delightful rewards for weary hikers.

The toughest part of the trail begins at Hanakoa and covers five miles to **Kalalau Beach**. Hike early to avoid the hot afternoon sun while traversing switchbacks up and down cliffs and

also to have plenty of time to stop here and there to enjoy spectacular views. The land dries out along the way. Kalalau is the largest and most beautiful of the valleys along the trail. Edged with a lovely ivory sand beach, camping is allowed on the beach, under trees near the beach and in caves at the west end of the beach (with a permit available from the Division of State Parks). A small waterfall at the west end of the beach provides *treatable* water.

From mid-May to early October, take a boat trip in relatively calm seas to see the wonders of the Na Pali Coast. Most tours are on heavy-duty 23-ft inflatable rafts made famous by Jacques Cousteau and started on Kauai by **Captain Zodiac**. **Lady Ann Cruises** has a 38-ft sailboat out of Lihue. Like the other companies, guests can snorkel ashore, tour ruins of an ancient Hawaiian village and have lunch on a Na Pali Coast beach. This unforgettable tour lasts $5\text{-}1/2$ to 6 hours. Shorter tours, including whale-watching in season (December 15-March 15), are provided year-round.

Hiking near Na Pali Coast.

and very good seafood also can be found at the **Hanalei Shell House**.

On the other end of town, behind **Waioli Huiia Church**, the **Waioli Mission House Museum** is the former residence of the Wilcoxes and other mid-18th century Protestant missionaries. Living rooms and bedrooms are full of interesting missionary artifacts and history. The museum is open Tuesdays, Thursdays and Saturdays until 3pm

Horseshoe-shaped Hanalei Bay's three parks – **Hanalei Beach Park**, **Hanalei Pavilion** and **Waioli Beach Park** – all share wonderful mountain and ocean views. Except near **Hanalei Pier**, swimming conditions at these beaches are dangerous.

Rounding a curve near the five-mile marker on Route 56, a memorable vista appears suddenly – **Lumahai Beach** set in a cove surrounded by lush green hills – the *Bali Hai* beach better known as *Nurse's Beach* in the classic movie *South Pacific*. The east (*South Pacific*) end of Lumahai is reached by a steep trek through dense foliage; and the west end can be reached by car.

One-lane bridges on Route 56, crossing places where water streams down from the northern mountain slopes, siphon traffic along the road to Haena and Kee beaches. **Haena Beach Park**, across from **Maninoholo Dry Cave**, occasionally gets crowded. More secluded **Haena beaches** are located off access roads along Route 56. Legend says that Maniniholo Dry Cave was created by *Menehunes*; whereas geologists say it is a

lava tube. Nearby **Waikapalae** and **Waikanaloa Wet Caves** are said to be the work of *Pele* seeking fire in the earth — only to find water.

Kalalau trail, **Haena State Park** and the park's **Kee Beach**, begin at the end of Route 56. Enclosed by a brilliantly colored coral reef full of tropical fish, Kee Beach offers the best snorkeling and often some of the best swimming on Kauai. A short hike to **Kaulu o Laka Heiau**, sacred to *Laka*, goddess of the *hula*, reveals a most important *hula* site where traditionally *hula* masters express devotion to their *hula* mistress. The stone shrine honors *Laka*. Young male dancers were trained in the ancient art on this sacred site. Many legends surround this revered *heiau* located behind the **Allerton House**. One says *Pele* transformed herself into a mortal to join the *hula* festival and fell in love with Chief Lohiau.

Day hikers can leave their cars locked at Kee Beach and walk a few arduous hours two miles to **Hanakapiai Valley**. A white sand beach at Hanakapiai appears in summer and disappears again in winter. For hikes beyond Hanakapiai, permits and appropriate camping gear are required.

Kukui Grove Center

On the outskirts of tiny Lihue is **Kukui Grove Center**. The redeeming feature of this otherwise featureless mall is **Stone's Gallery** displaying the largest collec-

Kauai's Art Celebrates Nature

The island's artists and craftspeople translate Kauai's natural beauty into many different styles and media — Hanalei Valley's taro pads; Hanapepe Valley in the old plantation days, pristine tidal pools and views of scenic hidden beaches, the Wailua River winding through lush valleys, spectacular Waimea Canyon and views from Kokee's trails, Wailua, Opaekaa and other waterfalls, the lush beauty of Na Pali seascapes and the Kalalau Valley wilderness from above and below and many more of the Garden Isle's scenery.

The art is in abstract, contemporary, figurative, impressionist and other styles — James Hoyle's vivid impressionism in pastels; watercolors by Patrice Pendarvis, Fredrick KenKnight, Silva Segrist, Jean Gregg and Maria Pacca; oils on canvas by Paul Yardley, Dane Clark and Reuben Tam (Kauai's most renowned and successful painter, whose oils and acrylic works are in the museum and private collections throughout the world). Celebration of the spirit of the island where he was born and grew up has been the goal of Tam's art.

Some of Stone's artists are exceptionally successful in depicting Kauai's mountains, clouds and water. Lanai-born Ande Lau Chen's landscapes, in mixed media monotypes and acrylic-and-paper collages, capture inspiration she has found hiking and back-packing throughout the island, driving almost every back road and flying over its remote areas in an airplane.

George Sumner's dolphins live in perfect harmony with the mist over the Na Pali and mother humpback whales and their children. Marine art is featured at **Kahn Galleries** in the **Market Place** at Coconut Plantation and a new gallery in **Anchor Cove**, next to the Westin Kauai.

Roy Tabora's seascapes, vibrant impressionistic landscapes by Jan Parker and bold still-life paintings by Steve Mei have been featured as local art in Kahn Galleries. Marty Kahn's three **Island Images** fine art print shops located in the Market Place, Koloa, and Hanalei are one of the better sources on the island for good value in prints and posters by local artists depicting the island's beauty.

tion of Kauai's most talented artists and artisans together with a tasteful selection of gift items.

Stone's Expresso Cafe in one corner of the store serves tasty light meals, pastries and a rare experience on Kauai, excellent capaccino. **See You in China** is Kukui's other interesting gift shop specializing in hand-painted clothing, cloisonné and other jewelry.

Kilohana and Grove Farm Homestead

Located nearby on Highway 50, **Kilohana** completely contrasts with

Kukio Shopping Center and lives up to the meaning of its name. This elegant plantation home was once the most expensive house built on Kauai. Owner Gaylord Wilcox, nephew of the founder of **Grove Farm Homestead**, made it the center of uppercrust social, cultural and business life in the mid-1930s, the heyday of Hawaii's sugar industry.

Take lunch *al fresco* in Kilohana at **Gaylord's** covered courtyard restaurant facing a grassy lawn — one of the most comfortable and delicious meals on Kauai. One light choice might be local papaya stuffed with bay shrimp, accompanied by vegetables or fruits picked in season from Kilohana's own garden,

A homestead that is in contrast with its surroundings.

and a delicious dessert. Cheese blintzes with Kauai Portuguese sausage for Sunday brunch, consumed in the surroundings of Gaylord's museum furnishings and Kilohana crater etched majestically against the horizon, is a very special way of beginning an unhurried day of touring.

Open to the public as a house-museum and posh shopping place, Kilohana has been painstakingly restored with many of its original furnishings and artifacts. The Wilcoxes' bedroom is now full of art by Hawaiian artists in **Kilohana Galleries**. Chic shops offer some of the most worthwhile browsing on the island — **Cane Field Clothing**, with the island's best selection of contemporary sportswear; Niihau shells and Hawaiian jewelry in the **Hawaiian Collection**; along with hand-painted clothing and Japanese-style gift items like *tansu* chests and kimonos.

Island Memories in Kilohana, one of the better little shops in Hawaii for one-of-a-kind Pacific Island and Hawaiian gifts, displays a large variety of superb feather hatbands and hand-carved woods featuring Robert Hamada's turned-wood bowls, vases and free-form works. The **Artisan's Room** downstairs sells unusual wood carvings and ceramics. Upstairs, **Sea Reflections** carries rare and unusual shells from around the Pacific. In the former Wilcox Guest Cottage, **Stone's at Kilohana**, a branch of the main gallery, specializes in arts and crafts from around the Pacific.

Thanks to Miss Mable, George Wilcox's neice, the **Grove Farm Homestead**, was carefully preserved and converted into a museum in 1971 for guided tours. The tour is offered only on Mondays, Wednesdays and Thursdays, and lasts about two hours (starting at 10am and 1pm.).

Koloa

Along Highway 50 heading for the turnoff to Koloa, the beautiful route from Lihue aims at Knudsen Gap between the Haupu Range and the Kahili Ridge, Kawaikini and Waialeale peaks usually vanish into thick clouds. Highway 52 or *Maluhia* ("Serenity") Road turns toward Koloa through a mile-long **Tree Tunnel** — Australian eucalyptus trees planted in 1911 by Walter McBride to form a dramatic gateway to his sugar plantation domain.

A picturesque plantation town dating back to 1835, **Koloa** declined with the sugar industry until tourism started its rejuvenation in the early 1970s. Rusty tins roofs, sagging and bulging walls, dilapidated porches, weathered timber and other remnants of economic decline still visible in the 1980s have been painted over and gentrified into **Old Koloa Town**. Ruins of Kauai's first **sugar mill** remain as a picturesque relic of days when owners paid workers in scrip redeemable at the mill's grocery store. Down Hapa Road, off Weliweli Road, in the churchyard of **St Raphael's Church**, Kauai's oldest Roman Catholic Church, are the burial plots of plantation workers and their families.

About three miles north of Poipu, picturesque Koloa today is a thriving shopping village with over 40 stores and restaurants. A few shops in Koloa stand out for discrimination and quality. **Kahana Ki'i Gallery** has had an artist-owner, Dawn Steinhart, for over 11 years. Steinhart's collagraphs, etchings and acrylics of Kauai's landscapes and other subjects are very evocative and memorable. She has brought many fine artists from Kauai and other islands into this showcase for local art and crafts: fused glass, ceramic sculpture, pottery, hand-painted silks, turned-wood bowls and more. Around the corner, Bob and Sutji Gunter's **Indo-Pacific Trading Post** gathers very interesting fine art and gift items from around Asia and the Pacific.

Poipu

Sun-drenched beaches line Poipu's old sugarcane coast, boasting excellent swimming, snorkeling, diving and surfing. Hotels and condominiums cluster along Poipu's playground of the *alii* where Hawaiian fishermen still mend their nets and "talk story" at popular **Poipu Beach Park**. The *mahimahi* tee-shirts clinging to so many playful bodies on nearby **Brennecke's Beach** come from a popular lunch and drinking spot with beachgoers, **Brennecke's Beach Broiler**.

Dipping at Poipu's beaches.

From the lush tropical park-like setting of the condominium **Kiahuna Plantation**, once part of Hawaii's oldest sugercane plantation, locals beachcomb among shore rocks for edible *opihi*. Meanwhile, inside deluxe shorefront restaurants, local seafood is served without this delicious tent-shaped mollusk — ironically because *opihi* is too expensive (almost $200 a gallon). Amidst the prolific greenery of palm trees, ferns, bamboo and monkeypods at Kiahuna's **Plantation Gardens** restaurant, the "Hawaiian Wedding Song" can often be

sort next to the park fits the architecturally restrained image of beachfront development. By ordinance, buildings in Poipu cannot exceed the height of a coconut tree (four storeys). More relaxed than the adjoining **Sheraton Kauai**, the Waiohau also caters to guests seeking quiet candle-light suppers of continental cuisine and distinctive European wines, fulfilled perfectly by **The Tamarind**.

Next door, even the more casual, family-oriented **Stouffer Poipu Beach Hotel** has candlelit tables for romantic dinners at its **Poipu Beach Cafe**. The view from the adjoining Sheraton's beachside **Outrigger Room** restaurant takes in a restored early 17th century *heiau* built of lava rocks in front of the Waiohai.

The unpretentious **Stouffer Poipu Beach Resort** is much cheaper than its elegant neighbor, **Stouffer Waiohai Beach Resort** and shares many of the same facilities, including the tennis club, **Kiahuna Golf Course** and a stretch of Poipu Beach out-front.

Just a few years ago, beautiful **Keoneloa Bay** and its **Shipwreck Beach** were reached off a cane road where the new luxury **Hyatt Regency Kauai** now stands. The remainder of Shipwreck no longer qualifies as a secluded beach but is still a mecca for sunbathers and body surfing. With its own 1,500-ft beach, sited against a background of sugarcane fields and mountains, the Hyatt is built around open air courtyards and gardens, reminiscent of another era. An-

heard as couples marry or remarry in these secluded gardens. A wedding gift to daughter Alexandra Moir from her sugar-daddy, the scent of romance and flowers have flowed together here for many years.

Except for dry weather and superb beaches, Poipu obviously is no Waikiki. Low-rise **Stouffer Waiohai Beach Re-**

other fantasy resort in the genre of the Westin Kauai, the Hyatt has five acres of saltwater swimming lagoons with their own islands, a complete health spa, its own stables and every other imaginable amenity.

Mahaulepu, several miles further down the main cane road beyond Shipwreck, still possesses its "hidden" status. Enjoy scenic views of the coastline and mountains from a beach lined with ironwoods and the pleasures of swimming in tranquil ocean waters during summer months.

Kiahuna Shopping Village in Poipu has another **Elephant Walk Gift Shop and Gallery** with a typically eclectic mixture of quality craft items including **Bob McWilliams'** pottery, **Martin & MacArthur's** handcrafted *koa* furniture, **Holly Yashi** earrings, Niihau shell jewelry, hula dolls, wildlife sculpture. **A Thing of Beauty-The Gallery at Waiohai**, in the Waiohai hotel on the beachfront, displays a few of the better artists of Kauai and Hawaii including Reuben Tam, paintings and prints reflecting medieval Japan and China by Carolyn Young and artistic woodcraft by Robert Hamada.

In the opposite direction from Poipu Beach, a submerged lava tube regularly produces the **Spouting Horn** geyser. Old timers say that this geyser does not spout or moan as vigorously as it used to but it still remains a major attraction for tourists. Jewelry stands near the geyser's viewpoint offer some of the best deals on the island for coral shell jewelry and

Spouting Horn geyser.

Niihau shell *leis*.

Obviously the Poipu area invites staying more than one or even two days. One itinerary suggestion is to complete a two or three-night stay in the Poipu area and spend the last evening on the leeward side of Kauai at one of **Kokee Lodge**'s cabins in Kokee State Park, gaining additional time for hiking Kokee trails or taking an adventure van tour with **Kauai Mountain Tours** into remote forest reserve areas.

Thousands of different kinds of flowers and plants can be seen in the **Kiahuna Plantation Resort and Gardens** in Poipu. Garden lovers also should make reservations for a tour of the neighboring **National Tropical Botanical Garden** (see below). En route to Waimea, plan to stop at the 12-acre **'Ola Pua Gardens** on Highway 50, just past the picturesque village of **Kalaheo**.

West Kauai

West of Poipu, there are as yet no resorts and hotels. At the frontdoor to the west coast, one of the world's foremost gardens was created at **National Tropical Botanical Garden** , home of the beautiful **Allerton Estate**.

Driving west from Koloa on Route 53 (also called 530 just to be confusing), turn left on Hailima Road for a few miles to the National Tropical Botanical Garden in Lawai Valley. A three-hour tour of this 186-acre garden estate takes in **Queen Emma's Summer Cottage**. Res-

ervations are essential for one of the twice-daily tours (weekdays at 9am and 1pm and Sundays at 1 pm).

Back on Highway 50, past the **Kukuiolono Golf Course**, which has a delightful Japanese garden and outstanding coastal views, **'Olu Pua Gardens** spread over 12 acres half a mile past Kalaheo (on the *mauka* side). An estate originally built in the 1930s for the Alexander family, founders of Kauai's largest pineapple plantation, the house, its interior and its magnificent gardens and tree groves have been delighting visitors for years.

Now 'Olu Pua Gardens is shaping an exciting new direction as the Hawaiian cultural center for Kauai – *Ka 'Imi Na 'auao Hawai'i Nei*, the school of *hula* and Hawaiian culture. Special tours of the grounds combine Hawaiian lore and botanical information. Don't miss the **Saturday Heritage Garden Tour** (10 am and 1pm). In what used to be the estate's garage, the *'Olu Pua Blooms Gift Shop* displays very attractive *pareau*, *lauhala* earrings, hand-made *kupe'e* shell necklaces, fine woodwork, *pahu* drums and other island-made gifts not easily found elsewhere.

Follow Highway 570 toward the **McBryde Mill** and turn on the cane road toward the ocean to find **Wahiawa Beach**, one of Kauai's loveliest and most protected beaches. A panoramic view opens from **Hanapepe Lookout** over lush and scenic **Hanapepe Valley**. Several cruise boats operate out of **Port Allen** in Eleele.

Hanapepe

The remarkable little town of **Hanapepe** certainly has come a long way since 1924 when 20 people were killed in a battle between police and striking Filipino sugarcane workers. In the 1940s, Hanapepe reputedly was the largest and liveliest town on Kauai.

Today, Hanapepe is slowly reviving and perhaps will become another spruced-up plantation shopping village like Koloa.

Already renown as the factory-outlet for Hawaii's premier ice cream, **Lappert**'s. Mango, passion fruit and guava cheesecake ice cream are delicious flavors for beginners merely passing through Hanapepe.

Visiting *aikalima* (ice cream) epicureans will have to try *Kauai pie*, made from Kona-coffee ice cream topped with fudge, shredded coconut and macadamia nuts.

The **James Hoyle Gallery** and **Andy Lopez's Gallery** and a few up-scale clothing shops – **Tropical Tantrum** and **Art and Soul** – are previews of coming commercial attractions. Using oils in studio and pastels outdoors, Hoyle tries to capture Kauai's sun-drenched richness and vibrancy of light in a manner similar to Van Gogh. His painting style and talent have already brought recognition and success.

Lopez works with oil on canvas to preserve images of Kauai's fragile and endangered beauty, reflected in his paintings of the old town and its historic buildings.

Waimea

Former Polynesian capital of the island, **Waimea** possesses an interesting mix of early Kauai history.

Kauai's pre-Polynesian race of little people – the *Menehunes* – supposedly were hired by King *Pe* to perform the amazing engineering feat of building a stone aqueduct – the **Menehune Ditch** – to bring water several miles from the mountains to fields around Waimea. The result is a low stone wall of cut and keyed masonry opposite the suspension bridge on Menehune Road.

Captain Cook's Monument – an inconspicuous marker on the beach – in Waimea commemorates his first landing in Hawaii on January 20, 1778.

The Russians sent trading ships to Waimea's deep-water harbor and an employee of the Russian American Trading Company of Alaska managed to build **Fort Elizabeth**, in 1816, on a collection of false pretenses. He promised Kauai's King Ka-umu-alii that the Czar of Russia would help him get rid of King Kamehameha I in return for land and assistance in building a fort. Found out none too soon, this imposter was kicked out of Hawaii. (This remarkable adventurer also built a fort in Honolulu, where Aloha Tower stands and two others on Kauai's North Shore.) All that's left of the old Russian fort today is a pile of lava stones (next to some rest rooms). A few years later, in 1820, Kauai's first missionaries landed in Waimea.

A half block beyond the turn-off for Waimea Canyon Drive, **Waimea Plantation Cottages** – restored to sugar plantation architecture with period furnishings and modern amenities – are side-by-side with sugar camp houses still occupied by Hawaiians. One of Kauai's best kept secrets, these cottages are perfect for visitors who want to relax for a few days, explore West Kauai and its high-country state parks, picnic and perhaps surf at Wahiawa Bay , Pakala, Kekaha beaches and Waimea Plantation's own lovely beach, or **Polihale Beach** and catch a spectacular sunset over Niihau.

Waimea Canyon & Kokee State Park

Driving from Poipu, leave early, fill the car's gas tank, bring a sweater, binoculars, water or beverages, a picnic, a loaded camera and plenty of extra film. Fantastic views into **Waimea Canyon** open from several points on the way up to **Kokee State Park** and **Kalalau Valley Lookout**.

Depending on the time of day and light, browns, greens and pinks, blues, purples and lavenders predominate in the Canyon. It's hard to believe that this scene is less than 40 miles from Lihue. Eight miles further on, Kokee State Park offers 45-miles of hiking trails with vary-

ing degrees of difficulty. Along these trails, watch for delicious *lilikoi* (passionfruit) and Methley plums growing wild.

For those wise enough to make advance reservations, **Kokee Lodge Cabins** await on chilly nights with wood-burning stoves, rustic furnishings and room for as many as seven in each

Close to nature at Kokee State Park.

cabin. A homey dining room at nearby Kokee Lodge serves bounteous fare for dinner on weekends and breakfast every morning.

Besides plenty of tasteful gifts and souvenirs, **Kokee Park Gift Shop** displays Sheryl Ives-Boylon's watercolor paintings of Kauai's rare and endangered bird species, such as the Kauai *akialoa*.

From **Kalalau Valley Lookout**, the tropical forest drops 4,000 ft down to the sea and knife-like ridges run down the *pali*, easily the most impressive pano-

A little charmer.

rama on Kauai and arguably in all of Hawaii.

From this point, no matter what you've heard elsewhere, there is no trail down the mountain to Kalalau beach! The **Pihea Trail** does follow the rim of Kalalau Valley to Pihea, the last overlook into Kalalau before entering muddy trails into **Alakai Swamp**. This boggy seven-mile round-trip to Kilohana Lookout above Hanalei Bay, usually through pouring rain and swarms of mosquitos, is only for the most determined and prepared hikers.

Hikers will find that, among Kokee's trails, the 3.3-mile **Awaawapuhi Trail**, which starts north of Highway 55, halfway between the Kokee Museum and the Kalalau Valley Lookout, offers the most scenic views of Na Pali and surrounding rain forests. Be sure to bring a picnic along for a break at the overlook 2,500 ft above sheer cliffs to the ocean. This trail connects with **Nualolo Trail** for an 8.5-mile loop.

Down the mountain again to Route 50, you have the option of driving on Highway 55 to **Kekaha**, past **Barking Sands** on a military reservation (Pacific Missile Range Facility) and the dilapidated town of Mana, to reach the glorious white sands of **Polihale Beach**. Know that **Polihale Beach** lies at the end of a long (five mile) dusty road that probably should be driven in a four-wheel drive vehicle. Picnic pavilions and fire pits are sited near tall cliffs rising from this secluded beach.

Leis galore.

Very Special Events

Prince Kuhio Festival is held at the end of March honoring native son Prince Jonah Kuhio Kalanianaole accompanied by Hawaiian pageantry, canoe races, and a royal ball.

Buddha Day on Kauai enjoys extra special festivities, including pageants, flower festivals and dance, because Japanese-Americans constitute the largest segment of the island's population.

Lei Day on May 1 brings everyone out with *leis* and inspires fierce *lei*-making competitions usually held at the Kauai Museum.

Japanese O-Bon Festival from mid-June through August consists of a series of weekend ceremonies and dances dedicated to sending ancestors' souls back to Buddha.

With *cho-chin* (Japanese paper lanterns) hanging over head to light the path of deceased souls, persons of all races dressed in Kimonos and happi coats dance inside a roped-off circle to the beat of O-Bon drums and taped background music. Food flows from concession stands and games are played until the O-Bon dance ends at midnight.

The next day (Sunday) at sunset, boats stocked with food provisions and rafts carrying *cho-chin* are launched into Kukuiula Small Boat Harbor to symbolically send ancestors' souls back to Buddha.

T

Cuisine

he food in Hawaii, like the people, is a blend of American, Japanese, Chinese, Hawaiian, European, Portuguese, Korean and other dishes, styles of cooking, ingredients and presentation. Certain types of foods and ways of serving food are very common. During happy hours and before dinner, you'll sample *pupus* (appetizers) served on a platter that can vary from exquisite tidbits of seafood to vaguely recognizable munchies. Throughout the islands, local eateries serving lunch offer the Hawaiian staples of plate lunch or *Bento* lunch which comes in the form of a meat or fish entree served with one or two scoops of sticky rice and a scoop or macaroni salad in heavy mayonnaise dressing.

Ironically, unless you look for it, one of the cuisines of Hawaii that you are likely to miss (except at *luaus*) is Hawaiian food — *poi*, *kalua* pig (steamed in an underground oven or *imu*), *laulau* (*ti* leaves stuffed with salt fish, pork,

Catering to the oriental palate, noodles churn a brisk business.

351

Good cuisine and elegant surroundings are plentiful in Hawaii's resorts and restaurants.

sweet potatoes (*'uala*), bananas and taro shoots, all steamed), *pipikaula* (jerked beef), *lomi-lomi* salmon (salmon marinated with tomato and chopped onion) and *haupia* (coconut pudding and pineapple) for dessert. There is also *limu* or seaweed, fish and seafood, dog and fowl. Red pepper and salt were the main seasonings. The heart-shaped leaf of the taro plant was the main green in Hawaiian cookery. Tender sweet potato leaves were also boiled and eaten as greens. Seaweed provided many of the vitamins and minerals as well as the fiber that otherwise would come from vegetables. Raw *aku* or *ahi* fish combined with *limu manauea* (*ogo*), a red chili pepper and Hawaiian salt is still the popular *aku poke* (cubed or sliced

raw tuna mixed with pounded *limu*, seaweed, tomatoes, onions and kukui nuts).

With one notable exception, restaurants serving Hawaiian food typically are nothing fancy: small, plain, and family-style like **Ono Hawaiian Food** , only ten tables and excellent for Hawaiian plate lunches as is **Helena's Hawaii Food** . **The Aloha Poi Bowl** (2671 King Street, 944-0798) and the **People's Cafe** (1310 Pali Highway, 536-5789) are a couple of other small local favorites, especially for plate lunches.

Thursday lunch or Sunday brunch at the nearly 50-year-old **Willows** is the place on Oahu for tourists to sample Hawaiian dishes like *poi*, steamed *laulau*, chicken *luau* and *lomilomi* salmon. Flow-

Luau, the Hawaiian barbecue, is a great social event.

ering trees, thatched roofs, a koi pond and strolling Hawaiian musicians add a delightful Polynesian atmosphere.

The New England missionaries brought salt salmon, beef jerky and other foods to Hawaii, today called "typically Hawaiian dishes". Pineapple, papaya, guava, passion fruit, mango and other fruits also are non-native. *Ohelo* berry is one of the few native fruits in Hawaii and on the Big Island, limited amounts of the native Hawaiian raspberry or *akala* grow in the vicinity of Kilauea, but these large, juicy berries are bitter and unfit to eat unless, like early Hawaiians, you're on the cold, wet mountain with little else to eat. Early Polynesians wisely brought bananas, coconuts and bread-fruit with them to plant.

The distinctive cuisines in local and hotel restaurants combine the seasonings and cooking techniques of China, Japan, Thailand and Vietnam, as well as Europe, with Hawaiian and especially, Big Island produce and products. At the same time, the resulting recipes step beyond traditional oriental seasonings and food presentations to make their own original statements.

On each island, a network of people, including many part-time farmers and cottage-industry owners, grow herbs, vegetables and fruits and produce preserves, cheeses, ice cream and other products for the kitchens of Hawaii's best restaurants and cafes. Sometimes these natural and manufactured items are produced to orders from local chefs creating exciting new menu items.

The culinary adventures underway in West Hawaii's resorts, for example, are neither sudden occurrences nor are they specific to the Big Island and Hawaii. As Chef Glenn Alos of the Kona Village points out: "The so-called Pacific Rim cuisine that is faddish in California today has been in Hawaii for a long time."

East-Meets-West Cuisine

What is happening in Hawaii's cuisine can be viewed as the liberation of ancient Asian cooking methods and materials by creative chefs of both Asian and non-Asian heritage, many with classical European training, great travel experience and strong food design capabilities.

In a sense, the art of ancient Chinese cooking seems to have come full circle in Hawaii's East-Meets-West cuisine. Marco Polo returned from China in the 12th century with a Chinese pesto sauce already in existence for thousands of years. From Chinese food reflecting four distinct regional styles of cooking (Mandarin, Szechuan, Shanghai and Cantonese) we have come to expect many superb sauces and condiments, each with subtle and delicate differences. Very familiar and popular Cantonese stir-fries are only a small part of this vast and diverse Chinese culinary tradition.

Distinctive elements of Chinese (and also Japanese) cooking supply many of the basic cooking rules and techniques of Hawaii's Pacific-style cuisine:

• Many dishes, rather than one, make up the most satisfying meals.

• Relatively few seasonings are used sparingly to enhance natural flavors.

• Vegetables are more important than meat in many dishes (which means that fresh vegetable produce is a necessity year-round), and the variety of vegetables and herbs is seemingly endless.

• Fish, shellfish and other sea products are favored and must be fresh, ideally, ocean-to-saucepan measured in hours, if not moments.

• Appearance is as important as the taste, and foods are presented artistically and decoratively.

• Cooking time is remarkably minimal compared to lengthy preparation time.

• Exact measurements of fish or meat portions are made in relation to servings of delicious sauces.

• Ingredients are cut in ways that promote quick and even cooking, and, at the same time, enhance the presentation.

• Tenderness, crispness, color and nutrients in meat or vegetables are retained with quick and even stir-frying on a high, temperature-controlled heat, or by steaming.

With some minor differences, the cooking methods for Southeast Asian foods are similar to Chinese – stir-fry, simmer and steam. Vietnam makes lighter stir fries and not in a *wok*. Vietnamese cooking reflects French tech-

Pastries and sweet snacks for take-away.

niques and ingredients, learned from over 100 years of French occupation. For example, shallots and lemon grass used in Vietnamese cooking and rarely in Chinese cuisine, are favored by French chefs.

Thai cooking is heavily influenced by Indian cooking in its use of curry and other spices. Lemon grass, cilantro or Chinese parsley, fresh mint, chilli peppers, garlic, shallots and fresh or dried ginger, all favorites in Hawaii's East-Meets-West cuisine, are commonly used in Southeast Asian cooking.

Finally, throughout Southeast Asia and also the Pacific Islands, from Fiji to Samoa, coconut milk is important in cooking. This is not the juice of the coconut itself, but rather milk extracted from the white meat of the coconut, grated and processed with water. The modern cook makes a coconut meat purée in a blender, which is then placed in a thin cloth to squeeze out the coconut milk (or simply buys canned Thai coconut milk). Expect to find coconut milk in a variety of Hawaii's Pacific-style dishes.

Nouvelle Organic Cuisine

At the culinary heart of Hawaii's "*nouvelle* organic cuisine" is an abundance of locally grown raw vegetables, tropical fruits and fresh greens, mostly familiar herbs and spices (such as Chinese parsley, also known as coriander or

Seafood appetisers.

Main attraction at luaus.

cilantro, fennel, chives, sweet marjoram, sorrel, cucumbers, dill, edible flowers and ginger) and some less familiar ones such as lemon grass, Thai basil, lemon thyme and others. In addition to tongue and palate, this is a cuisine of the senses – eyes, nostrils and even ears become increasingly involved in the meal. The food is light, refreshing and the taste of many dishes is unexpected and in subtle ways, intoxicating.

You will be spoiled by Hawaii's East-Meets-West chefs who strive to preserve the pure flavors of shellfish while, at the same time, integrating imaginative combinations of flavors reflecting Asian influences. As with other cuisines from sunny climates in the Southwest, Caribbean and elsewhere, vibrant colors in presentations and bold flavors predominate East-West fusion cooking.

Try to imagine what happens, for example, when Chinese parsley, pineapple, mango salsa and macadamia nut pesto are combined with a spiny Pacific lobster curry. From this kind of dish you know that sweet and sour flavors are favorites of Alan Wong, chef of the Mauna Lani Bay Hotel's **Canoe House**.

In addition to Chef Wong, the role-call of outstanding East-West chefs includes: Mark Ellman, **Avalon Restaurant** and David Paul, **David Paul's Lahaina Grill**, Maui; Peter Merriman, **Merriman's** in Waimea and Philippe Padovani, **Ritz-Carlton Mauna Lani**, the Big Island; and Roy Yamaguchi, **Roy's Restaurant**, Oahu; and Jean Marie Josselin, the **Pacific Cafe**, Kauai.

There is so much to see and do in the Hawaiian Islands—much more than you know—and, for most visitors, usually so little time.

The best known attractions, resorts and hotels in the islands are easy to find and don't require the help of a guidebook: Waikiki, the Polynesian Cultural Center and the USS *Arizona* Memorial on Oahu; Poipu Beach, Wailea Canyon, Princeville and Hanalei on Kauai; Lahaina, Wailea and Kaana-pali-Ka-palua Resorts, Haleakala Volcano and Hana on Maui; Hawaii Volcanoes National Park, Kailua-Kona and Kohala Coast resorts on the Big Island.

Having all of the essential travel information at your finger tips doesn't necessarily ensure that it will be used to plan a thoroughly enjoyable vacation which takes advantage of the best experiences that Hawaii has

Na Pali Coast on Kauai.

Vacation Ideas

359

Great & Near-Great Golf Courses

Golf has to be one of the top attractions of Hawaii. Hawaii is unsurpassed in the world for its combination of weather, scenery and variety of golf courses designed for both beauty and challenge. Only a dozen of Hawaii's more than 60 excellent courses are private, like the Waialae Country Club in Kahala and the Oahu Country Club in Honolulu. For the rest, all non-guests need is up to $125 for a round with a cart and to be able to keep your head down despite knockout views.

Oahu

George Fazio's course (18 holes, par 72, 6,366 yards) at the *Turtle Bay Hilton and Country Club* closes for rebuilding when Arnold Palmer's course opens in 1991.

Deep in **Makaha Valley**, cut into the **Waianae** range, William Bell designed two courses: the tougher *West Course* (18 holes, par 72, 6,398 yards), managed by the **Sheraton Makaha Resort**, and rated number one on the island by *Golf Digest*; and the challenging *Makaha Valley Country Club* (18 holes, par 72, 6,091 yards). At the huge *Ko Olina* resort on **Ewa Beach**, Ted Robinson placed water hazards at eight different holes to add interest to this new course set on a beautiful plain in scenic surroundings.

Maui

Against the background of the West Maui mountains, tourist-filled sugarcane trains chugging to and from Lahaina cut through the **North Course** (18 holes, par 72, 6,704 yards) designed by Robert Trent Jones Sr., in the *Royal Kaanapali Golf Course.*, the first championship course in the state. The first hole gives fair warning as it bends around an S-shaped lake aiming for a trio of bunkers cunningly guarding the green. A slice results in a splash that could set a dismal tone for the rest of the day.

Drives have to not only find fairways but the correct sides of them. Golfers on the North Course's fairways know that their real chal-

lenges start on the undulating greens up ahead.

After criss-crossing sloping foothills for nine holes, the par-4, 444-yard 14th hole returns to sea-level which is where Arthur Jack Snyder's shorter and easier **South Course** (18 holes, par 72, 6,250 yards) starts. Arnold Palmer and Francis Duane teamed up to design the spectacular **Bay Course** (18 holes, par 72, 6,160 yards) at the **Kapalua Golf Course**. The Bay Course skirts an old Hawaiian village (4th hole) and pushes onto a lava peninsula encircled by white sand beaches (5th hole) from which you teè-off over a lovely bay dotted with snorkelers.

Palmer then teamed with Ed Seay to design the even more challenging Village Course (18 holes, par 71, 6,194 yards—6,820 yards from the championship tees), home of the *Isuzu Kapalua International*. Ranging through two lakes towards the West Hawaii mountains, the 5th, 6th and 7th holes encompass steep drop offs and a fairway indented with a profusion of sandtraps. Both championship courses offer dramatic vistas over to Molokai and Lanai and into surrounding Cooke pines and Kapalua ironwoods. A third course, designed by Bill Cooke and Ben Crenshaw, opened in 1991.

On the one side of Wailea's two 18-hole championship golf courses designed by Arthur Jack Snyder, the sun rises over Haleakala and on the other side of *Wailea Golf Club's Orange and Blue Courses*, humpback whales cavort just beyond five white-sand beaches. Besides great mountain and ocean views, the Orange Course's (18 holes, par 72, 6,304 yards) more challenging inclines, fairways, forty bunkers and other assets have earned it accolades from professionals. Gentler inclines on the Blue Course (18 holes, par 72, 6,152 yards) are offset by almost twice as many bunkers and four artificial lakes. Further down the road at **Makena**, Robert Trent Jones Jr., designed 18 holes at the beautifully landscaped *Makena Golf Course* (par 72, 6,389 yards) that skirts the ocean's edge, looking out on Molokini.

Kauai

The pair of 18-hole courses at the *Westin Kauai*

rocks in its center – unique 20 years ago.

The *Prince* course's 18 holes (par 72, 7,309 yards!) is one of the most spectacular in Hawaii or anywhere because Jones Jr paid so much respect to the dramatic site. With Hanalei Hills and the Waialeale mountains in the background, and Hanalei Bay glistening below, the scenic beauty visible from the Princeville courses is unsurpassed in Hawaii.

Your best golfing weather will be found at the *Kiahuna Golf Club* (18 holes, par 70, 5,631 yards) in the **Poipu Beach** area where the links-style course is built on the site of and skirts around, an ancient Hawaiian village in a plain adjoining some of Hawaii's best beaches. A nine-hole addition opened in 1991. You may hear a rumor that the back nine of the *Wailua Municipal Golf Course* between Lihue and Kapaa is one of the best in the state. See for yourself.

Big Island

Superb scenery and weather help to make up for some frustrating black lava roughs designed by William Bell into courses at the *Keauhou-Kona Country Club* (27 holes, par 36 nines, approximately 6,800 yards)..

Having found one of the most potentially beautiful resort sites in the world, Laurance Rockefeller naturally recruited the best known resort golf creator in the world at the time, Robert Trent Jones Sr, to shape the course at **Mauna Kea Beach** (18 holes, par 72, 6,365 yards) out of pulverized 5,000 year-old lava flow. Against the backdrop of 13,825 Mauna Kea, his masterpiece offers an oceanview from every hole. The famous third hole (par 3) requires a shot over a finger of the Pacific to a large kidney-shaped green on two-levels guarded by no less than seven traps. Lest too many golfers find themselves overmatched facing this kind of challenge while following plunging fairways and holes swinging left and right, twenty-two alternative tees were set up. Players now have four sets with markers that match their games. Mauka Kea is completing a second course in 1991.

Built on the estate formerly owned by half-

Golfing in cool breezes and scenic courses.

designed by Jack Nicklaus are built around man-made lagoons surrounding greens. Named the best new resort course in the US in 1989 by *Golf Digest*, *Kaui Lagoons Resort*'s *Kiele* course consists of a rugged inland front nine holes and a back nine with especially challenging twelfth through sixteenth holes along a gorgeous stretch of the Pacific. The inland *Lagoons* course built on more windswept agricultural land is also a difficult course with its own personality.

The original three nines (par 36 each, 3,058, 3,098, and 3,018 yards) of the *Princeville Makai Golf Club* – the distinctly different *Ocean*, *Woods*, and *Lakes* – were designed by Robert Trent Jones Jr.

The refurbished *Ocean* heads for the ocean through two outstanding par-3s: the 142-yard third hole and the 157-yard seventh, where jungle or ocean awaits mistakes. Like many Hawaiian courses today, the *Woods* nine has a "Zen rock" bunker – a trap with three volcanic

...Great & Near-Great Golf Courses

Hawaiian and half- Scots Francis H. I'i Brown, Mauna Lani *Bay* wins the award for the best and most beautiful course in the islands (which it does annually from *Golf Digest*). On the **North course**, the par-3 17th hole surrounded by lava rock provides typical Mauna Lani visual exhilaration even as golfers court punishment for poor shots.

Perhaps most important for the average player, however, the gentle, broad green contours of the Mauna Lani Bay's fairways yield satisfying results even for those with less than championship skills. Two new nines have been integrated into this magnificent layout. The former oceanfront hole number 6 now is the par-3, 163 yard 15th hole where golfers privileged to play on the **South Course** tee from a lava platform and play across a surging Pacific inlet to a huge green encircled by coconut palms and cloverleaf traps.

Robert Trent Jones Jr integrated lush palm trees, bougainvillea, oleander, wedelia and plumeria into the W*aikoloa Beach Resort Golf Course's* fairways adjacent to the *Royal Waikoloan* (18 holes, par 70, 6,500 yards). Jay Morrish and Tom Weiskopf's new and tougher **Kings Golf Club** layout also uses lava fields as elements to contrast with Eden-like green grass

(18 holes, par 72, 6,594 yards). Up the mountainside, you'll find the *Waikoloa Village Golf Club*, also designed by Trent Jones Jr., in the midst of a rapidly growing condominium development. If playing next to the finest black sand beach in Hawaii appeals to you, select the **Seamountain Golf Course** on the south side of the island in the **Kau District**. The *Volcano Golf and Country Club* sits on the edge of Volcano National Park.

Molokai

One of the best kept secrets in Hawaii, the first-rate *Kaluakoi Golf Course* (18 holes, par 72, 6,618 yards) designed by Ted Robinson at the western end of the island, has some of the best weather, ocean views and beaches in the islands.

Lanai

Ted Robinson teamed up with Greg Norman to design the *Koele Golf Course* (18 hole, par 72) outside of Lanai City and near the plush *Lodge at Koele* with marvelous scenery on the forested slopes of Lanaihale's ridges.

---

to offer. Here is some advice on vacation planning that hopefully will help you to make even better choices about where and especially how to spend your precious time in Hawaii.

• Spend at least some vacation time off-the-beaten path – a few hidden beaches on Kauai, Molokai or Lanai, whose names no one can or cares to remember like they do Waikiki and Poipu; see some of "unspoiled" and accessible Hawaii, such as Lindbergh's Kipahulu, the Big Island's Waipio Valley, or Molokai's Halawa Valley. Take a four-

wheel drive on Lanai's Munro Trail to the summit of Lanaihale; on Molokai's Main Forest Road to the Molokai Forest Reserve and to Kahakuloa on the northwest side of Maui or to Kaupo on the southwest side of Maui and ride up the horsetrail to Haleakala National Park. Drive to Yokohama Bay on Oahu's Leeward Coast and hike around Kaena Point to Mokuleia Beach. On the way drive up Waianae Valley Road to Kolekole Pass for spectacular views over the Waianae Mountains.

• Visit Hawaii's glorious gardens on

Tourists are extremely well catered to in all of Hawaii.

each island or any island – Foster Botanic Gardens just north of Chinatown in Honolulu; the Lyon Arboretum in Manoa Valley (outside Honolulu); Waimea Falls Park on Oahu's North Shore in Waimea; the walk-through protea gardens of Maui's Upcountry; the National Tropical Botanical Gardens and nearby Allerton Garden in Lawaii Valley on Kauai; the Hawaii Tropical Botanical Garden in Onomea Bay, north of Hilo and Hilo's tropical gardens of orchids and anthuriums on the way to Puna and Volcano are worth

Best Unofficial Beach Camping Places

Kauai

The Garden Isle offers the most glorious collection of hidden beaches for camping in Hawaii and the US. The ironwood grove at the far end of Poipu's **Shipwreck Beach** is less secluded today than before the Hyatt Regency Kauai was built. Consequently, move on to **Mahaulepu Beach** several miles down the main cane road from Shipwreck.

About a mile from Hanamaulu, several miles of beach fronting the *Wailua Golf Course* can be reached by a dirt road off Route 56. Further along, across the road from **Kealia**, the wide strand leads north to good camping spots. If beach nudity doesn't offend you, stay on Route 56 to **Donkey's Beach**, between Kealia and Anahola and camp among the tall ironwoods. Much more seclusion can be found further north at **Larson's Beach** off Koolau Road or at **Kahili Beach** off Kilauea Road. Kauai's "Makena" – the mecca of unofficial camping – is **Secret Beach**, reached by following a steep path from Kauapea Road near **Kilauea Lighthouse**. Continue on to camping under the ironwoods at **Kalihiwai Beach**, reached by the first Kalihiwai Road, or several miles beyond **Anini Beach Park** along Anini Road to more private camping spots on secluded beaches.

Beyond Hanalei, dirt roads off Route 56 **around Haena** lead to beaches that beckon campers. Along the **Kalalau Trail**, **Hanakapiai** with its excellent sand beach and scenic valley surroundings, is a perfect stopping place. Except for voracious mosquitoes, **Hanakoa Valley** is the next best choice before **Kalalau** itself. (Camping anywhere along the Trail requires a state permit.)

Oahu

Sand dunes along **Kahuku Golf Course Park** shelter you from prying golfers. For more privacy, on a calm day at low tide, put on a pair of sneakers, hold your gear overhead and wade across the strait from Kalanai Point (**Malaekahana State Recreation Area**) to **Goat Island** (*Mokuauia*). Of course, free camping with a state permit in the seldom crowded **Kalanai Point** section of Malaekahana is a more practical but less adventuresome option.

Unpopulated **Mokuleia** beachfront, the jewel of the North Shore, stretching west toward **Keana Point** off Farrington Highway,

a trip to the Big Island.

• Savor the natural beauty of some of the most scenic parts of Hawaii while hiking and camping between sub-tropical shores and frosty mountain-tops.

• Try an activity that's completely new for you – kayaking on Neighbor Islands, the Wailua River or even Na Pali on Kauai; a horseback ride on a remote beach down Kauai's sugarcane fields or up the backside of Maui's Haleakala-Kaupo Gap; fishing for marlin or other gamefish off the Kona Coast of the Big Island; birdwatch at Kilauea Lighthouse on Kauai's north shore; beachcomb on Lanai's remote Polihua or Shipwreck beaches; take a free *hula* lesson from Auntie Ma'iki Aiu Lake's daughter at the Royal Hawaiian Center or with the crowds at the Kodak Hula Show near the Waikiki Shell.

• Get in closer touch with Hawaii's incredible natural environment on both windward (wetter) and leeward (drier) sides of the islands – the Kamakou Preserve in the Molokai Forest Reserve; the Manoa Falls Trail above the University of Hawaii is less than a mile long pleasant

offers wonderful camping possibilities.

Maui

Maui offers relatively few official campsites so the unofficial ones become even more important. Circling the northwest end of the island on Route 30, stop past DT Fleming Park for the night at **Oneloa Beach** where you can enjoy views of Molokai from a protected white sand beach at the end of a cove, or continue on Route 30 to another cliff-rimmed beach at **Honolua Bay**.

On the other side of Maui, off Makena Alanui Road near Makena, the white sand of lovely **Poolenalena Beach** invites camping. Two miles further south, the salt-and-pepper **Black Sands Beach** sits adjacent to a cinder cone (**Red Hill**) along with **Little Makena's** white sand (Maui's nude beach). On the other side of Red Hill, beautiful **Makena Beach** is very popular with long-term unofficial campers.

Big Island

The Big Island has plenty of official camping

spots for $1 per person per day in country parks. Two unofficial camping choices are on the wet side of the island and one on the dry, Kona side.

At **Richardson's Beach** in Hilo you can swim from the black sand beach and camp along ironwood-fringed Hilo Bay's south shore. After exploring **Waipio Valley**, continue on the seven-mile **Waimanu Valley** Trail to some of the most secluded camping on the Big Island. Plenty of water waits in the valley for purification as well as lovely beachfront camping spots.

North of Kailua-Kona and the Honokohau Small Boat Harbor, **Honokohau Beach** is bordered by a lagoon and protected by a shallow reef. Take your pick of camping spots, near or away from nude swimmers.

Molokai

Few beaches in Hawaii are more off-the-beaten track than rock-studded **Moomomi Beach** on the northwest coast and on the **south coast**, a string of sand beaches, coconut groves and fishponds reached by a dirt road through Molokai Ranch paralleling the shoreline. (Molokai Ranch does charge a $5 per person per day fee on the south coast.)

walk along a stream through dense vegetation; Tantalus Drive above Honolulu leads to some wonderful and easy walks; the swimming hole at the bottom of Sacred Falls on Oahu, or the pools in Oheo Gulch ("Seven Pools") near Maui's Hana; Waimea Canyon State Park and Kokee State Park on Kauai and their several lookouts including Kalalau Valley.

• Above water, view the magnificent whales from an appropriate distance during their breeding season. See Hawaii's fabulous underwater environ-

ment, too.

• Take a helicopter tour, especially over Kauai, the Big Island or Maui.

• Learn as much as you can about Hawaiian culture and history.

• Time your visit to Hawaii with one of the major festivals or special events.

• Combine the best of Hawaii's sightseeing experiences with outstanding local dining, eating and snack pleasures.

• Plan at least one picnic on each island visited.

• Attend at least one outstanding luau and one Sunday brunch.

Water Safety & Precautions

Everyone knows that Hawaii is unsurpassed for swimming, skin diving and surfing, beachcombing and exploring tidepools. The beauty and fascination of the sea, however, has to be tempered with understanding of the ocean's awesome and treacherous power. The dangers of Hawaii's coastal waters, the many deaths and serious accidents every year, are avoidable.

Never turn your back on the ocean, even for a moment, especially when you're in waters with breaking waves. "Rogue" waves of abnormal size occasionally rise up unexpectedly. Sets of small and harmless waves are often followed by higher waves that can drag you into powerful currents. If you get caught in a rip current while swimming, which runs from the shore to the sea, don't try to swim against it. You'll get nowhere and exhaust yourself. Swim across the current, parallel to the shore.

Duck under big waves. Don't swim through heavy froth. Obey all warning signs. Ask lifeguards or beach attendants for information about the waters. Keep your eye on locals to see what they're doing based on years of experience at the beach.

Don't swim alone. If you insist on swimming alone, swim near other people. Don't swim after eating. Even though nothing has happened to you before, there's always that first time when cramps hit you. Watch out for jellyfish and Portuguese man-of-war. If stung, mix unseasoned meat tenderizer with alcohol and leave it on the sting for up to 20 minutes.

Don't try to learn to surf or bodysurf by doing it. Learn something about these sports from experienced surfers. Be careful of coral and high surf. Before entering the water for swimming, snorkeling or surfing, study it for rocks, breakers, reefs and riptides.

Coastal beach areas that are dangerous or require extreme caution are: **Oahu** — Windward coast when the sea is rough, North Shore in winter and Yokohama Bay when the sea is rough; **Big Island** — Hamakua Coast, North Kohala, Kau and Puna Districts; **Maui** — Paia (northeast coast); **Kauai** — north of Waimea is dangerous in winter, north of Kapaa use extreme caution in the Hanalei and Haena areas.

Fun in the sun.

Whales making trails.

- Play a round of golf on one of Hawaii's challenging golf courses. (See Box)
- Purchase a *lei* from one of shops or persons that makes especially beautiful ones.
- Dine at a few outstanding but expensive restaurants of Honolulu and Waikiki, Maui and the Big Island.
- Pamper yourself for at least one night at one of the Hawaii's plush beach resorts.
- Stay at a cozy Bed & Breakfast offering lots of *aloha* and save money for dining and other adventures.
- View a sunrise from some marvelous (romantic?) location (and a sunset, too).
- "Talk story" with local people.
- Above all, make an effort to experience the serenity that is so much a part of Hawaii's lifestyle and character.

TRAV' TIPS

AIR TRAVEL

Airfares to Hawaii are as competitive as any-where in the United States and the world. The fares and deals change constantly. In high sea-son, buy your ticket as early as possible, but with your eye out for special fares (and the solvency of the airline). Usually this means canvassing most of the major airlines to find the best fare available.

From the West Coast, no frill fares are under $400 for a round-trip, with an extra $45-$60 to Maui, Kauai or Kona. Add another $200 for flights from Chicago or New York. Economy deals and packages can get you to any island for about $110-$150 per night, per person, double occupancy, for a room and an air conditioned economy car with unlimited mileage. Mid-week prices are usually less and restrictions always apply.

Book an aisle seat so as to be able to get up as often as you like during the five-hour flight without disturbing the passenger next to you. You are allowed two large suitcases and one underseat-carry-on weighing a total of no more than 70 pounds. Usually carry-ons are not weighed but might be if the combined weight of your checked baggage exceeds 70 lbs. For a charge of about $30, many airlines allow bicy-cles on board as oversize baggage not included in your regular baggage allowance. You will find the main problem is the inter-island transport of bicycles.

Usually traditional *lei* greetings at airports are included in air-hotel packages and also the cost of transportation to your hotel if you're not picking up a rental car.

MAJOR NORTH AMERICAN CARRIERS

Your choice of airlines is a matter of personal preference and frequent flier credits you may want to earn or spend. All major airlines offer non-stops out of West Coast terminals and con-necting flights from most major cities. If you are heading directly for Maui, Kauai or the Big Island, book with a carrier that flies to these islands without a change of airplanes in order to reduce layover and baggage retrieval time and incon-venience. If possible, avoid transfering in Hono-lulu from a major carrier to an inter-island carrier.

United Airlines has the most nonstops flights weekly to Honolulu from Los Angeles, San Fran-cisco, Denver, Seattle, and Chicago and to Maui from San Francisco and Los Angeles, to Kona on the Big Island and Kauai from San Francisco, Los Angeles and Chicago. In addition to the most flights daily, most United flights are DC-10s. *America West* has non-stop service from Phoe-nix and Las Vegas to Honolulu (and has financial problems as of this writing); *American* flies non-stop from San Francisco, Los Angeles, Chicago, and Dallas/Ft. Worth. to Honolulu and Maui; *Canadian Airlines International* flies from Van-couver or Toronto to Honolulu; *Continental* flies non-stop from Los Angeles, San Francisco and Vancouver and weekly non-stops from Denver and Newark to Honolulu; *Delta* flies non-stop from Los Angeles, San Francisco, Dallas and Atlanta to Honolulu and from Los Angeles to Maui. *Hawaiian*, *Northwest*, and *TWA* fly non-stops daily out of West Coast terminals.

CLIMATE

Spring months in Hawaii, April through mid-July, are usually beautiful. During these months, the weather is as good as it gets. September to mid-December, before the high season's Christmas-New Year's crush, also has wonderful weather. April and October, the "shoulder" months, be-tween peak seasons, are excellent months to visit Hawaii. Avoid February and August, especially if you want to visit Oahu. The weather is not as good as other times of year and tourist-counts are at a peak unless you head for the outer reaches of the Neighbor Isles. With the help of *TRAV' BUG HAWAII*, you can always find accommodations and sightseeing choices off-the-beaten path.

Showers are more frequent in November-to-March and temperatures are a bit lower, in the mid-70s, sometimes in the 60s, depending on the elevation.

Unpredictable Konas blowing in from the south or west will increase the humidity. When you're making reservations, assume that the weather will be near-perfect, even in the off-season. Then, just before leaving for Hawaii, from any touch-tone telephone, dial 900-WEATHER-808 and receive the **American Express Travel Services Worldwide Weather Report** for Honolulu, Hilo, Kona and Lahaina. With this latest weather information, you can fine-tune your packing.

CLOTHING

Travel light for a warm climate. Life is very informal in Hawaii and you won't need many changes of clothing. Two bags per person are allowed on airplanes but try to get your belongings down to one suitcase (with some space left over for things you'll buy in Hawaii) and a carry-on bag.

Bring sandals (or be prepared to buy them), comfortable walking shoes, jogging shoes (if you own them), and heavy-soled shoes for serious hiking. Shoes are not worn inside private homes, which is another reason for bringing sandals. Bring two bathing suits.

Don't shop for everything in advance. Save some shopping for Hawaii, especially resort clothes. Men and women can bring light slacks, a pair of jeans or two, and shorts, which can be worn everywhere except in fancy restaurants. Have a sweater, down jacket or even a parka along for trips up to Haleakala, Volcanoes National Park, or Mauna Kea.

ELECTRICITY

110 volts, 60 cycles, same as the Mainland.

IMMIGRATION REGULATIONS

A valid passport with a USA visa, and a non-expired vaccination certificate.

INTER-ISLAND CRUISES

As of this writing, only one major cruise line offers luxury-liner cruises solely in Hawaiian waters: **American Hawaii Cruises' SS Constitution** (550 Kearny Street, San Francisco, CA 94108,

800-765-7000). Each vessel carries no more than 800 passengers. The cost of the cabin is determined by its size, whether it has a porthole and what deck it is on. Cabins higher up are more expensive, but cabins lower down provide smoother sailing.

Leaving Honolulu on Saturday night, the cruise ship docks at Kahului, Maui, Hilo and Kailua-Kona, the Big Island and at Nawiliwili on Kauai, arriving back in Honolulu the next Saturday morning. Its sister ship, the **SS Independence**, sails in the opposite direction, stopping at the reverse order of islands. **Be sure to check on the choices of optional excursions on each island and their costs and land packages if you wish to extend your stay, especially special promotional land packages, including car rentals**.

INTER-ISLAND AIRLINES

Usually it is difficult to choose between the two main inter-island carriers—**Hawaiian Airlines** (HAL) and **Aloha Airlines**. HAL flies DC-9s and Aloha flies Boeing 737s. DC-9s are quieter and have a better seat-configuration but inquire about the airline's latest on-time performance. Both airlines have outstanding safety records. All flights are about 20 minutes so minor differences in comfort on theses flights really doesn't matter much. For bargain fares, talk to the airlines directly. Fares on both airlines are almost always the same. First and last flights of the day are usually the least expensive, about $80 round-trip. Otherwise, round-trips between any island costs about $105. Standby usually works on any flight but avoid standby and checking baggage on the last flight of the day. It might cost you an extra night at a hotel on the wrong island without any clothing or other personal effects.

Aloha Island Air (previously Princeville Airways), related to Aloha Airlines, flies 18-passenger De Haviland Twin Otters. The company provides service to Princeville, Kapalua, Hana, Kamuela, Molokai and Lanai. Fares are higher than the larger airlines but reliability and service are outstanding.

INTER-ISLAND FERRY

The **Maui Princess** (533-6899) between Lahaina and Molokai is the only commercial inter-island boat transportation at this time. The trip is wonderful (when the channel is not choppy!).

NEWSPAPERS AND MAGAZINES

On Oahu, the *Honolulu Advertiser*, in the morning, and the *Honolulu Star Bulletin* in the afternoon, and local papers on each island.

Public Holidays:
New Years Day, January 1
Martin Luthur King, Jr., Day (3rd Monday in January)
President's Day (3rd Monday in February)
Prince Kuhio Day, March 26
Easter Sunday
Memorial Day
King Kamehameha Day, June 11
Independence Day
Admission Day (3rd Friday in August)
Labor Day
Election Day
Veterans Day
Thanksgiving Day
Christmas Day

SEA TRAVEL

There are no ships flying the U.S. flag that offer regularly scheduled cruises to the Hawaiian islands. Under the Jones Act, foreign ships cannot carry passengers between U.S. ports and Hawaii without intervening or ultimate foreign stops (for example, Hawaii as a port of call on a Pacific cruise). Therefore, no cruise tour begins or ends in Honolulu.

Some ship lines, like **P&O Lines** and **Cunard**, get around this restriction by sailing from Ensenada, Mexico, to Honolulu on a world cruise. One-way fare to Hawaii on *Cunard's* **QE2** begins at $900 per person, double occupancy. **Royal Cruise Lines**, **Princess Cruises**, and the **Royal Viking Line** also have world cruises and Pacific cruises.

You can fly to Honolulu and board a cruise sailing around the islands. For $1100 to $4200 per person, double occupancy, you can see four islands in seven days.

Check on **American Hawaii Cruises's** air/cruise packages, and **standby cruise fares**. Air transportation has to be included in the air/sea package to get you to Hawaii and home, which costs less than the normal round-trip fare. However, usually you're stuck with the flight schedule attached to the ocean portion of the package, which may not be convenient. **Be sure to specify convenient flight times to your travel agent and check on optional excursions and their costs on each island.**

TAXES

When you pay your hotel bill, you will find a 9.43% hotel tax and a 4% sales tax added.

TELECOMMUNICATIONS

Direct dial to almost anywhere in the world.

TIME ZONES

In standard time, there is a two-hour time difference to the West Coast, three-hours to the Rocky Mountains, four-hours to Chicago and the MidWest, and five-hours to the East Coast. Add one hour where daylight saving time is in effect, between late-April and late- October.

Hawaii never has daylight saving time. Remember that from the East Coast you will gain 5-6 hours on the way to Hawaii and lose them on the way home.

TIPPING

50 cents per bag, 10% to cab drivers, and 15% to waiters and waitresses.

TRAVEL AGENTS

Select a travel agency that is a member of *ASTA* (the American Society of Travel Agents), licensed by the *ATC* (Air Traffic Conference) and preferably a *CTC* (Certified Travel Counselor). After reading *TRAV' BUG HAWAII*, you should have a good idea of the itinerary that you want to follow. Write it out for a travel agent and take this book to your travel agent as a aid in putting your travel plan together.

Be specific about what you want to include in your inter-island travel plan, hotels, and car rentals. Discuss with your travel agent about the selection of a trip wherein you stay at a hotel or other accommodation not of your own choice because it is available with airfare and a car, as a package deal. Find out what the agent knows about the hotel and why it's better than the accommodations you prefer.

Price, of course, is important, but other considerations may be taken into account such as location. Be prepared to make your own reservations for each component of your trip.

USEFUL INFORMATION

Hawaii Area Code: 808 for all islands.
Banking hours: 8:30 a.m.-3:30 p.m.
Business hours: 8 a.m.-4 or 5 p.m.
Currency exchange: Honolulu International Airport Terminal, banks and local currency exchange companies.
Minimum drinking Age: 21

HAWAII TALK (li'dat)

372

aa	rough lava
ahi	yellowfin tuna
akamai	smart
ala	road
alii	nobleman
aloha	welcome, hello, good-bye, love....
brah	friend
da kine	that kind, watcha-macallit
ewa	West
halau	school
hale	house
haole	Caucasian, Mainlander
heiau	temple
holoholo	have fun, relax
hoolaulea	gathering
hula	traditional Hawaiian dance
imu	underground oven used in luaus
kahuna	Hawaiian priest
kai	sea
kamaaina	local resident, old-timer
kane	man
kapu	forbidden
keiki	child
kiawe	mesquite wood
lanai	terrace
lauhala	pandanus leaves used for weaving
lei	necklace made of flowers, seeds or other materials
luau	feast
mahalo	thank you
makai	direction of the sea
malihini	newcomer, visitor
mauka	toward the mountains
mele	song, chant
mele Kalikimaka	Merry Christmas
nui	big
ohana	family
pali	cliff
paniolo	cowboy
pau	finished
puka	hole
pupu	hors d'oeuvres
talk story	chat gossip
wahine	woman
wikiwiki	fast

DIRECTORY

AIRLINES
Aloha Airline – 367 5250
Aloha Island Air – 323 3345
American West Airlines –
800 247 5692
American Airlines –
800 433 7300
Canadian Airlines International
800 426 7000
China Airlines – 536 6951
Continental Airlines –
800 525 0280
Delta Airlines – 800 221 1212
Hawaiian Airlines –
800 367 5320
Japan Airlines – 521 1441
Northwest Airlines –
800 225 2525
Pan Am – 800 221 1111
Singapore Airlines – 524 6063
Trans World Airlines –
800 221 2000
United Airlines – 800 241 6523

BANKS
BIG ISLAND
American Savings Bank –
329 5281
Bank of Hawaii – 329 7033
Central Pacific Bank – 935 5251
First Hawaiian Bank – 329 2461
First Interstate Bank – 329 4481
HONFED – 329 2777

KAUAI
American Savings Bank –
822 3427
Bank of Hawaii – 822 3471

Central Pacific Bank – 245 3311
First Hawaiian Bank – 822 4966
First Interstate Bank – 245 3656
HONFED – 245 6902

MAUI
Bank of Hawaii – 871 8220
Central Pacific Bank – 877 3387
First Hawaiian Bank – 877 2311
First Interstate Bank – 877 5516
HONFED – 877 7373

OAHU
American Savings Bank –
531 6262
Bank of Hawaii – 847 8888
Central Pacific Bank – 5440510
First Hawaiian Bank – 525 7000
First Interstate Bank – 735 1711
HONFED – 546 2200

CAR RENTALS
Alamo – 327 9633
American International –
527 0707
Avis – 331 1212
Budget – 527 0700
Dollar Car Rental – 367 7006
Hertz – 654 8200
National Car Rental – 328 4300
Thrifty Rent A Car – 367 2277
Tropical Rent A Car – 367 5140

TOUR OPERATORS, BOOKERS AND OTHER INFORMATION
Akamai Tours – 922 6485
American Express Travel

Service – 367 2333
Hawaiian Holiday Tours –
367 5040
Pleasant Hawaiian Holidays –
(800) 2 HAWAII

CRUISES
American Hawaii Cruises –
765 7000
Cunard Line – 221 4770
Royal Viking Line – 422 8000

HELICOPTERS
Hawaiian Pacific Helicopters –
367 8047, ext. 142
Kenai Helicopters – 367 2603
Maui Helicopters – 367 8003
South Sea Helicopters –
367 2914

OTHER USEFUL TELEPHONE NUMBERS AND ADDRESSES
AAA Hawaii – 528 2600
Road Service – 537 5544

BUS INFORMATION
Honolulu/Oahu – 531 1611

Camping Permits
State
Telephone: 548 7455

City county
Honolulu
Telephone: 523 4525

CINEMAS
BIG ISLAND
Hualalai Theatre 1,2 & 3
Kailua Kona
Telephone: 329 6641

Prince Kuhio Theatres 1 & 2
Prince Kuhio Shopping Center
Telephone: 959 4595

Waiakea Theatres 1, 2 & 3
Waiakea Shopping Center
Telephone: 935 9747

World Square Theatre 1
Kailua
Telephone: 329 4070

KAUAI
**Consolidated Plantation
Cinemas 1&2**
Coconut Plantation Marketplace
Telephone: 822 9391

Kukui Grove Cinemas
Kukui Grove Shopping Center
Telephone: 245 5055

Roxy Theatre
4533 Kukui
Telephone: 822 0933

MAUI
Lahaina Cinemas
The Wharf
Telephone: 661 3347

OAHU
Holiday Theatres
87 2070 Farrington
Telephone: 668 8775

Miilani Theatre
95 1249 Meheula Parkway
Telephone: 625 3886

Pearlridge 4 Plex Theatres
Pearlridge Center
Telephone: 487 5581

Pearlridge West 12 Plex
Pearlridge Center II
Telephone: 487 0036

Kahala 8 Plex
4211 Waialae Avenue
Telephone: 735 9744

Koko Marina Theatres 1&2
Koko Marina Shopping Center
Telephone: 395 5503

CREDIT CARD COMPANIES
American Express –
(800) 221 7282
Bank of America –
(800) 227 3460
Citicorp – (800) 645 6556
Mastercard – (800) 223 9920
Thomas Cook MasterCard –
(800) 223 9920
Visa – (800) 227 6811
Customs – 546 5181

DEPARTMENT STORES/ SHOPPING CENTRE
OAHU
Ala Moana Shopping Center
1450 Ala Moana Blvd
Liberty House
Telephone: 941 2345

J.C. Penny – 946 8068
Sears Roebuck – 247 8360
Shirokiya's – 941 9111

Hyatt Regency Center
Hyatt Regency Hotel
Kalakaua Avenue
Telephone: 923 1234

Kahala Mall
4211 Waialai Avenue
Liberty House
Telephone: 941 2345

Ward Centre
1200 Ala Moana Blvd

Ward Warehouse
1050 Ala Moana Blvd

**Royal Hawaiian Shopping
Center**
2201 Kalakaua Avenue
Telephone: 922 0588

McInerny's
Telephone: 926 1351

Waikiki Shopping Plaza
Kalakaua Avenue
Telephone: 923 1191

Windward Mall
46 056 Kam Highway
Liberty House
J.C. Penny, Sears Roebuck

BIG ISLAND
Hilo
Prince Kuhio Mall – 959 3555
Liberty House – 959 3555
Kaiko's Mall – 322 3233

Kailua Kona
Lanaihau Center
Palani Road

Kona Coast Shopping Center
Palani Road

Keauhou Shopping Village
Alii Drive
Telephone: 322 3000

KAUAI
**Coconut Plantation
Marketplace**,
484 Kuhio Hwy

Lihue Shopping Center
Rice Street

Kilohana
Hwy. 50

Kukui Grove Center
2600 Kaumualii Hwy

EMERGENCY NUMBERS
Ambulances – 911
American Red Cross – 734 3101
Coast Guard, rescue unit –
536 4336
Dental services – 488 5200 or
536 2135
Doctors – 926 4777 or
533 NURS
Fire – 911

HOSPITALS
OAHU
Queen's Medical Center –
547 4311.
Pets – 737 7910
Pharmacy – 737 1777
Poison Center – 941 4411
Police Agencies – 911

FOREIGN MISSIONS
Consulate of Austria
1314 S. King
Telephone: 923 8585

Consulate of Belgium
250 S. King
Telephone: 533 6900

Consulate of Brazil
2148 Moura Place
Telephone: 536 5105

Consulate of Chile
Telephone: 949 2850

Consulate of Cook Islands
Telephone: 847 6377

Consulate of Costa Rica
Telephone: 395 7772

Consulate of Denmark
Telephone: 923 8884

Consulate of Finland
5000 Kahala Avenue
Telephone: 737 8788

Consulate of Germany
1069 S. Beretania
Telephone: 536 3271

Japanese General Consulate
1742 Nuanu Avenue
Telephone: 536 2226

Consulate of Malaysia
Telephone: 525 8144

Consulate of Mexico
2828 Pac
Telephone: 833 6331

Consulate of Netherlands

Telephone: 262 5644

Consulate of Norway
1585 Kapolani Blvd.
Telephone: 949 6565

Consulate of Peru
Telephone: 536 2680

**Consulate General of the
Philippines**
2433 Pali Highway
Telephone: 595 6316

Consulate of Portugal
Amfac Bldg.
Telephone: 537 2581

Consulate of Spain
Amfac Bldg.
Telephone: 537 2581

Consulate of Sweden
737 Bishop
Telephone: 528 4777

Consulate of Switzerland
4231 Papu Circle
Telephone: 737 5297

GOVERNMENT AGENCIES
STATE
**Commssion of Persons with
Disabilities** – 548 7606
Library – 548 4775
**Office of Consumer
Protection** – 548 2540

PARKS
Hawaii
Division of State Parks
P.O. Box 936
Hilo 96809
Telephone: 961 7200

Kauai
Division of State Parks
P.O. Box 1671
Lihue, HI 96766
Telephone: 245 4444

Maui
Division of State Parks

P.O. Box 1049
Wailuku, HI 96793
Telephone: 244 4354

Molokai
Telephone: 533 5415

Oahu
Division of State Parks
P.O. Box 621, Honolulu,
HI 96809
Telephone: 548 7455

STATE FOREST RESERVES
Hawaii
P.O. Box 4849
HI 96720

Kauai
P.O. Box 1671
Lihue
HI 96766

Maui
P.O. Box 1015
Wailuku
HI 96793

Oahu
1151 Punchbowl St.
Honolulu
HI 96813

State Department of Health
P.O. Box 3378
Honolulu, HI 96801
Telephone: 548 5862

COUNTY
PARKS
Hawaii
**Department of Parks and
Recreation**
25 Aupuni St
Hilo
HI 967201
Telephone: 961 8311

Honolulu
**Department of Parks and
Recreation**
650 S. King Street
Honolulu, HI 96813
Telephone: 523 4182

Kauai
**Department of Parks and
  Recreation**
4191 Hardy Street
Lihue, HI 96766
Telephone: 245 4982

Maui
**Department of Parks and
  Recreation**
War Memorial Gym
Wailuku, HI 96793
Telephone: 244 9018

Molokai
County Parks Department
Kaunakakai
HI 96748

Lanai – 565 7125

HAWAII VISITORS BUREAUS
Oahu – 923 1811
Hawaii – 961 5797
Maui – 871 8691
**Honolulu International Airport
Visitor Information** – 836 6413
Mailgrams – 521 1818
Postal Services – 546 5625
Surf Report – 847 1952

TELEGRAPH
ITT – 531 0561
RCA – 536 2521
Western Union – 537 6311

ISLAND BY ISLAND USEFUL TELEPHONE NUMBERS
BIG ISLAND
AIRPORTS
Hilo – 935 0809
Kona – 329 2484
Waimea – 885 4520

TOURIST INFORMATION
Hilo/Airport – 935 1018
Kona/Airport – 394 3425
Hilo/Chamber of Commerce –
  935 7178
Kona/Chamber of Commerce –
  329 1758

Other
Hilo – 961 5797
Kona – 329 1927
Directory Assistance/local –
  411
Interisland – 1 555 1212
Emergency – 961 6022

HOSPITALS
Hilo – 969 4111
Kona – 322 9311
Immigration – 961 8220
Marine Forecasts – 935 9883

POLICE
Hilo – 935 3311
Kona – 329 3311

POSTAL INFORMATION
Hilo – 935 2821
Kona – 329 1927

WEATHER
Hilo – 935 8555
Kona – 961 5582

TRANSPORTATION
Hele On Bus – 935 8241

ROBERTS
Hilo – 935 2858
Kona – 329 1688

GRAY LINE
Hilo – 935 2835
Kona – 329 9337

TAXIS
Hilo
A 1 Bob's Taxi – 959 4800
ABC Taxi – 935 0755

Kona
Kona Airport Taxi – 329 7779
Marina Taxi – 329 2481
Paradise Taxi – 329 1234

RENTAL CARS
Hilo
Alamo – 961 3343
Avis – 935 1290
Budget – 935 6878

Dollar – 961 6059
Hertz – 935 2896
National – 935 0891
Tropical – 935 3385

Kona
Alamo – 329 8896
Avis – 329 1745
Budget – 329 8511
Dollar – 329 2744
Hertz – 329 3566
National – 329 1674
Tropical – 329 2437

KAUAI
AIRPORTS
Lihue – 246 1400
Princeville – 826 3040

TOURIST INFORMATION
Visitors – 245 3971
Chamber of Commerce –
  245 7363
Directory/Local – 411
Inter island – 1 555 1212
Emergency – 911
Hospital – 245 1100
Marine Forecasts – 245 3564
Postal Information – 245 4994
Weather – 245 6001

TRANSPORTATION
Bus
Roberts
Taxi
Abba Taxi – 245 5225
Green Island – 245 2723
Kauai Cab – 246 9544
ABC – 822 7641
Poipu Taxi – 742 1717
North Shore Cab – 826 6189

CAR RENTAL
Alamo – 246 0645
Avis – 245 3512
Budget – 245 9031
Dollar – 245 3651
Hertz – 245 2256

LANAI
Airport – 565 6757
Directory Assistance – 411

Interisland – 1 555 1212
Emergency – 911
Hospital – 565 6411
Postal Information – 565 6517
Weather – 565 6033

CAR RENTAL
Lanai City Service – 565 7227
Oshiro Service – 565 6952

MAUI
AIRPORTS
Kahului – 877 0078
Hana – 248 8208
Kapalua/West Maui – 669 0228

TOURIST INFORMATION
Visitors – 871 8691
Chamber of Commerce – 871 7711
Directory/local – 411
Inter island – 1 555 1212
Emergency – 911
Hospital – 242 2036
Marine Forecasts – 877 3477
Postal Information – 244 4815
Weather – 877 5111

TRANSPORTATION
Bus
Roberts
Taxis
Alii Cab – 661 3688
Kaanapali Taxi – 661 5285
Kihei Taxi – 879 3000
Yellow Cab – 877 7000

CAR RENTAL
Alamo – 877 3466
Avis – 871 7575
Budget – 871 8811
Dollar – 871 2731
Hertz – 871 5167
National – 871 8851
Thrifty – 871 7596

MOLOKAI
Airport – 567 6140
Directory Assistance – 411
Emergency – 911
Hospital – 553 5331
Marine Forecasts – 552 2477

Postal Information – 553 5845
Weather – 552 2477

TRANSPORTATION
Molokai Taxi – 552 0041
TEEM Cab – 553 3433
Gray Line – 567 6177
Robert's Hawaii – 552 2751

RENTAL CARS
Budget – 567 6877
Dollar – 567 6156
Tropical – 567 6118

OAHU
Agricultural Inspection – 541 2951
Honolulu International Airport – 836 6413

TOURIST INFORMATION
Visitors – 923 1811
Chamber of Commerce – 522 8800
Directory/local – 411
Inter island – 1 555 1212
Emergency – 911
Hospital – 547 4311
Immigration – 541 1379
Marine Forecasts – 836 3921
Postal Information – 423 3990
Weather – 833 2849/836 0121

TRANSPORTATION
Airport Motorcoach – 836 3391
The Bus – 531 1611
Akamia Tours – 922 6485
Roberts Hawaii – 947 3939
Gray Line Hawaii – 833 8000
Waikiki Express – 942 2177

TAXIS
Aloha State Taxi – 847 3566
Americabs – 521 6680
SIDA – 836 0011
The Cab – 536 1707

CAR RENTAL
Avis – 834 5536
Budget – 922 3600
Dollar – 926 4200
Hertz – 922 1158

Thrifty – 923 7383
Tropical – 922 2385

HOTELS
BIG ISLAND
Kohala Coast
The Mauna Kea Beach Hotel
P.O. Box 218
Kamuela, HI 96743
Telephone: (800) 228 3000 or
    808 882 7222
Fax: 808 882 7593
310 rooms
Rate (European Plan): $250 $400
(Modified American Plan) $355
    $520

The Kona Village Resort
P.O. Box 1299
Kailua Kona, HI 96745
Telephone: (800) 367 5290 or
808 325 5555
Fax: 808 325 5124
125 rooms
$345 $565 full American Plan

**Mauna Lani Bay Hotel and
    Bungalows**
P.O. Box 4000
Kawaihae, HI 96743
Telephone: (800) 367 2323 or
    808 885 6622
Fax: 808 885 4556
354 rooms
Rate: $275 $395; suites $600
    $2,000

The Ritz Carlton Mauna Lani
50 Kaniku Drive
Kohala Coast, HI 96743
Telephone: (800) 241 3333 or
    808 885 0099
Fax: 808 885 5778
542 rooms
Rate: $255 $500

The Royal Waikoloan
P.O. Box 5000
Waikoloa, HI 96743
Telephone: (800) 537 9800 or
    808 885 6789
Fax: 808 885 7852
540 rooms
Rate: $155 $300

CONDOMINIUMS

**Mauna Lani Point
Condominiums**
P.O. Box 4959
Kohala Coast, HI
Telephone: (800) 642 6284 or
808 885 5022
Fax: 808 661 2737
50 units
Rate: $225 $400

**Mauna Lani Terrace
Condominiums**
South Kohala Management
P.O. Box 3301
Waikoloa, HI 96743
Telephone: (800) 822 4252 or
808 882 7676
Fax: 808 882 7676

**Kona Coast
Kona Hotel**
Mamalahoa Highway
Holualoa, HI 96725
Telephone: 808 324 1155
11 rooms
$23 per night for 2 persons, $15
for 1 person.

**Kona Hilton Beach & Tennis
Resort**
P.O. Box 1179
Kailua Kona, HI 96745
Telephone: (800) HILTONS or
808 329 3111
Fax: 808 329 9532
444 rooms
Rate: $119 $470

Kona Surf Resort
78 128 Ehukai St.
Kailua Kona, HI 96740
Telephone: (800) 367 8011 or
322 3411
Fax: 808 322 3245
535 rooms
Rate: $99 $155; suites $350
$850

Kona Tiki Hotel
75 5968 Alii Dr.
Kailua Kona, HI 96740
P.O. Box 1567
Kailua Kona, HI 96745

Telephone: 808 329 1425
15 rooms
Rate: $40 $45

Manago Hotel
P.O. Box 145
Captain Cook, Kona HI 96704
Telephone: 808 323 2642
42 rooms
Rate: $20 $49

Kanaloa at Kona
78 261 Manukai
Kailua Kona, HI 96740
Telephone: (800) 657 7872 or
808 322 2272

Colony Hotels & Resorts
32 Merchant Street
Honolulu HI 96813,
Telephone: (800) 657 7872
Fax: 808 526 2017
116 rooms
1 bedroom, $135, 2 bedroom,
$220

Sea Village
Sea Village Condominium
Resort
c/o Paradise Management
Corporation
Kukui Plaza C 207
50 S. Beretania St.,
Hon. HI 96813
Telephone: (800) 367 5205 or
538 7145
1 bedroom garden view, $70;
oceanview, $104 + $20 in
season

BED & BREAKFAST

Holualoa Inn
P.O. Box 222
Holualoa, HI, 96725,
Telephone: 808 324 1121
4 rooms
Rate: $75 $125
Hilo
Dolphin Bay Hotel
333 Ilahi Street
Hilo, HI 96720
Telephone: 808 935 1466
18 rooms
singles $31 $63, doubles $42

$74.

Hawaii Naniloa Hotel
93 Banyan Drive
Hilo, HI 96720
Telephone: 808 969 3333
Fax: 808 969 6622
325 rooms
Rate: $80 $120; suites $170
$500

CONDOMINIUMS

Waiakea Villas
400 Hualani Street
Hilo, HI 96720
Telephone: (800) 367 6062 or
808 961 2841
Rate: $75.

BED & BREAKFAST

Hale Kai
111 Honalii Pali, Hilo HI 96720
Telephone: 808 935 6330
Rate: $70

**Hamakua Coast
Tom Araki's Hotel**
c/o Sueno Araki
25 Malama Pl.
Hilo, HI 96720
Telephone: 808 775 0368
$20 per night per person

Linda Beech's Treehouse
P.O. Box 5086, Kukuihaele
Telephone: 808 775 7160

BED & BREAKFAST

Waipio Wayside B&B
P.O. Box 840, Honakaa,
HI 96727
808 775 0275
6 rooms
Rate: $55 75

**Waimea/North Kohala
Log House Bed & Breakfast**
P.O. Box 218
Honakaa, HI 96743
Telephone: 808 775 9990

Upcountry Hideaways
P.O. Box 563
Kamuela, HI 96743

Puu Manu Cottage
Telephone: 808 885 6247
Rate: $85

Waimea Gardens Cottage
Telephone: (800) BNB 9912 or
808 885 4550
Rate: $85

Hawaii Country Cottage
Telephone: 808 885 7441
Rate: $65

Volcano/Puna/Kau
Champagne Cove
Drs. Keith or Norma Godfrey
1714 Lei Lelua Street
Hilo, HI 96720
Telephone: 808 959 4487
Rate: $70 per day, three day
minimum

CONDOMINIUM
SeaMountain at Punalu'u
P.O. Box 70
Pahala, HI 96777
Telephone: (800) 367 8047 or
808 928 8301
27 rooms
Rate: $66 $140

BED & BREAKFAST
Carson's Volcano Cottages
P.O. Box 503
Volcano, HI 96785
Telephone: 808 967 7683
Rate: $50 $65

Kilauea Lodge B&B
P.O. Box 116
Volcano Village, HI. 96785
Telephone: 808 967 7366
8 units
$75 per couple and up

Volcano Bed & Breakfast
P.O. Box 22
Volcano, HI 96785
Telephone: 808 967 7779
Fax: 808 967 7619
Rate: $60

KAUAI
HOTELS

Lihue
Westin Kauai
Kalapaki Beach
Nawiliwili
Lihue, Kauai 96766
Telephone: (800) 228 3000 or
808 245 5050
Fax: 808 245 5049
1200 rooms
Rates: $150 $395; suites $350
$1200

Princeville/Hanalei/Haena
Sheraton Mirage Princeville
Telephone: 808 826 9644

CONDOMINIUMS
Hanalei Bay Resort
5380 Honoiki Rd.
Princeville
P.O. Box 220
Hanalei, Kauai, HI 96714
Telephone: (800) 657 7822 or
808 826 6522
Fax: 808 826 6680
255 rooms
Rate: $80 $435; suites $500
$1000

Hanalei Colony Resort
Condominiums
5 7130 Kuhio Hwy.
Haena
P.O. Box 206
Hanalei, Kauai HI 96714
Telephone: (800) 367 8047 or
808 826 6235
Fax: 808 826 9893
49 rooms
Rates: $100 $155

BED & BREAKFAST
Hanalei Bay Inn
P.O. Box 122
Hanalei, Kauai, HI 96714
Telephone: 808 826 9333
Rate: $45 $55
Kapaa

Makana Inn
Telephone: 808 822 1075
$50 $60
Keapana Center
Kapaa

Telephone: 808 822 7968
$50 $60

Koloa/Poipu
HOTELS
Stouffer Waiohai Beach Resort
2249 Poipu Rd.
Poipu, Kauai 96756
Telephone: (800) HOTELS 1 or
808 742 9511
Fax: 808 742 7214
426 rooms
Rate: $150 $325; suite $405
$1,285

Hyatt Regency Kauai
1571 Poipu Rd.
Poipu, Koloa, Kauai 96756
Telephone: (800) 233 1234 or
808 923 1234
Fax: 808 742 1557
605 rooms
Rates: $195 $390; suites $575
$895

CONDOMINIUM
Garden Isle Cottages
2666 Puuholo Rd.
Koloa, Kauai, HI 96756
Telephone: 808 742 6717
13 units
Rate: $75 $135

Kiahuna Plantation
R.R. 1
P.O. Box 73
Koloa, Kauai, HI 96756
Telephone: (800) 367 7052 or
808 742 6411
Fax: 415 283 3129
330 rooms
Rate: $145 $395

Koloa Landing Cottages
2704 B Hoonani Rd.
Koloa, Kauai, HI 96756
Telephone: 808 742 1470
4 units
Rate: $50 80

BED & BREAKFAST
Gloria's Spouting Horn B&B
4464 Lawai Beach Rd.
Koloa, Kauai, HI 96756

Telephone: 808 742 6995
Rate: 50 $90

Halemanu Guest Ranch
P.O. Box 729
Koloa, Kauai, HI 96756
Telephone: 808 742 1288
Rate: $45 $110

Poipu Bed & Breakfast Inn
2720 Hoonani Rd.
Koloa, Kauai, HI 96756
Telephone: 808 742 1146
$75 $135

Poipu Plantation
1792 Pe'e Rd.
Koloa, Kauai, HI 96756
Telephone: (800) 733 1632 or
   808 742 7038
Rate: $65 $105

Victoria Place
P.O. Box 930
Lawai, Kauai, HI 96765
Telephone: 808 332 9300
4 rooms
Rate: $60 $85

Waimea/Kokee
Kokee Lodge Cabins
P.O. Box 819
Waimea, Kauai, HI 96796
Telephone: 808 335 6061
12 units
Rates: $48 $59

Waimea Plantation Cottages
9600 Kaumualii Hwy.
Waimea, Kauai, HI 96796
Telephone: (800) 9 WAIMEA or
   808 338 1625
Fax: 808 338 1619
28 units
$75 $125

LANAI
Hotel of Lanai
Box A119
Lanai City
Lanai, HI 96763
Telephone: (800) 624 8849 or
   808 565 7211
10 rooms

Rate: $60 $75

Lodge at Koele
Lanai City, HI 96763
RockResorts
P.O. Box 774
Lanai City, Lanai, HI 96763
Telephone: (800) 223 7637 or
   (800) 321 4666 or
   808 565 7245
Fax: 808 565 6477
102 rooms
Rate: $275 $350; suites $425
$900

Manele Bay Hotel
Hulopoe Bay, Lanai City,
HI 96763
Telephone: (800) 223 7637 or
   (800) 321 4666 or
   808 565 7245
Fax: 808 565 6477
250 rooms
Rate: $295 $400; suites $400
   $1,000

MAUI
Hana
Hotels
Heavenly Hana Inn
Box 146
Hana, Maui HI 96713,
Telephone: 808 248 8442
6 units
Rate: $75 $100

Hotel Hana Maui
P.O. Box 8
Hana, Maui HI 96713
Telephone: (800) 321 HANA or
   808 248 8211
95 rooms
Rate: $460 $560 with three
   meals

Hana Plantation Houses
P.O. Box 489
Hana, Maui, HI 96713
Telephone: (800) 657 7723 or
   808 248 7248
Fax: 808 248 8240
7 units
Rate: $75 $185

CONDOMINIUMS
Hana Kai Maui Resort
Box 38
Hana, Maui, HI 96713
Telephone: (800) 346 2772 or
   808 248 8426
17 rooms
Rate: $80 $95

Kehei
Lihi Kai Cottages
2121 Iliili Rd.
Kihei, Maui, HI 96753
Telephone: (800) LIHIKAI or
   808 879 2335
10 units
Rate: $55 $65

Nani Kai Hale
73 N. Kihei Rd.
Maui, HI 96753
Telephone: (800) 367 6032 or
   808 879 9120
Rate: $32 $125

Nona Lani
455 S. Kihei Rd.
Kehei, Maui, HI 96753
Telephone: 808 879 2497
8 units
Rate: $60 $85

Sunseeker Resort
P.O. Box 276
Kihei, Maui, HI 96753
Telephone: 808 879 1261
Rate: $50 $80

Wailea/Makena
HOTELS
Four Seasons Wailea
3900 Wailea Alanui Drive
Wailea, Maui, HI 96753
Telephone: (800) 332 3442
Fax: 808 874 2222
Rate: $230 $350
**Grand Hyatt Wailea Resort &
   Spa**
Wailea Alanui
Wailea, Maui, HI 96753
Telephone: (800) 233 1234 or
   808 921 6015
Fax: 808 924 8753
787 rooms

Rate: $165 $275; suites $350 $1,200

Maui Inter Continental Wailea
3700 Wailea Alanui Dr.
Wailea, Maui, HI 96753
Telephone: (800) 367 2960 or
    808 879 1922
Fax: 808 879 7658
550 rooms
Rate: $185 $275; suites $350 $1,200

Maui Prince
5400 Makena Alanui Road
Kihei, Maui HI 96753
Telephone: (800) 321 MAUI or
    808 874 1111
Fax: 808 879 8763
300 rooms
Rates: $230 $350; suites $350 $700

Stouffer Wailea Beach Resort
3550 Wailea Alanui Drive
Wailea, Maui, HI 96753
Telephone: (800) HOTELS 1 or
    808 879 4900
Fax: 808 879 6128
347 rooms
Rate: $165 $360; suites $500 $1,200

CONDOMINIUMS
Wailea Condominiums
3750 Wailea Alanui Dr.
Wailea, Maui 96753
Telephone: (800) 367 5030 or
    808 669 6271
Fax: 808 669 5740
600 units
Rates; $130 $150

Kaanapali/Kapalua
HOTELS
Kapalua Bay
1 Bay Drive
Kapalua, Maui HI 96761
Telephone: (800) 367 8000 or
    808 669 5656
Fax: 808 669 4694
200 rooms
Rate: $205 $385; suites $750 $1,250

Hyatt Regency Maui
200 Nohea Kai Dr.
Kaanapali, Maui, HI 96761
Telephone: (800) 228 9000 or
    808 661 1234
Fax: 808 667 4498
815 rooms
Rate: $195 $355; suites $260 $2,000

CONDOMINIUMS
Kapalua Villas
1 Bay Drive
Kapalua, Maui HI 96761
Telephone: (800) 367 8000 or
    808 669 5656
Fax: 808 669 4694
143 units
Rate: $155 $390

Kaanapali Alii
50 Nohea Kai Drive
Kaanapali, Maui HI 96761
Telephone: (800) 642 MAUI or
    808 667 1400.
205 rooms
Rate: $175 $250

Kaanapali Beach Hotel
2525 Kaanapali Hwy.
Lahaina, Maui HI 96761
Telephone: (800) 367 5170 or
    808 661 0011
Fax: 808 667 5616
430 rooms
Rate: $140 $210

Napili Point
5295 Honoapilani Highway
Napili, Maui HI 96761
Telephone: (800) 922 7866 or
    808 669 9222
115 rooms
$105 $200

Napili Kai Beach Club
5900 Honoapiilani Rd.
Napili Bay, Maui, HI 96761
Telephone: (800) 367 5030 ot
    808 669 6271
Fax: 808 669 5740
162 rooms
Rate: $150 $195; suites $180 $450

Paki Maui
Honokawi
Aston Hotels & Resorts
2255 Kuhio
Honolulu, HI 96815
Telephone: (800) 922 7866 or
    808 669 8325
Rate: $110 $170

LAHAINA
HOTELS
Lahaina Hotel
127 Lahainaluna Rd.
Lahaina, Maui 96761
Telephone: (800) 669 3444 or
    808 661 0577
13 rooms

Lahaina Shores Beach Resort
475 Front Street
Lahaina, Maui, HI 96761
Telephone: (800) 628 6699 or
    808 661 4835
199 rooms
Rate: $110 $195

Maui Islander
660 Wainee Street
Lahaina, Maui, HI 96761
Telephone: 808: 667 9766
Fax: 808 661 3733
372 Units
Rate: $80 $105

Plantation Inn
174 Lahuainaluna Road
Lahaina, Maui HI 96761
Telephone: (800) 433 6815 or
    808 667 9225
9 rooms
Rate: $90 $125 with breakfast

Upcountry/Paia
Kula Lodge
RR 1
Box 475
Kula, Maui HI 96790
10 units
Telephone: 808 878 1535
$55 $95

BED & BREAKFAST
Bloom Cottage
Box 229

Kula, Maui, HI 96790
Rate: $75 $85

Gildersleeve's
2112 Naalae Rd.
Kula, Maui, HI 96790
Telephone: 808 878 6623
Rate: 50 $75

Kilohana
378 Kamehameiki Rd.
Kula, Maui, HI 96790
Telephone: 808 878 6086
Rate: $60 $80

McKay's B&B
536 Olinda Rd.
Makawao, Maui, HI 96768
Telephone: 808 572 1453
Rate: $60 $90

Salty Towers
Drawer E
Old Paia Town
Maui, HI 96779
Telephone: 808 579 9669

MOLOKAI
HOTELS
Hotel Molokai
P.O. Box 546

Kaunakakai
Aston Hotels & Resorts
2255 Kuhio Avenue
Honolulu, HI 96815
Telephone: 808 553 5347
(Molokai)
(800) 423 MOLO
52 rooms
Rate: $65 $125

Kaluakoi Hotel and Golf Club
Kepuhi Beach
P.O. Box 1977
Maunaloa, Molokai, HI 96770
Telephone: (800) 777 1700 or
808 552 2555
Fax: 808 526 2017
182 rooms
Rate: $95 $240
Pau Hana Inn
P.O. Box 860
Kaunakakai, Molokai, HI 96748

40 rooms
Rate: $45 $85

CONDOMINIUMS
Paniolo Hale
Kaluakoi Resort
P.O. Box 146
Maunaloa, Molokai, HI 96770
42 rooms
Rate: $75 $150

Molokai Shores
P.O. Box 1037
Kaunakakai, Molokai, HI 96748
102 rooms
Rate: $80 $110

Wavecrest Resort
Star Route
Molokai, HI 96748
Telephone: 558 8101
126 units
Rate: $61 $81

OAHU
Waikiki/Honolulu Area
HOTELS
The Breakers
250 Beachwalk
Honolulu, Hi96815
Telephone: (800) 426 0494 or
808 923 3181
64 rooms
Rate: $80 $105

Hale Pua Nui
228 Beachwalk
Honolulu, HI 96815
Telephone: 808 923 9693
22 rooms
Rate: $45 $60

Outrigger Coral Seas
250 Lewers Street
Honolulu, HI 96815
Telephone: (800) 733 7777 or
808 923 3881
Fax: (800) 456 4329
Rate: $50 $85

Outrigger Edgewater
2168 Kalia Road
Honolulu, HI 96815
Telephone: (800) 733 7777 or

808 922 6424
Fax: (800) 456 4329
184 rooms
Rate: $70 $115

Outrigger Reef
2169 Kalia Road
Honolulu, HI 96815
Telephone: (800) 733 7777 or
808 924 9857
Fax: (800) 456 4329
885 rooms
Rate: $95 $145

Royal Grove Hotel
151 Uluniu Avenue
Honolulu, HI 96815
Telephone: 808 923 7691
87 rooms
Rate: $60 $90

Diamond Head Beach Hotel
2947 Kalakaua Avenue
Colony Hotels and Resorts
32 Merchant Street
Honolulu, HI 96813
Telephone: (800) 367 6046 or
808 922 1928
Fax: 808 924 8960
56 rooms
$110 $130; suites $150 $400

Halekulani
2199 Kaila Rd.
Waikiki, HI 96815
Telephone: (800) 367 2343 or
808 923 2311
Fax: 808 926 8004
456 rooms
Rate: $175 $300; suites $350
$2,300

Hawaiian Regent Hotel
2552 Kalakaua Avenue
Waikiki, Hi 96815
Telephone: (800) 367 5370 or
808 922 6611
1346 rooms
Rate: $99 $185; suites $320
$700

Hilton Hawaii Village
2005 Kalia Rd.
Waikiki, HI 96815

Telephone: (800) HILTONS or
    808 949 4321
Fax: 808 947 7898
2523 rooms
Rate: $135 $310; suites $375
    $2,000

Kahala Hilton International
5000 Kahala Avenue
Honolulu, HI 96816
Telephone: (800) 367 2525 or
    808 734 2211
Fax: 808 737 2478
369 rooms
Rate: $165 $400; suites $450
    $1,500

**New Otani Kaimana Beach
    Hotel**
2863 Kalakaua Avenue
Waikiki, HI 96815
Telephone. (000) 657 7969 or
    808 923 1555
124 rooms
Rate: $71 $150; suites $135
$305

Outrigger Prince Kuhio Hotel
2500 Kuhio Avenue
Honolulu, HI 96815
Telephone: (800) 367 5170 or
    808 922 0811
Fax; 808 923 0330
626 rooms
Rate: $90 $140; suites $195
    $375

Sheraton Moana Surfrider
2365 Kalakaua Avenue
Waikiki, HI 96815
Telephone: (800) 325 3535 or
    808 922 3111
Fax: 808 923 0308
793 rooms
Rate: $180 $275; suites $335
    $475

Royal Hawaiian Hotel
2259 Kalakaua Avenue
Honolulu, HI 96815
Telephone: (800) 325 3535 or
    808 923 7311
Fax: 808 924 7098
525 Rooms

Rate: $195 $350; suites $270
    $2,700

CONDOMINIUMS
The Colony Surf
2895 Kalakaua Avenue
Waikiki, HI 96815
Telephone: (800) 252 7873 or
    808 923 5751
Fax: 808 922 8433
50 rooms
Rate: $130 $1200

Aston Waikiki Beach Tower
2470 Kalakaua Avenue
Waikiki, HI 96815
Telephone: (800) 922 7866 or
    808 922 7866
Fax: 808 926 7380
88 rooms
Rate: $199 $600

BED & BREAKFAST
Manoa Valley Inn
2001 Vancouver Drive
Honolulu, HI 96822
Telephone: (800) 634 5115 or
    808 947 6019
Fax: 808 946 6168
8 rooms
Rate: $80 $145

Paula Luv's B&B
3843 Lurline Drive
Honolulu, HI 96816
Telephone: 808 737 8011
Rate: $35 $45

Makaha/Waianae
Sheraton Makaha Resort
84 626 Makaha Valley Rd.
Waianae, HI 96792
P.O. Box 896
Waianae, HI 96792
Telephone: (800) 355 3535 or
    808 695 9511
179 rooms
Rate: $95 $165

Kahuku/North Shore
HOTEL
**Turtle Bay Hilton and Country
    Club**
57 091 Kam Highway

Kahuku, HI 96731
P.O. Box 187
Kahuku, Oahu, HI 96731
Telephone: (800) 445 8667 or
    808 293 8811
486 rooms
Rate: $120 $220; suites $270
    $895

BED & BREAKFAST
Ke Iki Hale
59 579 Ke Iki Road
Haleiwa, HI 96712
Telephone: 808 638 8229
Rate: $95 125

Windward Shore
Kailua Beachside Cottages
204 South Kalaheo Avenue
Kailua, HI 96734,
Telephone: 808 261 1653
6 units
Rate: $55 $70 per day.

NIGHTSPOTS
BIG ISLAND
Kailua Kona
Don Drysdale Club 53
Telephone: 329 6651
Eclipse
Telephone: 329 4686
Huggo's
75 5828 Kahakai Rd.
Telephone: 329 1493
Kona Inn
Kona Inn Shopping Village
Telephone: 329 4455

Hilo
Fiasco's
Waialea Square
Hwy 11
Telephone: 935 7666
Lehua's Bay City Bar & Grill
11 Waianuenue Avenue
Telephone: 935 8055

Reflections Restaurant
101 Aupuni Street
Telephone: 935 8501

Roussel's
60 Keawe Street
Telephone: 935 5111

Kamuela
Cattleman's Steak House
Waimea Center
Telephone: 885 4077

Kahilu Theater
Telephone: 885 6017

Parker Ranch Broiler
Parker Ranch Shopping Center
Telephone: 885 7366

Kohala Coast
Hyatt Regency Waikoloa/Spats
Telephone: 885 1234

Royal Waikoloan
Telephone: 885 6789

KAUAI
Hanalei/Haena
Charo's
5 7132 Kulio Hwy
Haena
Telephone: 826 6422

Tahiti Nui
Kuhio Hwy.
Hanalei
Telephone: 826 6277

Kapaa
Sheraton Coconut Beach Hotel
Coconut Plantation
Telephone: 822 3455

Lihue/Nawiliwili
Club Jetty
Nawiliwili Harbor
Telephone: 245 4970

Duke's Canoe Club
Westin Kauai
Telephone: 246 9599

Gilligan's
Kauai Hilton
Telephone: 245 1955

Inn on the Cliffs
Westin Kauai
Telephone: 246 9599

Paddling Club

Westin Kauai
Kalapaki Beach
Telephone: 246 9599

Poipu
Drum Room
Sheraton Kauai
Telephone: 742 1661

The Tamarind
Stouffer Waiohai Beach
Telephone: 742 9511

MAUI
Kaanapali
Banana Moon
Maui Marriott
Telephone: 667 1200

Makai Bar
Maui Marriott Hotel
Telephone: 667 1200

Spats II
Hyatt Regency Maui
Telephone: 661 1234

Sunset Terrace
Hyatt Regency Maui
Telephone: 661 1234

Lahaina
Blackie's Bar
Honoapillani Hwy.
Telephone: 667 7979

Longhi's
888 Front Street
Telephone: 667 2288

Wailea
Inu Inu Lounge
Maui Inter Continental
Telephone: 879 1922

La Perouse
Maui Inter Continental
Telephone: 879 1922

MOLOKAI
West
Ohia Room
Kaluakoi Resort
Telephone: 552 2555

East
Hotel Molokai
Kaunakakai
Telephone: 553 5347

Pau Hana Inn
Kaunakakai
Telephone: 553 5342

OAHU
Honolulu/Kahala
Ainahau Ballroom
Sheraton Princess
Kaiulani Hotel
120 Kaiulani Avenue
Telephone: 922 6811

Black Orchid Restaurant
500 Ala Moana Blvd.
Telephone: 521 3111

Compadres Mexican Bar & Grill
Ward Center
1200 Ala Moana Blvd.
Telephone: 523 1307

Cupid's Lounge
Outrigger Prince
Kuhio Hotel
2500 Kuhio Avenue
Telephone: 922 0811

Hala Terrace
Kahala Hilton
5000 Kahala Avenue
Telephone: 734 2211

Maile Lounge
Kahala Hilton
5000 Kahala Avenue
Telephone: 734 2211

Peacock Room
Queen Kapiolani Hotel
150 Kapahulu Avenue
Telephone: 922 1941

Studebaker's
500 Ala Moana Blvd.
Restaurant Row
Telephone: 531 8444

Waikiki
Bobby McGee's
Conglomeration

Colony Surf Hotel
2885 Kalakaua Avenue
Telephone: 922 1282

Esprit Lounge
Sheraton Waikiki Hotel
2255 Kalakaua Avenue
Telephone: 922 442

Great Hall
Hyatt Regency Waikiki
2424 Kalakaua Avenue
Telephone: 923 1234

Hard Rock Cafe
1837 Kapiolani Blvd.
Telephone: 955 7383

Hilton Hawaiian Village Dome
2005 Kalia Rd.
Telephone: 949 4321

House Without a Key
Halekulani Hotel
2199 Kalia Rd.
Telephone: 923 2311

Hy's Steak House Lounge
Waikiki Park Heights Hotel
2440 Kuhio Avenue
Telephone: 922 5555

Lewers Lounge
Halekulani Hotel
2199 Kalia Rd.
Telephone: 923 2311

Maharaja
Waikiki Trade Center
2255 Kuhio Avenue
Telephone: 922 3030
Monarch Room
Royal Hawaiian Hotel
2259 Kalakaua Avenue
Telephone: 923 7311

Nicholas Nicholas
Ramada Renaissance
Ala Moana Hotel
410 Atkinson Dr.
Telephone: 955 4466

Nick's Fishmarket
Waikiki Gateway Hotel

2070 Kalakaua Avenue
Telephone: 955 6333

Outrigger Main Showroom
Outrigger Waikiki Hotel
2335 Kalakaua Avenue
Telephone: 923 0711

Polynesian Palace
Outrigger Reef Towers Hotel
227 Lewers Street
Telephone: 923 9861

Rumours
Ramada Renaissance
Ala Moana Hotel
410 Atkinson Dr.
Telephone: 955 4811

The Point After
Hawaiian Regent Hotel
2552 Kalakaua Avenue
Telephone: 922 6611

Tropics Surf Club
Hilton Hawaiian Village
2005 Kalia Rd.
Telephone: 949 4321

Trappers
Hyatt Regency Waikiki
2424 Kalakaua Avenue
Telephone: 923 1234

Wave Waikiki
1877 Kalakaua Avenue
Telephone: 941 0424

PLACES OF WORSHIP
BIG ISLAND
Grace Baptist Church of Hilo
2575 Kilauea Drive
Telephone: 959 6711

St. Michaels Kailua
Holualoa
Telephone: 324 1477

Kona Church of Christ
74 4907 Palani Drive
Telephone: 329 1165

Church of Jesus Christ of Latter Day Saints

1373 Kilauea Avenue
Telephone: 935 6919

Hawaiian Congregational Church
76 6224 Alii Drive
Telephone: 326 2112

Christ Church Episcopal
Kealakekua
Telephone: 323 3429

Christ Lutheran Church
595 Kapiolani
Telephone: 935 8612

Hilo United Methodist Church
374 Waianuenue Avenue
Telephone: 935 2144

KAUAI
Eleele Baptist Chapel
339 Mehana Road
Telephone: 335 6154

Immaculate Conception
Kapai Road
Telephone: 245 2432

Church of Jesus Christ of Latter Day Saints
Lihue
Telephone: 245 3063

All Saints Church
1065 Kuhio Hwy.
Telephone: 822 4267

Lihue Lutheran Church
4602 Hoomana Road
Telephone: 245 2145
Kapaa Seventh Day Adventists
1132 Kuhio Hwy.
Telephone: 822 9230

Kapaa First Hawaiian Church
4 1325 Kuhio Hwy.
Telephone: 822 9931

Lihue United Church
4340 Nawiliwili Road
Telephone: 245 6253

MAUI

Bahainer Baptist
209 Shaw
Telephone: 661 3725

St. Anthony's
1627 Mill
Telephone: 244 4149

Church of Christ
810 Waiehu Beach Road
Telephone: 244 5886

Harvest Chapel Church of God
Luakini & Prison
Telephone: 667 1959

Holy Innocents' Episcopal
561 Front
Telephone: 661 4202

Emmanuel Lutheran Church
520 W. One
Telephone: 877 3037

First Presbyterian Church of Maui
(call) Telephone: 661 3114

Seventh Day Adventist Church
261 S. Pavene Avenue
Telephone: 877 5270

Keawalai Congregational Church
190 Makena
Telephone: 879 5557

Ala Lani United Methodist Church
505 Papa Avenue
Telephone: 877 0388
OAHU
Assembly of God
98 1125 Moanalua Rd.
Telephone: 488 3231

Aloha Baptist
94 496 Kahualena
Telephone: 677 0228

Calvary Church of the Pacific
90 400 Aiea Hts. Dr.
Telephone: 488 6825

St. Peter & Paul
59 810 Kam Hwy.
Telephone: 638 7676

Church of Christ at Waipahu
94 447 Apowale
Telephone: 677 4222

St. Barnabas Episcopal Church
91 429 Ft. Weaver Road
Telephone: 689 7464

Glorei Dei Lutheran Church
784 Kam Hwy.
Telephone: 455 1138

Mililani Presbyterian Church
95 410 Kuahelani Avenue
Telephone: 623 6663

Wahiawa Seventh Day Adventist
1313 California Avenue
Telephone: 622 3440

Olive United Methodist Church
108 California Avenue
Telephone: 622 1717
(Churches of historical distinction)

Big Island
Mokuaikaua Church
Alii Drive
St. Benedict's
Capt. Cook
Kalahikiola Church
Kapaau
Kauai
Maui
Church of the Holy Ghost
Waiakoa
Kaahumanu Church
Wailuku
Molokai
St. Philomena Church
Kalawao

OAHU
St. Andrew's Cathedral
Beretania St. at Queen Emma St.
Kawaiahao Church
957 Punchbowl Street
Telephone: 522 1333

Our Lady of Peace Cathedral
Fort St. Mall at Beretania Street

Queen Liliuikalani Church
66 090 Kam Highway

St. John the Apostle and Evangelist Church
95 370 Kuahelani Avenue

RESTAURANTS
BIG ISLAND
<u>American</u>
Hilo
Bears' Coffee
106 Keawe Street
Telephone: 935 0708

Harrington's
135 Kalanianaole
Telephone: 961 4966

Kailua Kona/Kealakekua
Aloha Cafe
Aloha Theater
Hwy. 11
Telephone: 322 3383

Keauhou Beach Hotel
78 6740 Alii Drive
Telephone: 322 3441

Kona Kai Coffee
Keauhou Village Shopping Center
Telephone: No

Kona Village Restaurant
Alii Drive
Telephone: 329 4455
Kona Ranch House
Kuakini Hwy.
Telephone: 329 7061

Ocean View Inn
Alii Drive
Telephone: 329 9998

Spinnaker's Sailboat Salad Bar
Waterfront Row
Alii Drive
Telephone: no

Kohala/Kwaihae

Harrington's
Kawaihae Shopping Center
Telephone: 882 7997

Kona Provision Co.
Hyatt Regency Waikoloa
Telephone: 885 1234

Chinese
Hilo
Ting Hao Mandarin Restaurant
Puainako Town Center
Hwy. 11
Telephone: 959 6288

Continental
Kailua Kona
Beach Club
Kona by the Sea Condominium
75 6106 Alii Dr.
Telephone: 329 0290

Jamison's by the Sea
77 6452 Alii Dr.
Telephone: 329 3195

Kamuela
Hartwell's
Hale Kea
Hwy. 19
Telephone: 885 6095

Kohala
Bay Terrace
Mauna Lani Bay Resort
Telephone: 885 0099

Cafe Terrace
Mauna Kea Beach Hotel
Telephone: 882 7222
Gallery Restaurant
Mauna Lani Resort
Telephone: 885 7777

Kona Provision Co.
Hyatt Regency Waikoloa
Telephone: 885 1234

Le Solei
Mauna Lani Bay Resort
Telephone: 885 0099

Pavillion
Mauna Kea Beach Hotel

Telephone: 882 7222

The Terrace Restaurant
Third Floor
Mauna Lani Bay Hotel
Telephone: 885 6622

Water's Edge
Hyatt Regency Waikoloa
Telephone: 885 1234

Creole
Hilo
Roussel's

French
Kailua Kona
La Bourgogne
Kuakini Plaza South
Kuakini Hwy.
Telephone: 329 6711

German
Kamuela
Edelweiss
Hwy. 19
Telephone: 885 6(800)

Indonesian
Kailua Kona
Sibu Cafe
Banyan Court
Alii Drive
Telephone: 329 1112t

Italian
Kailua Kona
Phillip Paolo's
Waterfront Row
75–5770 Alii Drive
Telephone: 329 4436

Kohala
Cafe Pesto
Kawaihae Shopping Center
Telephone: 882 1071

Donatoni's
The Hyatt Regency Waikoloa
Telephone: 885 1234

Japanese
Hilo
Nihon Cultural Center

123 Lihiwai Street
Telephone: 969 113

K.K. Tei Restaurant
1550 Kamehameha Highway
Telephone: 961 3791

Restaurant Osaka
762 Kanoelehua Street
Telephone: 961 6699

Tomi Zushi
68 Mamo Street
Telephone: 961 6100

Kohala
Imari
Hyatt Regency Waikoloa
Telephone: 885 1234

Pacific Rim
Hilo/Volcano
Kilauea Lodge
Volcano Village
Telephone: 967 7366

Kohala
Canoe House
Mauna Lani Bay Hotel
Telephone: 885 6622

The Kona Village
Telephone: 325 5555

Cafe and Ocean Bar and Grill
Ritz Carlton Mauna Lani Bay
Resort
Telephone: 885 0099

The Dining Room.
Ritz Carlton Mauna Lani Bay
Resort
Telephone: 885 0099

Kamuela
Merriman's
Opelo Plaza
Rt. 19
Telephone: 885 6822

Seafood
Hilo
Kailua Kona
Fisherman's Landing

Kona Inn Shopping Village
75 5744 Alii Dr.
Telephone: 326 2555

KAUAI
American
Lihue
Duke's Canoe Club
Westin Kauai
Telephone: 246 9599

Ma's Family Restaurant
Telephone: 245 3142

Waimea
Kokee Lodge
Kokee State Park
Telephone: 335 6061

Kapaa/Anahola
Duane's Ono Char
Kuhio Hwy.
Telephone: 822 9181

Kountry Kitchen
1485 Kuhio Hwy.
Telephone: 822 3511

Poipu
Brennecke's Beach Broiler
2100 Hoone Rd.
Telephone: 742 7588

Continental
Lihue
Gaylord's
Kilohana Plantation
Hwy. 50
Telephone: 245 9593

Inn on the Cliffs
Westin Kauai
Telephone: 246 5054

Prince Bill's
Surf Tower
Westin Kauai
Telephone: 245 5050

Poipu
Tamarind
Stouffer Waiohai Beach Resort
Telephone: 742 9511

Waiohai Terrace
Stouffer Waiohai Hotel
Telephone: 742 9511

French
Lihue
The Masters
Westin Kauai
Telephone: 245 5050

Hawaiian
Hanapepe
Green Garden Restaurant
Telephone: 335 5422

Kapaa
Ono Family Restaurant
4 1292 Kuhio Hwy.
Telephone: 822 1710

Waipouli
Aloha Dinner
Waipouli Complex
Telephone: 822 3851

Italian
Kilauea
Casa di Amici
Kong Lung Shopping Center
Telephone: 828 1388

Japanese
Lihue
Hamura Saimin
2956 Kress St.
Telephone: 245 3271

**Hanamauku Restaurant and Tea
  House**
Kuhio Hwy.
Telephone: 245 251156

Tempura Garden
Westin Kauai
Telephone: 246 5053

Mexican
Waipouli
Norberto's El Cafe
Roxy Theatre building
1375 Kuhio Highway
Telephone: 822 3362

Pacific Rim

The Midor
Kauai Hilton and Beach Villas
Telephone: 245 1955

Seafood
Hanalei
Tahiti Nui
Kuhio Hwy.
Telephone: 826 6277

Kapaa
Kapaa Fish Chowder House
1639 Kuhio Hwy.
Telephone:

Poipu
Plantation Gardens Restaurant
Telephone: 742 1695

Wailua
Seashell Restaurant
Telephone: 822 3632

Kapaa Fish & Chowder House
Telephone: 822 7488

MAUI
American
Lahaina
The Bakery
991 Limahina Place
Telephone: 667 9062

Lahaina Coolers
180 Dickensob St.
Telephone: 661 7082

Paia
Dillon's Restaurant
89 Hana Hwy.
Telephone: 579 9113

Kapalua
Plantation Verandah
Kapalua Bay Hotel
Telephone: 669 5656

Upcountry/Kula
Grandma's Coffee House
Hwy. 37
Telephone: 878 2140

Kula Lodge
Hwy. 37

Telephone: 878 2517

Wailea/Makena
The Prince Court
Maui Prince, Makena
Telephone: 874 1111

Chinese
Kahalui/Wailuku
Ming Yuen
162 Alamaha St.

Continental
Kaanapali/Kapalua
Kapalua Bay Club
Kapalua Bay Hotel
Telephone: 669 5656

Upcountry/Kula
Haliimaile General Store
900 Haiimaile Road
Telephone: 572 2666

Wailea
Raffles
Stouffer Wailea Resort
Telephone: 879 4900

Swan Court
Hyatt Regency Maui
Kaanapali
Telephone: 661 1234

Hana
Hana Maui
Hotel Hana Maui
Telephone: 248 8211

French
Lahaina/Olowalu
Chez Paul
Honoapiilani Hwy. (30)
Telephone: 661 3843

Gerard's
The Plantation Inn
Lahainaluna Road, Lahaina
Telephone: 661 8939

La Bretagne
562 C Front Street
Telephone: 661 8966

Longhi's

888 Front Street
Telephone: 667 2288

Wailea
La Perouse
Maui Intercontinental
Telephone: 879 1922

Hawaiian
Wailuku
Yori's
Telephone: no

Japanese
Lahaina
Kobe Japanese Steak House
136 Dickenson St.
Telephone: 667 5555

Wailua/Makena
Hakone
Maui Prince Hotel
5400 Makena Alanui
Telephone: 874 1111

Kahului
Ichiban
Kahului Shopping Center
2133 Kaohu St.
Telephone: 871 6977

Makawao
Kitada's
Telephone: 572 7241

Pacific Rim
Wailea
Café Kiowai
Lahaina
Avalon Restaurant
844 Front Street
Telephone: 667 5559

David Paul's Lahaina Grill
127 Lahainaluna Road
Telephone: 667 5117

Seafood
Lahaina
Lahaina Tree House
Lahaina Marketplace
126 Lahainaluna Rd.
Telephone: 667 9224

Paia
Mama's Fish House
799 Poho
Telephone: 579 8030

Thai
Wailuku
Saeng's Thai Cuisine
2119 Vineyard Street
Telephone: 244 1567

Siam Thai
123 N. Market Street
Telephone: 244 3817

MOLOKAI
Kanemitsu Bakery
Ala Malama Street
Kaunakakai
Telephone: 533 5855

Holo Holo Kai
Hotel Molokai
Kaunakakai
Telephone: 553 5347

JoJo's Cafe
Maunaloa
Telephone: 552 2803

Ohia Lodge
Kaluakoi Hotel
Telephone: 552 2555

Pau Hana Inn
Kam Highway
Kaunakakai
Telephone: 553 5342

MidNite Inn
Ala Malama Street
Kaunakakai
Telephone: 553 5302

OAHU
American
Honolulu
Garden Cafe
Honolulu Academy of Arts
Telephone: 531 8865

Ruth's Chris Steak House
500 Ala Moana Boulevard
Restaurant Row

Telephone: 599 3860

Sunset Grill
800 Ala Moana Blvd.
Restaurant Row
Telephone: 521 4409

Chinese
Honolulu
Dynasty II
Ward Warehouse
1050 Ala Moana Blvd.
Telephone: 531 0208

Hee Hing Restaurant
Diamond Head Center
449 Kapahulu Avenue
Telephone: 735 5544

King Tsin
1100 McCully
Telephone: 946 3273

The Mandarin
942 McCully Street
Telephone: 946 3242

Yen King
Kahala Mall
Telephone: 732 5505

Waikiki
Golden Dragon Restaurant
Hilton Hawaiian Village Hotel
2005 Kalia Rd.
Telephone: 946 5336

Continental
Waikiki
Bali by the Sea
Hilton Hawaiian Village
2005 Kalia
Waikiki
Telephone: 941 2254

Hanohano Room
Sheraton Waikiki
2255 Kalakaua
Telephone: 922 4422

The Hau Tree Lanai
New Otani Kaimana Beach
Hotel
Telephone: 923 1555

House Without a Key
Halekulani Hotel
2194 Kalia
Telephone: 923 2311

Kahala
Maile
Kahala Hilton
Telephone: 734 2211

Kailua
Swiss Inn
5730 Kalanianaole Highway
Niu Valley Shopping Center
Telephone: 377 5447

French
Waikiki
Bon Appetit
1778 Ala Moana Boulevard
(Discovery Bay Shopping
  Center)
Telephone: 942 3837)

La Mer
Halekulani Hotel
2199 Kalia Rd.
Telephone: 923 2311

Michel's
2895 Kalakaua Avenue
Telephone: 923 6552

The Secret
Hawaiian Regent Hotel
2552 Kalakaua Ave.
Telephone: 922 6611

Hawaiian
Honolulu
Helena's Hawaii Food
1364 North King St.
Telphone: 845 8044

Ono Hawaiian Food
726 Kapahulu Avenue
Telphone: 737 2275

The Willows
901 Hausten Street
Telephone: 946 4808

Italian
Waikiki

Baci
Waikiki Trade Center
2255 Kuhio Avenue
Telephone: 924 2533

Honolulu
Castagnola's Italian Restaurant
2752 Woodlawn Avenue
Telephone: 988 2969

Che Pasta
1001 Bishop Street
Telephone: 524 0004

Il Fresco
Ward Centre
1200 Ala Moana Blvd.
Telephone: 523 5191

Matteo's
Marine Surf Hotel
364 Seaside Avenue
Telephone: 922 5551

Philip Paolo's
2312 South Beretania
Telephone: 946 1163

Sergio's
Ilima Hotel
445 Nohomani Street
Telephone: 926 3388

Japanese
Waikiki
Furusato
Hyatt Regency Waikiki
Telephone: 922 4991

Irifune
563 Kapahulu Avenue
Telephone: 737 1141

Restaurant Suntory
Building B
Royal Hawaiian Shopping
Center
Telephone: 922 5511

Honolulu
Kamigata
Manoa Marketplace
2756 Woodlawn Drive
Telephone: 988 2107

Sushi Hirota
3435 Waialae Avenue
Kaimuki
Telephone: 735 5694

Yanagi Sushi
762 Kapiolani Blvd.
Telephone: 537 1525

Restaurant Sada
1432 Makaloa St.
Telephone: 949 0646

Pacific Rim
Waikiki
Orchids
Halekulani Hotel
2199 Kalia Rd.
Telephone: 923 2311

Bagwell's
Hyatt Regency Waikiki
2424 Kalakaua Ave.
Telephone: 923 1234

Honolulu
Roy's
6000 Kalanianaole Highway
Hawaii Kai
Telephone: 396 7697

Seafood
Honolulu
John Dominis
43 Ahui Street
Telephone: 523 0955

Waikiki
Nick's Fishmarket
Waikiki Gateway Hotel
2070 Kalakaua Avenue
Telephone: 955 6333

Thai
Honolulu
Chiang Mai
2239 South King Street
Telephone: 941 1151

Waikiki
Keo's Thai Cuisine
625 Kapahulu Avenue
Telephone: 7379250

Vietnamese
Waikiki
Saigon Café
1831 Ala Moana Blvd.
Telephone: 955 4009

Elsewhere on Oahu
American
Wahiawa
Kemoo Farm
Telephone: 621 8481

Haleiwa
Kua Aina Sandwich
Kam Highway
Telephone: no

Hawaiian
Haleiwa
Matsumoto's
Kam Highway

Mexican
Waimanalo
Bueno Nalo's
Telephone: 259 7186

Seafood
Kahuku
Amorient Aquaculture Stand
56669 Kam Highway
Telephone: 293 8661

THEATRES
BIG ISLAND
Hilo Community Players
141 Kolakaua
Telephone: 935 9155
Kahilu Theater
Kamuela
Telephone: 885 6017

Kona Community Players
Kainaliu
Telephone: 322 9924

KAUAI
Kauai Community Players
Telephone: 245 3408

MAUI
Maui Community Theatre
68 N. Market
Telephone: 242 6969

OAHU
Honolulu Community Theatre
Telephone: 734 0274
Kumu Kahua Theatre
Telephone: 737 4161

PHOTO CREDITS

392

Antiques of the Orient : 12, 22
James Ariyoshi : xiv, 90, 104, 173, 222, 239, 251, 272, 273, 288, 308, 350
Rita Ariyoshi : 32, 43, 47, 64, 78, 79, 80 (bottom), 83, 87, 93, 94, 96, 102, 106, 112, 121, 135, 137, 148, 149, 150, 151, 165, 168/169, 175, 194, 218, 247, 248, 249, 253, 270, 289, 297, 309, 353
Wendy Chan : 124, 128, 129
Gamma/Art Seitz : 76, 146
Hawaii State Archives : 11, 14, 15, 16, 17, 18, 19, 20, 21
Image Bank : 80 (top)
Image Bank/John Bryson : 361
Image Bank/Morto Beebe : 278
Image Bank/Tim Bieber : 320/321
Image Bank/Skip Dean : 356
Image Bank/Stuart Dee : 234
Image Bank/Kevin Forest : 136, 144/145, 363
Image Bank/Tracy Frankel : 197
Image Bank/Grant V Faint : 242/243
Image Bank/Larry Gatz : 66/67, 184
Image Bank/David W Hamilton : 8, 63, 85, 266, 291, 346/347
Image Bank/Jeff Hunter : 192/193
Image Bank/Gill C Kenny : 163, 274/275
Image Bank/Don King : Back cover (bottom), x (bottom), 36, 40
Image Bank/Kaz Mori : Front cover, ix (top), 2/3, 259
Image Bank/George Obremski : 208/209, 357
Image Bank/Charles C Place : Back cover (top right), 352
Image Bank/O K and A E Payne : 226/227
Image Bank/Steve Satushek : 156/157, 260, 335
Image Bank/Alvis Upitis : Back cover (top left)
Image Bank/Turner & De Vries : x (top), 65
Douglas Peebles : End paper (front), vi (top), vi (bottom), vii (top), vii (bottom), viii (top), viii (bottom), ix (bottom), xi, xii, xiii, 4/5, 7, 25, 26, 28, 31, 35, 38/39, 50/51, 52, 55, 56/57, 58/59, 60 (top), 60 (bottom), 61, 62, 74/75, 81 (top), 81 (bottom), 86, 88, 92, 95, 98/99, 101, 111, 114, 115, 116, 117, 118/ 119, 120, 134, 140, 152/153, 154, 155, 158/159, 160/161, 170/171, 178, 180, 183, 186/187, 188, 196, 200, 201, 203, 206/207, 212/213, 216, 217, 219, 220, 229, 232/233, 236, 246, 252, 254, 255, 262, 276, 283, 284/285, 286/287, 292/293, 295, 299, 300, 304, 305, 306/307, 310/311, 312, 314, 319, 322/323, 325, 329, 330/331, 332/333, 338, 340/341, 342/343, 348, 349, 355, 358, 366, 367, 368, endpaper (back)
Morten Strange : 69, 70, 71, 73

INDEX

INDEX

402

NOTES

NOTES